BERTHA KNIGHT LANDES OF SEATTLE

BERTHA KNIGHT LANDES OF SEATTLE

BIG-CITY MAYOR

by Sandra Haarsager

University of Oklahoma Press : Norman and London

Published with the assistance of the National Endowment for the Humanities, a federal agency which supports the study of such fields as history, philosophy, literature, and language.

Library of Congress Cataloging-in-Publication Data

Haarsager, Sandra, 1946–
Bertha Knight Landes of Seattle, big-city mayor / by Sandra Haarsager.
p. cm.
Includes bibliographical references (p. 315) and index.
ISBN: 0–8061–2592–6 (alk. paper)
1. Landes, Bertha Knight, 1868–1943. 2. Mayors—Washington (State)—Seattle—Biography. 3. Women mayors—Washington (State)—Seattle—Biography.
4. Seattle (Wash.)—Politics and government.
I. Title.
F899.S453L364 1994
979.7'77204'092—dc20
[B] 93-29485
CIP

Text design by Cathy Imboden.

The paper in this book meets the guidelines for permanence and durability of the Committee on Production Guidelines for Book Longevity of the Council on Library Resources, Inc. ∞

1 2 3 4 5 6 7 8 9 10

To my mother,
Melba Louise Rowlett Smith,
who made all things possible

CONTENTS

ILLUSTRATIONS

Figures

Maps

PREFACE

While reading histories of Seattle and Washington State, I was surprised to see only oblique references to the woman who had been elected mayor of Seattle in 1926, the first woman ever to be elected mayor of a large city in the United States. While some historians have omitted her name altogether from their lists of city officials, others have trivialized her as an aberration, a female who, yes, had been elected to office but was soon rejected by the voters for her bluenose policies.[1]

Bertha Knight Landes not only was the first woman to be elected metropolitan mayor; four years earlier she was the first woman to be elected to the Seattle City Council. In fact, this woman won her city council seat by an unprecedented margin out of a field of twenty candidates. I wondered, then, what lay behind the descriptions that dismissed her and what her history might reveal.

Research revealed a strong, intelligent, pragmatic woman who honed her leadership skills in women's clubwork and worked to advance the causes of urban reform and feminism, although she did not call herself either a reformer or a feminist. I found a woman who saw herself as others did—as a test case of what her gender could or could not accomplish in public office. I found an ambitious woman who seized power—albeit reluctantly—and used it. She upended the power structure to gain office, with the help of the women of Seattle.

"If the men will not show enough interest in their city government to get the right kind of candidates in the field, the women must," she said on the eve of her victory.[2] Once in office, she sought to make the city a larger home, then to neutralize the issue of gender in the management of public affairs. As a result, she moved away from her natural power base as she extended her influence to earn the endorsements of the usual power brokers of

Seattle. Even skeptical males—unused to women in office or in power—credited her for thinking as they did (like a man), at the same time that she focused their attention on "women's concerns" and social welfare.

Landes belonged to a reform-oriented marginal group at the periphery of the power structure. Urban progressivism led women to blur or obliterate the distinction between domestic and public welfare issues. Initially she focused on the clubwoman rhetoric of domesticity and woman's special sensitivities and on their relationship to politics. Later she tried to make women equal to men in areas where distinctions by sex were unnecessary, as in the management of a great city. In trying to have it both ways, she encountered the classic double bind that derailed the feminist movement following suffrage.

Landes abandoned the powerful metaphor of the social housekeeping ideal in her reelection campaign, fitting herself instead to the prevailing "businessman" discourse of politics and fitting that to communitarian ideals. She believed—mistakenly, as other women did later in the twentieth century—that once she had demonstrated her competence, she could leave gender behind. Landes walked a tightrope and ultimately fell from it. The man who defeated her in 1928 refused to discuss the issues or debate her. Instead he waged a well financed, mean-spirited, personal campaign, successfully attacking her class and gender, despite her endorsements from Seattle's daily newspapers and labor organizations. By then, the outsider had become a powerful insider. Despite her loss, she left her mark on Seattle, helping to shape its physical, social, and administrative environment. At age sixty she went on to speaking tours and other projects that continued to further women's interests.

Those who pay attention to history have a fascination with firsts. To be first is important because the act crosses a line, a barrier, creating a place and time that had not before existed. In some cases the fact of being first is merely a matter of timing, as a final link in a chain of events. Undoubtedly, if Landes had not been elected mayor of this metropolis at the edge of the West, some other woman would have been mayor of some other city, some other time. But the fact that Landes was first in 1926 was no accident of time and place. A collection of forces and events coalesced, fused with her personality and this setting, and led to her election. She was part of a series of political firsts who came out of the West, the region that was first to give women the right to vote. Along with Landes, the West produced the first female congressman (Montana's Jeannette Rankin) and first female governor (Wyoming's Nellie Tayloe Ross).

This book traces her rise, candidacy for public office, election, accomplishments, and defeat as they unfolded through the media and appeared to Landes herself. The final chapter connects her life's experiences to broader issues of power and politics in the twentieth century. Her story demonstrates how women's clubs redefined women's roles and how Landes and other leaders used what they gained in their clubs to redefine civic priorities in this pivotal time in women's history and the history of the United States. The book describes how Landes worked both with and against the powerful assumptions about gender and government that constructed society. What she did and what happened to her are very much connected to ongoing issues of civic and social reform and to gender and power at the end of the twentieth century. Landes and other activists have succeeded in turning the business of government from business to social welfare issues. Despite their general lack of official political power, such activists were critical in expanding the role of government to provide protection of citizens through government intervention and regulation, from urban planning to child labor laws.

As this book is published, we are seventy-four years beyond the national enfranchisement of women. Women constitute a 51 percent majority of the population. Yet women fill only 20 percent of the seats in state legislatures, despite the significant gains of 1992, dubbed another "Year of the Woman." Outside the realm of political office the continuing disparities are also striking. Fewer than 10 percent of the tenured professors on our college and university campuses are women. Although women make up the majority of employees working at newspapers, fewer than 10 percent of the top managers are women. Despite their gains in employment at all levels, women still earn, on the average, less than seventy cents for every dollar that men earn.

In the exchange of sex for dollars, women are criminalized, but their male customers (generally) are not. In divorce settlements affecting families, the standard of living of women and children involved usually falls, often to below the federally established poverty line, while that of the husbands and fathers typically increases. The statistics reflecting gender/power relations in this society seem to be a constant, despite the gains from 1920, when the clubwomen of Seattle began thinking about the possibility of putting a woman like their leader—Landes—into public office.

Landes, a famous first, was also a political pioneer who changed city priorities. She acquitted her offices with intelligence and grace, ever conscious of her representative status, but also clearly a product of the time and the struggles over what was acceptable behavior for women. She was visionary and principled; she could also be high-handed and impatient. Her pragmatic politics and long view led her into occasional political blunders. But her ability to grow with responsibility, her sense of humor, and her deep understanding that what concerned government both mirrored what society cared about and affected its institutions helped her create a Seattle different from the one she found.

Several questions relate to Landes's career. Once women won their seventy-two-year struggle for the right to vote and participate in politics, why was the promise of that participation by women—symbolized by her election to office—left largely unfulfilled? How was a Bertha Knight Landes able to defy tradition and make herself into a political force who won three elections and persuaded others to implement most of her programs? Why was she later rejected, despite widespread recognition for an outstanding, effective, and honest administration and ringing endorsements from the usual power brokers? Since women were responsible for putting her into office, why did they not sustain her there? What was the role of place—the West—in her success and "civic betterment"?

Bertha Knight Landes called for civic involvement as woman's right and responsibility as well as man's and then provided an example of how to do it in her fight for civic and social reforms. Her example also helped pave the way for those women who followed her into politics, on the Seattle city council and elsewhere in local government. She saw herself (and indeed others measured her) as an anomaly, but by the end of the twentieth century women routinely became council members, mayors of cities large and small, and even occasionally governors of states. And Landes's civic reform ideals continued to find expression in a host of social welfare programs and environmental measures, from zoning to health regulations. Fastened to the name Bertha Knight Landes and the first decade of women's suffrage are many strands that still tug on women who would seek political power and in many ways confine the men who have it.

In completing this work, I am indebted to other people. I want to acknowledge and thank colleagues Susan Armitage and Roy Atwood, and especially LeRoy Ashby, for their suggestions, support, and critical insights at an earlier stage of this project. I also am grateful for the financial support provided by the University of Idaho Research Foundation and its faith in and support of this work. Without the assistance and expertise of the archivists and librarians such as Richard Engeman and Karyl Winn at the University of Washington, the staff of the Seattle Public Library, Rick Caldwell at the Seattle Museum of History and Industry, Scott Cline at Seattle's City Hall, and Jeanne Wagner at the University of Idaho Interlibrary Loan office, I would still be looking through files. I also want to express my gratitude to the University of Oklahoma Press, and editors Kimberly Wiar, Barbara Siegemund-Broka, and Craig Noll, who made this book a reality. And finally, I thank my family—Dennis, Anna, and Andrew—whose tolerance of both Bertha and my computer was sorely tested in the process of completing this book.

SANDRA HAARSAGER

Moscow, Idaho

BERTHA KNIGHT LANDES OF SEATTLE

1

THE CITY IS BUT "THE LARGER HOME"

Seattle mayor Bertha Landes spoke in a firm voice from the podium. Beside her was an empty wooden chair, set there to accommodate her opponent, Frank Edwards. Once again he had declined her invitation to debate him during her campaign for reelection, preferring the cloak of mystery.

Nodding toward the chair, she called the missing man Mr. Blank. She occasionally chuckled as she spoke to the crowd, glancing at the chair from time to time. "What is he afraid of? Can it be true that a man is afraid of a woman?" she asked the crowd. "If we need a man for mayor of Seattle, why is it that the man nominated for this office is afraid to debate with me at the Metropolitan Theatre tomorrow at noon?"[1]

How did this traditional Massachusetts-born matron, this woman who was initially cool to the idea of women's suffrage, this Seattle pioneer with her vision of the city as a larger home, end up debating and brazenly seeking votes in 1928? This is the story of her career, of how the forces around her created her and how she changed their course, and of her legacy as the first woman to be elected mayor of a major city in the United States.

She demanded that Edwards come forward and identify his faceless, deep-pocket backers, who supported his campaign with "acres of billboards" and dozens of paid campaign workers. He claimed ignorance. But then how could she lose? This reserved, plain-speaking woman, who one of her unlucky employees said was more silent than silent Calvin Coolidge, had earned not only the respect but also the endorsements of Seattle's power brokers. Urging her election and Edwards's defeat were the three major daily newspapers, the unions, the influential Municipal League, most of the former and current candidates who had sought the prize of the mayor's office, and the clubwomen of Seattle.

Landes had come far in distance and time. She was born across the continent three years after the Civil War ended. In 1868 the popular *Harper's Weekly* published a cartoon consisting of two panels. Its sarcastic caption read, "How it would be, if some ladies had their own way." On the left were men awkwardly handling children, knitting, bending over sewing machines. On the right were women in hoopskirts and petticoats coming out of a saloon, smoking cigars.[2] That vision, of topsy-turvy gender roles and the symbols made of petticoats, cigars, saloons, and children, circumscribed Landes's life.

Bertha Knight Landes spanned the nineteenth and twentieth centuries. Like many people with a foot in each century, she looked both forward and backward—in her case, back to a traditional society and communal values and forward to a modernist vision of a scientifically perfectible future, free of civic corruption and backroom deals. Women had a unique role to play in fulfilling both views. When she left college in 1891, Landes entered a world of social ferment, technological revolution, and reformist visions such as temperance drives and civil rights for women. These alternative visions grew out of women's clubwork and found expression in suffrage.

Family and Early Home Life

Bertha Ethel Knight was born on October 19, 1868, seventy miles west of Boston in Ware, a small town in central Massachusetts about halfway between Amherst and Worcester. The year she was born, both the Sorosis Club in New York City and the New England Women's Club of Boston were founded, the first clubs in a movement that before the end of the century swept across the country.[3] In July of 1868 the Fourteenth Amendment had been added to the U.S. Constitution, guaranteeing citizenship to all those born or naturalized in the United States—except the half of the population that was female. Only three months after Bertha was born, Susan B. Anthony presided over the new National Woman Suffrage Association meeting in Washington, D.C. It marked a new beginning for what became a three-generation-long campaign to get women the right to vote, essentially the right to political recognition and power. Both movements picked up Landes in their forward flow and, for her, culminated when she crossed a boundary into new territory as the first woman elected to the Seattle City Council and, four years later, the first female mayor of a large city in the United States. The themes that

Bertha is pictured here with her parents, Charles Sanford Knight and Cordelia Cutter Knight. The family traced its lineage back to the Massachusetts Bay Colony and the Huguenots, who escaped religious persecution in Europe. After Civil War service, her father worked as a painter and later in real estate in Worcester. *Photo courtesy of Henry Landes Papers, University of Washington Libraries*.

she sounded, echoing from the nineteenth century, were family, duty, reform, benevolence, and civic involvement—and what it was to be female and what it meant to seek and find power within the constraints of being female.

Landes was born to Charles Sanford Knight and Cordelia Cutter Knight. Her mother was born in Enfield, Massachusetts, on May 26, 1828. Her father was born in Huntington, Massachusetts, on March 19, 1830.[4] Bertha was the baby of the family, which included a total of seven girls and two boys. Bertha's mother was forty years old and her father thirty-eight when she was born. Both the Knights and Cutters, quintessential New England stock, traced their families back to the Massachusetts Bay Colony. Landes's ancestors settled on this continent in 1630, some from Denmark, and some from England.[5] The ancestry of both the Knights and Cutters was primarily English.

The Cutters reportedly came from England to Watertown, Massachusetts, about 1626. A deed in the possession of the family transferred land at Watertown in 1630.[6] In an 1897 genealogy, the Knight side of the family was traced back to 1648, to Richard Knight in Newport, Rhode Island. He was a carpenter who died at age thirty-two, leaving three children.[7] Many descendants in the Knight line, including Bertha, displayed large black eyes and olive-toned skin. In his memoirs, her brother-in-law remarked on this feature in Bertha and in his own wife and daughter. He wrote that it reportedly came from "a Huguenot maid and her father, who fled from France to England to escape religious persecution."[8] When the French king revoked his protection of the French Protestants in 1685, a wave of Huguenot emigrants eventually settled in Rhode Island, Massachusetts and elsewhere, emigrants who created a thrifty and industrious middle class of merchants and artisans.

Bertha's father, one of the 159,000 men from Massachusetts who fought in the Civil War,[9] left his wife and five children to engage in battle. He was also one of the war's many casualties. In fragile health as a result, he worked for a time as a painter in Ware after leaving the Union army. Ware, with a population of 8,263 by the end of the century, housed cotton and woolen mills and an iron foundry.[10] However, the family did not remain in Ware long. When Bertha was five years old, the Knights moved thirty miles east to Worcester, the county seat and then the second largest city in the state.

Worcester boasted of having the largest wire works in the world, along with textile, shoe, and other manufacturing. When the Blackstone Canal linked Worcester to Providence, Rhode Island, in 1828, industrial growth rapidly accelerated. Worcester was a center for education as well as wire and cloth, with Clark University (1887), College of the Holy Cross (1843), and Worcester Polytechnic Institute (1865). It also was a center of resistance to slavery and the Fugitive Slave Law. Here Charles Knight began working in real estate rather than the craft of painting.[11]

The rest of Bertha's childhood and some of her years as an adult were spent in Worcester, which by 1900 supported a population of 118,000.[12] She lived with her family in the Sunnyside District, at Agricultural Street and Park Avenue, near Elm Park. Worcester also had a strong women's club tradition, a frequent outgrowth of women's collective activism in antislavery work before the war and benevolence during the war. In Worcester in 1880, when Bertha was twelve, a group of women met to celebrate what was already thirty years of women's organized efforts in that city on behalf of women "and their emancipation from legal disabilities."[13] From that meeting ensued the Worcester Woman's Club. It held its first formal meeting in December 1880, at the residence of Mrs. W. A. Knight, perhaps a member of Bertha's family.

The club had four committees—literature and history, art and science, work and education, and social entertainment—and in its early years gave much attention to education and the need for a hospital for contagious diseases. Unlike some women's clubs that limited membership, the Worcester club had a membership of four hundred women. By the end of the century it claimed credit for getting both manual training and kindergarten into the public schools and for establishing the hospital its founders wanted.[14]

By the time Bertha was eight years old, her father was an invalid (in her words, he "gave his health to this country during the Civil War"), and money was tight.[15] Despite her family's financial problems, she described her childhood as normal and happy. Its "slim family purse" caused her to develop resourcefulness and "a good understanding of life and its problems." She also said later that she played with the boys as much as the girls, crossing gender lines even as a child, and seeing it as not unusual.[16] She also developed a sense of humor about life and its vicissitudes that would serve her well throughout her political career.

The family was close, and Bertha admired her mother's care and devotion to children and husband. The sense of duty to family and country was strong. A man who later worked for Landes described her lineage and family background as "old American stock, of that sterling uprightness, and devotion to duty, that 'plain living and high thinking,' that has produced so many of our best in literature, arts and statesmanship."[17]

Education was also important to the family. Bertha's delicate health as a young girl made her school work irregular but did not keep her from getting an education. She attended Worcester's Dix Street School, passing the final exam in 1884 at age fifteen.[18] After two years of public high school at Worcester, she completed two years of college preparatory work in a private school.[19]

Bertha Ethel Knight is shown here as a young girl growing up in Massachusetts. The youngest child in a large family, she described her childhood as a normal and happy one in which she played with the boys as much as the girls. *Photo courtesy of Bertha Knight Landes Papers, University of Washington Libraries.*

Unlike most of her female contemporaries, who were denied any more than a basic education, she graduated from Classical High School in Worcester. At least one of Bertha's sisters also graduated and went on to attend college at Cornell (which opened its doors to women in 1872), an act that also opened horizons for Bertha.

Her older brother Austin, fourteen years her senior, gained fame of his own. He became commander of the Asiatic fleet and commanded the Narraganset Bay Naval Station from 1913 to 1917. He was also president of the Naval War College at Newport, Rhode Island. On his death, Navy officials credited him with bringing the U.S. Navy out of nineteenth-century methods into twentieth-century technology. Attending Annapolis Naval Academy when Bertha was only four, Austin M. Knight later as an admiral helped the navy develop modern guns, armor plate, electric instruments, and explosives for its vessels. Adept at mathematics, he used his skill in engineering to make the new equipment operational.[20] Back at Annapolis in charge of the seamanship department, he trained thousands of men. He also wrote the book *Seamanship,* which, according to the memoirs of his brother-in-law, was "an exhaustive treatise and accepted text on the subject."[21] He retired at the rank of rear admiral.[22]

Other siblings who grew up and left home before Bertha did had scattered across the country by the 1920s. Her other brother, Charles S. Knight, Jr., became a businessman in Chicago. Two sisters, Mrs. Asa O. Richardson and Mrs. Sadie Knight Price, remained in Worcester. Another sister, Mrs. Henry C. Austin, lived in Somerville, Massachusetts, while Mrs. Eva Collins lived near Bertha in Seattle.[23]

Fortunately for Bertha's future education, her older sister Jessie married the widowed David Starr Jordan, who was then the new president of Indiana University. Jessie married this ichthyologist and academic pioneer on August 10, 1887, in Worcester, when Bertha was eighteen. In his memoirs Jordan described Jessie as a Cornell student whom he had met in connection with a trustees' meeting at Ithaca earlier that same year. His first wife, Susan, had died of a sudden illness almost two years before in November 1885, leaving him with an eight-year-old daughter, three-year-old son, and a baby. The baby also died in 1886.[24] It was this family that Jessie and, one year later, Bertha entered.

At Indiana University

In the fall of 1888, not quite twenty, Bertha went to live with her sister's new family and enrolled as a student at the university. She arrived shortly before Jessie's first child was born and doubtless provided considerable help to her sister with the household and the other two children. Jessie and David S. Jordan had a daughter, Barbara, whom Jordan called a study in the heredity of the Knight line, with her large black eyes, olive skin, and native intelligence.[25] Those who later described the mature Bertha frequently commented on her arresting dark eyes and the sparkle of intelligence and humor in them.

Bertha studied history and political science in the university. The institution was taking a radical new direction under Jordan's leadership, away from classical studies and toward a more modern curriculum that incorporated findings in the physical and social sciences. Jordan had a vision for Indiana University when he came in 1885 and hired a faculty to match that vision and inspire students.

The year Jordan assumed the presidency, at the young age of thirty-four, Indiana had a total of 135 students. The school, founded in 1820, had seen only clergymen as presidents before Jordan came. In 1886 he realigned the curriculum, abolishing the fixed course of classical study in favor of adding the humanities, social sciences, and physical sciences. With a small committee, he came up with a plan that established a broad two-year curriculum to be followed by all students. That was then followed by work in the student's choice of specialty, or major, with study under a major professor.[26] More than one writer credited Jordan with revolutionizing higher education, taking it from the rigid classical approaches of the nineteenth century to a new curriculum, where eventually one-third of the courses consisted of required general courses, one-third of the courses were concentrated in a single field, and one-third were freely elected by the student.[27] It also brought him national attention.

Jordan filled faculty vacancies with far-thinking, well educated, relatively radical men who shared his vision and were willing to live in remote Bloomington. Trained under Louis Agassiz as a biologist, Jordan had a passion for science and reason and an instinct for politics. A former student called him a great teacher. "He was not merely a great scientist; he had the imagination of literary genius and he knew how to marshal facts and illumine theories so that they became alive to the dullest intellect."[28] Already recognized as an authority on fish, he developed skills in the political realm as well. He saw that Indiana University needed stable state funding in order to prosper, survive budget cuts threatened periodically, and attract the best students. He also saw that to gain state support and funding required him to go out on the stump to build support for the school, and he did. He visited virtually all of the state's ninety-two counties and learned how to lobby the legislature effectively on behalf of the university's interests.[29]

Jordan, recognized for his achievements and a frequent guest speaker on the new university education, was in a few years hired away by railroad financier Leland Stanford to found and run

Stanford University. He was recommended to Stanford by the president of Cornell, who himself had declined the offer. Later in his life Jordan also gained national fame for his activism in the causes of world peace and eugenics.[30] He and Jessie stayed in contact with Bertha over the years after their paths separated, and he was proud of the woman he mentored.

Being in the Jordan household must have provided its own education for Bertha. Along with a formal education in the new curriculum, she gained an education in faculty and state politics guided by direct involvement, a pragmatic approach, and reasoned analysis. It was training in an art that stood her well when she became a leader, first in clubs and then in city government.

Bertha finished her degree in history in just three years, graduating in 1891. The new Department of History and Political Science, influenced by the Johns Hopkins Seminar, stressed American history and politics.[31] In attending college at all, Bertha was unusual. In 1890 only 2.2 percent of all women between eighteen and twenty-one were in college, and women composed 36 percent of all students.[32] Those women in the vanguard of higher education at coeducational institutions sometimes did not have an easy time of it. They frequently were targets of ridicule, hostility, abuse, and—as their numbers increased—complaints that they were "feminizing" and thus weakening education.

Bertha was apparently also guided early in her life by a well-worn self-improvement and self-education handbook dating from the eighteenth century, *Isaac Watts' Improvement of the Mind*.[33] Isaac Watts (1674–1748), a tutor and minister in a Congregational chapel in London was a controversial writer. Landes was a member of the Congregational church, which affected her attitude toward civic responsibility and government. In 1725 Watts wrote *Logic; or, The Right Use of Reason in the Enquiry after Truth,* used for several generations as a textbook. He also wrote hymnals used for 150 years in dozens of reprints in England and America. His was a stern Calvinism touched with sympathy and kindness. It was also infused with rational thought.

The flyleaf of this edition of his treatise, published in Boston in 1833, was inscribed "Bertha E. Knight." It was the only such volume saved in either her or her husband's papers. Watts's treatise, which promised to assail "pride, egotism, prejudice, dogmatism, prating, reviling, etc.,"[34] focused on the powers of observation and logic in learning. His "ways to knowledge" included observa-

Bertha Knight graduated with a degree in history from Indiana University in 1891. She studied a new curriculum that had moved away from classical studies and toward the humanities and social sciences, in a new Department of History and Political Science. She also picked up ideas on politics from her brother-in-law, David Starr Jordan, then president of the school. *Photo courtesy of Special Collections Division, University of Washington Libraries, neg. UW7335.*

tion, reading, conversation, instruction, and meditation, each with specific rules. Watts advocated stretching the mind, using the methods of analysis to compare, contrast, and suspend judgments in the process of learning.[35] His methods, in a time and place remote from his, would lead practitioners toward science, efficiency, and objectivity as a means of perfecting human institutions.

Watts's guide contained "sixteen general rules for gaining knowledge and improvement," beginning with self-awareness and the value of learning from experience and including the need to guard against the frailties of human nature and effects of "unruly passions." Watts advised not relying on wit and genius, because "without labor and study [they] will never make a man of knowledge and wisdom." He advised thinking about what is read, rather than simply reciting, as was the common educational methodology of the time. Do not "hover always on the surface of things," he wrote, but seek depth, avoid quick judgments, and guard against dogmatism. Rely on evidence, because dogmatism leads to arrogance and a "censorious attitude," he wrote. "Never be too proud to change your opinion," and never fear charges of inconstancy. He also advised guarding against pride in one's own reason and conceit in intellectual powers, instead retaining humility and recognizing dependence on God.[36]

Watts's appeal to self-knowledge and sober service—and for openness and analysis in seeking alternatives and causal connections—helped Bertha face problems in the twentieth century that could not even have been imagined when she was growing up in the nineteenth. Written entirely with masculine pronouns and with a focus on reason, Watts's book was an unusual guide for a woman in the nineteenth century. Using it worked against the then-prevalent ideas about gender, much as *Pilgrim's Progress* did for Louisa May Alcott.

Marriage to Henry Landes

While a student at Indiana University, Bertha Knight met Henry Landes, the man who would have the most impact on the remainder of her life. The son of Samuel and Lydia (Dunkin) Landes, Henry was a geology student from Carroll, Indiana. He was born on December 22, 1867, the oldest of five children. His family was perhaps descended from Mennonites banished from Switzerland in the seventeenth century who settled in Pennsylvania.[37] Other sources said his ancestors came to Virginia from Germany before the Revolutionary War, later moving to Indiana Territory, where Landes's father enlisted to fight in the Civil War at the age of eighteen.[38] In any case, Henry Landes attended country schools in Indiana, and taught in them for three years before going to Indiana University, where he met Bertha. He took his senior year at Harvard and gained a bachelor's degree from both that school and Indiana University in 1891.[39] He and Bertha became engaged.

After her graduation in 1891 with a degree in history, she returned to Worcester. For three years she taught at her alma mater, Classical High School on Walnut Street, while living at home and helping her mother. Henry went on to graduate work in geology on a scholarship at Harvard, finally graduating in 1893. He spent his summers working for the U.S. Geological Survey and the New Jersey State Survey. The fall after he graduated he took a job at Trenton, New Jersey, classifying and arranging the rocks in the geological collection for the state museum.[40]

Once engaged, Henry and Bertha found their long separations difficult. He worked summers mapping, and their times together were brief. Doubtless she also missed the stimulation of her years at college and felt the confinements of living at home and teaching. The only letter from Henry that she left in her papers, written on July 9, 1893, came from Max Meadows, Virginia, on U.S. Geological Survey letterhead.

In the letter he responded to a reference she had made in an earlier letter to the difficulties of living at home, and he beseeched her not to work so hard as a result of her mother's illness.[41] He wrote of his own loneliness, and of the pain of waiting and being apart. "I am so glad that you find your life happier than you had expected. It takes a load off me. . . . You must not be blue dearie, it don't pay." He referred obliquely to her brother, Charlie, and May (possibly Bertha's sister or sister-in-law), and how good it would be if they came home and stayed, presumably to help her, and how then she could leave without guilt. "I am very sorry that mother is ill, and that you have to work so hard. Please do not do too much, but keep as strong as you can."

He called Bertha "dearie" and "old sweetheart." He wrote of his hope that they could marry during the holidays in 1893 and be together at least six months until July 1894, when he would leave for survey work again until November. The national economic depression and increasing unemployment left him worried about not being employed the following year. He also, in his sweet words, used language that reflected the role expectations of the time: "Dearie, if you are so true and faithful and loving now, how much more will you be to me as a wife. You are my only idol, dearie, and you I worship with my whole devotion. My life is nothing to me without being linked to yours. I cannot plan or even think of any work without taking you along as an interested party."

They were married on January 2, 1894, when Bertha was twenty-five. Bertha was somewhat unusual in marrying, as over

75 percent of the generation of women who graduated from college before 1900 remained single. In the eyes of many, their education made them unfit for marriage.[42] Bertha left her home, and the new couple first lived for a year at Trenton, New Jersey, where Henry finished processing collections for the New Jersey State Museum, as the assistant to the state geologist of New Jersey.[43] He then worked as the principal of the high school in Rockland, Maine, for the 1894–95 school year.[44] The following fall, with the help of a favorable recommendation from Jordan, Henry Landes got the job he really wanted. He became a geology professor at the fledgling University of Washington in Seattle, where he and Bertha spent the remainder of their professional lives.

Early Days in Seattle

Seattle and the campus that the Landeses found in 1895 were primitive but were changing quickly. In 1880 the university faculty had consisted of Dr. Alexander J. Anderson, the president, and his wife and daughter. They taught forty students. The university was then located in downtown Seattle at the site of the Olympic Hotel. Jordan had lectured in Seattle at the university in 1885 and was full of praise for the possibilities of Puget Sound.[45] A gift of land located between Union and Portage bays gave the university a new site of 355 acres on a remote wooded hill five miles northeast of downtown Seattle. The two years before the Landeses arrived had not been good to the Puget Sound. At the end of the 1893 depression, only nine of twenty-three King County banks survived, and Seattle's land values had depreciated by 40 to 80 percent. Further, the city treasurer fled after stealing $200,000, and the state budget was in disarray.[46]

The year Henry and Bertha Landes arrived, the new Denny Hall opened overlooking Union Bay. It had thirty-five rooms to accommodate a student body that had grown in fifteen years to just over two hundred. The library, faculty offices, music room, and ten classrooms were all located in the new building, along with a seven-hundred-seat lecture hall.[47] Landes taught his classes in a small room on the first floor and had a laboratory in the basement. He did his assaying of ores in a shack left over from construction.[48] The university, which paid some of the lowest faculty salaries in the nation, was frequently embroiled in political conflict and controversy.

Only two years after Landes arrived, the board of regents was threatening to fire both the president and the faculty. The faculty and students had objected to a board decision in September 1897 to make gymnasium work and military drill compulsory for freshmen and sophomores, for a hefty twenty-four credits. One faculty member was quoted as calling the regents "ward heelers and bum politicians," and the regents complained of insubordination in the face of a faculty petition objecting to the new requirements. Arguments over curricula ensued, with the founder of the *Seattle Times,* a home-owned paper that later would become one of Bertha Knight Landes's champions, objecting to the new catalog that Henry Landes had a hand in developing. Regent and *Times* publisher Col. Alden Blethen complained that a student could get a bachelor's degree under the new catalog without even looking at a Greek or Latin text or taking mental or moral science.[49]

The debate over the college curriculum reflected tensions over change in the city itself. More than the college curriculum was in transition. Seattle was raw, rough, and booming. By 1890 the population of Seattle proper had reached 80,671, over seventy times the frontier population of 1,107 only two decades before. By 1910 it had tripled, exploding to 237,194 people. By 1930 it neared 400,000 people. The completion of a transcontinental railroad linking Seattle to the rest of the nation contributed to the boom, as did the discovery of gold in Alaska. The city's infrastructure could hardly keep up with physical, let alone social, needs.

Despite the phenomenal growth and talk about progress, the city was still very much a part of the nineteenth century. Indeed, Washington had been admitted into the union as a state only six years prior to their 1895 arrival, and the city was still recovering from a disastrous fire about the same time. Mud filled the streets, and tall stands of timber shrouded the city. One writer observed that heavy traffic on the unpaved streets made "beds of dust when they were dry and mud streams when they were wet."[50] At that point in Seattle's history, city developers saw the timber as an impediment to building rather than as a resource for exploitation. Such a view would come later. Another impediment was the steep hills near the waterfront, which one by one were shaved off the city's scalp in extensive, expensive regrading projects as the city grew. Steep grades were evened out and building areas cleared, and the city's harbor became the gateway to both Alaska and Asia. Over a period of three decades Seattle removed an estimated 50 million tons of earth to eliminate the steep hills in the downtown area. Denny Hill eventually disappeared, carted away by endless shovels, belts, horses, wagons, and rail carts to Elliott Bay barges that took it to the bottom of the sea.[51]

The city sprawled over seven hills, with the rugged Olympics to the west and the Cascades to the east. Hemmed in by those mountains and faced with shaving the smaller hills to create building zones, Seattle became dependent on its harbor to the north and trade with exotic places on the way to the Orient. When gold was discovered in the Yukon and Alaska, Seattle promoted itself as the commercial jumping-off point and the merchant that met miners' needs. The miners—and sailors and loggers—came to Seattle to meet other needs as well, in a collection of businesses segregated south of Yesler Way. Seattle had one of the most transient populations in the nation in the closing decades of the nineteenth century, with a seedy district devoted to hard-core vice. Unemployed and seasonal workers flooded into Seattle, looking for bright lights and warm places in the absence of work.

The city soon had a civic opera, a symphony, a string of city parks, the University of Washington, dozens of neighborhood churches, and an abundance of natural wonders. It also collected even more of the Northwest's casual workers and its unemployed, attracted by ads from the Chamber of Commerce and the railroad companies and by the lure of gold to the north. They took advantage of dance halls, cardrooms, poolrooms, shooting galleries run by painted women in scanty clothes, and "theaters" with theater boxes where illicit activity sometimes went on behind drawn curtains. All manner of gambling, drinking and prostitution enterprises set up lucrative shop in a place dubbed Deadline, the Lava Beds, or Skid Road (for the logs that once skidded their way from the mill to the waterfront).

The University District, initially known as Brooklyn, represented a very different image of Seattle. It was accessible by streetcar tracks but difficult to reach from downtown. As a result, it developed its own self-sufficient community. From 1890 to 1920, the University District drew many working-class families, who were supported by small truck farms and the small industries in the area. In 1901 a university administrator said the district consisted of wooden sidewalks, some unpaved streets,

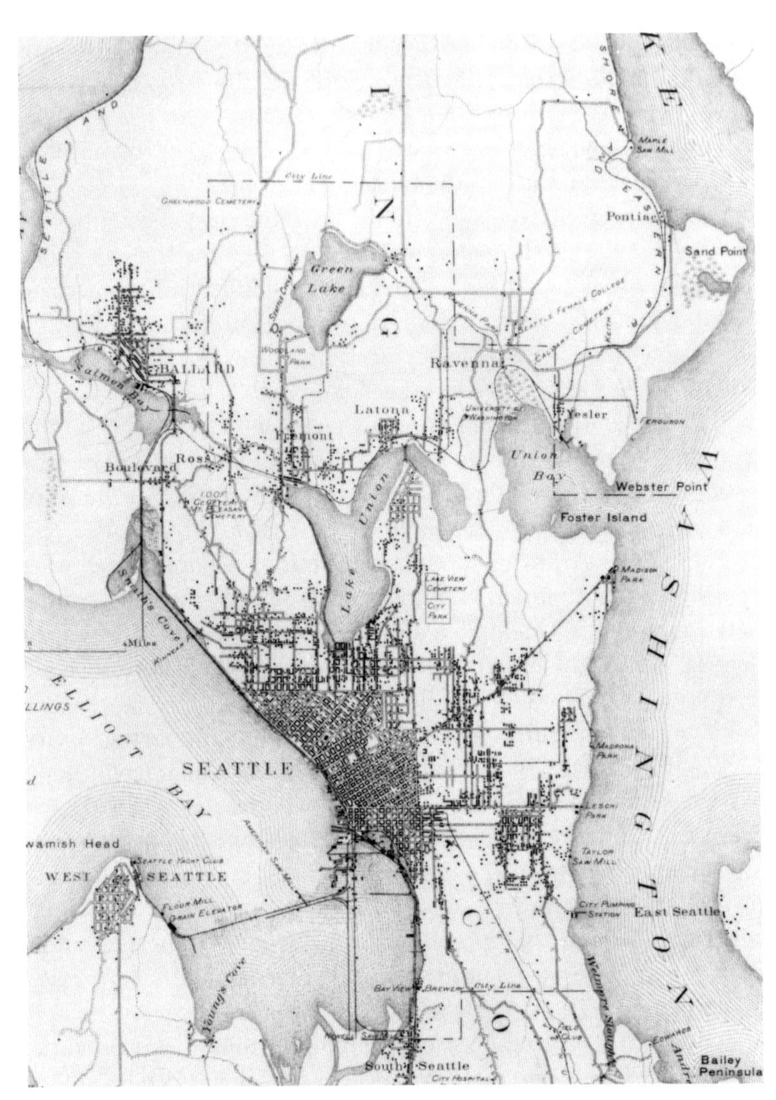

The Seattle to which the Landeses moved was concentrated along the city's waterfront. Yesler Way, the dividing line for the small city's gambling and prostitution enterprises, was like a belt across the city's waist. It was fairly remote from the North End area around the University of Washington, seen here between Lake Union and Union Bay in this 1894 map. *Map courtesy of the Museum of History and Industry, Seattle*.

cottage homes with "bits of lawn on which the cows from the Green Lake farms were daily trespassers, a cluster of stores at the corners, and a little community church." The community was made up of people in their twenties and thirties, "all of them from somewhere else, and all ambitious and confident of achievement."[52]

In 1902 the first seven of the houses in "Greek Row" were built. The Alaska-Yukon-Pacific Exposition of 1909, trading on supplying the burgeoning needs of Alaskan gold fever and showing off the Queen City, was located on the campus as the result of a proposal by Prof. Edmond Meany. He hoped it would get some campus land cleared and buildings needed on campus out of a strapped legislature. It did both. In all, the university kept twenty buildings from the exposition, including a new Women's Building, although many of them were only temporary structures. The exposition also resulted in a real estate boom for the area.[53]

The Landeses chose to live near the new campus, eventually building a home at Brooklyn Avenue and Northeast Forty-fifth Street. It was a two-story frame house with an inviting front porch circling its base.[54] Their house was located on the future site of the Hotel Meany, which later became the University Tower Hotel. Two of Henry's younger brothers followed him west to Washington. Charles became a teacher at Roosevelt High School in Seattle, and Thomas became a rancher at Wenatchee, Washington.[55]

Bertha and Henry Landes joined the University Congregational Church, a church geared to the university and a focus for the isolated community. By 1899 Henry was its treasurer and a trustee, and Bertha, in 1903 and again in 1918, served two terms as president of its Women's League. In 1928 she served as moderator of the Washington Conference for the denomination, perhaps the first woman to do so.[56]

The Congregational church, which in the eighteenth century dominated New England, infused the culture of that region. It held that the highest human authority was the members themselves, who had to prove themselves worthy. They did this not through fulfilling decrees from on high but through a contractual agreement from below through fellowship. It was an individual duty to live the right way, and it was woven into daily life. The Congregational religion was "locally owned and operated" and until the nineteenth century was legally intertwined with Massa-

The Landeses built their home near the University of Washington campus, where the University Tower Hotel now stands. Bertha fed hungry and homesick students Boston baked beans and bread in this home every week for years. She also helped her husband host department Sunday dinners and alumni receptions as he moved from professor to dean to acting president. When Landes was elected they moved to the Wilsonian Apartments nearby, where meals and housekeeping help were available if needed. *Photo courtesy of Special Collections Division, University of Washington Libraries, neg. US7332.*

chusetts' government.[57] It remained mentally intertwined with ideas about government, civic involvement, and education, long after the legal ties were cut. It also had a reputation for leading the way in civil and educational rights.

Only fifteen years before Bertha was born, Oberlin-educated Antoinette Brown Blackwell pursued and won her ordination to the ministry of the Congregational church. She was the first female to gain the authority of the ministry in one of the major denominations,[58] and she worked for recognition of women's rights. The church thus established, if not a tradition, at least an opening for women to influence public affairs through seeking office. Congregationalists were often connected to social reform

Bertha was twenty-seven years old when her daughter Katherine was born, one year after she and Henry had moved to Seattle. Katherine died tragically when she was nine years old. *Photo courtesy of Henry Landes Papers, University of Washington Libraries*.

causes, as a matter of individual responsibility in civic as well as church affairs.

The West offered new opportunities to Congregationalists, as it did other denominations. In fact, Congregationalists formed an alliance with the Presbyterians (the Plan of Union of 1801) for missionary work in the westward expansion. From the time when Congregationalist minister Lyman Beecher settled in the western frontier town of Cincinnati in 1832 until the church reached the Oregon Territory at mid-century,[59] members of this church felt a responsibility to bring order to anarchy, and civilization to barbarism, while capitalizing on the bounty of the West. Seattle was the last outpost of the West and had several Congregational churches by the end of the century.

Bertha was soon busy with children as well as church. A daughter, Katherine, was born in 1896, only a year after they arrived, when Bertha was twenty-seven years old. Son Roger followed, but he died in infancy. A second son, Kenneth, was born in 1899. In 1905, Bertha and Henry again suffered the pain of losing a child. Nine-year-old Katherine died tragically and unnecessarily at the end of March as a result of preventative surgery by an unnamed physician. The purpose of the surgery was to reduce the size of Katherine's tonsils and ward off danger to her throat. The home operation was successful, but the girl never awakened from the chloroform administered as an anesthetic. Her heart simply stopped beating. The parents had been talked into the surgery as a prophylactic.[60]

A family friend described the child as a "beautiful, strong and helpful character," and "the most intelligent and motherly child I have ever known."[61] The parents' bitterness must have been enormous. Bertha later spoke or wrote about most of the other parts of her life, but she was silent on the loss of her children. She must have suffered terribly, however, centered on home and family as she was. The loss may have influenced her later focus on the importance of motherhood and of women staying at home when their children were small. Staying at home with their children, however, was a luxury not available to many mothers in Seattle, even then. Almost 20,000 women were working for wages in Seattle in 1910, many of them in other women's homes.

Two years after Katherine died, the loss was evidently still very much on Bertha's mind. In 1907 she and Henry adopted into their family a girl the same age Katherine was when she died, a nine-year-old named Viola. Viola grew up and was working at a Seattle bank by the time her mother made her first run at the city council. Viola later married Edwin J. Peach, a clerk at Seattle First National Bank, and they resided at 2021 Miller Street.[62] Late in her life Viola Peach lived in Seattle, as a widow in an apartment on Lake Washington. She always spoke highly of her mother and her accomplishments, calling her "grand."[63]

Bertha's son Kenneth attended the University of Washington, graduating in 1921, the year before his mother took her seat on the city council. Like his father, he also attended Harvard graduate school, and he taught at Wellesley for a time. He followed in his father's professional footsteps, becoming a professor of mineralogy at the University of Kansas and later at the University of Michigan. He took a concurrent position as state geologist in both

Kansas and Michigan, as his father did in the state of Washington. He also published books on petroleum geology and mineral resources (one with his father) and a variety of geological surveys.[64] Kenneth married Susan Beach, daughter of Dr. Walter Beach of Stanford, and they had three children—Walter Henry, Robert Kenneth, and Katherine Flora.[65]

While her children were small, Bertha participated in school and university activities and supported her husband's blossoming career. She was long noted for feeding hungry students Boston brown bread and baked beans in her home. Every Saturday for years she fed young men who, she said, "were 'baching' and struggling to make both ends meet on very little money." She remembered in particular one man, who later became a wealthy professional in Washington, "who lived for sixteen weeks one year on $16, largely because he knew he could count on brown bread and beans."[66]

Bertha did this, she added, to brighten the lives of young men and women at the university who were lonely, and evidently hungry. "One might say that the boys and girls of the university at that time and ever since have been my 'second family,' " she said later. After she won the primary election to the Seattle City Council, she said she suspected the Boston brown bread she baked for all those students during these years might have won her one thousand of her votes.[67]

In 1912 her husband was named dean of the new College of Science, the first and only dean. Up to that point the sciences had been poor cousins to the languages and classical study; but with the help of votes from faculty in science and engineering, Henry had led the university into establishing the college. He instituted high standards for the college and gave it needed visibility. He also served as chairman of the Committee on the Course of Study for the university and established the survey courses for non-majors now taken for granted. His course, Geology 1, Survey of Geology, was the first. His leadership led to greater cooperation and good feeling among departments at a time when such rapport was hard to come by.[68]

His reputation was such that the board of regents named him acting president following the forced resignation of Thomas Kane. Kane had lost the confidence of both students and regents in conflicts over free speech and other issues. Henry held the position for about eighteen months in 1914–15, taking office dur-

Henry Landes, a professor of geology at the University of Washington, was for eighteen months acting president of the school, when this portrait was taken. Landes always supported his wife's endeavors, wanting for her as "rich and full" a life as he had. As the author of dozens of reports on the state's dam sites, mineral resources, and topography, Landes had a significant impact on the development of Washington. *Photo courtesy of Special Collections Division, University of Washington Libraries, neg. UW504.*

ing a time of open warfare among the governor, university regents, and legislators. Landes filled the post capably enough to be talked about as a permanent president and to be nominated for president of Washington State College (later Washington State University). Superior Court Judge James Ronald of King County wrote the governor praising Landes's ability in applied science and his technical experience, qualities needed at the latter institution. Such qualities, along with his "lovable personality and ease of approach, together with his fine sense of humor," could ease the friction between the two schools.[69] However, outsider Henry Suzzallo got the University of Washington presidency, only to be fired a few years later.

The board of regents, however, unanimously praised the Landes administration. The board said it had been marked "by consummate tact and judgement," with a "high degree of intellectual ability and executive capacity." The board, sensitive to past criticisms, also noted that his conduct "has been such as to avoid all friction and controversy and to command the loyal support of the faculty and student body."[70] Under President Suzzallo, Landes was president of the Instructor's Association and worked diligently for salary increases for the university's beleaguered faculty. He also founded the University Commons and was sensitive to student needs. He was noted particularly for his "unswerving devotion to democratic principles and policies."[71] He was careful to submit proposals to the right committees before a faculty vote, and those who talked to him about issues always felt they could do so in utmost confidence. He could "listen to the advocates of all sides of a problem and yet scrupulously preserve the confidence of each individual," showing "a gentleness and a sense of humor that are hard to equal," colleagues said.[72] In fact, he was a champion of both student and faculty free speech rights, basic civil rights that were sometimes abrogated at the school, especially during the First World War. In 1934 he proposed a sandstone monument on the campus as a gathering spot for students to exercise complete freedom of political expression.

Henry Landes, at 5′10″ a dashing figure with an impish goatee and smile, always supported his wife's endeavors. He was an admired and popular figure on campus, noted for providing support to women on the faculty in nursing and home economics and firm but friendly guidance to students. The student newspaper described the professor as fond of driving tractors, growing red apples, and constantly whistling. He was also famous for his skill at kidding students.[73]

Henry also played a significant role in the development of the state, in his allied position of state geologist during the years 1897–1931. Landes was editor of and contributor to the dozens of annual reports and bulletins of the Washington Geological Survey. He founded the Puget Sound Academy of Science in 1928 and served as its president until 1936.[74] In the late 1920s he produced a series of well-received monthly broadcasts for KOMO

Radio, with titles such as "The Story of a Lump of Coal," "When Puget Sound Was Filled with Ice," and "The White Bearded Volcanoes of Our Mountains."[75]

Landes published major works on the geological history of the Columbia River, analyzed dam sites in many places in the state where dams were subsequently built, and cataloged the mineral resources of the Columbia River basin and parts of northern Idaho.[76] He also founded a successful consulting engineering firm, taking on work that later complicated his wife's political career. Like his wife, he was also a member of many professional and community groups, including the Kiwanis Club and Masonic Lodge.[77] Unlike his wife, he called himself a Democrat. She called herself a Republican and was at least a nominal member of the party that held a tight grip on Seattle and Washington politics until Roosevelt.

Bertha contributed to her husband's career in many ways. Besides feeding lonely and hungry students, while he was acting president she helped him host members of one of the university departments by inviting them to Sunday dinner, and later in the afternoon she would entertain the students of that department. She went with him on a number of field trips, leading groups of students into the Cascades and beyond. She also accompanied him on geological study trips to places such as Yellowstone and Glacier national parks, even to Alaska. She described their match as a partnership, in which he wanted for her as full a life as he had for himself. "My husband and I formed a partnership a good many years ago, and the partnership is still working in full force," she said in 1927. He "is as interested in having me live a full, rich life as he is in having one for himself."[78]

Work in Women's Clubs

Her full, rich life increasingly included work with other women in clubs. She began her club career in her thirties, beginning shortly after her daughter died in 1905. Clubwork, especially for middle-class women, opened a window on the world outside home and family. Most women at the turn of the century found themselves caught in the cusp of the transition between the timeless ideals of the nineteenth century and rapid-fire changes of the twentieth century. Most women practiced and held tightly to the idea that woman's role centered exclusively on home and family. They accepted or resigned themselves to the legal, social, and political structures that reinforced that view of reality.[79]

Yet many women envisioned a less restrictive definition of "woman," pushing the boundaries (sometimes by extending the definition of "home") to take a more active role in politics and society. They also began to move into professions outside women's traditional professions of teaching and nursing, which were extensions of home service. Even those who held fast to the prevailing domestic ideology recognized that to protect that sphere required their involvement in civic affairs.[80] Despite significant gains for women in legal and economic rights by 1900, there were few avenues open to women who might want to step outside the domestic realm to become involved in civic affairs at the turn of the century and beyond. One of the best was women's clubwork.

The clubs developed a sense of "female consciousness," to borrow a phrase from historian Nancy Cott, and gave women a vehicle through which to act in the larger world. For instance, the constitution of the Worcester Woman's Club, adopted in 1880, declared that the women of Worcester believed "the present and prospective status of woman" imposed upon them a need to inform themselves on "the more important special questions . . . pressing upon all peoples everywhere for a just solution . . . involving the welfare of humanity."[81] In 1896 a member of that club described what the club had given them, using words that applied to most clubwomen: "A habit of working together; an appreciation of people whose social and other relations differ from our own; a higher intellectual standing." It also enabled members to study questions "to which our attention might not otherwise have been called—resulting in the formation of definite opinions and a confidence in expressing our views." Members also gained "tolerance, greater thoroughness in our work, a mental stimulus which no mere reading could supply, [and] a closer touch with other bodies of earnest women throughout the land."[82] Clubs offered education, a network, and a vehicle that gave women confidence in themselves and their opinions. They also offered a means for action, a pathway to collective power.

Clubs for women provided the kind of organic network that sustained the individual and provided a context to use in absorbing and interpreting change.[83] Like groups formed around ethnicity, the women's clubs provided a unique social structure, a place to discuss and test ideas and explore the tensions between continuity and change, and a means of forwarding a community of interest and shared hopes. To borrow from anthropologist Victor Turner's theories about social change, they offered open-ended opportunities to critique existing models and structures and to test alternative visions. They gave participants a sense of what Turner called *communitas,* where they could forge a sense of common identity, purpose, and friendship outside the confines of the home.

Women's clubs also provided a conduit for transition from family and kin to professional and bureaucratic alliances. Perhaps most important, they provided practical experience in running meetings, raising money, lobbying, securing speakers, organizing committees, putting together campaigns, and doing research. They also established an arena where women's impulse to power, their will to power, could be realized, although the women themselves would never admit to having such desires or interests.[84] Many clubs moved from simply studying problems to actually resolving them. Despite their lack of formal, sanctioned power, women fostered the implementation of an impressive list of bills and ordinances and civic and social services through club action. The role of women was seldom recognized, however, since any final actions were taken by bodies with formal power. And the clubs found and made leaders.

Landes credited the women's clubs for whatever political success she had. She said clubwork gave her not only poise and confidence but also the ability to work with people "of many minds and temperaments" and a knowledge of the city and its people. Without club training, she said, she would not have been on the council. Without having been on the council, she would not have been mayor.[85] She later advised women with political aspirations to use that same avenue, the one guaranteed to be open to all women. "Clubwork offers the woman the best method of advancing themselves, of learning how to work harmoniously with other people and to make progress along the line of civic welfare and civic betterment."[86]

Clubs and their leaders, however, often stirred the wrath of men such as Grover Cleveland, who in the *Ladies' Home Journal* in 1905—about the time Bertha began joining such clubs—attacked women's clubs as a menace to the integrity of the home.

"There are woman's clubs whose objects and intents are not only harmful, but harmful in a way that directly menaces the integrity of our homes."[87] The safest club for a woman, he said, was her home. Nevertheless, women's clubs flourished in the 1890s and early 1900s, spreading quickly from the clubs that first developed in New England in 1868.[88] The clubs were federated in 1890 under the umbrella organization, the General Federation of Women's Clubs.

Membership in the General Federation of Women's Clubs exploded from 100,000 in 1896 to 800,000 by 1910 and passed the million mark by 1920.[89] Constituted primarily (but not exclusively) of middle-class women, the clubs fostered a heightened sense of civic consciousness, activism, and leanings toward reform, even within relatively conservative groups. Made up of diverse organizations, the General Federation itself finally adopted a resolution supporting the political tool of women's suffrage in 1914. That step occurred several years after the issue had been brought before the federation by Carrie Chapman Catt and delegates began arguing for it, and several years after western states enfranchised their female residents.[90]

Like other growing urban areas in the West, Seattle was the site of much club activity, dating from the nineteenth century. As cities grew, clubs became small enclaves where common interests and concerns were shared. Landes's earliest and most significant club involvements included a forerunner of the Parent Teacher Association, the University Club, the Century Club, and the Red Cross. She joined her first clubs when her son was eight. By 1911, when her son was twelve, she was thoroughly caught up in Seattle's women's clubs, although she had not yet assumed leadership roles.

Bertha and Henry were part of a social, although not economic, elite that moved into Seattle at the close of the century. The education and occupational status of these newcomers meant new social ideas and a changing agenda for Seattle's future. Landes's early activities, according to the 1911 *Seattle Society Blue Book,* included memberships in the Woman's Century Club, the Rainier Club, and the University Club. Within a few years she rose to the head of social services (1916–17), then the presidency (1918–20), of the influential Women's Century Club.

She also became president of the Seattle Federated Women's Clubs in 1920–22, which by then represented thousands of women. The federation in Seattle included a mixture of literary, professional, women's rights, and social clubs in overlapping networks.[91] Women who became active in one club often were pulled into others. The clubs themselves invited visitors from sister clubs in the city and in the region. The national federation priorities became local and regional club agendas and vice versa. In Seattle varied clubs and women from varying backgrounds found they could agree on a plan of action to meet specific needs in Seattle. They learned the process of creating consensus and found that they could exercise collective muscle. That Landes joined and became the leader of the Century Club and later the Seattle Federated Women's Clubs was particularly significant, given the history of women's clubs in Seattle. It was the women of Seattle, working through clubs, who often forced social and cultural concerns on the pro-development agenda of the city's official establishment.

One of the first clubs was the Century Club. It was founded in 1891, four years before Landes arrived in Seattle. One of this Seattle club's founders was Carrie Chapman Catt, who gained national and international fame as the head of the National American Women's Suffrage Association (NAWSA) in 1916,[92] replacing Susan B. Anthony, and who in 1925 helped organize the National Conference on the Cause and Cure of War.[93]

Catt, born Carrie Clinton Lane in 1859, had studied law at the University of Iowa and worked as high school principal and superintendent of schools in Mason City, Iowa.[94] In 1885 she married newspaper editor Leo Chapman there. He died of typhoid fever a year later, and she ended up in San Francisco, broke and working occasionally in journalism. A gifted speaker, Catt—as Landes did later—put together a national speaking tour. She wrote three lectures centered on the ever-popular topic of the dangers of aliens to American institutions, hired an agent, and began speaking to large audiences.[95] In 1890 Carrie Lane Chapman, then thirty-one, found herself on a speaking tour of the Northwest and settled in Seattle. There she married wealthy civil engineer George Catt, a man she had met in college who now was in charge of the extensive Washington State operations of the San Francisco Bridge Company.

On July 31, 1891, Catt met with a half-dozen exceptional women residing in Seattle. Together they founded the Seattle Woman's Century Club, out of the belief that the coming century would be the woman's century.[96] The club's initial purpose in meeting was "for intellectual culture, original research, and the solution of the altruistic problems of the day."[97] Each member was expected to complete one original paper during the year, a terrifying prospect for some members. Catt, elected president, gave the first, "The Evolution of Woman," on the progress of "the sex out of primitive barbarism and slavery into the freedom of today." Other papers included "The Present Status of Woman, Social, Industrial, Legal," "Working Women and Their Wages," "Women in Science, Literature, and Art," "Pauper Wives and the Remedy," "Divorce," and a half dozen other subjects written from a distinctly female perspective.

This club's founders formed a nexus of leaders in women's club activity, who in some cases became leaders of social and political activism in Seattle. Besides Catt, the first members included Julia Kennedy, a woman who had been on the Illinois State Normal School faculty for nine years and was the first superintendent of Seattle schools; Alice Blake, the first woman to receive a degree from Yale University; Sarah Kendall, one of the city's first female physicians, who later became an officer in the state and national federations of women's clubs; Kate Turner Holmes, a university graduate who later founded the Seattle Federation of Women's Clubs and was the second president of the Washington State Federation of Women's Clubs; Harriet Parkhurst, a Women's Christian Temperance Union activist; Mary Barrett Hagan, a writer who had been published in Ohio; Anna Fishback, who was also president of the Seattle Board of Friendly Visitors and Chautauqua Alumni; Elizabeth MacIntosh, who in 1869 had become enrolling clerk of the Washington territorial legislature, the first female in the nation to hold that position in a state legislature; and Elizabeth Lyle Saxon, a southern-born worker in temperance and social reform.

Leaders of the Century Club crossed class lines. For instance, Carrie Hill, one of the Century Club's first presidents, founded and presided over the Women's Industrial Club, established in 1895 for self-supporting women. Hill also published *Washington Women,* a paper devoted to club interests and later women's suffrage. She subsequently became president of the Washington Equal Franchise Society.[98]

The Women's Industrial Club, with annual dues of fifty cents, had as its object "mutual improvement, bettering of physical conditions and the elevation of tastes." Its membership included primarily women working as domestics, an avenue of work many women, especially immigrants, pursued in order to survive. In the club they practiced elocution, drilled in parliamentary procedure, and debated current events. At the first state federation meeting, Hill, one of four women named to represent the state federation at the national meeting, made a plea for laying aside all social differences in clubwork.[99] Another example was an action taken by Century Club founder Julia Kennedy at the second meeting of a working class group called the Ladies Protective and Beneficiary Association. She resigned over the issue of becoming a secret society, one that ultimately split the membership. She opposed making the membership exclusive. "In a working girls' union there should be no line of demarcation," she said.[100]

The Century Club initially renounced political activism and claimed no devotion to any particular philanthropy or reform, but it soon became involved in corollary political issues that affected women. One of the measures for which it proudly claimed success was getting the legislature to raise the age of consent for sexual activity in Washington from twelve years of age to fifteen. In Delaware as late as 1891 the age of consent for sexual activity was a shameful seven years old. The average in the United States at the time was fourteen years.[101]

The club led a spirited but unsuccessful effort to get a woman on the Seattle School Board before the turn of the century. It also helped start the Martha Washington School for Girls, paid the salary of the first librarian for a year, and, in Landes's era, started Travelers Aid, for the protection of newly arrived immigrant girls and women.[102] It used volunteers and sometimes a paid staff to connect newly arrived citizens to social services and employment and protect them from being victimized. In 1909 the Century Club established an institution called Girls Parental School, running it through private charity until the Seattle School Board took it over in 1914. It offered vocational and industrial training for girls in trouble in juvenile courts. Club women frequently tried to apply domestic and maternal values not only to schools but also to the handling of delinquency. They lobbied for systems, programs, and alternatives outside the punitive, adult-oriented court system. The club also secured Revenna Park and preserved its huge trees. Members also established a Daughter's Auxiliary.[103]

The club's constitution set three goals: "to promote intellectual growth of its members, to stimulate investigation in social and political ethics, and to lend its influence toward the solution of the altruistic problems of the day."[104] Although the club included connections with working women, it was at first elite in its membership, at least in terms of education, if not wealth. Members were nominated by a secret committee and were voted in by the membership. Within a couple decades, however, the Century Club had opened its doors to welcome hundreds of Seattle women as members. Members paid $1 for initiation and $2 in annual dues to the club (much less than in many social clubs), and the club bestowed honorary-member status to women of distinction. As a comparison, the Woman's Club in Olympia, the first woman's club in Washington and a founding member of the state federation, charged a $10 initiation fee and $3 annual dues, plus pro rata distribution of the cost of social affairs.[105]

The Century Club was also one of the earliest clubs to affiliate with the General Federation of Women's Clubs, itself founded only in 1890 nationally and in 1896 in Washington State.[106] Landes joined the Century Club in 1907, when her son was eight years old and she was thirty-nine. Jennie Cunningham Croly's massive 1898 history of the women's club movement described the Seattle Woman's Century Club as "a strong club, more aggressive in its methods than the purely literary clubs."[107]

It was here that Landes's political philosophy began to crystallize. The club's early roundtable groups included art, current literature, education, hygiene, philanthropy, politics, religion, science, temperance, woman's progress, and the World's Fair. She was part of the new social service department in 1911–12 and headed it by 1916–17. By then the club had a dozen departments, including art, child study (which included junior guilds), current events, drama, French, German, literature, music, parliamentary procedure, travel, and social service, which studied sociology and "current social problems."[108]

The women in her social service department used books—Elwood's *Sociology and Modern Social Problems* and Zueblin's *City*—as their expert guides. The social service department subdivided into ten committees, which undertook the following specific projects: child welfare, progress, child labor, juvenile court, schools and playgrounds, institutional work, hospitals, penal, education and philanthropy, and immigrant station. In addition to hearing lectures from a variety of experts, the department met monthly. In her report on the department Landes said the work included visits to charitable and penal institutions to contribute food, clothing, a little money, and time, furnishing thereby the "means of social relaxation" to the inmates.[109]

Landes began working with women from other clubs. She signed the register at the biennial Washington federation meetings as a representative of the Woman's Century Club (in 1916, 1918, 1919, and 1920), as did other members who later became Landes's campaign leaders in the 1920s. By 1933 the Century Club had three hundred members and eventually its own three-story building at Roy and Harvard North, with its own small theater.[110]

President of the Seattle Federation

When she became president of the Seattle federation in 1920, Bertha became part of the leadership of the Washington federation. The Washington State Federation of Women's Clubs had both culture and politics in its purview. Its object was "to unite the Women's Clubs of the State for the study of cultural and altruistic subjects, for the consideration of public issues and to secure such concerted action thereon as its members may desire."[111] Its first half dozen presidents, like Landes, came from New England, where the women's club tradition developed. Early dubbed the Housewife's University, the clubs of the state federation offered the opportunity for women to learn, meet socially, and work collectively toward goals.

At the first federation meeting, President Amy P. Stacy defined the nature and purpose of Washington's women's clubs: "We discuss practical questions, economics, home decoration, the care and training of children, the betterment of schools, the improvement of civic conditions, the problems of ethics, and the thousand and one questions as vital to women as to men." Increasingly, those concerns reflected reform efforts later lumped under the term "Progressive." She added that the "flippant charge can no longer be made that we 'care only for dress and amusement.' " The clubs, she said, were necessarily altruistic, and a woman "of greater culture must share her benefits with her listening, less-favored sister; and as always, the most generous giver gets greatest good." She then listed dozens of civic accomplishments of member clubs in their respective cities, including the Century Club.[112]

During the first decade of its existence the state federation moved into a feminist mode that plunged into politics, displaying an activism that would sharply diminish by the end of the 1920s. Its early resolutions included calls for dramatic changes in the legal and political framework of the state and for giving attention to social rather than business concerns. The women sought national uniform divorce laws and supported patronage of only those establishments employing women "where they are paid living wages." They were active in efforts to prohibit saloons near schools, put officials and employees of Washington's institutions under a merit system, change legislation that had weakened the new age-of-consent law, enforce the state anticigarette sales law, elect at least one woman on every school board in the state, and add pragmatic "domestic science" and "manual training" to what became junior high curricula. The federation called for the employment of women to teach physiology "and kindred subjects" to girls and to become teachers of science in high schools. It also attacked a state education official's recommendation that men supersede women as high school instructors in Washington, arguing that "women are endowed equally with men in all that pertains to the making of competent teachers."[113] Pressure from the women's clubs led to classes being established in Seattle and elsewhere for deaf, blind, and mentally challenged children.

Like the General Federation, the Washington State Federation also promoted libraries, the child labor amendment, higher standards of education, care and housing for children, protective laws for women and children, and the construction of special facilities for women. In Washington, the last item involved a protracted campaign for a training school for girls, which had to overcome a governor's veto even after the legislature authorized it. In 1901 the federation helped establish a ten-hour work day limit for women. In 1903, in concert with the Grange and the Washington State Federation of Labor, the federation managed to get several reform measures through the legislature, including a child labor law, an initiative law, and an eight-hour day for employees on publicly funded projects.[114]

In 1913 the federation was credited for getting introduced into the Washington legislature a spate of social legislation, including a minimum wage for women and minors, a teachers' pension bill, a mother's pension bill, a consumer bill to protect citizens from bogus employment agencies, and bills for vocational schools, support of destitute women, control of liquor and "red light" districts, and an eight-hour-day law for coal miners.[115] Several of the measures passed, although some were delayed. The fraudulent employment agencies problem, for example, was addressed by the next session of the legislature.

The Seattle and state federations had long pushed for a separate asylum for women, an industrial home at Medical Lake. Although their intense lobbying got the facility established (the act passed in 1919), in 1921 Governor Roland Hartley vetoed any appropriation for it. Eighty-seven women were to be dumped on their counties with only five dollars in their pockets. Seven women's clubs took matters into their own hands. They filed a writ of mandamus to force the state to open the facility and fund it. Landes was one of the signatories among the plaintiffs, as were Theresa Griswold, Greta Weeks, and other women who would be part of her later political campaigns. Their writ petition failed, however, and the issue was deferred for two years.[116]

Under the leadership of Kate Turner Holmes, one of the cofounders of the Century Club, the federation's agenda included making it a crime for a man to desert his family, building a state reformatory for girls, closing saloons and gambling, and building traveling libraries. In recognition of her efforts, Holmes was named one of the original members of the Washington Library Commission.[117] Besides gaining protection for working women, the federation sought better conditions for female prisoners, established scholarships for young women, and worked to get women on the University of Washington Board of Regents as well as on school boards.[118] In fact, Washington became the first state to put a woman on the university's Board of Regents when Ruth Karr McKee joined it in 1917. Actively involved in clubwork and a past president of the Washington Federation of Women's Clubs (and a UW graduate), McKee also became the first female president of a major American university's board when she was elected president of the UW board in 1923.[119]

A few years before Landes took the office of president of the Seattle federation, federation president Viola Crahan organized clubs for female laundry workers. These women, who averaged $5.87 a week in pay and endured difficult working conditions, were on call at all times and furthermore were prohibited from joining a union.[120]

The state federation's broad agenda also included an early and ongoing focus on environmental issues, including reforestation, environmental and species protection, and eventually highway beautification and support for establishing Olympic National Park. In the 1920s, under Esther Maltby, the federation raised funds for the purchase and development of sixty-three acres of old-growth timber for the Federation Forest State Park on Snoqualmie Pass.

In the years 1915–17 the federation added a Committee on Immigration to aid "the struggling immigrant mother." It offered classes in English for foreign women and provided care for their children during the classes.[121] During World War I, like thousands of other clubwomen, Landes turned to patriotic duty and assisting in the war cause. Here again she took a leadership role. She was on the local Red Cross board and organized five Red Cross auxiliaries;[122] she said she bought war savings stamps and bonds "till it hurt."[123] The Seattle-King County chapter of the Red Cross raised money, provided transportation for soldiers and supplies in and out of Seattle, sewed surgical dressings and socks, and supported military and civilian relief.[124]

As a founding member of the Washington Minute Women, Landes helped raise money to provide assistance to needy families of soldiers. The group also gave a "cheering send off" of lunches, candy, and cigarettes to draftees passing through Seattle, provided mess funds and reading matter for soldiers, and even offered meals for sailors and soldiers in a local clubhouse.[125]

The allied Minute Men took on a more nefarious role—that of policing patriotism. Among many others, they targeted "alien" teachers or those who resisted "impressing patriotism" on their students, which led to the firing of six teachers.[126] In fact, fearing the excesses of patriotism, the Federation of Women's Clubs and State PTA went on record opposing "military addresses . . . or any addresses of a political nature in the public schools."[127]

In 1917–19, shortly before Landes took over the Seattle federation, the state federation continued its forays into political action. It supported thirty-one legislative measures in total, such as equal pay for female teachers, and a remarkable seventeen of them passed the legislature.[128] After the war ended, the minutes of the 1919–21 biennium for the state federation reflected a growing worry about the mixture of immigrants and politics, as recounted by a later president of the Washington federation. "As many as 5,000 foreigners entered the country in one day and assimilation was impossible. There was a danger to our own state of an alarming increase in illiteracy and this in turn furnished tools for unscrupulous political bosses."[129] The idea that corrupt politicians could manipulate the immigrant vote concerned urban reformers across the country, under its one-man, one-vote representative democratic system.

The federation also supported and praised the University of Washington's efforts in offering credit in sociology for work "done among the foreign born" in teaching English and civics. In fact, by 1920 Seattle's population was 26 percent foreign born, with most of the immigrants having come from Sweden, Norway, and England,[130] an influx that also affected Seattle city politics. Many ethnic groups settled in distinct areas of the city and formed their own neighborhood clubs.[131]

Federation accounts from this period were consistently silent on the other hot political issue of the day—women's suffrage, the ultimate collective political power.[132] Even Landes, shortly before she began joining her clubs, was uncertain about the drive for enfranchisement for women, concerned that a mother's direct involvement in politics might damage the family.

An old friend recalled that Landes was not exactly an early advocate of women's rights. "In fact, she was decidedly opposed to the Woman Suffrage movement when it was launched, believing that a woman's place was in her home, with her children," said Mrs. H. O. Stone. However, her opposition did not last long. Her view on women's involvements outside the home and suffrage changed when her first child was ready to leave home and enter school. She became the organizer and first president of the University Heights Parent Teacher Association and was later president of the Lincoln High PTA besides being active in the Century Club. Her club career (and political career) was born.[133]

In the early 1920s, when Landes was president of the Seattle federation, its divisions included Americanization, citizenship, conservation, safety, education, the motion picture, child welfare, health and narcotics, and state and industrial relations. The annual report for 1919–20, spanning the time Landes was president, showed that the Washington federation endorsed the

Sheppard-Towner Act for protection of women and infants, called for a strengthening rather than an end to wartime prohibition, and complained that now that the war was over, women were in danger of losing the wider opportunities they had enjoyed. The state federation wanted women to have the "freedom to choose their occupation without restriction through custom and prejudice." It also sought equal pay and equal opportunity for advancement. Female high school teachers were paid less than male teachers until 1919, when the board was forced to equalize pay after the legislature passed an equal pay bill.[134] The federation also wanted a federal Women's Bureau, and it established a motion picture committee "to work for better and cleaner pictures, and particularly for pictures suitable for children."[135] In 1923 the state federation's membership included women in 245 clubs, the heyday of the federation's collective power. In contrast, sixty years later, the clubs in the federation totaled only 117, despite the state's increase in population in the intervening years.[136]

Landes's political skills and agenda were formed in this milieu, but it does not represent the full extent of her club activities and involvement in Seattle's civic affairs. Her extensive connections and experience made her a formidable force and strengthened her sophistication and resolve, sometimes to the irritation of those not headed in the same direction. Besides helping organize the PTA and Travelers Aid, she for twelve years was one of the few women on the board of the Seattle Community Fund, founded in 1920.

Bertha also was a director of the campus YWCA and served as its president early in the century. It ran an employment bureau for women students and classes on leadership training and marriage.[137] She joined the P.E.O. (known by its acronym) and Business and Professional Women. The BPW in Seattle, founded in 1921 with four hundred members, was the successor to the 1913 Seattle Business Girls' Club.[138] She was president of the Coterie Club and University Heights PTA. She founded the Women's City Club for the express purpose of crossing class lines in the study of civic activism while she was on the Seattle City Council, and she became one of six females on the thirty-person advisory council of the Seattle Chamber of Commerce.[139] Landes became president of the Washington State League of Women Voters (the successor to the NAWSA) and moderator of the Congregational Church Conference in Washington. She was national president of the American Federation of Soroptimist Clubs in 1930–32.[140]

She was also a member of the influential University Club, active with the YWCA in hosting the women's activities at the 1909 Alaska-Yukon-Pacific Exposition, held the year before women gained suffrage in Washington. The Women's University Club combined in 1914 with the College Women's Club and included fully nine hundred members in the 1920s. Members discussed book reviews and world problems, held lectures, and founded a popular drama group called the Handbag Players. Speakers included luminaries such as Carrie Chapman Catt, writer Ida Tarbell, explorer Roald Amundsen (hosted by Landes), and First Ladies Hoover and Roosevelt.[141]

Landes found power and a voice through her work in clubs, a fact to which her daughter Viola alluded in a 1965 interview. "She was the grandest woman you could know. There was no one kindlier or more tolerant. But she just had to keep busy. She wasn't aggressive, but if she wasn't engaged in planning something or other, she was bored to tears." According to Viola, "There was hardly an organization she joined of which, within a short time, she didn't become president. We had to smile at that, just a little."[142]

A reporter from the *New York World* said that Landes outwardly seemed anything but aggressive. "She is quiet-spoken and suggests a domestic background—regular housecleaning, prompt meals, neatly labeled preserves," he wrote. "As she talks, however, her hand drumming restlessly on the desk, the air of placidity disappears. The quiet manner develops into calm tenacity and reveals a lively mind." The police chief she fired later in her career described her reserve and tenacity another way: "Compared with Mrs. Landes, 'Silent' Cal Coolidge is a circus spieler."[143]

Bertha Knight Landes became a powerful presence in the sphere of women's clubwork, as demonstrated through her multiple memberships and election by her peers to offices and boards of these organizations. One of Seattle's newspapers said of her that she was "probably the best known clubwoman in Seattle,"[144] although her sphere of influence was limited to Washington's largest city, itself hardly known in the East where the club movement began. She clearly relished working at this "profession," leaving her mark and meeting her goals in ever-wider circles, in the places where women could simultaneously learn about the larger world and have some impact upon it through club projects.

The Suffrage Movement in Washington State

In a dynamic relationship heightened by successful efforts to gain state suffrage (1910) and then national suffrage (1920), some of these women saw even grander opportunities emerging. They saw the potential for extending the sphere of their activism and influence across the gender boundary lines into areas formerly controlled by men. If they gained the vote, they would have a new means of realizing their political agendas. Some of them might even then run for office and win; with the vote they might make their priorities the system's priorities.

The path to full political participation for women was difficult. As doors remained tightly closed in the East and Midwest, however, they began to open in the West. One state after another in the West gave women the right to vote and even elected a few to office. In fact, one could build a case that women in the Northwest enjoyed greater freedom than women in either the East or South, where traditions were more entrenched and had deeper roots. One of those important freedoms was access to education. In 1891 a professor at Vassar and Wellesley praised the West for its coeducation before the National Council of Women meeting in Washington, D.C. "In the West especially has the higher education of women been well supported by the government of the separate States and by institutions that have been founded under the auspices of private individuals." The speaker said that in the West, of 212 institutions, 165 were coeducational, and some of those were even founded by women.[145] The new land-grant colleges established through the 1862 Morrill Act offered unprecedented educational opportunity to both men and women (although some schools, like the University of Wisconsin, put women into separate curricula once they came to school).[146]

Women in Washington State had a long history of engagement with the idea of suffrage, going back even before the Civil War, when a suffrage bill failed on a 9-8 vote. After the Civil War, the Washington territorial legislature's new election code of 1866 gave all white citizens the right to vote, which two judges interpreted to include women, at least until the legislature specifically denied women the vote in 1871.[147] New efforts followed but failed in 1873, 1875, 1878, and 1881. In Washington as elsewhere, giving women the vote was inextricably bound up with taking away access to alcohol.

The Washington territorial legislature, as happened in several frontier territories looking in part to boost the votes that would lead to statehood, finally gave women the right to vote in 1883. In 1887, however, after a series of local option prohibition elections passed, the Washington Territorial Supreme Court declared women's right to vote unconstitutional. The outcome of those elections had been blamed on women's having and using the ballot. Since a state constitution was being written at the time, the provision for women's suffrage could easily be included, and there was considerable debate by convention delegates over two central issues: suffrage and prohibition. It continued the trend of linking the reforms of women's rights and prohibition when they came before the voter.[148]

Ultimately the delegates decided to let white male voters, who would have to ratify the constitution, decide the questions of both woman suffrage and prohibition. Both were defeated—women's suffrage by a two-to-one margin, and prohibition by a smaller margin. The proposed constitution passed by a four-to-one ratio, leading to Washington's entry into the union on November 11, 1889.[149] Washington's first state legislature, however, did extend to women the right to vote in school elections, limiting their participation in government to an arena traditionally deemed appropriate for them.[150]

By 1900, Wyoming, Utah, Colorado, and Idaho had granted women full voting rights. In Oregon, women's right to vote was on the ballot as an amendment six times before it was passed in 1912, and then not before both Washington and California had adopted similar measures. Nevada followed in 1914.

The ultimate success of the 1910 suffrage campaign in Washington State, supported by many of the women's clubs Landes had joined, resulted from a highly visible campaign and political grass roots work. Suffragists canvassed every precinct and each county, following a national strategy promoted by Catt. The member from each county on the central committee appointed a worker in each precinct who would try to determine each voter's stand on suffrage. Those records were then turned over to the state office so campaign leaders could determine where to concentrate their efforts on the unconverted.[151] This campaign strategy also avoided confrontations like demonstrations and thus backlash.

Dubbed a hurrah campaign, with highly publicized events and speakers, the effort gained considerable coverage in the press. The National American Woman Suffrage Association held its national meeting at the 1909 Alaska-Yukon-Pacific Exposition in Landes's neighborhood, on the University of Washington campus. Movement leaders boarded a "suffrage special" train at Chicago bound for Seattle and held meetings along the way. Speakers at Seattle included Abigail Scott Duniway, Charlotte Perkins Gilman, Florence Kelley, and *Woman's Journal* editor Henry B. Blackwell and his daughter Alice Stone Blackwell, all lending force and attention to the suffrage effort in Washington.[152]

One day at the exposition near the end of the NAWSA meeting was called the Woman's Suffrage Day. All who entered the fair passed under a huge "Votes for Women" kite, and visitors received a green-ribbon badge representing the Evergreen State's Equal Suffrage Association.[153] Other groups holding conferences in conjunction with the exposition that also were forwarding the cause of women included the National Council of Women, the Washington Federation of Women's Clubs, the Washington Teachers and Washington Nurses associations, the WCTU, and even the Eastern Star.[154]

Oregon used a similar strategy to gain passage in 1912 as western states together advanced the cause of women's rights. Women's club leaders and Landes herself would learn to use "hurrah" campaign and precinct canvassing techniques to help accomplish their own political goals.

The first state victory in fourteen years, Washington's move started a wave of enfranchisement in the West, spreading south, then east, culminating in congressional action in 1919. The national importance of the victory in Washington State was not lost on suffrage leaders (although it was on some later historians). Carrie Chapman Catt called it critical: "In point of wealth, population, and political influence, Washington is the most important state yet won."[155] In other words, Washington State was more like one of the states in the East; it could not be ignored as a sparsely populated, backward wasteland frontier, as many in the East believed about most western states. By 1918 all the states in the West except North Dakota, Nebraska, Texas, and New Mexico had given women the universal right to vote. In 1917 New York became the first eastern state to do so.

Immediately after Washington granted women the right to vote, it also passed other reform legislation. By 1911, Washington had other weapons of reform—the initiative, referendum, and recall—also passed as amendments to the state constitution. In fact, thanks to a coalition that included the federated clubs, that same year the Washington legislature also enacted an eight-hour day for women workers, workmen's compensation, pure food and drug measures, and ratification of the new federal income tax amendment.[156] Women's clubs had played a key role in getting women the right to vote and influencing passage of the new reform measures, although they did not get much credit.[157] But it would take more than suffrage and reform to make full political participation possible.

Women's clubwork gave women such as Landes an opportunity to hone leadership and political skills while researching social and political issues. Clubs initially engaged in literary and artistic endeavors began to concern themselves with social welfare issues and reform. In doing so, they generally accepted prescribed behaviors for men and women, seeing their causes as selfless and linked to a higher good. Such involvement heightened women's sense of moral superiority and concern for social issues that had won some men (and some women) over to suffrage in the first place. Members of both sexes saw it as a golden opportunity to better the world through women's moral, nurturing, "better" nature, an assumed superiority that would prove to be double-edged. Women's alleged better nature became bound up with ideas of reform and purity. Suffrage, as a result, was likewise linked—or chained—to the issues of temperance and prohibition, despite the efforts of some women's rights advocates, such as the indefatigable Abigail Scott Duniway in the Pacific Northwest, to separate the two issues.

Duniway warned in 1899: "We will never get the ballot . . . if we persist in demanding it as a whip with which to scourge the real or apparent vices of the present voting classes. . . . Here is where woman has . . . made her greatest blunder. Whenever she demands the ballot, not simply because it is her right to possess it, but because of its use . . . she only succeeds in driving nails into the closed coffin of her own and other women's liberties."[158] Although women did eventually get the vote, there continued to be tension of the nature that Duniway described, and a persisting link, both real and imagined, between temperance and suffrage. It sometimes resulted in a backlash against women in politics, as happened in Washington.

Prohibition and Reform

The argument of women's superiority, of social purity and the "white life" (a euphemism for living purely, beyond social reproach), became a cornerstone in the positions of both the WCTU and the NAWSA, but it also established a link between women and an old-fashioned morality in the twentieth century.[159] Temperance as a cause became particularly important to women, for they had little or no power over their lives, and lived and struggled without property, legal, or civil rights. The argument for temperance and reform represented a defense of the family's interests within the framework of male dominance. Domestic ideology and the idea of reform established a base for subsequent social and political action that went beyond temperance, closing saloons, and promoting self-control. Indeed, even at the turn of the century, feminists such as Charlotte Perkins Gilman had begun to look less at "moral failings" and more at problems caused by capitalism itself and its existing structures, such as child abandonment, prostitution, and the exploitation of women in sweatshops.[160]

Seattle's women's clubs, like women's clubs elsewhere, frequently supported temperance if not outright prohibition. There appears to have been relatively little overlap in Seattle, however, between the Women's Christian Temperance Union leadership and leadership of the clubs, at least based on membership directories. In Washington, the WCTU, established there in 1883 with 20 members after Willard and her successor Anna Gordon came to Seattle, counted 629 members in King County and 2,300 statewide by 1905.[161] Landes, however, and other club leaders were generally not listed as members in the WCTU directories.

The WCTU reflected a moral zeal and single-mindedness that apparently put off women like Landes, who approached their activism from a broader historical and social context. Women's clubs attracted a more urbane type compared with the religion-based movement that gave rise to the WCTU membership. WCTU's watchwords, however, could have been used to describe other women's civic reform groups—"agitate, educate, organize."[162] The goals of politically active women's clubs and the WCTU often paralleled one another, however, when it came to women and abuses in the home sphere and other social welfare issues.

Like other women, Landes justified moving into a more public sphere by linking that involvement to the protection of home and family, while at the same time denying any personal ambition or will to power.[163] For instance, Landes always described her hard-fought political victories as the result of her being tapped for service by others and the need to protect "the larger home"—the city of Seattle. "Home standards should be city standards, and this man has not realized," she wrote right before her first election.[164]

Urban progressivism led women to blur or obliterate the distinction between domestic and public welfare issues. In addition, concepts of cities as reservoirs of disease and vice, as unfit environments for women and families, propelled women to action. Through women's clubs they combined forces to work on social welfare projects such as enforcement of laws regulating drinking, prostitution, and gambling and those that provided for more equitable treatment of women and protection of children. These efforts sought to regulate the behavior of men to the benefit of women and children, who were the frequent victims of abuse at the hands of men engaging in illegal, illicit, or ill-tempered behavior, rather than to re-create some pastoral, agrarian ideal as some historians have argued.

Clubwork on social welfare issues also provided a useful forum for Landes and others for defining and promoting their ideas of progressive civic leadership and for reordering civic priorities. Such civic leadership would remove city administration from the realm of party machine politics and cronyism in favor of the ideals of professionalization, merit, efficiency, and governmental stability. These ideals were also fundamentally connected to realizing social rather than economic priorities. Corollary issues were working for public control and development of utilities to ensure they operated in the public interest and for the expansion of government services to meet critical social needs.

For women like Landes, however, taking on civic leadership and reform issues early in the century did not have much connection with seeking jobs and careers. Women's eternal tension—balancing home and career—made it difficult for many women and men to accept the idea that women—especially married women—might work outside the home for reasons other than economic necessity. And the exploitation that most working women suffered made wage work a rather unattractive option, for they were relegated to lower-echelon, lower-paid positions. As historian Alice Kessler-Harris put it, when women "strode bravely into the work force, they landed in its lowest places, without coercion, with their full consent and understanding and even encouragement."[165] Their roles at work—as domestics, in the garment industry, or as teachers and nurses—dovetailed neatly with their expected roles at home. Until those traditional roles and expectations changed, women's work experiences generally would not and did not change. In their support for equal wages, job protection, and increased opportunities for women, Landes and clubwomen like her helped bring about that change.

Wage work for women was neither empowering nor liberating in the view of most women of Landes's time. Married American women seldom worked outside the home until the twentieth century, and then only in large numbers after the first few decades of the century. Nationally, only one white married woman in forty was in the wage labor force in 1890, and only one in seven as late as 1940.[166] Of all women who worked for wages, one-half were immigrants or daughters of immigrants. One-third of all working women nationally ended up as servants or waitresses, and one-fourth were in the mills or factories. Only 10 percent could be classified as professional, and almost all of them were in teaching and nursing.[167]

Seattle's experience was similar. Between 1900 and 1920 in Seattle, the proportion of married working women rose four times faster than the city's burgeoning population, although it still represented only 2.5 percent of the population in 1920. Married women (excluding divorced and widowed women) constituted 18 percent of Seattle's total female wage workers in 1900, and 25 percent in 1920, as more and more women came into the work force. However, over 40 percent of Seattle's female wage earners were involved in domestic service in 1900, a proportion that dropped to 26 percent by 1920. The drop in domestic service was matched by a rise in clerical employment. By 1920, about a fourth of all working women were employed in clerical work in Seattle, compared with about 13 percent in 1900.[168] Women in Seattle seldom worked in male-dominated industries, such as lumbering and shipbuilding, and when they did, as during World War I, male unionists often reacted hostilely. Women were perceived to be diluting men's wages, undermining men's skilled labor ranks, or breaking strikes.[169]

To women of means, work outside the home in the early years of the century held few attractions, despite significant gains in women's educational levels. Clubwork instead became a profession for many educated women generally excluded from professional work, and reform gave these women their goals and fulfillment. Although 90 percent of women were married and over 95 percent of those did not seek outside employment at the turn of the century, women were less and less prisoners of the rigors and responsibilities of bearing and rearing children and had more time for other activities, a development not all found good or healthy.

Women progressively bore fewer children in the nineteenth century, when the birthrate dropped to half what it was at the beginning of the century, but this trend brought on fears of race suicide and its resulting pressure on women to have less schooling and more babies. Despite the complaints, the declining birthrate, along with changes in educational opportunity, industrial production, and the agricultural economy, changed women's lives in important ways but left the domestic ideology largely in tact. Long before they could vote, women mustered political power by capitalizing on unique female institutions to pressure men's institutions to change and compete for control over distribution of resources. In championing gender-related causes and issues, female reformers often advanced class-related causes during times of social and economic turmoil, such as women's rights to employment.[170]

Applying domestic ideology to the city also indirectly offered women an opportunity to criticize existing structures of patriarchy, materialism, and laissez-faire capitalism.[171] Furthermore, in the clubs new cultural scripts, based on research, pragmatism, and club networks, could be drafted; feminism coexisted there with a maternalism that was not expressed as an either-or relationship. Clubs also conferred on their members higher status and greater power in the struggle over city priorities and public policies.

At the turn of the century, discussion of suffrage as the inalienable right often gave way to suffrage as the opportunity for woman's selfless nature and virtue to rescue society and democracy through beneficial legislation.[172] Cleaning up political and civic corruption, restoring morality and order to urban chaos, and implementing much-needed reforms for the social welfare were envisioned if women gained the right to vote. Women's suffrage in Washington State was thus part of a larger package of voter reforms that ultimately changed the political process. Besides the referendum and recall provisions, they included the direct primary, popular election of senators, and social legislation such as antisaloon measures. On the eve of the suffrage vote in Washington, the Washington newspaper *Votes for Women* inserted a series of posters trumpeting women's right to vote. One read simply, "Give Women the Ballot for the Sake of the Children."[173]

Using the Vote

One of the first exercises of political muscle for women after gaining the franchise in Washington was the recall of Seattle mayor Hiram Gill in 1912.[174] Gill, an attorney who often represented Seattle's vice lords, had promised to confine the city's vices to south of an artificial line on Yesler Way, the belt across Seattle's midsection. Instead he allowed gambling to spread and to go on openly day and night. He also sanctioned the construction of a new 250-stall combination brothel and boardinghouse downtown on Tenth Avenue, with another 300-room house and an "amusement" district planned. The Hillside Improvement Company, with several big-name investors, even got an easement from the city council when it was discovered the brothel encroached eight feet on the adjoining street. The council also passed an ordinance to give the company a fifteen-year lease on the street. Stock in the venture was sold openly and was seen as a good investment.

Seattle's clubwomen and other citizens were appalled and outraged. More than any other manifestation, the plan reflected the acceptance by the power structure of a spreading downtown district of vice as both inevitable and profitable. The WCTU, Seattle Federation of Women's Clubs, and Mothers' Congresses combined forces with Seattle's Municipal League to campaign for recall of Gill—and won. Out of 23,000 women newly registered to vote in Washington, 20,000 voted, and they did not vote to keep Gill.[175]

It was only the second time in the country that a city had used the new recall provisions pushed by Progressive reformers to throw a mayor out of office. Gill was gone, and the house never opened as a brothel. It was turned into a legitimate rooming house instead. Besides offering these women their civil rights, suffrage represented a strong, new vehicle for urban reform—a development crucial to Bertha Knight Landes. One magazine said that without the women's votes the election would have been very close. "With them, the victory for good government was a certainty."[176]

In this milieu Landes and other female candidates came of political age in their clubs. At the same time it reinscribed the lines around hearth and home, with woman's life defined by children, home, and the civic acts needed to strengthen that domestic realm in the larger world. Such a connection redefined politics. Landes herself used the connections, citing a woman's need to confront issues outside the home if she wanted to protect it. According to Landes, the home, with its idealistic spirit of service, sacrifice, and ministering to one another, should be the spirit of the city.[177] Those indeed were new priorities for city management, especially for seaport Seattle.

Landes said that a mother such as herself had to go outside the home to know what conditions her children would face and to "do my share to make them better." As a result, "community and civic problems began to interest me through club work and welfare work," she said. "And let me say this right here to the mothers who are reading this," she warned. "Do not let your immediate task of raising a family so completely absorb your time and interest that when your work along that line is finished you have nothing else to which you can turn for future life interest and work."[178]

Motherhood was idealized, even in the halls of government. Congress, by unanimous resolution, established Mother's Day in 1914. Anna Jarvis, whose own tireless mother of twelve started clubs to improve health care for members' families and to patch the enmities created by the Civil War, had campaigned vigorously for the idea, and it eventually caught hold.[179] Not surprisingly, the metaphors and analogies likening motherhood to social welfare, and efficient governmental administration to civic housekeeping and cleaning house, would be repeated frequently. The words "municipal housekeeping," in reference to social services and legislative reforms, emerged from the General

Federation and WCTU traditions before the turn of the century.[180] Landes used them herself repeatedly to build the bridge between women and civic activism and sometimes played with the metaphor.

In an article Landes referred to how much men "always hate house-cleaning." They prefer to allow "social vice" to be conducted in a way as "quiet and businesslike as possible." Women, however, know what has to be done, although "the best and most modern method is not by occasional upheaval but by keeping house properly, day by day. Women also are less conservative than men."[181] Like "petticoat government," the term "municipal housecleaning" conveyed powerful images and emotions. The term also described a direction that diverged from the usual understandings of the Progressive Era. When they talked of "municipal housecleaning," women referred to a process of making the values and priorities of the home supersede the corporate, free-enterprise values and priorities of typical city management.

By 1921, Landes had spent about fifteen years of her life in clubwork. After having presided over the 270-member Woman's Century Club for two years, Bertha was ready for a larger assignment as president of the Seattle Federation of Women's Clubs. By then the Federated Women's Clubs counted 20,000 women as members in Washington State, and over a million women nationally. In Seattle, the federation had grown to thirty-four clubs from twenty-four only a decade earlier.[182] By 1920, clubs exercised considerable power within the limitations of women's club activities and were pushing those limitations in order to affect a wider public arena. That arena, for Landes, meant orchestrating a major exhibit for Seattle, using her organizing skills to display the new wonders available to that new consumer—woman.

Domestic Technology and the Seattle Exhibit

If women by the 1920s could move out of the home and away from domestic life, it was in no small measure due to something besides clubs—technology and commercialization of chores formerly reserved for the home.[183] In addition, the advent of communications technology such as radio, telephone, and even rural mail delivery linked women together and helped end their homebound isolation. So did the automobile and public transportation.

As Landes noted, the availability of the electric stove and oven, the refrigerator, the vacuum cleaner, the clothes washer, the electric iron, the sewing machine, and other labor-saving devices in the 1920s had a liberating effect. Others have argued that although such devices relieved hard work and drudgery, they also raised housekeeping standards and expectations and emphasized class differences. Landes spoke of the impact of these changes on women's daily lives when she entered politics. She said that the woman's movement was the logical outcome of suffrage and "commercialization of many of the activities which formerly centered in the home, such as the laundry work, baking, sewing and so forth." Removing from the home "a good deal of the drudgery of housework has given women in general more time for outside activities." But women needed to put that time to good use. "If she is not to be a parasite, something abhorrent to her nature, she must turn her energies to public service of some kind—social welfare, community service or civic betterment," she wrote.[184]

Home technologies, the rise in manufacturing in states like Washington, and the growing attention to efficiency gave rise in the 1920s to a consumer economy, complete with advertising aimed specifically at women. This trend created yet another definition of "woman"—the woman at home now was an important industrial consumer, the person responsible for the health and development of the family through the purchase of particular products. Landes revealed her attitude on the new consumer products marketed to women through advertising. She wrote that women were grateful for "all these wonderful household helps" and were striving to run their homes "as a business proposition, as a man runs his factory, his store, or his office." Thus they needed to be informed—truthfully—about the virtues of new products. "Tell us how much time and how much labor it will save us, but don't tell us that a washing machine takes care of the washing, a mangle does the ironing, a vacuum cleaner keeps the house clean, a patent dishwasher clears the table, washes and wipes the dishes and puts them away." Products meet needs, but "don't insult our intelligence," she chided advertisers.[185]

That same approach infused her handling of the exhibit. Bertha Knight Landes came to the attention of the male power structure in Seattle through the intersection of man's domain of business and manufacturing and woman's domain of family guardianship and consumption, meeting in a neutral zone—an exhibit. Her recognition came as the result of her demonstrated leadership in organizing this extensive show around the idea of woman as consumer of this new technology and the shiny, wondrous new products available to her, all manufactured in Washington. In her new role as leader of the federation, Landes again challenged traditional gender lines when she completed this difficult organizational task on behalf of Seattle's business community and its manufacturers in a novel way.

Her task as federation president in 1921 was to organize the Women's Educational Exhibit for Washington Manufacturers. There 130 manufacturers displayed their wares in exhibits staffed by a thousand members of the Federated Women's Clubs.[186] Although organized, promoted, and viewed primarily as a means of boosting business at home in Seattle, the exhibit also marked the importance of women as powerful consumers, able to choose from a startling array of technological innovations and products that promised to make their difficult home labor easier—or at least make them a better caretaker of home and family. For Seattle, it symbolized the state's emergence as a sophisticated, modern metropolis.

Landes ran the exhibit by organizing small groups of women to act as educators and to host demonstrations for particular manufacturers or kinds of manufacturers at the exhibit. Each team of eight to twelve women visited and studied the manufacturer in advance in order to answer any questions that might arise from the public. They also used information from surveys of each manufacturer, addressing business-related issues of size, market, raw materials used, payroll, taxes, and the future of the industry. That information was also collated and made available to all clubs or organizations.[187]

Exhibits showcased Washington manufacturers of furniture, tires, appliances, clothes, and foods, displaying products ranging from phonographs to yeast cake. The show had some dramatic staging, including a cross-section of a coal mine and a waterfall cascading real water. The exhibit ran April 18–23, 1921, in the Seattle Arena, with attendance so large people sometimes had to be turned away. Twenty-five manufacturers were also shut out for lack of exhibit space. For her efforts, Landes and two other women were heaped with praise in a special ceremony and presented locally manufactured bags made of sharkskin lined with whaleskin.

"Seattle Rises, Rubs Eyes, and Makes the Discovery That It Is Now Grown Up," trumpeted a headline on the exhibit in the

Seattle Post-Intelligencer. This event gave Landes the opportunity to assume personal leadership, test her organizational skills, and display management potential.

The exhibit also gave Landes recognition throughout a good share of the established business community. Letters of praise often included a tone of surprise at her ability to organize such an extravaganza and at her sagacity in interviews. For instance, the president of the Seattle Chamber of Commerce and Commercial Club was one of many to add his praise for the Women's Educational Exhibit at the Seattle Arena. He wrote Landes that he was especially impressed "with the character of the interviews you have given out," which had shown clear vision of "civic usefulness and responsibility" in support of Seattle's business and industry.[188]

These were unusual words for a man to use in describing the efforts of a woman in connection with business. They represented, however, growing recognition of the role women could play in civic betterment as an extension of the role women had always played as mothers and society's caretakers. Through the exhibit Bertha articulated female consumer power in such a way that men had to take it seriously, but they were not threatened by this display of power. The setting—a carnival-like event where traditional roles were put aside—offered a safe place open to experimentation and new cultural scripts. It also opened at least some business and industry managers to the idea that municipal housekeeping might include more than bothersome moral reforms, that it might also support economic growth and development.

A manufacturer of phonographs wrote Landes after the exhibit, expressing the hope "that someday you will be rewarded by seeing greater prosperity in Seattle, and that you will then feel fully repaid for the untiring efforts you have put forth."[189] Letters came to Landes from businesses like the National Baking Company, which congratulated her "on the splendid organizing ability displayed," adding that the show was much better attended "than any of us anticipated," and hundreds were turned away.[190]

Letters praising her efforts, which she evidently felt were significant enough to save, symbolized her initial entry into a different sphere of activism for women. As a result of the visibility and success she had attained in this endeavor and her reputation, Seattle mayor Hugh Caldwell in 1921 named her to the

Mayor's Unemployment Council. He had for some time been aware of her growing visibility. He earlier had offered her a seat on the city's library board, a post she had declined.[191]

The unemployment councils had been suggested by U.S. secretary of commerce Herbert Hoover. Their purpose was to find possible remedies for the intractable problem of unemployment in Seattle, the result of the seasonal nature of Washington's major industries, including agriculture, logging, shipping, and construction. Seattle typically had a floating population of ten thousand jobless men during the winter, a number that grew year by year with the burgeoning population of the city.[192] Landes was the only woman sitting with the four men in the local group. The timing of Caldwell's appointment of Landes proved to be propitious. She was in the right place at the right time, with the right background, ready for the women of Seattle to tap her for larger service.

II

THE WOMEN'S PSYCHOLOGICAL HOUR

The 1920 *Official Register and Directory of Women's Clubs in America,* published in Massachusetts, listed clubs and officers state by state. It also carried ads for lecturers, musicians, dramatic readings, books, magazines, stereopticon shows, and the latest consumer goods, all promoting their wares to the educated, liberated New Woman of the 1920s in hopes of tapping into the lucrative circuit of women's clubs, which regularly supported such endeavors.

Page 8A of the register was filled by two ads. They themselves reflected the competing ideas both inside and outside the world of women's clubs in the 1920s regarding the appropriate behavior for women. On the top of the page appeared an ad for a book entitled *Woman Triumphant:* "The story of our struggles for freedom, education and political rights. It is, as all critics agree, the most spirited book ever dedicated to womanhood. No intelligent man or woman, seeking information about the most important question of all times, should fail to read it. 300 pages with 63 beautiful illustrations. $1.75."

Immediately below it was an ad for a parents' guide entitled *What Will Your Child Become?* It sold for $2 and carried cartoon drawings of girls and boys, and the following copy for the girls:

> At 13: bad literature or study and obedience?
> At 20: flirting and coquetry or virtue and devotion?
> At 26: a fast life and dissipation or a loving mother?
> At 40: an outcast, or at 60: an honored grandmother?[1]

A few pages later appeared an ad for the buyer's choice of three important lectures by reproduction-rights advocate Margaret Sanger: "How to Tell a Child the Facts of Sex"; "Sex Hygiene for Young Girls"; "Birth Control—Why—How—and to Whom?" The ad promoted Sanger's lectures as being "of vital interest to women, dealing as they do with subjects no woman, conscious of her responsibility to the race, can afford to neglect."[2] The wording of the three ads seemed to distill the options for girls and women; according to these ads, it was up to the woman to choose.

What was a proper woman to do? What was a proper woman? What was proper? Who would decide? These were important questions with no clear answers in the 1920s, the decade in which Bertha Knight Landes rose to power. The more disputed the territory of "woman" became, the more polarized were the answers proposed by factions battling for control of the definition. At the forefront were coalitions of women organized into clubs, who were developing, testing, and promoting alternative and traditional visions of "woman" and her proper role.

Landes, in a meteoric rise after years of hard work in and through the clubs of Seattle, capitalized on the emerging political interests and strengths of women in the 1920s. She and other such women hoped to implement their vision of a modernist future and, through the ideals of efficiency, education, and professionalism, solve the old ills of society. The decade of the 1920s was connected to the grand social experiment of women's vote, and it was also connected to that other grand social experiment—prohibition. In this exalted vision of a reformed world, women had a vital role, but it was one grounded in the perceived differences between men and women and in the moral superiority assumed in the traditional understanding of "woman."

Rooted as it was in the nineteenth century, this vision of a new world was a logical extension of woman's traditional interests as she moved through suffrage toward full political participation. The vision was also a trap. The philosophy of equal but separate, easily espoused, was difficult to maintain. In such a climate Bertha Knight Landes herself became a symbol that for many embodied the promise and the fears of this decade.

In 1920, when the nation's constitution finally included females as citizens, the directory of women's clubs listed the "purely social" clubs. It also listed enterprising, goal-oriented groups such as the National Federation of Business and Professional Women, the National League of Women Voters, the National Consumer's League, the National Association of Colored Women, the National Women's Christian Temperance Union, the Council of Jewish Women, the Women's International League for Peace and Freedom (chaired by Jane Addams), and, by 1924, the

National Women's Trade Union League of America. In Washington State, the Federated Women's Clubs in 1920 included no fewer than 198 clubs with a total of 20,000 members, which by 1922 (shortly after Bertha Knight Landes took over leadership of the Seattle Federation) had grown to 241 clubs and 27,000 members.[3] Women's clubs, although hardly unified and monolithic, were powerful voices in the national and regional debate over the definitions of "woman" and "social welfare." In the 1920s Landes played her own role in that debate.

Changing Images of Woman in the 1920s

Cultural and social turmoil marked the extravagant, excessive decade of the 1920s. "Woman" became emblematic of societal upheaval. She was alternately society's salvation and stabilizing refuge, or with her undisciplined behavior she was the cause of its turmoil. From flapper to venerated mother, gender models were symbolic and in transition. The forces of stability, status quo, and dominance offered and enforced their own definitions of "woman" through the language and standards of medicine, psychiatry, sociology, religion, and elsewhere.

Behavior codes and language codes have always limited the emergence of new ideas and behaviors. Even where the language did not yet accommodate radical shifts, new and symbolic forms of behavior challenged existing norms. They gave rise to the verbal expression of the ideas they represented. Some women shortened their hair and their skirts; at the same time that the cultural police criticized such wanton behavior in the 1920s, social norms changed to accommodate less restrictive clothing and behavior codes for women.

Popular culture reflected another model for female behavior—the flapper. Along with jazz and the speakeasy, the flapper became a symbol for the age. The flapper was the cloche-hatted, boyish-built, cigarette-smoking young woman who defied the codes of convention. It was the flapper who most challenged the traditional constraints of gender, not because she was dedicated to social betterment causes, but because she was chasing the fast life, the good life of hedonism. She (and there were far fewer of her than people believed) laughed in the face of tradition, flouted it, and in her open sensuality if not sexuality made both men and women fearful of the future she represented. That future contained not only hedonism but also cynicism and selfishness. For women to behave this way was deemed much more serious than for men. Over and over the Seattle media, reflecting this national concern, felt it necessary to reassure readers that Landes in no way had any connection to this model of womanhood. Few did.

The forces of stability and status quo set definitions of duty, domesticity, and family against women's rights and participation. Yet others used those same ideas to promote women's rights and participation. Mixed into the maelstrom around gender definition were debates about reform, politics, and professionalization, all connected in complex ways to women's suffrage and politicization. Some women like Landes exercised their newfound power to promote their agenda for civic betterment. That agenda often involved making new social welfare programs the responsibility of the state, reforming government, and enforcing vice laws—including prohibition. The three tracks—suffrage, prohibition, and urban reform—became the touchstones for civic betterment.

Women Enter Politics

On a national scale, this activism resulted in the Sheppard-Towner Act of 1921 for the protection of women and infants, congressional passage of the Child Labor Amendment, and the first federal social security legislation. It was also felt in the lobbying of the powerful Women's Joint Congressional Committee, formed on November 22, 1920. The WJCC was organized through the League of Women Voters and seven other organizations, including the Federated Women's Clubs, the WCTU, National Business and Professional Women's Clubs, WTUL, and others, as a powerful phalanx of women's organizations reportedly representing 10 million women.

The WJCC priorities were summarized as the six Ps: prohibition, public schools, protection of infants (its primary goal), physical education in the schools, peace through arms reduction, and protection of women in industry.[4] Its support helped establish a long list of reforms, including the Packers and Stockyards Control Act in 1921, the U.S. Coal Commission in 1921, the Cable Act in 1922 giving independent citizenship to married women, banning the shipment of coconut-oil-laced milk in 1923, a federal prison for women in 1924, congressional support for the Child Labor Amendment in 1924, compulsory school attendance for the District of Columbia in 1925, and other measures. It also lobbied against the Equal Rights Amendment, fearing loss of the hard-fought legislative gains protecting women from exploitation.[5] Most of its successes came in the years 1920–25.

When women finally saw the Nineteenth Amendment ratified in 1920, there was an idealistic assumption that woman's "better nature" would repair the gaping tears in the social fabric. Once women had the right to vote, there was an assumption—creating euphoria in some quarters and dread in others—that women would move into positions of political power. If there would not be complete political equality, at least there would be significant representation from women on issues of particular importance to women. But by the end of the 1920s, however, many of the expected gains for women had failed to materialize.

There was no woman's bloc vote, which political parties and the power structure had feared as a potential threat to their way of doing business. Woman as gender remained divided by class, race, region, and special interest. Women walked the same road to suffrage but parted company over the issues of equality, protective legislation, political participation from within male structures, the status of working women, and many others. There never had been a woman's bloc, especially once the galvanizing goal of suffrage was finally realized. The divisions had long histories.[6]

Gaining the vote and other civil rights, important as they were, hardly made women the quick political equals of men, who lived and worked in an interlocking network of patriarchal structures in politics, government, the courts, and business and industry, in Seattle as in most cities. Women's suffrage did not offer women even full citizenship. State constitutions and the courts continued to bar women from jury duty and from holding some offices in some states, and a husband's nationality continued to determine the nationality of his wife.[7] Working out those issues required yet further campaigns.

Those women who advocated equality and the dropping of gender distinctions in public affairs—as Landes began to do later in her political career—lost a natural constituency born of those differences. In the 1920s, the distinctly female culture held over from the nineteenth century, idealized then, now was devalued by women who were trying to climb into the male bastions of power or into the professions. Tensions over protectionism developed within the cause of feminism itself and exacerbated a rift along class lines. Race lines had divided the movement long before. Federated women's clubs across the country supported black women's clubs but kept them at arm's length.

In Seattle, the Culture Club was organized by Mrs. W. D. Carter for fifty "colored girls" in 1916, and in 1919 the Colored Branch of the YWCA opened a house at 1807 Twenty-fourth Avenue to offer a "haven and social center for colored girls," especially for new arrivals to the city. Carter also ran a placement service for employment and worked as a volunteer in Seattle's juvenile courts for five years.[8] In 1920 Seattle's black population numbered about 3,000, or less than 1 percent of the city's population. In contrast, the number of residents of Japanese ancestry rose to almost 8,000 by 1920.[9]

The National Association of Colored Women's Clubs had been established in 1899, paralleling the General Federation and angry about being excluded from it. The General Federation, despite acrimonious debate, denied credentials to delegates from black women's organizations, although the issue came up repeatedly. It finally adopted a compromise in 1902, dropping the race problem into the laps of the state federations. If their constitutions allowed clubs with black memberships to join, then they were eligible to join the General Federation.[10] The delegates to Washington's Federation meeting debated the issue in 1901 but reaffirmed the exclusion. The clubs themselves were and remained racially segregated, as separate in Seattle as they were nationally. The color line, for clubs as well as the rest of society, was broadly drawn.

The clubs were more sensitive to the problems of class lines and working women, and the Seattle and Washington federations worked closely with working class groups on certain issues. For instance, the Seattle Women's Union Card and Label League, the Washington Federation of Women's Clubs, and the Seattle Women's Trade Union League all linked arms to pursue legislative changes that benefited women, such as minimum-wage laws and an eight-hour workday. They also jointly sought a repeal of union policies against married women's employment, but that plea fell on deaf ears.[11]

Working women, as Landes came to recognize, had difficult lives. They were exploited in factories and offices with long hours and low wages before and after the 1920s. In 1929 Landes said that she willingly conceded female physical inequalities and believed that protective laws to regulate hours and conditions of labor were necessary, "not particularly for woman as woman, but in the interests of the future family."[12]

Their protectors—if not all the workers themselves—continued to favor gender-based protective legislation to lighten their burdens. Other women, usually middle and upper class, divided over this issue. Some, believing that gender-based legislation kept women from full equality, fought against protective legislation. They favored the Equal Rights Amendment introduced by the National Women's Party in 1923.

More women were like Landes. They had fought hard for protective legislation for women and children, and now they took a more short-term view. They thought that such protection was necessary to end their exploitation.[13] Rather than push for systemic changes in the economic and political structures that made exploitation of women and children not just possible but desirable, these reformers tried to change the rules governing participation in the existing structure through protective legislation.[14]

As a result of the hard work of both clubwomen and trade unionists in a coalition, Washington State had an impressive record of labor laws by 1919. The legislature had passed laws regulating the both the hours and minimum wages of working women (set at $10 a week minimum for women in 1910). The state supreme court upheld them, and labor commissions appointed by the governor attempted to make sure they were put into practice. This was unlike the experience in other states, where employers frequently ignored such laws.[15]

Both clubwomen and the working women's groups tended not to see the contradictions others saw in protective legislation. They favored equal rights for women at the same time as they sought protective legislation.

Women's coalitions for causes continued to reflect classic women's concerns. Manipulators, builders, and exploiters were masculine; those who were selfless and who protected home, virtue, and democracy were feminine, and they were good for society. Women would not yield to party control but in voting would bring selflessness and purity to politics and social reform, both women and men believed. Although this view gained a few women power and access—and indeed perhaps won women the vote—it also imposed on women the responsibility for the moral conditions of society.

"Here indeed was work for a woman," Landes later commented about the city council's problems with Seattle's all-night dance halls, assuming this was naturally the women's concern and problem to solve.[16] This view continued a trend that actually reached back to the nineteenth century, one that excused men from taking responsibility for home and city life conditions. This freed men for production of vital goods and business capital, the material expression of progress and prosperity. Men and women both generally viewed women's concerns as specifically and fundamentally different from those of men.

In the 1920s women continued to be idealized as pure, pious, and domestic by nature; conversely they were accused of violating that ideal if they seemed venal or competitive. By nature they were supposed to be more moral and more compassionate than men, although cracks were appearing in the idealized portrait.

Like many other women, Bertha Knight Landes found herself in the double bind of mutually exclusive categories of definition. If women were passive, irrational, and biologically determined, as Freud and men long before Freud told them they were, then they could not be "like men" when it came to professional and economic self-actualization and independence. Yet if they could not be like men, they could never be truly equal. And if they chose not to be like men (as some feminists of the late twentieth-century would advocate), then they could never gain power. Landes herself was described with admiration by the men who surrounded her as thinking like a man.

In the 1920s, New Women more and more tried to enter male institutions and cross their increasingly professionalized and disciplined boundaries—in education, medicine, politics, and science—often finding themselves in hostile territory. Female institutions suffered from the absence of these new women and in some cases began to disintegrate.[17] Gradually a new generation of women began to adopt men's professional and political values and those discourses as an effective means of finally finding equality.[18] Those women who abandoned the unique discourse surrounding domestic life and women lost much in the exchange. They sacrificed an important traditional language that made it difficult to link their lives either to the past or to future generations of women.[19]

Landes herself experienced an erosion of female support of her candidacy, in part because she adopted the dominant discourse of men as reflected in business and public administration and tried to minimize the role of gender. "The question of sex should not be raised in electing persons to offices . . . but only fitness and ability," Landes told the *Chicago Daily Tribune* before her last campaign.[20]

Prohibition, Vice, and Politics in Seattle

The other great social reform dream—prohibition—was proving to be problematic. At the beginning of the decade, prohibition was a rising tide, hard either to contain or turn aside. A long parade of reformers who saw that women and children frequently were powerless victims of men's intemperance had pushed for abolition of alcohol and saloons for almost a century.[21] Clubwomen like Landes were generally sympathetic to their cause, even if they failed to join their campaigns. More recently, others who wanted to put boundaries around the behavior of immigrants and the working classes had joined the cause. They wanted to rid communities of "defects" such as institutionalized drinking houses like saloons, where gambling and prostitution sometimes flourished as well. Prohibition headed the reform agenda because reformers viewed alcohol as the agent of corruption. Prohibition—like suffrage—took on symbolic value as a potential watershed in moral and social progress.[22] It became a national priority with the passage of the Eighteenth Amendment and the Volstead Act by 1920, which were broad-scale attempts to prohibit the production and purchase of alcohol. Prohibition came in with women's suffrage and went out with the Great Depression.[23]

City officials like Bertha Knight Landes were faced with enforcing unpopular "dry" laws in areas where bootlegging and violations of drinking laws, frequently with the complicity of law enforcement, were rife. In Washington State, the Anti-Saloon League had been successful in getting legislators to vote the state dry—in a manner of speaking—as early as 1916.[24] The state had already outlawed the largely unregulated saloons in 1916. The Anti-Saloon League bragged that 1,100 saloons, twenty-four breweries, and one distillery were thus put out of business. The result was, according to many historians, that Seattle and other areas simply had a head start on establishing the institution of bootlegging to meet high consumer demand.[25]

The prohibition amendment to the state constitution had

passed in thirty-three of the state's thirty-nine counties, with Seattle's King County voting no.[26] But the law had a loophole that allowed mail order liquor to slide through. It allowed an individual to import up to two quarts of liquor or twelve quarts of beer each twenty days via an import permit from the county auditor. Full-page ads for mail-order alcohol quickly appeared, and in August the King County auditor issued eighteen thousand such permits to Seattle residents alone.[27] Illegal traffic in alcohol, often through soft-drink shops that opened as fast as mayors closed them, escalated rapidly. Also, physicians by law were authorized to issue prescriptions for bottles of drug store whiskey.[28] In the first three months of 1916 no fewer than sixty-five new drug stores opened in Seattle. This was the climate in which Landes and other civic activists—male and female—found themselves living. Hypocrisy abounded.

Following the 1916 dry law, however, arrests for public drunkenness and violations such as tax delinquencies were reportedly down substantially. Even the *Seattle Times,* which had fought hard against prohibition as interference with civil rights and free enterprise, was converted to the cause.[29] Initiatives that would have eased liquor restrictions increasingly lost favor. In 1917 the state legislature ended the permit system (except for clergymen and druggists) by a huge majority in both houses. And on December 22, 1917, Congress proposed an amendment to the Constitution to prohibit "the manufacture, sale, or transportation of intoxicating liquors." Washington passed it two to one in a small voter turnout in 1918, on the heels of a devastating influenza epidemic.[30] The Washington legislature ratified it in January 1919, shortly before the general strike.

Although virtually all those in public life professed support for the law, the law from the start was violated privately and widely. It was common knowledge that a small room off the upper corridor in the Olympia statehouse was used to fortify legislators with Canadian liquor.[31] People increasingly believed that the law was inequitably enforced—locally and nationally—for rich and poor, probably with good reason. When prohibition was strengthened with the passage of the Volstead Act in 1920, penalties were stiffened for the manufacture of and trade in alcohol, but the consumer was not liable for federal prosecution. Corruption grew. Even in Olympia, the city council, meeting in emergency session in 1921, found itself recommending the dismissal of its chief of police and two patrolmen who were selling confiscated whiskey.[32] The federal Prohibition Bureau, responsible for enforcement in the Pacific Northwest, was woefully inadequate. There were seldom more than twenty agents for the entire area. They were unprofessional, underpaid, and underequipped,[33] and they often were thwarted by local law enforcement, especially in Seattle.

Stemming the liquor traffic across the border from Canada was virtually impossible, particularly around Puget Sound. The situation was so out of control that one hundred bootleggers and rumrunners held an open convention in a Seattle hotel in 1922, the same year Landes was elected to the Seattle City Council. They adopted resolutions condemning narcotics traffic, set prices for liquor, and established a code of ethics for "approved business methods."[34]

Clearly the federal government could not handle enforcement, and city and county officers and politicians frequently shrugged off the matter, feeling it was a federal responsibility to enforce the federal laws. Washington governor Louis Hart (1919–25) absolved himself and his state of responsibility for enforcement.[35] The man who succeeded him, Roland Hartley, was fanatical about reducing public expenditures. During his eight years in office, he thwarted all attempts to use the state's police powers to enforce prohibition.[36] For example, a Hartley appointee to the University of Washington Board of Regents was picked up in a liquor raid and fined. Asked to remove him from the board, Hartley responded by saying, as Lincoln did about Grant, that if he knew what brand of whiskey his appointee drank, he would send some to the other regents.[37] Not surprisingly, those who believed in civic betterment through law enforcement—as Landes did—would find mostly frustration in Washington State. Enforcement in Washington would have to come at the city and county level in cooperation with federal agents. City governments seldom even tried vigorous law enforcement, faced as they were with the usual difficulties of schools, sewers, utilities, traffic, crime, taxes, and governance—and the limitations on their jurisdiction.

Yet there was rising concern in Seattle, well before Landes ran for office, about the city's inability to enforce vice laws and its wide-open reputation. Its reputation for lawlessness escalated in the years after prohibition passed. Added to that concern was fear over the complicity of law enforcement and city officials in bootlegging and gambling. Many citizens were demanding, more than ever, a return to moral uplift and "good government" and felt they were losing their Seattle to lawlessness, vice, and "the interests." Civic reform became the other track to structural change, and a prerequisite to enforcement of prohibition.

Those who took seriously the ideals of civic responsibility and urban reform felt that "municipal betterment," as well as economic and social health, depended on a law-abiding population, public control of utilities, and an efficient and clean government. In this matter they were part of a national trend glorifying the ideals of efficiency and purity, and denigrating party politics where decisions were made not in the name of rationality and progress but on the basis of favors and political patronage. In cities throughout the United States, tensions between politics and reform measures ended up in a tug-of-war on city government turf.

One such reformer—Washington Gladden, a Congregationalist pastor in Columbus, Ohio—had decided to run for the city council to attend to such abuses. Although he had what he called "no special fitness" for the office, he won. Gladden identified two problems at the root of municipal politics, ideas that Landes repeated. First, responsible citizens felt it was beneath them to get involved in local politics; second, city authorities were not as much corrupt as they were incompetent, and the former problem exacerbated the latter. He set forth his ideas in almost forty books, including the popular *Applied Christianity: Moral Aspects of Social Questions* (1886).[38] Landes shared some of the same values, as did many civic and social reformers. Gladden's books frequently appeared in club study lists.

Old-style politics, with its deals, patronage, and potential for corruption, was anathema to civic reformers. In its place the reformers wanted to put administration by trained, nonpartisan experts who would be hired on the basis of merit rather than favors, bribes, and connections. One such remedy was the city manager system, which Landes and others pushed for Seattle. It had been used experimentally in Cleveland, Cincinnati, and other cities in the 1920s as a rational solution to the growing problems of city management and lack of continuity in city governance.

Landes believed that all citizens had a duty to participate in the political process to keep democracy alive, but she too was critical of politics per se, at least as traditionally practiced. As part of several reforms, Seattle in 1911 had decided its city elections would be nonpartisan and at-large, a decision reached at one of the first elections held after women won the right to vote.

The movement leading to this charter amendment reflected alliances of liberal Democrats and liberal Republicans dating from 1904, seeking reform and an end to railroad domination and machine control of politics. The council reform movement caused a liberal/conservative split in the Republican party in Washington. Leaders formed the City Party, which set the tone for civic reform. It promoted a "city for the people" rather than for corporate interests or professional politicians, leading to the 1910 proposed charter amendment.[39] The size of the council was thus reduced from fourteen to nine, and the amendment curtailed the standard practice of making ward political deals to favor one's constituents. Direct democracy, the antivice movements, municipal ownership of utilities, and government efficiency all frequently enjoyed broad popular support across class and political lines, at least until the postwar years.

In addition, Seattle was a city of transplants, immigrants, and transients. Almost 26 percent of the city's population was foreign-born in 1920, and another 50 percent had been born out of state, a higher proportion than all but three other cities in the United States.[40] Out of all 412 candidates running for city offices between 1911 and 1923, only 4 were natives of the state. Only 11 of these 412 candidates were female—2.7 percent—although women gained statewide suffrage in 1910. All were unsuccessful until Landes ran in 1922.[41] The high proportion of outsiders, combined with the gaps in law enforcement and the serious urban development and management problems created by Seattle's explosive growth, alarmed city residents and, in turn, city officials.

The urban experiment, with its bright lights and material progress, was also home to the crime, disease, and poverty of the urban slum. The slums were pockets of exploited misery that threatened to spill out into the streets. Unemployment, factory exploitation, and miserable working conditions for men, women, and children led to increasing labor unrest and to bitter strikes and repression of strikers, some of which led to violence. Other forces for reform, rising from concerns about crime, corruption of government, and corporate greed, used a newfound faith in the social sciences and efficiency that in turn galvanized civic reform efforts. Outrage of elected officials over manipulated transportation rates, over electricity rates, over water supplies and quality, and over sale to the public of bad merchandise led to measures to curb corporate arrogance and abuse. That outrage fostered regulation, control, or even ownership of vital public utilities, as was Seattle's pattern. It also found expression in imposing licensing requirements and in drafting rules and regulations to protect the public welfare in the modern metropolis, in everything from zoning to traffic to entertainment. Landes took on all of these causes on behalf of Seattle.

The twin cults of efficiency and expertise flourished in reform ideas from the city manager system to the training and licensing of professionals. Professionals isolated and controlled the factors that governed behavior and experience. Professionals, and the rising middle class from which they came, had authority and command.[42] Power and knowledge, as historian and theorist Michel Foucault described, became inseparable concepts. If ignorance produced disease, education and legislation was its cure. Discipline of mind, of body, and of body politic was necessary to enforce efficiency and contain behavior and irrational impulses. These ideals, emerging from a faith in pragmatism and administrative science coupled with moral reform, guided reformers like Landes in the twentieth century. Like engineers, they felt they were the doctors for an ailing society. In fact, technocracy had particularly strong adherents in Seattle.[43] Their armies of experts, acting in the public interest, could solve all the public's problems.

These professionals and experts, representing the new power/knowledge link, aroused the suspicion and ire of the working classes, who sometimes exercised their democratic muscle to reject reformers' interference in their lives. Their ire was especially aroused when they suspected that interference was designed to continue working-class exploitation and reduced status in a land where there was the promise, if not the existence, of a classless society.[44]

The most vehement opposition to antisaloon measures in Seattle came from the downtown wards, which contained higher proportions of lower-income workingmen and transients, many of them immigrants. One writer described them as "men who traditionally enjoyed their pail of beer or bottle of wine at lunch and after work. The middle class voted overwhelmingly in favor of all antisaloon measures, the upper class less so."[45] The saloons were also centers for neighborhood politics, and they excluded women—most women, anyway. However, the neighborhood saloons—although symbolic—were not nearly so egregious as city vice districts, and Seattle's own rivaled San Francisco's infamous Barbary Coast in reputation. Clearly, government intervention was needed to effect a change in Seattle's vice district and the city's politics, and women wanted power and influence to to effect that change and a host of others.

Landes Enters the Primary

Knowing Landes's standing with the clubwomen of Seattle and sensing the potential of the women's vote, some men on the mayor's Unemployment Commission (perhaps also unwilling to face the time requirements and obligations of service if any of them should run) urged her to run for one of the open seats on the Seattle City Council. Other women also pressed her to become a candidate. Leaders of Seattle's Federation of Clubwomen let the word out to the media that the clubwomen might have a candidate of their own and were asking "Mrs. Henry Landes . . . to come out as their standard bearer."[46] They also hinted they would find another candidate if she declined. Nearby Kirkland had elected a former teacher, Carrie Shumway, to its city council in 1911, the first in the state,[47] and it was past time for Seattle to put a woman on that important body. Landes was a natural. However, she professed both surprise and reluctance, not an unexpected response for a nineteenth-century woman asked to become the first woman to take a seat with all the men on the Seattle City Council.

Ironically, the clubwomen's hints about Landes diminished the entry that same day, February 28, 1922, of another woman into the city council campaign—Kathryn A. Miracle, who, in response to a question, admitted she did not have the support of any women's club. The newspapers automatically gave credibility to Landes as the female candidate who had the backing of the clubs, indicating the legitimacy and power the women's clubs held.

In fact, Miracle was a working woman, a widow who for the past four years had run a real estate business out of her home and for a dozen years had run a Seattle boardinghouse. Miracle, like Landes, lived in the University District, but she claimed to be running specifically as a businesswoman. She said she had experience as a legal stenographer and a realtor and had done "some banking."[48] Her candidacy, the *Times* said, "heralded the entry of women into the coming municipal contest."[49] While the newspaper ran Miracle's announcement on page 3, Landes's announcement was treated much more grandly, with front-page space in the *Times* and inclusion of a lengthy statement.[50]

In a statement published later, Miracle said that as women began to take places in government, "men will recognize in their intuitive knowledge a great asset of assistance in many branches. Her pride in civic and moral betterment will have expression."[51] Born in Ontario, Canada, Miracle said she was a graduate of Montana State College, that she had traveled extensively, and that she had been a "self-sustaining business woman the greater part of my life."

She reportedly managed a roominghouse "in a nice residence district of Seattle" and for eighteen years had "rubbed elbows with men in supporting herself." Miracle had a nine-year-old son who frequently helped her distribute "her modest little cards" at her campaign stops.[52] Her husband was never mentioned. Miracle clearly was of a different class than was Landes, and Landes stole her thunder as additional stories appeared about how hard the women were campaigning for "their" candidate—Landes.

Before she entered the campaign, Landes discussed her candidacy at length with her husband and others. Only two hours before the deadline on March 2 she filed her declaration of candidacy for the April 18 primary election. She listed herself as Mrs. Henry Landes, of 4511 Eighteenth Avenue, N.E., wrote in the word "councilman" in the appropriate blank, and turned over a $30 filing fee to the city comptroller.[53]

In her published statement, Landes used the domestic metaphor, saying that it was time the city family had women's viewpoint and influence in city affairs and public questions. "The City of Seattle represents a great big family, consisting of men, women and children, each with their own peculiar needs and desires which must be attended to in addition to the general welfare of the city."[54] A city has to be run like a business—and like a home—or it will not meet all human needs. "The women feel that there are many details of municipal housekeeping where a woman's influence should be felt." She continued with the separatist ideology, using it to buttress the novel idea of a woman's sitting on the council who was quite naturally focused on issues relating to public health, morals, and welfare. "Woman is particularly suited to deal with these matters and she should have an opportunity to find expression in the policy and laws of the city," she said. Although this was woman's particular niche on the council, "a woman of reasonable intelligence would not find it beyond her ability to function along the more strictly business lines."[55]

Bertha Knight Landes was certainly not the first woman to be elected to office, even in Washington State. The first women to run for office there were Margaret Pontius, for school director, and Lovetta Denny, for school clerk, in 1879. Both women lost.[56] Julia Kennedy, one of the founders of the Century Club, was appointed superintendent of schools as early as 1887.[57] The controversial journalist Anna Louise Strong was the first female to be elected to the Seattle School Board in 1916 with the support of the University Club and others, but she was recalled two years later for her radical activities and support of an avowed anarchist.[58] Perhaps the first female mayor in the United States was elected in 1887 in Argonia, a small town in south-central Kansas.[59]

Women began surfacing in numbers as candidates about 1915, at least where it was legal for them to surface. The numbers made it clear that enfranchised women were not able to open the doors that they anticipated would be unlocked for them. The first woman elected to Congress was Jeannette Rankin from Montana in 1917. As an undergraduate at the University of Washington, she had worked there for women's suffrage.[60] In fact, her first political speech was at a rally at Ballard, an area of Seattle, speaking to an audience of seven.[61] She served only one term, losing her bid for a Senate seat in 1918. By 1920, twenty-three states had elected at least one woman to their legislatures or some other office, although the women generally had little impact. Not many women chose to run for office, and even fewer won. As of 1925, women held less than 2 percent of the 7,542 seats in the nation's legislatures.[62] Being a prominent suffragist was not an advantage in either state or national races, a fact of political life that women like Bertha Knight Landes did not fail to recognize.

The slow pattern of female firsts was not encouraging to those who had high hopes for women in office, and some women who were elected were quickly discredited for real or imagined failings or faults. In Washington State, two women were elected to the legislature as early as 1912. They were Dr. Nina Jolidon Croake, a forty-year-old doctor of osteopathy from Tacoma, and Frances Axtell, a forty-seven-year-old Bellingham housewife. Axtell, as president of the Whatcom Ladies' Cooperative Society in 1893, had shown a capacity for creative leadership. She and her organization had tried to establish a flax industry, a creamery, and playgrounds there.[63] The reception Axtell and Croake received at the legislature was cool. Their colleagues and the press trivialized or ridiculed both of them when they spoke on the floor of the house.[64]

Despite Washington's early support for suffrage, women had a difficult time getting elected. In the dozen years between 1912 and 1934, only seventeen women were elected to the Washington legislature, only one of them from King County.[65] Most of the women were Republican, reflecting the political tenor of the times. In 1922, when Landes was first a candidate, five women were elected to the legislature, and four remained in 1924. But by 1927, Seattle's Maude Sweetman was the only female to be found in the Washington legislature. A woman was not elected to the Washington senate until 1928, when outspoken Spokane attorney and prohibitionist Reba Hurn was elected. However, her male colleagues labeled her brassy and relegated her to obscurity after she ran for a leadership position in the senate as a freshman senator.[66]

Successful women candidates in Washington, as elsewhere, could be counted on one's fingers. Clearly the prospects in 1922 for two women running for seats on the all-male city council were not promising. Landes and Miracle entered a crowded field of twenty-one candidates, including two incumbents, who were vying for three at-large positions on the nine-member city council. Landes ran her nonpartisan campaign with a small group of clubwomen. Her campaign committee included names that frequently appeared in connection with politically active women's clubs, both before the campaign and for a decade after.

The list included Greta (Mrs. R. F.) Weeks, wife of a railroad agent, who had been a delegate from the Century Club to the 1914 Washington Federation of Women's Clubs biennial meeting;[67] Ethel C. (Mrs. W. H.) Utter, parliamentary procedure expert who was described as a born teacher with an enthusiastic personality;[68] Mrs. S. J. Lombard; Theresa (Mrs. W. S.) Griswold, wife of a physician and Landes's neighbor, who also was a Century Club delegate to the state federation meetings in both 1913 and 1917; Anna (Mrs. George) Dalton, wife of an accountant and another neighbor; Helen Ames (Mrs. J. Herbert), wife of a bookkeeper; Mrs. H. A. M. Bonner; Frances (Mrs. George) McLoughlin; Mrs. J. B. Hill (perhaps Emma, wife of John B. Hill, who also lived in the University District).[69]

This collection of women, inexperienced with political campaigns but savvy in organization and lobbying as the result of their clubwork, put together a massive, precinct-by-precinct effort through other clubwomen, canvassing house by house, to build support for Landes. They used informal techniques that either bypassed the regular campaign channels or simply overwhelmed them.

Along the way, the clubwomen picked up important endorsements for Landes. The Bolo Club, a political organization of war veterans, endorsed Landes. "During the world war she organized five Red Cross auxiliaries and gave unsparingly of her time and energy," the group decided. "She is now a trustee of the Seattle Chapter of the Red Cross and as such has shown herself to be a woman of exceptional ability as a counsellor and representative."[70] In addition, some of the sitting members of the city council urged Landes's election as the woman's candidate to the city council.[71]

The results of the army of female volunteers was stunning. In the April 18 primary Landes achieved a spectacular success, the likes of which Seattle had never before seen. Running against twenty candidates, Landes garnered 31,000 votes, a number almost equal to votes cast for candidates running unopposed for other city positions. She was a record 17,830 votes ahead of her nearest council opponent. The *Times* editors were so impressed they decided to run a three-column–wide oval portrait of Landes on the front page, captioned "Mrs. Henry Landes."

A Landslide Win

Everyone, including Landes, was surprised at the size of her plurality. Miracle, with 10,937 votes, came in fourth behind two men, but that was enough to put her in the general election. After the primary, Miracle's comments were intended to set her apart from Landes. "It is up to the working men and women of Seattle to gather behind the one voice that will speak for them and

Seattle. . . . I have earned my own way as a business woman in Seattle. I love the city and every stone in it, and if elected councilwoman will give my best services for everyone."[72]

At a meeting following Landes's stunning primary victory, supporter Lombard described the campaign leaders' strategy for Landes. From Landes's friends and supporters, Lombard had obtained lists of women in organizations. She then gave each organization member a list of ten names of women from the voter registration lists in each precinct and asked for help. Only two of the clubwomen "were not interested in women in politics," she said. Thus nearly every female voter and household was visited, and those reluctant to back Landes sometimes were seen twice. Even mothers with small children were interested in helping and took their children with them as they canvassed.[73]

Campaign leaders also sent out a chain letter supporting her candidacy, asking each recipient to mail a copy to four friends. "Talk Mrs. Landes . . . lose no opportunity to further the interests of this Seattle woman who will be successfully elected if all Seattle women get behind her," clubwomen were told.[74] Although the clubs themselves generally did not participate in political campaigns, there were no restrictions on members. The grass roots effort, heavy on personal contact and light on costly advertising and brochures, worked.

Others at the postelection meeting discussed the importance of getting media coverage for her campaign. Ethel Utter, who headed publicity for the campaign, noted at the meeting following the primary that this was the first time that women in Seattle had been able to get "conversation" (i.e., coverage) into the papers. Some newspapers had run columns written by her supporters boosting Landes and women in politics. They appeared on news pages outside the pages usually devoted to women's news. At the meeting Theresa Griswold defined the symbolic value that Landes held for realizing women's rights and mapped out some of the contested terrain in women's behavior. Both men and women patrolled the boundaries of appropriate behavior for women, and they often disciplined transgressors by trivializing those women who did run for elective office, as Griswold noted indirectly, by pointing to appearance and clothing.

"There used to be silly arguments about what kind of clothes women candidates ought to wear, and criticism because they wore blue instead of brown, or because they talked with their rubbers on, as someone said about our candidate." She said she believed that should not happen. "It is our part to be generous with other women in politics. In other places they had bitter experiences. We should be grateful and generous to those who pioneer this work." She added, "We do not want a women's party, but we want an expression of women's opinion in government."[75]

Her comments about criticism of what women wear reflected the objectification of the female body that characterizes the category "woman" in patriarchal systems, which view woman as "the other." Rather than focus on the subject as candidate, and on the candidate's ideas as object, many observers focused on the woman candidate as object, in a self-conscious fashion, especially on what she wore and how she looked.

Knowing the right code for dress in such a system constituted a significant power/knowledge link enforcing what was "correct" behavior, and women were and are among the best enforcers. To know and follow the code is itself an expression of power, no matter what the challenges are to that power and that construction of gender. Even Griswold was careful not to step too far outside the established forms; she favored "women's opinion in government," not a women's party.

Landes's words, on the occasion of her primary election success, revealed her sense of newfound power. They also revealed her awareness of and humility about becoming a symbol for all women, one who was traveling into foreign political territory to accomplish her goals—namely, the material improvement of conditions for women, children, and men in her community. "You have shown what women can do if this beginning is to be followed. You have established yourselves as a power that has to be reckoned with," she said.

She commented on her symbolic value to women. "If I am elected it will not be Mrs. Henry K. Landes, nor Mrs. Bertha Knight Landes, who occupies a chair on your city council, but a visible personality of the women of Seattle." She also noted the link between her performance and other women's opportunities. "I am bowed down with the responsibility, friends, because if I fail, the women of Seattle fail. I ask your advice and friendly criticism and your suggestions. Do come to me and show me my mistakes," she told the women. "Above all, I know you want justice, a prosperous city, where if possible everyone will have employment, and where we all may live in peace, comfort and happiness."[76]

Clearly Landes was conscious of creating a new paradigm, a new model of behavior for women, and she was likewise aware that her support came from women. Her campaign stationery carried the words, "Campaign Headquarters of Mrs. Henry Landes, the Women's Candidate for the Seattle City Council." Despite being "the women's candidate," she felt constrained by custom to use her husband's name rather than her own.

The newspapers also were unsure of what to call her. Usually they used "Mrs. Henry Landes," but increasingly they called her Mrs. Bertha Knight Landes. In fact, the issue of what to call her actually resulted in a challenge to the legitimacy and legality of her campaign. She had registered to vote as Bertha Landes, as required by law, but had filed for candidacy as Mrs. Henry Landes. However, prosecuting attorney Malcolm Douglas, calling the complaint frivolous, rejected this early effort at ostracizing her and her unusual candidacy. He said that as far as he was concerned, she was on the ballot unless the court ordered her off.[77] It declined to touch the matter.

The assumptions implicit in the male-dominated power structure (which also excluded most men) soon led to questions about whether this woman—or any woman—could or should enter the all-male domain of Seattle city government. The battle in the political arena was fought in part over and through contested symbols. For instance, Landes told a meeting of the Coterie Club during the campaign that a story was being circulated among "the men" that having a woman on the city council would mean a curtailment of their personal liberties, including the institution of smoking. She in turn tried to trivialize their exclusionary symbol, one that had long associated politics with smoke-filled rooms and beefy, cigar-puffing political bosses. "It seems to me," she responded deftly, "that the work of the city council is of such importance that there should be no thought of paltry personal liberty entering the campaign. If men can think better by smoking, they had better smoke. Women don't require it." She added, recognizing gender assumptions of her own, "Every department of the city council's work is an elaboration of the same problems that a woman meets in her own household, from budgeting her finances on down to buying the winter's coal supply." She added it was only natural that women should be involved in the making of laws that affect them and their children.[78]

Her campaign platform reflected her transitional status as a female candidate and her attempt to bridge the home and politics. The platform included "the right of 40 percent of voters to representation," and the presence of the woman's viewpoint on matters affecting city business, the home, children and moral issues. But it also included issues not related to gender, such as reduction of taxes compatible with effective public services, business administration in civic government, and the development of municipal-owned utilities "along sane and reasonable lines."[79]

The issue of class, as well as gender, always a dividing line among women, was an element in this campaign. Landes clearly came from a middle-class, women's club environment, as did many of her supporters. Working-class women sometimes resented the leisure time activism of women who gained that time by having domestic help with their home responsibilities from other women. The use of servants was one of the most visible symbols separating women from other women. Publicity Chairman Utter felt it necessary to comment that neither Landes nor any of the women running her campaign had servants coming into their homes.

Landes was aware of the potential class divisions and also tried to counter the image (often pushed by opponents) of her as upper class. After the primary, reporters and photographers found Landes in the basement of her campaign headquarters. She was reportedly discussing working-class problems with the cleaning lady and finished that conversation before turning to them. In a rather self-conscious way, she told them she had always "been interested in women workers because I'm a worker myself and have always had five or six in the family to look after, and have done my own housework. I am a woman of the people, nothing else."[80] She also took it upon herself to include black women in her campaign. One evening she made an appearance before both the Federation of Colored Women's Clubs and the Sojourner Truth Club.[81]

One of Seattle's newspapers (probably the labor-owned *Union-Record*) commented on her lack of class consciousness, despite her middle-class background, although class would be used against her in years to come. Race, again, was not raised as an issue. The writer noted her egalitarian attitude. "And for all her university and club connections, she is of a democratic nature, free from snobbishness, and the leader of a movement to establish a large downtown club for women without regard to social lines."[82]

Landes also felt it necessary to provide some reassurance to men after she won the primary election, giving them recognition for whatever role they played in helping her win. She promised them they would have no reason to regret supporting her, adding that she planned to concentrate on the welfare of women and children, protection of the home, and moral issues.[83] In this way she could stay "safe" and traditional, despite her unusual candidacy. Noting that she planned to "lie low" and learn, the *Seattle Times* said, "Mrs. Landes takes her victory in the first battle of her political career with becoming modesty, without elation, and with the calmness of a veteran in the game of politics."

Adding that she made a plea to represent both men and women, representing all citizens first and then "women citizens," the writer quoted Landes: "I shall expect no special consideration on account of my sex and do not wish it. Naturally I shall give special attention to all legislation and questions of government that relate to the welfare of women and children and to the home and moral issues."[84] Equality and difference were raised in the same breath.

The city's major newspaper also felt it necessary to provide reassurance about Landes's femininity and her seriousness in the wake of her primary victory. The newspaper explained that Landes was not "the 'chattering' kind [of woman], and in that hour of triumph she showed it," instead choosing her words carefully. "It appeared that Mrs. Landes has that which is rare among women, a judicial mind." Furthermore, she was "a plain, unassuming church-going woman," a woman who was "not at all like the popular conception of clubwoman."[85] She was safe, sane, secure, and traditional. In her club activities and in politics, "she is Mrs. Henry K. Landes, not Bertha K. Landes. There is nothing of the new woman about her in her looks, speech, or actions."[86]

All this made her a trustworthy candidate, constrained by gender and her acceptance of gender roles, yet able to counter negative expectations of women with her "judicial mind." Here she reflected existing biases dating from the domestic ideology of the nineteenth century; later she began to push against this definition, to keep it from trapping her and to enable her to pursue real political equality and added power. But for this campaign she held tight to the metaphors of extended domesticity and women's proper behavior, and others held to them in talking about her.

Noting that both Des Moines and Kansas City had recently elected women to their city councils, Landes wrote in a newspaper column that women were uniquely qualified for office. "Woman is today the official money-spender for the family; why should she not have some say as to how the money shall be spent for the larger family—the city?" In addition, families were dependent on the city for protection of water, milk, and food supplies, "the sanitary conditions of our homes and of our city—in other words, for the health and happiness of ourselves and our families," she wrote. "Surely woman can qualify as an expert . . . can take her place on an equal footing with man and speak in many instances with even greater authority."[87]

She and her campaign leaders repeated the litany of analogies between running a home and running a city, and so did many in the media who endorsed her candidacy. Publicity Chairman Utter would say that of course a woman's first duty was to family, and if she could not keep house and go into politics at the same time, she had no business in politics.[88] Articles by Landes's supporters focused on the idea that running a home and leading women's clubs gave women unique qualifications for running a city, because they had learned how to manage problems. As a result they knew how to budget, how to finish unpleasant tasks, how to make do and improvise, and how to make decisions.

Landes recognized, perhaps at an unconscious level, that for women to enter a realm from which they were normally excluded required taking familiar elements and reconstituting them. Women could be politically successful and remain secure within themselves and their identity as women in only one way: by making women's private sphere—home and family—into a kind of public domestic sphere, in this way providing a bridge between the two, while at the same time emphasizing selflessness and denying political ambition.

Landes and other female candidates thus in a sense grafted power and public involvement for women onto the prevailing beliefs about women, which included rigid codes of behavior. The variations of this theme echoed again and again as she gained in political and administrative sophistication and power in the coming years. She was the "right kind" of woman to be accepted into clubwork and attain leadership, and she became the "right kind" of woman to open the door by running for office. One of Landes's contemporaries, writing for the *Nation,* described the rigors and legitimation that women found in the arena of clubwork: "A rapid rise in club circles denotes unbounded energy, intelligence, executive acumen and limitless tact and charm. It also denotes an impeccable personal life: a home and family that will pass the most rigid inspection and a reputation for being an excellent wife and mother. It denotes 'the right ideas,' the 'right clothes,' membership in a Protestant evangelical church, and New England ancestry."[89]

Landes had them all. Being the "right kind" of woman would serve her well now, but not so well in years to come. Nevertheless, in May, she enjoyed the spoils of victory as a woman who created a "social drama," breached a societal norm, and was welcomed into the system.

After Landes's primary landslide, nobody in Seattle really expected her to lose. In fact, one of the local newspapers said odds on election bets were being posted downtown, of $100 "or any part of it that Landes is the next councilman," and $100 "or any part of it that Landes leads any candidate you name."[90] Landes saved the article in her papers.

The morning of May 2, 1922, Bertha Knight Landes found herself elected to the Seattle City Council, having achieved a record plurality of 22,000 votes in an election in which 70,645 voters went to the polls (a record 82.5 percent of those eligible to vote). Miracle also won a seat on the city council, perhaps carried in by Landes's landslide, with 33,587 votes to Landes's 55,638. The third councilman, incumbent E. L. Blaine, drew 25,970 votes. Landes later said it must have been "the woman's psychological hour in Seattle politics." Blaine joked that apparently the reason he won was because only two women were in the field.[91]

Landes's success with her "amateur" campaign managers was fodder for analysis for long after the election. Her campaign committee got most of its coverage in two smaller newspapers, finding the large newspapers at least initially noncommittal. The committee printed one poster and had some cards printed, which was the extent of their campaign materials. In addition to the neighborhood canvassing, Landes made a number of speeches, addressing primarily women's organizations. The night the returns came in to the auditor's office, two members of her campaign committee had great fun watching the dumbfounded expressions of the men, "the old politicians," as Landes's numbers kept going higher and higher.[92]

Landes's campaign expenses totaled less than $500, most of it for printing, postage, and advertising, including $21 for a street banner.[93] On May 8, 1922, the city filed her "Appointment and Oath of Office," the first to be filed for a councilwoman.[94] She described herself as "absolutely without political experience," and so were "the women friends who helped in the office." When she ran, she said the politicians laughed. "We did not. We worked. We decided wisely to keep free of all entangling alliances, political or others." She said several were offered them, especially after the primary. "We proceeded on our way, rejoicing and alone."[95]

Here was a woman who had not even been able to vote on the issues that concerned her until she was forty-one years old, when the state of Washington adopted women's suffrage in 1910. She did not see women elsewhere able to vote on issues important to them until she was fifty-one years old, with the ratification of the Nineteenth Amendment in 1920. Now, at age fifty-three, she found herself just beginning her political career, about to take a place (with Kathryn Miracle) inside the previously all-male bastion of city power.

RACING A FAST TRAIN

The first ordinance the Seattle City Council ever passed prohibited noisy cows. The city fathers voted to prevent people from allowing cows to run at large while wearing bells. Every family in Seattle at that time seemed to have a cow, and the noise from the bells was "distressing at night," according to Albert Smith Pinkham, a merchant who came to Seattle in 1859.[1] He was one of the first in a long line of councilmen to try juggling individual liberties and collective good with issues of private property. Balancing them was not easy then, and it was not going to be easy for Landes and her backers.

Bertha Landes was now in a position to try. She had a place at the table, giving her a chance to play in the game of power politics guiding Seattle's development. She began her term as a team player on the council and built her credibility and power base within that group by learning and following its accepted procedures and codes. Yet within two years she had put her own stamp on city politics and administration, gaining enough acceptance to be elected president of the council.

After she became the council's president, she sampled a different kind of power when she became acting mayor while the mayor was away. And on one occasion while she was acting mayor, she entered another transitional state—she seized power in a most unladylike, unexpected fashion. As acting mayor, she made strategic administrative moves that confounded her opponents and gave her a local and even national reputation as a feisty, no-nonsense caretaker of the city's legal and moral health.

Landes's Expectations

Shortly before the May 2, 1922, general election that elevated Bertha Knight Landes to the status of council member, the "women's candidate" had outlined in a newspaper column what she now expected of women and herself. Fully aware of the long battle to gain women the right to vote, she chided women for not taking a more active role and exercising their new rights to address issues of special concern to their gender—even if it meant voting differently from their husbands. "Women worked hard for the right of franchise in this state. What have they done with it? Some vote. Some do not. . . . Some vote according to their husbands' dictation, too lazy mentally to decide for themselves." She concluded that women were "little better off than we were before we had suffrage." Being able to vote was not an end, but a means to an end, and "representation on the governing bodies of the state and city is necessary if suffrage is to accomplish the desired result." The vote brings with it heavy responsibilities in civic education, to learn the forms and functions of city government, she wrote.[2]

She also touched on one of the tensions in women's clubs, the clubs that were her own source of legitimation and power. What was the proper role of such clubs in this new political configuration? The women "have been slow in preparing themselves for this in their clubs, departing little by little from the purely cultural clubs to the study of social welfare and civic problems," Landes believed. "Woman must either do this—play her part in the game—or give up on her hard-earned prerogative of suffrage and cease her criticism of man's administration of public affairs."[3] Here was an example of the double bind in which enfranchised women found themselves. Women were systematically excluded from the power structure before and after suffrage, but if they were not able to make significant inroads, then somehow it was their fault.

Landes and others gave the vote more power to change political and social institutions than it actually had. Female activists, like Landes, who saw such potential in it, incorrectly assumed that all women shared the same concerns and would organize and vote to address those concerns. Their own faith in democracy, reform, and the vote meant that women—again—carried more than their share of the responsibility for the moral and social health of the community.

Landes argued that balance—the views of both men and women—were necessary for proper equilibrium in government. But at the city level, the standards of the home should be the standards of the city. While emphasizing in her campaign that woman's correct role was creating home and family and rearing future citizens, she argued that women must have civic involvement once that task had been accomplished.[4] She later said that involvement outside the home was also important for the psyche of the woman.

Her statements reflected domestic ideals but extended them. She believed that the sphere where women held the most power should be superimposed on city governance, making the city the larger home—safe, clean, protective, supportive, and moral. Other models of city governance at the time focused on the corporation and efficiency and on making the city run, not like a home, but like a business, where growth, economics, and private property ideals under law and order prevailed.

Progressive models centered on the civic reforms that limited the influence of politics and political appointments and that fostered the rise of a civil service system where jobs were filled according to ability rather than connections. One of Landes's frustrations about city government was its revolving door for individuals in key positions, who served at the whim of a mayor elected every two years. However, Landes had made a campaign promise—her first—to "support the moral and welfare projects in which women are primarily interested."[5] In subsequent campaigns her agenda would change to include other kinds of goals too, but this one campaign promise remained central to her understanding and use of gender in coming political power struggles, even as her own political understanding evolved.

The physical manifestations of the city, she said, "most vitally affect the well-being of the home, and in them the woman has as great, if not greater, interest than the man." On that list she included some unusual items, although they were common fodder for councils: grading and paving, the laying of water mains and sewers, sanitation, food inspection, garbage removal, building inspection, regulation of utilities, the making of budgets and raising of taxes, public safety including police and fire departments, and moral conditions.[6]

Landes began from a power base in the women's clubs of Seattle but gradually built a broad coalition of support that crossed class, economic, business, labor, and professional lines. At the end of her political career, she kicked off her final campaign with the endorsements of 350 individuals belonging to a variety of business groups, women's clubs, community organizations, and professional associations.[7] She was virtually the only candidate for the Seattle City Hall who consistently managed to garner labor, Municipal League, and newspaper support.

At 2:00 P.M. on June 5, 1922, Landes and Kathryn Miracle, along with the reelected member, took their seats at city hall. At that meeting Landes was elected to four of the council's eleven standing committees: License Committee, Judicial and Department Efficiency Committee, City Utilities, and the Fireman's Pension Board.[8] Three of the four assignments would prove to be particularly significant in her later political career.

The Seattle City Council, 1922

The Seattle City Council comprised nine individuals elected at large. They had diverse backgrounds, and some had lived out long careers on the council or in other elected positions. Landes and Miracle joined a council that was experienced, established, diverse, and more Democrat than would be expected during a Republican-dominated era in Seattle and Washington. Several of its members had survived several elections, and there were no clear dichotomies such as businessman-Republican or labor-Democrat. They routinely crossed those lines.

One such member was Robert Hesketh. President of the city council when Landes ran for mayor, he urged her election, in itself significant, given Hesketh's background. Hesketh, a member of the cooks union, first filed for election to the city council in 1911, when he was the only one of four labor candidates to win.[9] Born in Scotland, he became vice president of the Washington Federation of Labor, spent three years as a traveling organizer for the American Federation of Labor, and managed catering organizations prior to that. Yet he called himself a Republican and often had the support of conservative interests as well as labor. He was a perennial member of the city council, serving as its president in 1912, 1913, and 1925.[10]

Another of the labor council's endorsements was Oliver T. Erickson, sixty-two years of age when Landes ran for office. First elected to the city council in 1917, he resigned to run against Brown for mayor in 1924, losing both that race and his seat on the council. However, he was reelected the following year, defeating Miracle. Born in Minnesota, Erickson was a businessman involved in the manufacture of electric machinery and was founder and president of the Washington Elevator Company.

Erickson had been a construction superintendent and an elected commissioner in Minneapolis before coming to Seattle in 1900. He advocated public ownership of utilities before the war and was president of the Super Power League. He was a Democrat and, with Frances Axtell, formed the Washington Non-Partisan League in 1916, making Otto Case its executive secretary. The league was unsuccessful, but Axtell went to the legislature, and Case was elected to the city council when Landes ran for mayor.[11]

Another veteran was William T. Campbell, first elected to the council in 1914. Also from Minnesota, he was the first principal of West Seattle High School before going into real estate. He too was a Democrat.[12] Another venerable politician on the council as of the 1924 election was William H. Moore. Seattle's mayor from 1906 to 1908 and a state senator for four years, he was initially elected to the city council in 1916 with the backing of the Municipal League. A St. Louis-born lawyer with degrees from universities in Kentucky and Michigan, he too was a Democrat.[13]

On the more conservative side was E. L. Blaine, a business-oriented member whom labor had actively opposed in 1922. Born in Oregon, Blaine had resided in Seattle over thirty years. The council also included perennial candidate Philip Tindall as well as A. Lou Cohen, a merchant who had lived in Seattle thirty-five years, who was elected to the council the same year Landes was. The group included another businessman, Cecil B. Fitzgerald, manager of Federated Industries of Washington and another former mayor. He sat on the city council from 1914 to 1919, took the mayor's seat 1919–20, was back on the council 1921–24, and served as chairman of the Republican State Central Committee 1924–26.[14] Lawyer John E. Carroll, a Republican born in Louisiana, came to Washington in 1879 and was a justice of the peace 1907–17. He was elected to the city council in 1919.[15] Last on the list was Ralph Nichols, also active in Republican party politics and a leader in the Super Power League.

The Seattle City Council met weekly, and most of its business involved routine improvements, assessments, and condemnations, all the administrative detail connected with the construction of sewers, grading, sidewalks, pavement, and lighting. Landes, even on issues she would later address with reform proposals, generally voted with the majority on the council.[16] Her initial behavior, and the fact the council saw fit twice to elect her its president, indicated that she did not see herself or conduct herself as a marginal gadfly but rather as a student of better government, despite the fact that she and Miracle were outsiders by virtue of their gender and background.

Landes and Miracle voted together on many issues, but certainly not all. For example, business-oriented Miracle presented to the council the resolution in support of the Bone Power Bill, which would have allowed the city to sell public power outside city limits to small towns and farming sections. It was an important and ongoing issue in the struggle between the public and private power companies that wanted to expand their power grids. Landes had long been an active promoter of the bill and public power. Although private power interests succeeded in defeating the bill in the Washington legislature during her term, it ultimately became law in 1930.

Miracle, however, tended to be more protective of business interests from government interference than was Landes, voting against, for instance, the comprehensive planning and zoning code and commission that Landes spent so much time developing and defending.[17] Remarks Miracle made later indicated that the qualities that made Landes a club leader—her education, expertise, and connections—also made her somewhat overbearing. On the comprehensive zoning plan, which squeaked through the council by a 5-4 vote after boisterous hearings, Miracle was joined by Carroll, Nichols, and Tindall. Nichols later was one of Landes's best allies in trying to clean up Mayor Edwin Brown's administration of Seattle.

City planning—the idea that regulation and zoning could create an orderly, harmonious whole by regulating growth rather than irrationally responding to pressures of private interests—grew out of the idea of a comprehensive plan for cities. Such plans should include boulevards, parks, classic architecture for public buildings, plazas, and an eye for future aesthetics as well as regulation of present growth. Urban planners, members of an emerging profession, held their first conference in 1909, the culmination of years of work on the idea of city beautification. It represented a faith that through physical planning, a new civic spirit would arise, a physical manifestation of harmony and order as opposed to "chaotic, individualistic striving or disruptive social and ethnic conflict."[18] Standards of decency, morality, and the common good became connected to standards for city beauty and good government. Seattle, many recognized, certainly could benefit from the imposition of urban standards and planning.

Landes clearly advocated using government regulation to meet her goals for civic betterment, but even more, she generally succeeded in persuading other council members to her point of view on the mechanisms that would accomplish those goals. She did not find it easy, however. "With maturity should come wisdom. I know it brings courage. Ten years ago I doubt if I could have stood for what seemed right as I have been able to do," she said. "It has not been easy. Many measures have taken months of strenuous effort, but right does win. After all, it is only the breaking down of prejudices and conservatism. These must be eliminated before we can hope to accomplish much."[19]

There were few apparent factions on the council, although certain sets of members tended to vote labor interests or reform interests or business interests a little more often than did their colleagues. They more often demonstrated unanimity than division, however, partly as a result of the hearing process and modifications of proposed ordinances before votes were cast, partly as a result of their ongoing conflict with Mayor Edwin Brown, and partly as a result of the routine nature of the business they most often conducted. Such divisions as there were frequently centered on the licensing or delicensing of certain cabarets.

For instance, a few months into Landes's term, the city's corporate counsel recommended the city council pull and review for reconsideration the cabaret licenses for the Butler Hotel, the Lodge, the Alhambra, and the Bungalow as a result of alleged problems in them. The motion failed, with Cohen, Hesketh, and Landes voting for suspending their licenses.[20] Only two weeks earlier Landes had again been on the losing side in voting against several cardroom licenses, this time with Carroll on her side.[21]

What also helped unify the council was an unwieldy administrative structure that exacerbated conflict with the mayor, and several perennial, critical problems that took up most of its time. One was building and expanding Seattle's infrastructure in order to keep up with the city's booming population, which went from 80,000 in 1900 to 315,000 in 1920. Another was the problems of the street railway system, a deteriorating white elephant the city had unwisely purchased at an inflated price a few years before.

Yet another was what direction Seattle's public utilities should take to meet the city's future power needs. Finally, the city council was also united by a concern for law enforcement in Seattle and trying to keep vice and corruption at bay or at least corralled, particularly under prohibition.

Throughout the 1910s, city government in Seattle had been criticized on two fronts: the city's lax morality and the council's fiscal irresponsibility, with an undercurrent of fear about the rise of radicalism and labor unrest.[22] To some in power, social criticism meant reform, and reform meant radical, and radical meant subversion, revolution, and bolshevism. Mainstream labor consciously divorced itself from organized labor's more left-leaning elements, especially after the ill-conceived 1919 general strike that gave Seattle notoriety.

The Central Labor Council (which evolved from the 1888 Western Central Labor Union) was an aggregation of over 100 unions. It had a membership of about 35,000 trade unionists. In addition, the new Civil Service League, organized in 1916, represented almost 4,000 municipal employees and became an unrecognized, underground force in Seattle politics in the 1920s.[23] Seattle had a long and vibrant history of organized labor power and influence, culminating perhaps in the 1919 general strike. The strike polarized the union memberships, the union leadership, and the response of Seattle's middle class to union demands. The strike also hardened a conservative shift in the electorate and dimmed organized labor's fortunes in subsequent elections, although labor still cast a long shadow.[24]

Uneasiness about radicalism remained. The 1919–20 election was one where class consciousness seemed to create a great divide, where middle-class and working-class residents of Seattle had previously formed easy coalitions. In 1919 labor's endorsed candidates lost, and those the Chamber of Commerce endorsed won. Labor presented a strong candidate for mayor in 1920, supported by an alliance of farmers, railwaymen, and organized labor. However, a tough business-backed group called Associated Industries soon countered what was called the Triple Alliance. Its goal was to discredit organized labor and to eliminate unions altogether.[25] This time, neither group's candidate won. Seattle's electorate, in its wisdom, chose moderate Hugh Caldwell instead, the person who gave Landes her first push into city politics. In the meantime, Landes, as Seattle's leading clubwoman, came onto the council with fewer preconceived notions about labor and a bent toward conciliation.

The council faced several important forces in Seattle politics, including organized labor. Candidates for city positions were expected to fill out Central Labor Council questionnaires and make appearances before its representatives in the Political Welfare Committee. Labor endorsements were important, in both the negative and positive sense. A 1928 analyst found that, although labor's endorsed candidates frequently won elections in Seattle, those who won elections usually also had the endorsement of other groups as well, as did Landes.[26] As labor gained in stature and influence in Seattle, it also became more and more conservative, especially after the hotly contested mayoralty race of 1920 and the first complete rejection of labor's candidates.

The Municipal League

Also important in Seattle city politics was the Municipal League, which published the *Seattle Municipal News,* just as the Labor Council published the *Union-Record* and the federation supported *Washington Clubwoman*. Even the Civil Service League had its own newspaper used as a vehicle to influence readers toward its political positions. The Municipal League was created in 1910 by eight individuals hoping to use reform to remedy problems created by the massive increase in the city's population and the ever-growing vice and corruption and to make city management more professional and efficient. Its broad goals were municipal improvements, better living conditions, selection of competent officials, preparation of the city's citizens for active involvement in city affairs, and dissemination of information about Seattle.[27] In this respect it was representative of the "good government" clubs that appeared all over the country, formed to combat urban problems of all types.

Landes's political philosophy incorporated many of the league's initial tenets, and the league supported her in her campaigns, although it stopped short of specific candidate endorsements. The league, nonpartisan and educational by design, worked on policies and problems through various standing committees. Generally members were in their late thirties or early forties, comparatively well educated, affiliated with the Republican party, and self-identified as middle class.[28] They were for progress, reform, efficiency, and order, and they were against "the interests" and urban blight.[29] Early on they attacked prominent businessmen and financiers for monopolizing the city's political and economic institutions, but they also were suspicious of labor-born strife.

Just as the clubs used domestic ideology, so the league used civic consciousness to bridge class, occupational, and ideological differences in Seattle.[30] Both organized labor and the Municipal League were joined in seeking reforms such as an end to partisan city politics and city corruption. League members also sought rational planning in city design, budgeting, employment, and various services and developed proposals to implement ideas such as the city manager plan. Gradually, however, the group shifted to supporting more economy in government and began to cooperate with the large business interests it had shunned from 1910 to 1912.[31]

The Municipal League took a nativist turn in the years surrounding World War I, and its president went on a patriotic rampage. But after the war, the league, like many groups, moderated its nationalist stance and turned its attention to taxpayer complaints in the face of postwar employment contractions.[32] It continued its tradition of developing and promoting city structure reforms, such as the comparatively new city manager system. It also passed and circulated judgments on candidates for office as to their background, qualifications, and positions, without directly endorsing them. Landes, who garnered the support of labor, also had the support of the Municipal League throughout her career and her campaigns for civic improvements.

Improvement Clubs

Civic betterment, often of a close-to-home variety, was also the target of another significant force in Seattle city politics—namely, the dozens of community clubs or improvement clubs. They came and went, often pulled together for the specific purpose of building a particular bridge, park, or other amenity in a neighborhood or of relocating a red-light district. Seattle, perhaps more than other cities, was divided by geography and immigrant communities into discrete neighborhoods. They developed their own networks of support, including clubs with clubhouses and neighborhood newspapers.[33]

The community clubs also filled a vacuum in organized pressure politics when Seattle adopted nonpartisan, citywide elections. The end to ward and party representation had the effect of occasionally substituting another kind of pressure politics that Landes and other elected officials had to acknowledge. Naturally, the community clubs also became an important avenue for candidates to use to reach voters—and vice versa.

Seattle had a patchwork of neighborhoods. Hills, view sections, and lakefront composed more exclusive residential sections, while the lowest land tended to be occupied by economically disadvantaged and immigrant populations. The North End, including the University District, Green Lake, and Ballard, was relatively homogeneous and contained about 32 percent of the city's electorate.[34] It was an area that consistently backed Landes. The central district, south of Lake Washington Canal and north of Yesler Way, with businesses and apartments and neighborhoods ranging from poor to wealthy, had about 43 percent of the electorate. The district south of Yesler Way had lots of topological divisions and industry; its scattered, varying residences constituted 25 percent of the electorate.[35] It also had a higher proportion of the lower-income working class and transient neighborhoods.

Geographically, the North End persistently had more power than other parts of the city. It consistently had proportionally more representatives on the council than the South End. From 1911 to 1923 only three councilmen had resided south of Yesler Way.[36] Each section of the city had strong representation in one or more community clubs. Neighborhood sentiment was expressed—sometimes loudly—through these neighborhood clubs, and when angered and coalesced around some issue that affected them, they exerted considerable issue-oriented pressure on the council that the council, not surprisingly, often tried to accommodate.

In fact, Landes once complained about the special interests and all their special pleas coming before the council. "What first impressed me when I took my seat on the city council of Seattle was the utter selfishness of individuals. It was every interest for itself," she told an Oregon audience of five thousand at a Chautauqua.[37] One councilman interviewed in 1928 commented on the "raids" such clubs made on city funds. Large delegations appeared at council chambers and, by force of numbers, could make the council approve an expenditure it might not otherwise

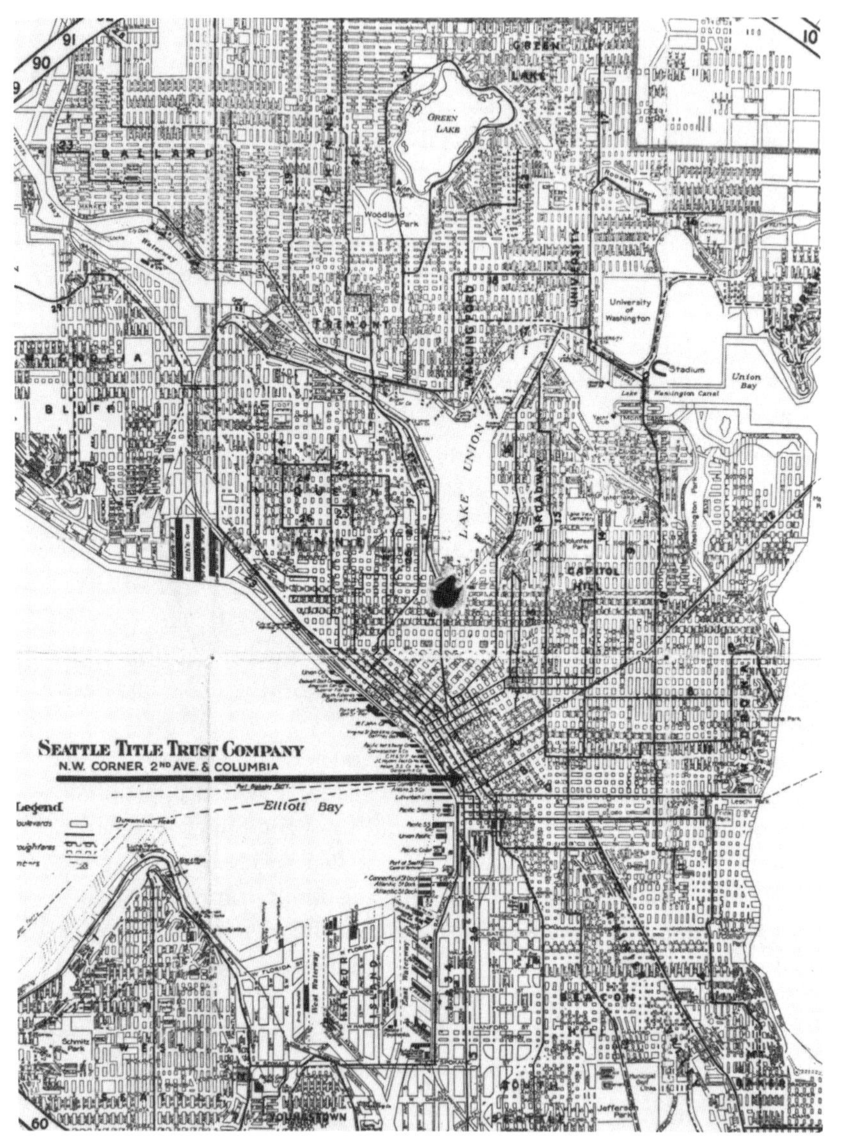

This 1926 "E-Z Guide" map demonstrates the growth of Seattle from the time the Landeses arrived three decades earlier. It shows the city's increasingly important neighborhood districts. The arrow appearing under the words "Seattle Title Trust Company" points just above the dividing line of Yesler Way, from which illicit enterprises threatened to spread. *Map courtesy of the Museum of History and Industry, Seattle.*

approve.[38] Pressure politics, in Landes's view, did not make for good government.

Not unlike the women's clubs, such groups formed informal yet powerful coalitions and learned to lobby, although their interests and goals were frequently self-serving. In fact, at one point there was a proposal to change the structure of city government to create nominations of two councilmen from each of seven districts, with at-large elections. Landes criticized the plan, primarily on the basis of the influence of the communities and their clubs. "I know by sad experience the pressure which communities now exert on the members of the Council. Don't increase this power. It would be disastrous to good government."[39]

Coalitions of such clubs could indeed be powerful. It was the North End federation of community clubs that took on the public power issue a few years hence, whose leaders engineered and forced the recall of Seattle's then-mayor through the power of referendum and petition presented through the city council.

Anxious to increase women's understanding and involvement in politics and to diminish class barriers, Landes created a new women's club. It was designed specifically to involve women in civic affairs across class lines and became known as the Women's City Club. Landes called a few women together in the fall, only a few months after she took office, to launch "The Women's Civic League." She was elected its first president in December. By then it had already attracted an astounding 640 members, who decided to change the name of their group to the Women's City Club. The size of the membership in such a short period of time indicated widespread interest in the club and in its founder. Bertha Landes remained its honorary organizing president until her death.

The group's membership included some of the women who had worked on her campaign and a broad cross section of Seattle's women. The nonpartisan group held weekly downtown luncheons, during which civic problems were discussed and the departments of city government described. It also held classes on Tuesdays on municipal citizenship and city government and sponsored monthly lectures. Its committees included legislation, Americanization (teaching English and history to the foreign-born and helping with naturalization), recreation, better films, welfare, and civic health and housing, which worked for the city/county hospital and a home for the aged. It had a girls' service committee to deal "with the problem girl and community resources for meeting her needs." Dues were $1 a year.[40]

The City Club's stated purpose was to work for "the moral, social, industrial and civic welfare of the city without political influence," and it had a custom of not allowing controversy unless both sides of the issue were discussed.[41] Landes's idea was to bring together all women interested in the welfare of the city, across social lines, to make scattered social and civic efforts more effective and to expand knowledge of public affairs among women. Every meeting for decades after its founding began with the idealistic oath once led by Landes: "I pledge allegiance to every movement that will make my city better, and I promise to register and vote at every election unless prevented by illness or absence from the city."[42]

Carrie Buell, the Chicago welfare worker who later comanaged Landes's mayoral campaign, followed Landes as president in 1923. Buell had been a welfare worker in Chicago and, like Landes, had particular concern for housing for "women of limited means," an issue the City Club under Landes and Buell, and the YWCA, had worked to remedy in Seattle in the early 1920s.[43]

Landes's Council Agenda

Landes was concerned about substandard housing in parts of Seattle and the growth of slums, and their effects on the people who lived in them. In a speech to the King County Humane Society during her first council campaign, she said a woman's place "is wherever things happen that touch the home." But she also told the group she was concerned about Seattle's growing slum district and poor housing for its residents.[44]

Landes continued her civic welfare agenda—and her own education—on the council. She also found she was developing her own political understanding as a result of her experiences. "I found my hands full of most interesting problems," she wrote later. "They kept me busy from nine in the morning until five at night, and many evenings were spent in giving talks to civic groups." She found that she was formulating a political philosophy in "meeting challenges to intelligence, sanity, and common sense. I also learned that there was a big difference between being on the outside looking in and being on the inside looking out."[45] She noted that she encountered no problems being accepted by the men who surrounded her. In fact, they disregarded their assumptions about women to describe her as like them, which they intended as a compliment. She was understandably ambivalent about their view of her as "not like" women. She was once asked if they resented her. "They did not. I never tried to force my ideas on them. We were all responsible, not to each other, but to the electorate," she said. "In fact, one of them told me once that my mind worked more like a man's mind than any other woman he had ever met. Was that a compliment, or was it not? I never did decide one way or the other."[46] On another occasion, she said she learned early that a woman who went into political life without claiming special privileges "or trying to reform the men among whom she labors is likely to be accepted as a co-worker without much ado." This insight banished, for her, the "popular bugaboo that men in politics resent women and try to double-cross them."[47]

However "integrated" she was, Landes did not hesitate to dissent when she disagreed with the majority of the council. Her first negative vote (which she lost 7-2) occurred at only her second meeting. It was against the mayor's appointment of the relatively inexperienced George Russell as the city's superintendent of public utilities.[48] It was an opening skirmish in the war that would eventually erupt with Landes and other members of the council united on one side and Seattle mayor Edwin ("Doc") Brown on the other. Brown himself had just been elected, having made it through the primary election by the thinnest of margins—a mere thirty-two votes.[49]

Members of the city council frequently introduced their own or their committees' ideas in the form of what were called member bills, and Landes had been on the council only six weeks before introducing her first—for the elimination and prevention of fire hazards in Seattle.[50] Within a few months, she began following the agenda she roughly sketched in her campaign, introducing proposed ordinances designed to control (although not eliminate) cardrooms, dance halls, and cabarets; improve efficiency in (and safety of) traffic and other municipal affairs; and strengthen enforcement of liquor laws. By November she had proposed her own amendment to the cabaret licensing ordinance and put on the table a proposal to regulate public dance halls through issuing permits.[51] Both were aimed at stiffening existing procedures and background checks before licenses could be granted.

Landes's stance on Seattle's morals and her support for women clashed headlong with economic realities facing some women in Seattle. These were women Landes otherwise would never have met, and meeting three of them one day changed her views. Landes moderated her position on Liberty Dance Hall and the dance hall ordinance following a visit from three women—two of them mothers—who explained that they saw their work less as licentious and more as economic necessity. May Stanford, Winnifred Durgin, and Gladys Nelson one day came not to her office but to her home at 4511 Eighteenth Avenue Northeast. They represented thirty-one women employed at the dance hall. The confrontation between the dance hall girls and the New England matron who happened to also sit on the council made the press.

Stanford later told the *Post-Intelligencer* about their visit. She said she identified herself as a woman with three children to support who had formerly sanded chairs in a factory for $13.85 a week, or about $720 a year. "What girl can live on that amount of money—much less support a family of three children and a sick husband?" she asked Landes. "I told Mrs. Landes all about it and I believe she understood the problem that I have to solve," she said.

Durgin, mother of two small children, said she preferred five hours at a dance hall for $4 or $5 a night in percentages paid compared with the $2.40 for eight hours work she formerly made at a restaurant. Nelson, who was single, said Landes seemed most interested in the two women who had families. "She seemed to understand us, and she said that for the present, the dance hall would not be closed—not by her efforts."

As for Landes, she said of the visit that the women "did not make a bad impression," and they had a pleasant talk. Her eyes were opened by what they had to tell her, speaking mother to mother as much as citizen to councilman. "I got their viewpoint," she said. "It was just between ourselves." The economic strictures of their gender were obvious. Clearly she was touched by their visit, but she was also boxed in by the publicity they generated over it. She backed down. She indicated she would pursue licensing rather than outright closure, with one of the points being an earlier closing time. (The hall's normal hours were 8:00 P.M. to 1:00 A.M.)[52] She proposed the licensing ordinances in November 1922.

Within eighteen months after she took office, as she gained confidence and expertise, she went into a higher gear to work on her political agenda. It grew to include professionalization of city management functions, which suffered from frequent turnover, political appointments, a lack of continuity, scattered and duplicated efforts, and incompetence if not outright corruption. She introduced a proposal to strengthen a Women's Division of the Department of Police with its own superintendent; in the spring she voted repeatedly against the issuance of more dance hall licenses.

She continued to draw a ring around Seattle's wild side and its profiteers through administrative regulation. In April she introduced a proposal for an ordinance to regulate movie theaters, shooting galleries, bowling alleys, and penny arcades, setting closing hours for them and penalties for offenses. In May she advocated licensing and regulation of massage parlors and public bathhouses, regulating the conduct in them and defining offenses and penalties, with an emergency enactment clause. One week later she proposed adding patrolmen and clerks to the police traffic division.[53] Most of her proposed ordinances passed, sometimes after lengthy and noisy hearings.

Another Presidency—the Council

At the council's organizational meeting on June 2, 1924, she was elected president, the first woman to gain that recognition and responsibility. The newspapers made note of the fact and her perennial "first" status, but without the surprise in the headlines her primary election had elicited. Her committee assignments had grown. They now included the License, Department Efficiency, Public Safety, and Finance committees, and also she chaired the Conference Committee.[54] Following the custom of the day, she continued to sign her name on documents "Mrs. Henry Landes." Her "civic betterment" agenda through the power of government regulation continued.

At the meeting after her election as council president, she introduced a proposal to condemn an area of Seattle for creation of parks and boulevards, to be paid for from the park fund. She proposed replacing the ineffective Zoning Commission with a City Planning Commission, outlining its structure and duties, one of her most significant contributions to city management.[55] In August she proposed an ordinance providing for the inspection of "animals, carcasses and meats intended for human consumption."[56]

As president of the Seattle City Council, Landes became acting mayor whenever Mayor Edwin ("Doc") Brown went out of town, an opportunity she used to her benefit. Here he is congratulating her in council chambers on her election. Brown, a "tolerance" mayor, was Landes's target when she ran for the office. He ran against her when the job came open again, but came to her side when she was under attack by candidate Frank Edwards. *Photo courtesy of the PEMCO–Webster & Stevens Collection, Museum of History and Industry, Seattle.*

In 1910 Seattle had named a commission to plan for the future expansion of the city. It hired civil engineer Virgil Bogue, who had worked with Frederick Law Olmsted, creator of New York's Central Park. Earlier the city had hired Olmsted's son, J. C. Olmsted, to produce a boulevard plan. That 1903 plan called for a winding parkway of about twenty miles to link existing and planned parks, most of which was implemented. Olmsted's goal was to place a playground or park within one-half mile of every home in Seattle. In 1911 Bogue produced a visionary two-volume *Plan of Seattle* based on Olmsted's work, which also included extensive arterial, park, and boulevard development for the city and the surrounding area.[57]

The voters rejected his plan in 1912 as too costly, and the city abandoned it. But this vision and beautification plan continued to have considerable influence on later officials such as Landes. In October, after a long hearing process, her forward-looking City Planning Commission was established, on a 5-4 vote, with Miracle voting against her idea.[58]

Another planning tool Seattle needed was a zoning code. A zoning commission, initially created by the council in 1920, had hired a St. Louis engineer to do some preliminary work on a zoning plan.[59] It was to be up to the council to draft the appropriate ordinances to direct the city's growth as part of a comprehensive planning effort that Landes supported.

Like city council members from time immemorial, Landes found that attempting to regulate residents' dogs generated more vitriol than many more difficult issues. In a town where packs of dogs barking all night had long irritated residents, the council at one point proposed to restrict the size of dog kennels. Landes recalled the stormy hearing. "Feeling ran so high during the discussion that I once threatened to adjourn the hearing and clear the room unless the people would behave like human beings, not like the canines under discussion," she said. "I wondered if it would not be safer to legislate against people's children than against their dogs."[60]

In September she became involved in an issue that was perhaps the first to mark a negative relationship with Civil Service employees—a relationship that would give her considerable difficulty later. As a result of a petition by representatives of the firemen and policemen association, another member of the council proposed a November 4 election to vote on a $25-a-month raise for police and fire personnel, plus a 15 percent raise for all general fund employees, effective January 1. Four councilmen voted yes, and four—including Landes—voted no. She declared the vote lost and then went on a two-week leave.[61] Nine days later, however, with labor representative R. B. Hesketh acting as president pro tem, the council approved holding an election in November for a $25 raise for certain police and fire personnel, and this time only Blaine opposed it.[62] It carried the city by 7,600 votes after a well-organized campaign by the Civil Service League.[63]

In the meantime, sporadic fighting began between Mayor Brown and the council, with factions both in the community and on the council accusing him of various collusions and violations of the law. He in turn accused members of the council of being politically ambitious and out to sabotage whatever he proposed in order to further their own political careers.

Mayor Brown and the Dance Halls

Mayor Brown, also elected in 1922, was a Seattle dentist who advertised himself as painless. His ads sometimes began with a medical message and ended with a political one. "I do not compete with cheap quack dentistry, I do not operate on your pocketbook, nor sell conversation," read his ad in the 1921 city directory. "I give you $2 worth of dentistry for $1. Then you will come back and send your friends to me. This Pays!"[64]

He was one of the few Seattle businesses to advertise consistently in the Washington suffrage newspaper, *Votes for Women,* before women got the vote in Washington in 1910. A Democrat, he initially had been a member of the Socialist party and later "reformed" in 1916. Once a manager of a Kansas City barbershop, he studied dentistry and then took up the study of law in 1882–83, graduating from a Kansas City school of law in 1899. In 1901 he came to Seattle.[65]

During his lifetime, Brown had worked as a newsboy, a bootblack, a bellboy, a shingler, a sailor, and a barber. He developed a talent for public speaking as a soapbox orator along the Skid Road District. In fact, Brown, then an active socialist, a dozen years before he was elected mayor was arrested for speaking downtown, on the inflated charge that the crowds he drew obstructed the streets.[66] He was expelled from the Socialist party in 1908 for publishing interviews "in capitalistic dailies derogatory to the party and its policies" and for his remarks about two socialist leaders.[67] Brown's experiences on the street gave him sensitivities to policemen on the beat and to small businessmen, leaving him somewhat cynical about both, particularly in the face of prohibition.[68] Brown, the reformed socialist, also owned mining property in three states and an orchard and farm at Ephrata, Washington.[69]

Known widely as a tolerance mayor, Brown supported keeping Seattle a place where men with change in their pockets would feel comfortable coming and spending their tourist dollars, as he put it. "Loggers and other laboring men don't come here now as they used to," he said. "The city is thereby losing a great deal of money." He claimed Seattle used to have 5,000 of them a year spending $500 each, or a total of $2.5 million, "left among our businessmen."

Unlike Landes, he tried to work with cabaret owners in a cooperative fashion, once suggesting that they hire special patrolmen whom he would name special investigators.[70] This was equivalent to throwing down the gauntlet to those members of the city council who wanted to clean up Seattle and was a factor in the push for cabaret licensing. Landes had initially leaned toward closing the dance halls, where women danced with patrons in return for a piece of the profits for each soft (and sometimes hard) drink ordered, but she softened her stance after her visit with the three dance hall workers.

Landes came into conflict with one of Washington's few female legislators, Maude Sweetman, on the dance hall issue. The target was again the infamous Liberty Dance Hall, at 217½ Second Avenue South, which paid women a percentage of the profit on each dance and each drink sold to men. Sweetman said it was simply a place where laboring men in overalls danced with middle-aged women, and that it employed thirty-one women.[71] The dance hall was in her district, and she was running for election. "Men can go there—working men who are not welcome in uptown dance halls. They are under bright lights and police protection."[72]

Landes told her license committee that the hall had been closed for months, but that it was reopened by Brown and his police chief, William Severyns. She had also been told, "Things are pretty wild down there."[73] A week later the head of Seattle's Council of Churches demanded closure of Liberty and another hall, Dreamland, at Fifth Avenue South, following his own investigation. He said he had found "males of all colors and manner of dress and many women of all ages," where "girls" made 40 percent on drinks ranging from $1 to $2.50 and $1 on bottles of wine.[74] Dreamland had been shut down before as a source of prostitution in 1910, under pressure from the Seattle Federation of Women's Clubs.[75]

Seattle may have had good reason to be concerned about commercial dance halls, gauging by the experience in another port city, New York. While most dance halls were indeed simply opportunities for working- and middle-class men and women to meet and entertain one another, others—especially commercial ones—were fronts for prostitution, for violations of prohibition laws, and even traps where young women were captured and held against their will in brothels.[76] After 1905, so-called tough dancing spread to commercial dance halls from the brothels of San Francisco. It featured close physical contact and involved partners clinging to each other while they moved suggestively. Ribald language and bawdy behavior were encouraged or ignored at some commercial dance halls.[77] All this also violated standards of community decorum if not the law, leading to widespread efforts in Landes's time to control the halls. Commercial halls with commercial hostesses clearly exploited women and their bodies, even where there was no illegal behavior. However, they also provided badly needed economic relief to some women, as Landes found out.

"When I went on our city council, our dance halls were practically a law unto themselves," she said later. Although the council majority was against her in the beginning, "I fought for three months for the passage of a dance hall ordinance. We had public hearings every week, but at last we voted to license the dance halls, to close them at a decent hour and to keep them under sensible supervision."[78]

Landes encountered both abuse and praise for her efforts to put brakes on the dance halls and enforce more acceptable codes of behavior. Superior Court Judge James Ronald, known as the patriarch of King County Superior Court (and himself a former mayor back in 1892) wrote her, praising her push for the ordinance while suggesting legal refinements in the language.[79] Others were less kind. During the public hearings, Landes later said she was vilified and even threatened with death, but she held fast to her goal of ridding the city of the unregulated and unsupervised all-night operations, which fostered prostitution and consumption of alcohol.

"The men were not losing any sleep over [the all-night dance halls], but ought to have been," she later said of her efforts.[80] She and the License Committee had the new ordinance drafted and called in proprietors but got no cooperation. Ultimately her License Committee recommended that all-night dance hall parties and Sunday dances should cease and that chaperones should be required at the dance halls. The ordinance as drafted required a suvervisor of dances (a position to be filled by the police chief) and matrons. It established a minimum age of eighteen, an application process for licensing, and a ban on "shadow and moonlight" dances. It required an admission fee and prohibited a per dance fee.[81] After weeks in public hearings, some of them riotous, the package passed the council, but it was with a cost, she felt. "I thus began sowing the seed which later was to develop into organized opposition to me."[82]

In this issue involving class and gender, Landes came face to face with some of the economic realities that made her begin to moderate her reformist stance. She gained an understanding of some of the pragmatic issues involved, and her growing sensitivity to the complexities of management and effects of power surfaced again as she gained political sophistication. She recalled those days later. "Things are not always so simple as people on the outside seem to think. I became much more tolerant of other law makers and civil servants."[83]

The council was not, however, showing much tolerance toward Mayor Brown. In the meantime, Brown, annoyed at what he saw as interference by the council in his executive powers, was trying to get rid of the whole council as a nuisance. Seattle had a history of frequent conflicts between the mayor's office and the city council, but it was usually less vociferous than the present battle. At the end of October 1922, Brown proposed a new city charter for Seattle, one that would abolish the council as a part of consolidation of city and county government. "Give me a commission of three men, not more," he said, because the council had become both a legislative and an administrative body, usurping the powers of the executive branch.[84]

In fact, Seattle had what municipal government experts called a weak mayor system, where the council could veto the mayor's appointments, had responsibility for preparing the budget, and exercised considerable control over the administrations of all mayors.[85] Not surprisingly, the result was often deadlock and friction, especially where the council and mayor disagreed philosophically and politically. If the council refused to confirm an appointment, the department could be left without a supervisor for several months, as happened with Brown's superintendent of streets and sewers. All appointments by the mayor, except the police and fire chiefs and the civil service commissioners, had to go through the council.[86]

As a result of this structure and the personalities in Seattle politics, conflict with the council was the traditional pattern for a mayor during the early twentieth century (with the notable exception later of Landes).[87] Compounding the problem, the key administrative positions of comptroller, treasurer, and corporation counsel (city attorney) were also elected, further complicating any effort at efficient, centralized administration. Their terms were four years, the council's three years (with three members elected each year), and the mayor's term only two years. Most of the administrative heads went out with the outgoing mayor, causing considerable disruption and discontinuity in vital public services, a complaint that Landes voiced repeatedly. Seattle at the time had eleven administrative departments, plus six divisions of the Board of Public Works as the result of the city owning so many public utilities.[88] However, this compared favorably with Boston's forty departments and Chicago's thirty in terms of administrative complexity and political patronage.

In 1923 the city council, with Landes's concurrence, put forth its own plan to remedy some of the intrinsic problems in Seattle government, one that also would do away with their problems with Brown. They proposed simply doing away with the mayor. The plan would establish a professional city manager, whom the council would hire. The council voted 6-3 to go forward with a plan that would put the idea on the March ballot. According to the proposal, approval of the city manager idea included the election of fifteen freeholders who would then revise the city charter according to voter preference. The plan would also have allowed the council to elect one of its own to fill the role of mayor, and it would reorganize the city's offices into six departments, each headed by the manager's appointees.[89]

Earlier that month, Brown again raised the council's collective ire when he expressed doubt that the present nine council members—who were, he said, "elected in a wave of political hysteria and fashionable intrigue"—could ever select a satisfactory city manager.[90] Although the idea was supported by the Municipal League, the civic and business leaders organized for the betterment of Seattle, it found potent opposition in the Civil Service League, some labor circles, and a few veterans' groups. The Civil Service League objected most to the charter revisions, arguing that civil service would effectively disappear because the manager under the new system would decide appeals and dismissals.[91] This time around, the city council ultimately backed away from the proposal, which needed to return to the drawing board. Landes said time was too short before the March election.[92]

Complaints about Brown's administration and confrontations over the dance halls, gambling, and drinking continued to fester. Brown had been in office only four months when U.S. Attorney Thomas Revelle criticized Brown's employment of a Nellie Hartford as a "special investigator" after she was arrested for smuggling narcotics to a prisoner in Monroe State Reformatory. She was driving a city auto at the time.[93] Shortly after that scandal, Brown suggested that dance hall entertainers form a union and regulate their own profession. Angry citizens initiated a recall effort at that point, but it failed. The pugnacious Brown then threatened to run for governor.[94]

By the following year, the second of Landes's three-year term, Brown was going on the offensive against some of his many detractors, including Landes. He filed a $10,000 lawsuit against a member of the Republican State Committee who reported seeing him furnish illegal drinks at a meeting of Democrats in the Butler Hotel.[95] The charge that Brown either served drinks or was present where alcohol was served surfaced again and again. Its symbolic value in the crusade for law enforcement and control of illegal behavior in Seattle provided a catalyst for Landes, enabling her to usurp the power of the mayor's office a few months later to clean up corruption and put an end—at least temporarily—to the double standards in following the law.

Acting Mayor Landes

Landes first tasted the power of the mayoralty soon after her election as president of the city council in June 1924. Brown in the meantime had been reelected, despite all the charges and rumors swirling around him. In June she became acting mayor for a brief time while Brown was out of the city, according to provisions of the city charter. It was the first time in the United States that a woman acted as mayor of a major city. It came the day after another first, the day she became the first woman in Seattle's history to be voted president of the city council.

The leading newspaper, the *Seattle Times,* reported the event this way: "Woman Acts as Seattle Mayor; Precedent Set by Mrs. Landes," with the subhead reading, "New President of City Council Denies Any Ambition to Become Executive and Advocates

City Manager Plan."[96] Here again, the media portrayed Landes as an aberration, but a "safe" aberration without political ambitions of her own. She never disputed the interpretation. The framing of the article demonstrated her transitional nature as a first by focusing on the novelty of it. The lead read, "For the first time in Seattle's history, a woman was acting as mayor today. Mrs. Landes, voted president of the city council yesterday, the first woman to hold that position, was called upon today when he went out of town."

At Brown's desk, the article continued, she signed over twenty bonds and performed other routine duties. "Despite her experience today, Mrs. Landes does not consider her new position as a stepping stone to the mayor's chair. In fact, she doubts whether the city will have a mayor in years hence," since she favored a city manager plan. She took the opportunity to note, in support of the plan, that only one man on the Board of Public Works had more than two years' experience, and she blamed the existing system.[97] It was a dress rehearsal for a role-reversal confrontation that followed a few weeks later. That confrontation brought her national attention and resulted in her being drafted to run for the mayor's office herself almost two years later.

Shortly after her first experience as acting mayor, Landes found she would be occupying the mayor's office for an entire month later that summer while Brown attended the national Democratic convention at Madison Square Garden in New York City and visited cities in Illinois and Michigan. "I'm going to leave the city in good hands," he told the *Times*. "I don't think anyone is going to try and slip anything over on her."[98] In point of fact, it was she who slipped something over on him.

Acting mayors usually operated only as caretakers, but the potential for seizing power was there, since the city charter said the mayor had authority only when the mayor was physically within the city limits. In 1910 the power of the mayor's office had been seized once before by an acting mayor when Max Wardell fired Mayor Hiram Gill's chief of police and appointed a replacement, a move well publicized at the time.[99] The door was thus ajar for Landes to seize power to promote her own agenda.

For the first several days, she merely handled routine responsibilities while sitting in Brown's chair, signing dozens of official documents. Then she began to do a little more. A staunch supporter of the public ownership of utilities, she took it on herself to issue an official proclamation. She declared June 18 "Public Power Day." It was part of a campaign to get on the ballot a bill that would allow cities that owned municipal power plants the right to sell off excess power outside the city. The bill also would allow municipalities to condemn the properties of privately owned power and light companies where necessary, a clause that quickly mobilized the private power operators and companies and their investors. The private power interests were not pleased either with the bill or her stance on it and campaigned actively against the measure. Puget Sound Power and Light Company ultimately spent $125,000 to kill it.[100]

Landes's declaration, and her ongoing support of public power interests to the potential detriment of the comparatively well-heeled private power interests in Seattle and the Pacific Northwest, would influence the remainder of her political career. She confronted utility interests again in the legislative arena, and finally in the political arena. Not satisfied with "Public Power Day," she decided to rehire public power proponent J. D. Ross as the city light superintendent. Ross, who began working on Seattle's public power system at the turn of the century, had been in and out of favor with various administrations over his career. Brown had failed to reappoint him when he took office. A formidable foe to the private power interests, Ross had been waiting in the wings. Bertha brought him back into the spotlight and made it clear where she (and the council) stood on the issue of public versus private power.

Having made her point about the utilities, she decided to take action on another situation that she found intolerable—widespread police corruption. A few months before Brown left for the East Coast, his police chief, William B. Severyns, made a casual remark in the presence of a reporter that there were probably one hundred men on his police force who should not be there. He implied they were taking payoffs, but he was not to blame because they were under Civil Service protection.

On June 23, 1924, Acting Mayor Landes, just over five feet tall, called the burly Severyns into her office. She handed him a letter dated June 23, 1924.[101] In it she said that "businessmen and our citizens in general" were disturbed over the lack of law enforcement in Seattle. "Bootlegging and gambling are carried on openly and apparently with no fear of the consequences. Violations of law in the pool rooms and the card rooms are not reported to the

License Committee [which she chaired] of the City Council as they should be. Burglaries and hold-ups are of daily occurrence." She said holdups occurred in daylight with the perpetrators showing no fear of being caught. This and other crimes led her to two conclusions: "Either there is collusion between members of the police force and criminals, or else the police department is so inefficient that law violators neither fear nor respect its power."

She added that "the patience of the general public is about exhausted," noting that Severyns's request of the council for additional patrolmen found opposition "for fear of merely increasing inefficiency or something worse—especially in the face of your own public statement that there are many men on the police force who should not be there." She said she would be loath to use taxpayer money to add men to the department "until there has been a house-cleaning in the department."

As Seattle's chief law enforcement officers, the mayor and police chief had a joint responsibility for the bad conditions, and it was now her duty to do something about it. "While it is true that I am Mayor only in a temporary capacity, at the same time it is my duty while Mayor to insist upon a policy of law enforcement and to protect the public as far as lies in my power." Then she got to the heart of her letter. She wrote that if his statement were true, "then it must follow as a logical conclusion that one hundred men should be removed." The officers should be fired, and taxpayers should not continue to pay their salaries.

"Furthermore it is only fair to the efficient and worthy men in your department that those who bring disgrace upon the police force should be weeded out. The Police Department has lost the confidence of the people. The innocent men are under the stigma of graft, bootlegging and connivance with crime as well as the guilty." She concluded by ordering him to fire the officers. "For these and other equally potent reasons I feel obliged to issue an order that you remove from your department, without delay, the men whom you believe to be protecting law violators or who are themselves law violators." Her use of the word "potent" was interesting in this context.

She added that she wanted immediate action and a written statement—within twenty-four hours—from him acknowledging receipt of her orders and the results. "If there are any obstacles within or without your department tending to prevent or impair the effectiveness of such a move on your part, please include such a report in your communication to me." Here she apparently referred to the Civil Service Commission. She had other plans for them.

She signed the letter Mrs. Henry Landes, Acting Mayor. Aware that she was taking aggressive, unladylike action, she wanted to make the letter as strong, perhaps as masculine, as possible. In her draft of the letter, which she preserved in her papers, she had eliminated the phrase "as many as" in front of the reference to one hundred men, apparently to strengthen the wording and its challenge to Severyns and, through him, Brown.[102] The letter was direct, clear, and forceful. In it, "housecleaning" took on an almost rugged, masculine quality.

She then gave him twenty-four hours to respond before releasing the letter. But somehow the letter found its way into the papers shortly after being handed to Severyns, along with an account of her ultimatum. This further antagonized him, and he wrote a somewhat flippant response, daring her to take over his department.

Severyns, himself an attorney and University of Washington graduate and, at thirty-seven, the youngest man ever to hold the job of Seattle's police chief,[103] was not used to this kind of treatment, especially from a woman. However, it culminated months of direct and indirect criticism of his police department. He once said in another context that prohibition was unenforceable, the cause "of more police delinquency than all other laws put together." It also was "violated more often than all laws put together." He said that people "do not vote as they drink," that politicians "do not drink as they vote," and that the law bred hypocrisy.[104]

In his response to Landes, he may have been simply expressing his irritation, or he may have been daring her to follow through on her unexpected inversion of the traditional gender roles. In any case, the tone of his letter to her was both condescending and angry. "Yesterday afternoon you telephoned and asked me to come to see you, and in obedience thereto I appeared at your office at about 5:30 o'clock. . . . I had no opportunity to read the letter in your presence." He complained that she had given him her "firm and solid promise not to hand your letter to the press nor disclose its contents until you received my reply. I have just learned that you have released your letter to the press." However, he said her "hasty action" would not affect his response. The rest of his letter contradicted that statement. He noted that she seemed "disturbed and somewhat alarmed" over conditions in Seattle, and the tone of her letter would make one think "a great calamity" of some kind was imminent.

"May I not most respectfully call your attention to a provision in the City Charter which authorizes the Mayor or Acting Mayor to take immediate steps in the event of impending danger. Article V, Section 2, provides in substance that the mayor of the City may take charge of the Police Department at a moment's notice in times of public stress." He believed Landes should "find solace and consolation in that wholesome provision."[105]

His letter continued at length, reviewing her charges point by point. He blamed her and the License Committee for issuing licenses to cardrooms and poolrooms with which she now found fault. He blamed the former police chief and administration for the personnel in his police department, contending that he had removed twenty-six officers since he began and disciplined many others. He said that her complaints of businessmen and citizens being disturbed about law enforcement in Seattle were groundless, since it was these same citizens who reelected Brown in 1924, despite "vile, venomous and groundless attacks." He added, "I presume that these same political defamers are having difficulty in forgetting their defeat."

He obliquely accused her of playing politics ("I wish to say that I always have discharged the duties of my office in a spirit of fairness and fearlessness"). And he said he would "continue to do so in the future, undismayed and unintimidated by the vociferous and venomous bickerings of the disgruntled and disappointed." He concluded by hinting that she could not have taken this action plaguing him on her own, but only as "the result of a composite deliberation of various individuals, some of whom I have reason to believe are conspiring against me." Furthermore, he was "unafraid and undisturbed" and would continue on his present course.[106]

It was, Landes would later call it, an insolent response to her ultimatum that she said left her no options. "As any bridge player understands, the only thing left for me to do was to follow his lead and take the trick," she recalled. "It was not a pleasant thing, but it was inevitable."[107] The next day she wrote him another letter: "It is very generally known by citizens that the conditions to which I referred in my letter openly prevail in this city. It is the duty of the police to maintain a reasonable trend of lawful conduct, and since this is not being done by you, whether through inability or unwillingness, it becomes necessary to place in charge of the police department someone who can function with greater effectiveness."[108]

She said the records of his department showed no "appreciable inroads on the liquor ring whose leading spirit is a man who is a frequent and apparently welcome visitor at police headquarters" (she presumably referred here to former police lieutenant Roy Olmstead, who was Seattle's leading bootlegger at the time). She added that other men connected with law violations of almost every type were in frequent conference with high officials of the police department. "Such fraternizing with the lawless is constantly tearing down the morale of your own department whatever there may be left."

Severyns's public statement that the Civil Service Commission tied his hands was untenable. "Here was your opportunity to at least put the test squarely before the Commission, but in not doing so, you have failed to protect your own interest." She added that his attack on the licensing of pool and card rooms "is unworthy of you because you know as a matter of fact that no licenses are granted until your own department has made recommendations for these places, and almost no adverse reports reach the committee from your office." Her ultimate challenge to him came in the last paragraph: "Your reply to my letter is very unsatisfactory, being not only evasive but defiant as well, and leaves me no alternative but to relieve you of your command. You will please turn over your office immediately to your second in command, Inspector J. T. Mason." The ten-day mayor then proceeded to appoint Severyns's lieutenant as chief of police.

Joseph Mason, a thirty-year veteran, was in an awkward position, to say the least. He had been on his way to play golf when he got the word he was now in charge. He defended his boss and the department, arguing it "is in the best condition it has been in for some time." He added he did not expect to be chief very long and that "I will not fire one hundred cops or any number of cops just on hearsay."[109]

Acting Police Chief Landes

When Landes realized that this appointment would work no better to meet her goals and put him or any other appointee in career jeopardy, she took Severyns's sarcastic advice. She issued a proclamation declaring an emergency and appointed herself Seattle's Chief of Police:

> An emergency having arisen by reason of the removal of former Chief of Police William B. Severyns, and it not being deemed advisable at this time to appoint his successor, and such emergency in my judgment justifying the same, I, Mrs. Henry Landes, Acting Mayor of the City of Seattle, pursuant to the provisions of Article V, Section 2, of the Charter, do hereby assume command and control of the whole police force of the City for the time being, and for the period of such emergency.[110]

Seattle city government was now topsy-turvy, and Landes was assuming a role no woman—and few men—dared assume before. Here indeed was a public crisis.

Landes called in as her assistant former police chief Claude G. Bannick, Seattle's police chief from 1911 to 1914. He had a reputation for honesty and was then working as a police captain banished to the Ballard District north of the city. Within hours, police had closed down Seattle's most flagrant law violators. Lotteries were closed, punchboards disappeared, and speakeasies were raided.[111] Some closures were voluntary once the word about what had happened at city hall hit the street.

The effect of this challenge was dramatic. The episode, stage by stage, was carried in the front-page headlines throughout Seattle. It resulted in a flurry of telegrams to Mayor Brown, who was attending the deadlocked Democratic National Convention in New York City. He returned a telegram advising Chief Severyns to take a fishing trip until he could get back, and he asked his secretary to prepare a letter of reappointment for him to sign when he returned. Brown quickly boarded a train for the three-day return trip to Seattle.

His secretary, Henry Dahlby, attacked Mrs. Landes on Brown's behalf for acting on what he called gossip and for statements in her letter to Severyns. He wanted to call her a liar but thought better of it. "If the statement had not been made by a woman I might add that it is also untrue. But if you place a loaded pistol in the hands of some people somebody is liable to get hurt." He called her move rash.[112]

Meanwhile, Landes continued with her efforts to make Seattle less lawless than it had been. Coincidentally, she gained considerable local, regional, and national publicity from a bemused press corps for her efforts. "Landes Races with Fast Train" exemplified the tenor of the articles, which generally reflected, first, amazement that a woman would seize power in this way, then surprise at what the woman was doing with it, then a kind of tacit cheering at the audacity of it, and finally amusement at the race between the matron and the mayor.

It was a shrewd if somewhat risky political move on her part. It reflected the nature of this woman, whose outraged sense of justice and political leadership training allowed her to rise up and take advantage of such an opportunity. It was also the courageous if obstinate act of an offended woman, despite the fact that she had so carefully made herself part of the power structure rather than operate as a radical outside the system. What she did in this showdown was also theatrical.

However, Landes, the pragmatic and calculating city official, was not acting in the completely individualistic and emotional fashion that it may have appeared. She said later she had spent an afternoon and evening thinking over her plan and discussing it with her husband. Before going forward (and during her brief tenure as police chief) she gained advice from several people who entered and exited via the back door of the mayor's office. They sneaked in and out to keep their identities secret from Brown's secretary, who was keeping the mayor posted on these perplexing events by telegraph. Some of those individuals included Thomas Kennedy, corporation counsel (city attorney); Ewing Colvin, deputy prosecuting attorney; A. A. Oles, a Chamber of Commerce leader; the Rev. G. Chatterton, head of the Seattle Federation of Churches; and, of course, her husband.[113] She clearly had broad-based support for her actions, which also served to embarrass Brown and his backers.

Many places that had conducted illegal activities remained closed voluntarily, waiting out the storm. Others saw their slot machines, liquor, and money confiscated. Bannick named a special detail to investigate beat officers for graft, and where there was evidence of graft or bribes, officers were fired or disciplined. The city council quickly authorized hiring additional patrolmen to help him.[114]

Landes had more in mind. On the administrative front, she planned to fire two civil service commissioners for malfeasance and for allowing the mayor to interfere with hiring decisions. The council's own Department Efficiency Committee—a thorn in Brown's side—had identified those problems earlier. Moreover, as Landes knew, vacancies on the Civil Service Commission, whose members were initially appointed by the mayor, could be filled only by the city council, giving the council some measure of control if she were successful in removing some existing members.[115]

What happened when Brown's personnel learned of her plans for this last act is possibly an apocryphal story, but it was repeated in virtually all subsequent articles about Bertha Knight Landes although with different endings. Supposedly Brown's secretary, Henry J. Dahlby, hoping to put an end to Landes's career as mayor, hatched a ruse. He arranged for two of Brown's suitcases to be left at a restaurant Brown commonly frequented and directed the mayor's chauffeur to pick them up before picking up Landes to take her to the mayor's office. The chauffeur innocently commented, "It appears that the mayor is back in town," when Landes asked about them. Then, in the mayor's office, Landes supposedly found another suitcase lying open containing a pair of Brown's shoes, up-to-date New York newspapers open on his desk, and on the desk Brown's cherished autographed photograph of William Jennings Bryan. And in the ashtray was a smoking cigar. One version ended this way: "Convinced by all the evidence that Brown had indeed returned, Mrs. Landes called off any further reformist moves."[116] Brown did return the following morning.

Other versions of the story have the two suitcases sitting beside the desk, smoke from a cigar curling in the air, and one of Brown's hats on top of the desk, with Dahlby issuing a press release purportedly from Brown that Brown had no statement to make on the situation,[117] which of course he did not have at that point, since he was still in transit. Still other versions have Landes not falling for the ruse but hanging on to the office until she saw "the redness of Doc Brown's eyes after his cross-country train trip."[118]

What was significant about these tales of the acting mayor episode was the frequent focus on the cigar and cigar smoke, which constituted a strong symbolic differentiation between the genders. Also, many of the stories took on a kind of imperialist adventurer approach to what she did, making her the hero of a story that she had crafted. They were appreciative of how she acted "like a man" (or unlike a woman) in her grab for power, implying that here was a diminutive, matronly "woman" who could get the better of the condescending and corrupt men around her in her quest for civic decency. They assigned to her a certain kind of heroism that transcended her gender status and what was deemed appropriate behavior for women in a time when considerable conflict surrounded this issue. For instance, the *Los Angeles Times* praised her bold move. "Men in the past have been wont to talk patronizingly of 'woman's instinct' as opposed to 'man's reason,'" the editorial said. "Seattle seems to prove that an instinct for getting things done is far more useful in the world than an intellect that only talks about them."[119]

Landes found herself not only the focus of a good deal of national media attention as a result of her actions but also increasingly a symbol in the skirmishes in the war over who would be victorious in deciding what was legal behavior. There was a widely held perception that general lawlessness and crime was on the rise everywhere and that no less than the future of the country was at stake. Not only was Landes suddenly a model for what women could do in public office, but she was also a model for what cities could do to restore law and order. Seattle had long had a national reputation as lawless and wide open to purveyors of vice. Landes said that Seattle suffered from adverse publicity across the country "for conditions here and wrangling among public officials."[120] As *Sunset Magazine* put it in September 1924: "What do you want, a 'liberal' town where Scotch is cheap and easy to get, where the bright light of cabarets twinkle behind dark velvet curtains, where the taxi business flourishes and visitors from the country have a 'good time,' or do you want a town where bootleggers slink round furtively, where booze is poor and expensive, where everything is dark at 11 and visitors from the country transact their business, go to bed and go home early?"[121]

Other cities in the United States, it said, had made bad choices, a mistake Seattle—under Landes—could avoid. "San Francisco has traditionally preferred the first-mentioned type of easy-going, semi-blind law enforcement; Los Angeles has endeavored to have a 'home' city with the minimum of vice, of nocturnal and spirituous entertainment." But Seattle had been wavering. "Half the town longed for the good old days of easy virtue, open gambling, abundant liquor and ample profits of a certain variety," while the other half "frowned on liquor and gambling with their trail of corruption and graft, but the frowners steadily lost ground."

Seattle, it said, had acquired a bootlegging machine that was highly organized, widespread, "and almost respectable," despite the wishes of the majority—at least until Landes took action as acting mayor. Noting that Brown undid what she did when he returned, the piece concluded that the desire of the majority for law enforcement was not enough. "The desire has to be transformed into continuous political action to become effective. And the minority which is financially affected by strict law enforcement is always active."

Although generally favorable, not all the press Landes received was laudatory. In words that indicated how she as woman should be disciplined, the editor of *Argus* stated that had she "sat tight and kept her mouth shut she might have been elected mayor one of these fine days . . . but she proved conclusively that woman's sphere is in the home or at any rate that hers is not at the head of the city government."[122]

Landes herself modestly downplayed what she did. She said there was nothing sensational in the way she acted, and that the police chief "really fired himself by talking too much and too indiscreetly." But she was pleased with what she did with her ten-day coup. "I think there has been a satisfactory demonstration of what can be done toward law enforcement. I do not think Seattle can be closed down completely, but I do believe it is possible to demand a general respect for the law."[123]

It was a point of view that she stressed then and later in her political life, as her opponents increasingly tried to paint her as an absolutist bluenose. She repeatedly responded that, with human nature being what it was, she did not want a Seattle that was completely "closed down," but she did want a community with order and respect for the law—including the liquor laws.

An out-of-town reporter described her response to the sudden media attention that her moves generated: "Her early actions in the mayor's chair naturally caused the newspapermen to swarm to her office, where they were all met with a smile and were called her boys; she said that they pestered her, but she liked to tease them." She also exhibited political skill with the press, in the reporter's view. "She deftly parried all manner of questions as to her future course of action, saying that she wished all such questioners would go fishing until after she got through being Mayor."[124]

This description, and others of her as well, portrayed someone with considerable political acumen, at ease with herself, and amused, rather than a wild-eyed reformist zealot. In any case, she continued to profess having no political ambition. "Her three-year term as councilwoman already has run two years, and she has no career in public life in view. 'I have no fences to keep up,' she says, 'and no ax to grind, so that I can do what I see fit, free-footed.' "[125]

Descriptions of Landes from this era and after continued disingenuously to stress her lack of political ambition, generally crediting her rise to club presidencies, city council, and mayoralty to the urging of others, to her selfless devotion to duty, never to an interest of her own in gaining power to realize any personal or professional goals. Once again, "woman" was objectified as someone being acted upon, not even the subject of her own life's drama. She was represented as merely having been in the right place at the right time, with a set of unique skills that made her the best possible candidate for leadership in the eyes of others—not in her own.

Part of the gender construction that keeps women from being acting subjects in their life stories is that the codes of acceptable behavior for women traditionally have not allowed for personal ambition; rather, they have favored the external call to service as their avenue to power. Landes did not gain office from a series of fortuitous accidents. She put herself in the right place at the right time by exercising intelligence, developing a vision, making others see it, and building leadership skills throughout her career. Based on her actions and what she as a subject wrote about herself, Landes, like other civic leaders working for reforms, held deep convictions about civic duty. Civic duty, in Landes's case, however, was not subsumed in politics.

Politics, connected as it was and is to personal ambition and patronage, was several notches below the idea of selfless civic virtue on the values scale. Landes, who favored the reform trend toward professionalization and expertise in important positions, despised political patronage and worked hard to minimize its place in Seattle politics. Some years later she said a career in government "should be a profession, not a mere series of jobs for the person who grabs hardest."[126] The city council and mayor positions were already nonpartisan (although she identified herself as a Republican), but she increasingly became an antipolitician, despite her faith in democracy. She used that apolitical stance in subsequent campaigns, focusing on her lack of financial ties to any group and enhancing thereby her attractiveness to voters who shared her concerns. From a political standpoint, there were contending models—the outsider versus the career politician. Landes's gender, her background on the council, and her agenda, however, put her in a weak position in the role as an outsider, which would become more of a factor later in her career.

Mayor Brown Under Attack

Once Brown was present in body as well as spirit, Landes went back around the corner from the mayor's office and resumed her seat on the council. Apparently her bid for power and its subsequent embarrassment of the Brown forces did not diminish her standing with the council. It reelected her as chair the following year, in June of 1925. In the meantime, Brown's fortunes continued to deteriorate. Another drive to impeach him started. The Reverend U. G. Murphy, a missionary to Japanese and Chinese residents, in his August petition bid to get Brown out of office cited flagrant violations of liquor and gambling laws. Furthermore, they went on with the full knowledge of the mayor and police, he said.[127] In December, the head of the YWCA also demanded his impeachment.[128]

Finally, the city council referred to its Brown-baiting Department Efficiency Committee a document filed on December 27, 1924.[129] In it, C. L. Maxfield outlined the citizens' complaints against Brown and the joke he was making of Landes outside the council's earshot. "I believe that you must share with other citizens deep humiliation because of the conditions existing in our city with regard to gambling, robbery, bootlegging and graft," he wrote the council. He said he and thousands of others were convinced the mayor was "either a party to the corrupt practices or he is incompetent to enforce the law and ordinances." He cited news reports of even high school boys promoting "booze parties."

Worse, he said, was the open violation of law at the opening of the new Olympic Hotel in downtown Seattle. "I understand that the mayor and the chief of police were both there. The *Post-Intelligencer* state[d] that the mayor said that those who participated in the revelry could go as far as they liked, as far as he was concerned, but they would have to settle with Mrs. Landes." This disrespect for the law, Maxfield said, was

> greatly increased by the fact that many who violate the Volstead Law believe that the mayor violates the same and is in cordial sympathy and probably abetting those who traffic in booze. . . . You could not have been unmindful of the continuous discourtesies shown to members of the Efficiency Committee, to witnesses who were called, to Mrs. Landes, and the Chairman of the Committee. Committees who call upon him to suggest ways and means of civic betterment are accused of wanting to be mayor. If attention is called to rottenness in his administration the accusation is made that we are defaming Seattle.

He closed by volunteering to circulate petitions if necessary and asked the council to impeach Brown.[130]

Petitions were soon printed, accusing Brown of failing to perform his duty in enforcing the laws, illegally disposing of liquor, openly permitting gambling to go on, refusing to cooperate with other law enforcement agencies, and "knowingly permitting solicitation to prostitution to be carried on, on the public streets and from buildings devoted to that purpose." Furthermore, private citizens were bombarded with "spielers" for lotteries. Gambling and prostitution were openly conducted on the streets of Seattle, and Brown and police officers were often present during illegal activities. Finally, in violation of civil service rules, they kept on the payroll employees charged with serious offenses, the petition said. "We do not expect Seattle to be a 'spotless town' or demand the impossible, but we have reason to believe that these laws and ordinances can be reasonably enforced because it has been done during a period of five days when the mayor was absent from the city."[131]

Landes's period of provisional power was used by the groups circulating these petitions, which gained almost six thousand signatures. To them, she had demonstrated that enforcement of law and order was possible, even in Seattle.

Brown was called before the Efficiency Committee of the city council—again—to defend himself against charges that he interfered with police and civil service appointments and failed to destroy liquor that had been seized. He had an interesting response about the confiscated liquor for the press. "No booze gets out illegally . . . but as long as I am mayor I'll give good liquor away to save lives. Whenever a hospital or an ill person requires liquor which may save his life, it is my moral duty to provide the liquor, if possessed. It may be against the law, but it's for humanity's sake." As for the other charges, he termed them yet another political plot on the part of politicians who wanted his office.[132]

Early in 1925, Brown found it necessary to leave Seattle, this time for California, again putting Landes in his office. Although she did not cause an uproar this time, she addressed another of her concerns—safety. She called in department heads for a traffic conference, concerned that there had been nineteen traffic deaths in the six weeks since the beginning of the year, compared with four at that time the year before.[133] She formed a Public Safety Committee made up of citizens and public officials, who hoped to reduce fatalities through education of both pedestrians and motorists.[134] Brown could not abide even this mild-mannered program and criticized its education focus, calling instead for more patrolmen. The group continued to meet, however, without his support.[135]

Landes was not above teasing Mayor Brown and his staff. When he returned to his office, he had to take down some decorations she left. He removed from the walls, in view of the press, clippings recounting Landes's days as acting mayor in 1924, when she fired his police chief.[136]

Landes ran again for the city council in 1925, saying there was more work to do in the city. She expanded her campaign agenda to include ideas for protecting the children and youth of Seattle. She said she would support a Park Board charter amendment that would give the board latitude in spending for public welfare for children.[137] She continued to support the city manager form of government, which was being tried in Cleveland at the time, and gained widespread endorsements for her candidacy, including an indirect one from the civic-minded Municipal League. It called her "conservatively progressive," "independent," and someone who had shown "unusual aptitude" for the position of city council member.[138]

When she ran for her next office, she cited what she viewed as her achievements on the city council: the City Plans [Planning] Commission, codification of licensing laws, Seattle's model traffic code, support of public utilities, and development of the Skagit project, a far-sighted endeavor for construction of Diablo Dam on the Skagit River to supply Seattle's power needs in the future.[139]

The primary election saw only a 25 percent turnout at the polls, compared with almost 70 percent in the previous primary. The poor showing translated into an erosion of votes for Landes. Landes received votes from 51 percent of the voters, putting her third in a field of six candidates for the council. The general election of March 2, 1925, saw her margin increase slightly to 55 percent, but she remained in third place.[140] She and Blaine had been reelected. Miracle had not. Miracle was replaced by Oliver Erickson, who earlier had run for mayor against Brown.[141]

Brown, still facing possible impeachment and rumors of a grand jury investigation, by August was telling reporters that instead of running for the U.S. Senate, as he had hinted, he might run for the city council to help revise the charter, because the council needed improvement. The council "does nothing but trip me whenever I start something constructive. Their blockades are little more than the machinations of vainglorious politicians who try to get famous overnight by throwing monkeywrenches at me."[142] It seemed to contain an oblique criticism of that "overnight sensation," Bertha K. Landes.

By October, other complaints piled up against Brown. One was that he was too cozy with the political department (i.e., lobbyists) of the private Puget Sound Power and Light Company. However, the council, including Landes, declined to impeach Brown at that point, aware that a grand jury investigation was going forward.[143] However, the King County Grand Jury, although sharply critical of him, failed to find enough evidence to impeach him. The petitions demanding his ouster were then turned over to the Judiciary Committee. Ultimately, the council, on the committee's recommendation, decided to let the voters decide his fate in the upcoming March election. Some members noted that it was unfair for the council both to accuse him and to sit as his judge. The vote, at a noisy meeting in December, was 6-3 against impeachment, with Landes, Ralph Nichols and W. T. Campbell on the losing side.[144]

Landes Enters the Mayor's Race

It was in this discordant setting that Landes again heard her name mentioned as a mayoral candidate. Giving some credence to Brown's charges of council politicians being after his seat as well as his hide, two council members besides Landes talked of running against him for the office, as did corporate counsel

Thomas Kennedy. Landes was pressured to run as perhaps as the only candidate who could beat Brown in the elections in the spring of 1926, despite the erosion in her support compared to the landslide of 1922. However, the ever-reluctant candidate declined repeatedly to enter the race unless it became clear to all that she was the only one who had a chance of defeating him, in spite of the fact that his political ship had been sinking.[145] She recognized that running for mayor of Seattle was awkward and out of character for a woman, to say the least. It was also much closer to politics than running for the council had been.

Another part of the stage set in 1926 was the arrest and trial of former police lieutenant Ray Olmstead, the king of Seattle's rum-runners, and sixty-five of his closest business associates. They were caught by federal agents as a result of the new wiretapping methods, dubbed "whispering wires" by the press. Olmstead had maintained his contacts in high places. He was highly regarded as an astute businessman, one who would not cheat his loyal customers, and as the bootlegger who stabilized the price of bootleg whiskey in Seattle, which he accomplished by evading Canadian tax on exports of liquor. The bays and inlets of Puget Sound, and the area's proximity to Canada, offered ample opportunity for smuggling liquor.

In 1920 Olmstead, then thirty-four and the youngest lieutenant in the police department, discovered he could sell his respectability to those who faced prison because judges would often listen to his recommendations. He invested that income in bootlegging, only to be caught soon after, unloading cases of liquor on a beach. He was fired but got off the federal charge with a $500 fine. When eleven backers staked him with $1,000 each, he soon began to monopolize the King County market, even avoiding the $20 a case excise duty imposed by Canada on exported liquor by routing it via Mexico. Thus he was able to undercut the prices of his competition. He hired an attorney and a staff of navigators, dispatchers, bookkeepers, salesmen, and dock workers, including some former Canadian police officers, and drove out the competition. He used a large ocean freighter and worked with bootleggers up and down the West Coast.[146]

He and his wife established Seattle's first radio station and were later accused of broadcasting coded messages involving his primary business during children's programs from his home transmitter.[147] He was brazen, often unloading his shipments at downtown docks in the middle of the day. He bribed policemen, followed good business practices, and was said to have grossed over $200,000 a month for several years, using his own fleet of fast boats and shrewd planning to evade capture, often with the help of advance warning of police actions. In fact, his wife once tried to call the police when agents raided their home.

Ultimately the wiretaps proved to be his downfall, and in January of 1925 a federal grand jury indicted him and the other defendants. However, Olmstead posted bail and went back to work bootlegging until the 1926 trial.[148] The trial played out daily on the front pages of the Seattle papers, right up to the March election, complete with hints that the mayor's office was implicated in Olmstead's extensive operation.

In the meantime, the city council had decided to put the city manager plan on the ballot again, modified slightly, in fond hopes of bringing rationality and professionalism to Seattle politics and city administration—and, coincidentally, more power to the city council. The revised plan, developed by the Municipal League, differed slightly from the prior one, in that more power was vested in the elected city council and less power in the appointed city manager. Corporate Counsel Thomas Kennedy was asked to prepare the question for the March 9 election.[149] Landes and others had long been on record supporting the professional city manager plan that was adopted by 430 cities by 1930, but previous attempts to get it passed in Seattle had failed, by substantial margins.

As the candidate filing deadline grew near, Landes was under pressure to enter the race. One argument was that her candidacy would improve the chances for passage of the city manager proposal if a candidate for mayor actively supported it while campaigning for mayor. She initially decided against running. On the day of the deadline, she told reporters of her decision, then had second thoughts. She called their offices a short time later to say that she was reconsidering and might indeed file.[150]

Torn initially about entering the race and thrusting herself into such a public arena, she had decided against it. But when the press carried announcement of her decision, it caused such a deluge of protests that she ultimately changed her mind at the last minute. She described her decision to run in a management magazine. "I filed for Mayor much against my own personal inclinations," she said, upon realizing that the form of government she advocated might not pass. "Friends argued that if the City Manager plan did not carry, Seattle might thus obtain an executive familiar with city business, one who could work in harmony with the Council," she said, "and one committed to the purpose of selecting capable heads of departments, regardless of personal or political entanglements." She also told the magazine that if she were elected, she would run the office "as nearly like a city manager as the laws will permit."[151]

Once again, only two hours before the deadline she paid her filing fee and entered the campaign, having talked herself into running in part out of the belief that this time the city manager plan would pass. If it did, the office of mayor would become largely ceremonial. And as president of the council, she likely would assume the role while retaining her powerful position.

Years later she offered another explanation of why she finally decided to run for office. Despite Seattle's nature as a seaport town, "with all that signifies," within Seattle's borders "were, and are, a host of law-abiding citizens, young people of the finest type, who deserved protection, children who should not be surrounded by evil conditions but given a fair chance to develop into the best," she insisted. "Those were the decisive factors which motivated me finally in going into the race."[152]

As the campaign got underway, the saga of the Olmstead trial gave credence to her campaign statements about law and order, and it also gave her law and order as an easy campaign issue to organize her speeches around. In contrast to her first campaign, which centered on representation in government for women and the promotion of home and family welfare, her mayoral campaign emphasized the need to clean up city corruption and crime, an always-popular political pursuit.

For instance, she told the Seattle Business Women's Club that "general police and criminal conditions here are intolerable." Her remedy was clear. "If elected mayor I promise to wage a relentless warfare on all crooks, thieves, bandits, burglars, stick-up men and other law-defying characters . . . too many policemen are taking their orders from bootleggers."[153]

Her primary election opponents were Brown, Kennedy, John B. Shorett, and Clifford Clark. Shorett, an attorney, was responsible for much of the waterway litigation and development in western Washington.[154] Attorney Kennedy, who entered the University of Washington in 1903, had been born in Minnesota. He was a deputy prosecuting attorney before becoming city attorney and the city's elected corporate counsel.[155] Clark was the retired founder and owner of a wholesale produce business.[156]

Landes's campaign managers were Carrie (Mrs. Frederic) Buell, former president of the Women's City Club, the club Landes founded shortly after her election to the council, and W. R. (Dick) Faris, former chief clerk in the auditor's office, who also lived on Brooklyn Avenue, with Caroline Horton, daughter of the late Dexter Horton and secretary of the Horton estate, as campaign treasurer. Buell had also been a state organizer for the Red Cross and active in Community Chest drives, organizations that Landes had helped direct as a member of their boards of directors. Buell had been a welfare worker in Chicago and had particular concern for housing for "women of limited means" and other social welfare issues.[157]

Ethel (Mrs. William) Utter and Harriet (Mrs. M.) Elias, who helped manage her two previous campaigns, completed the management team.[158] Utter and Elias were also consummate clubwomen, and Utter gained additional recognition after Landes was gone from the political scene. Utter, wife of a salesman,[159] became a noted expert in and teacher of parliamentary procedure, even giving classes on parliamentary law for legislators. She held the parliamentarian post in various organizations and was active in the Washington Federation of Women's Clubs in several capacities over the years.

Utter, born Ethel Comings, also came from Chicago, where she helped establish a juvenile court and became a probation officer in St. Louis. She helped organize a Women's Council and a Women's Economic League in the Midwest. In 1918 she moved to Seattle and did Red Cross work, becoming a member of Landes's committee of five in her run for the city council and the mayor's office. Ultimately she was appointed by Washington's governor to the State Welfare Commission, which was charged with administering the minimum wage law for women.[160]

Landes continued to use these comparative political neophytes, rejecting traditional politics. As an example, she began her campaign by promising the voters that she would make no appointments before the election and that she would remain free of the influence of any organized body.[161]

She began making dozens of club appearances in her campaign, working for passage of the city manager plan as well as the success of her own candidacy. She called for a manager and department heads who could "continue in office as long as they make good will mean greater efficiency and eliminating the necessity of training new department heads possibly at the end of every two years." She repeated her offer to relinquish the mayor's job for the city manager "because I firmly believe that plan means better government and that it offers immense savings to the taxpayer."[162]

In the meantime, Mayor Brown's fortunes were declining, revelation by revelation. The prosecution presented testimony at Olmstead's trial based on a 1924 wiretap conducted while Landes was making her move on lawlessness as acting mayor. Olmstead's office manager on the tape warned somebody not to take too many chances "until Doc Brown comes back" because city hall was heating up. When asked how long, the assistant said only a day or two.[163] Testimony presented the next day quoted Olmstead as informing his associates that he had "seen Doc and everything is OK." In the next two days the wire tap indicated that two hundred cases of whiskey were smuggled into Seattle in preparation for July 4 celebrations.[164] Landes and the other candidates were quick to capitalize on Brown's alleged failings. Landes was in the best position to point to his complicity because it was her actions while Brown was out of town that worried the bootleggers on the tapes implicating Brown.

The campaign was not long, but it was arduous. The days of pre-broadcast campaigning and limited transportation were grueling. Landes made as many as twelve to eighteen speeches or appearances in a single day toward the end of the brief but intense primary campaign. The newspapers followed her footsteps, citing appearances, but generally gave her remarks significantly less coverage than those of the other candidates in the campaign.[165]

The primary election saw a record 72 percent turnout, but with the vote split several ways, Landes only squeaked past Brown, 25,762 to 24,672 votes. Corporate Counsel Kennedy, who had been endorsed by the Central Labor Council, was third, with 20,208 votes.[166] Despite the revelations and allegations about Brown, perhaps the surprise was the number of votes he received. This indicated a citizenry divided on the issue of law and order when it came to alcohol consumption and the imposition of codes of behavior from above. Or perhaps it indicated citizens' concerns about boosting a woman into the office of mayor.

Nevertheless, with the general election only two weeks away, the campaign was now between the incumbent, Doc Brown, and Bertha Knight Landes. Suddenly, Landes was a novel force in Seattle politics. She was entering a new phase, that of being the leading challenger to unseat the mayor of Seattle. She was not the first female candidate for mayor of a major city in the United States, but she would be the first to win.

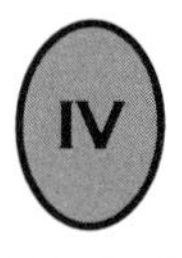

THE "FREAKISH" MAYOR

Landes felt sick to her stomach. She sat in the back half of an open biplane, taking what was supposed to be a short flight. The air and noise pummeled her face, despite her leather helmet and goggles. This was considered no place for a woman, but it was where the mayor was supposed to be. The mayor was taking the first passenger flight to Bremerton's Ward Station, twenty miles from Seattle. It was for her yet one more ceremonial function, a day in the life of the mayor of Seattle, with photographers in tow. When she landed, pale and not very dignified, she called for her husband.[1]

Landes did not realize what becoming mayor might entail, in its physical as well as its mental challenges. She might have reconsidered had she known about that airplane flight when she entered the last two arduous weeks of her campaign for the office.

On the Campaign Circuit

The general election was only a couple of weeks away. It had suddenly become a race between the incumbent, Edwin Brown, and Bertha Knight Landes, the female candidate who had created an upset by pulling away from him and the other candidates in the primary election. The final two weeks of the campaign saw a different attitude and discourse toward Landes. All recognized that Bertha Knight Landes, the candidate, might actually become Bertha Knight Landes, the mayor of Seattle. The thought was exciting—and disturbing.

Before the 1926 election Landes continued to push for passage of the city manager plan as a rational alternative in city governance. Her unflagging support of the plan, which would eliminate the office of mayor as presently constituted, became an asset to her political campaign. Many voters and power brokers viewed it as evidence of selflessness and a welcome absence of political ambition. It also made support of her "safer." Few noted, publicly anyway, the possibility that as president of the city council, she might well become the council's chosen mayor if the city manager measure passed. Few noted either the power that would accrue to her and the city council if the measure passed. Most of the criticism of the plan centered on the potential loss of voter control over a city manager as compared with an elected mayor.

In numerous editorials, E. B. Ault, the editor of the labor-owned *Union-Record,* warned that the league wanted to substitute "a King" for the mayor. This king would "deprive the people of their right to be heard."[2] In an ironic twist, given Landes's unflagging support of the city manager plan, organized labor threw its support to Landes rather than the Democrat Brown after the primary. Given her advocacy of the city manager idea, labor leaders apparently saw her as a more professional, honest, fair—or perhaps pliable—leader for the city than Brown. Their statements of support referred to Landes's record on the city council, her upstanding reputation, and her preparation for the office of mayor. Undoubtedly labor leader Hesketh, who had worked closely with her on the council for four years, played a key role in labor's endorsement.

Following the primary, her campaign received a significant boost when another man who had worked closely with her, Corporate Counsel Thomas Kennedy, the third-leading contender for the office of mayor, also threw his active support to Landes's campaign. So did City Comptroller Harry W. Carroll, running for reelection. Furthermore, U. S. Attorney Thomas Revelle initiated a frontal attack on Brown eight days before the election.

In a speech to the Municipal League entitled "The Shame and Danger of Seattle and the Way Out," Revelle said Seattle was "handicapped by inefficiency and incompetency." The long-term, bitter feud between the federal officials and Brown's administration of the city was breaking wide open as the result of the Olmstead trial. Revelle complained that bootleg joints and gambling houses in Seattle were permitted to run wide open, and he blamed Brown's lax administrative policies for allowing the city to get infested with imported lawbreakers, adding that the "few good men" in the police department were thwarted.[3] Brown, as usual, accused Revelle of playing politics.[4]

In contrast, a few days later Kennedy gave a speech praising Landes's selflessness and honesty in urging adoption of "a better form of government" that would prevent her from taking office. "There is no such record anywhere of a politician placing public interest above the quest for office. . . . This self-sacrificing spirit, this public altruism, this political abnegation convinces me that Mrs. Landes is the person we want for mayor."[5]

Landes's campaign, meanwhile, had begun capitalizing on new technology: she made nightly radio broadcasts. In addition, she was making twelve to eighteen appearances a day in the closing days of the campaign. Throughout her campaign, she made whatever appearances were expected of the mayoral candidates. She even showed up—wearing a long skirt—for the photographs taken at the golf meet that the *Seattle Star* traditionally sponsored for the men who ran for mayor.[6] The major newspapers continued to dog her footsteps, but they gave comparatively little space to her remarks and plans. The *Seattle Times* repeatedly editorialized for the city manager plan but was silent about its preference of candidates in the mayoral election.

In the last week of the campaign Seattle's newspapers also carried ominous news for supporters of prohibition. A presidential commission headed by Lincoln Andrews, the assistant secretary of the treasury, was named to establish an inquiry to examine prohibition's economic, social, and other phases. In the six years since the Prohibition Amendment had been adopted, this was the first large-scale move to question the efficacy of the law.

Landes's campaign materials in 1926 focused on her singular achievements on the city council, the need for utility development to foster business development, and a promise to improve civil service. She promised to support safeguarding Lake Washington from sewage, protecting Green Lake for recreation, constructing the High Line bridge, and yet one more regrading of Denny Hill.[7]

Following her campaign promises in her primary campaign brochure came her position on "civic decency." In her statement she seemed to be trying to counteract, or at least moderate, a perception that she was primarily a female bluenose reformer. That image lingered from the ten days she seized the power of the mayor's office to close down many of Seattle's night spots and from her consistent efforts to regulate dance halls and cabarets:

> In an age when the pendulum of public morality swings between extremes, Mrs. Landes is a happy choice for Mayor. Advocating a

> sane, steady enforcement of the law but NOT A FRENZY OF REFORM; broad minded in her views but unrelenting towards graft.
>
> Mrs. Landes is a clear thinking practical woman, having had years of experience in civic work before she was elected a member of the City Council. Recognizing the rights of the private citizen, she has always supported properly conducted public places of recreation and amusement.[8]

Her view of what Seattle needed focused on efficiency and business, along with equitable enforcement of the law. Under the headline "Not WHO but WHAT does SEATTLE NEED?" she listed what was important for the "superstructure of this world city." The list included "Business Prosperity, Business Activity, Business Stability, Industrial Activity, Employment, Homes Built, Homes Paid For, Homes Safeguarded, Business Integrity, Business Assurance, Investment of Eastern Capital."[9] But a city, she continued, must always have "respect for—obedience to—enforcement of the existing laws." She added that the mayor cannot open or shut a town. "The Mayor may only administer the laws as they exist. Either the people want an honest administration of the law—or they don't. The Mayor is chosen accordingly."[10] She had left her domestic ideology ideas at home.

Only at the end of her campaign brochure did she address directly the issue of gender, appealing to modern thinking on the issue of women in political power. She also tried to solidify her appeal to both men and women, unlike her initial campaign for city council, when she promoted herself as the woman's candidate. "The fact that Mrs. Landes is a woman is not the issue. Ten years ago it might have been but not now. In the present campaign it is only used to divert interest from the vital things at stake. Women who support Mrs. Landes will do so because—as a human being—she stands for good and efficient government. Men everywhere are supporting her because—as a human being—she stands for the impersonal and best interest of their city." The passage also attempted to minimize and attenuate the issue of gender in the election, with its references to "human being." Here and later she began to move away from the gendered construction of "domestic" woman to a more gender-neutral reconstruction of "woman" suitable for equal participation in all aspects of political office. Where she and others had entered politics in the name of motherhood and "municipal housecleaning" activism, she was now beginning to act in a more radical way,

We urge you to
Work and Vote For

BERTHA K. LANDES

We ask your support

All Seattle needs LANDES for Mayor

Our Public Utilities
Our Industrial Future
Our Growing Children
Our City's Good Name

Each and every one a reason why you should

WORK AND VOTE

We indorse LANDES FOR MAYOR:

W. E. FORKNER	MRS. HAM BONNAR
DR. DAVID C. HALL	MRS. J. W. MARLATT
JOHN H. REID	MRS. E. F. PUGSLEY
BYRON PHELPS	MRS. NORMAN COMPTON
W. WALTER WILLIAMS	MRS. WYLIE HEMPHILL

5

When Landes ran for mayor, she did not run as the women's candidate, as she did before, but as a human being who would work for all citizens of Seattle. In addition to social welfare and law enforcement, her agenda included expanding public utilities and industrial growth. Using a campaign team composed of politically inexperienced women, she won by the largest margin Seattle had seen in a mayoral election. *Photo courtesy of the Museum of History and Industry, Seattle.*

within the system, with her own challenge as a human being to the existing structure.

On the same page of the brochure, a passage setting apart her candidacy from all others provided further evidence. It said the voters of Seattle had a clear choice. On one side were those "who desire in their Mayor such dignity that will remove him from the possibility of bickering—badinage—buffoonery." And they wanted "not so much the temporality of 'an old-fashioned house-cleaning' as a steady, everyday, dependable administration."[11] The brochure ended with a statement quoting the positive reception she received from the Central Labor Council.

The issue of her gender, although seldom addressed directly by her opponents or the press, was an ever-constant presence affecting the conduct of the election. She herself had said she got into the race for gender-related reasons. "If the men will not show enough interest in their city government to get the right kind of candidates in the field, the women must," she had said when she entered the city council campaign.[12] Now in this campaign, others sometimes addressed the issue directly on her behalf.

The wealthy philanthropist H. C. Henry, identified only as "capitalist" in the *Seattle Times* (he was president of the National Bank of Commerce),[13] released a statement that he had heard intelligent men say they would not vote for women. They said that Landes's election "would mean disaster and added, unpleasant notoriety to the city." He responded that women now had the right to vote and hold office, and if exclusion were carried to its logical result, the nation would end up with two parties, one male and one female. "With the advent of women into office, the character of the service will be greatly improved. No grand jury again will report 80 indictments in a single session," he was quoted as saying, referring to the Olmstead bootlegging ring trial.

He added that Landes would be a splendid addition with her contrasting "female" style, although he did not support the city manager system she advocated. "Because one distant 'Ma' in Texas has proven unsatisfactory is not sufficient reason to condemn all women forever."[14] He referred to the embarrassment of the 1924 election to governor of antisuffragist Miriam A. Ferguson, who ran in place of her husband after he had been impeached. "Pa" Ferguson manipulated her term in office, and she was threatened with impeachment also, but she lost her party's nomination in 1926.

At least one publication had already equated Landes with Ferguson. "She would make no more marked success as mayor of Seattle than has 'Ma' Ferguson as governor of Texas," the *Argus* complained.[15] After the primary, the publication also complained that running a city like Seattle was a man's job.[16] It became clear even before the election that Landes, like Ferguson, would become a benchmark against which other female public officials were measured.

Henry's warning about the creation of gendered political parties if women continued to be frozen out of office reflected a national concern. Landes had signed the same oath of nonpartisan candidacy that all political hopefuls signed, declaring that she was "not becoming a candidate as the nominee of, or because of any promised support from, any national or state political party . . . or acting for any such political party."[17] However, many civic leaders remained concerned about party machines of any stripe—including female—influencing city elections. Landes herself later served as president of the Washington State League of Women Voters, but by the end of the decade the league had generally backed away from advocating candidates, focusing more exclusively on strict voter education, partly as a result of these concerns about women's vote.

As the election neared, another pinhole appeared in the prohibition dike. The *Seattle Times,* one of the strongest converts to the cause of statewide prohibition, said editorially that now, six years after the state went dry, it was not so sure that prohibition did not need modification, that maybe wine and beer were not so bad after all. It noted that fifty-three people had died in Washington State in 1925 from consuming bad alcohol. It announced a contest for anonymous columns with $1,000 in prizes, with the winning "dry" and "wet" columns to be printed. Readers would then vote on the issue.[18]

Meanwhile, the day before the election, the verdicts of the jury in the Roy Olmstead trial became page 1 news. Olmstead received a four-year prison term and an $8,000 fine, while nineteen others in his bootlegging ring got fifteen months or more in federal prison.[19] Landes and Brown both harped on the issue of law enforcement in the final days of the campaign, although Brown was clearly in a weak position to do so. Landes said the issues in the election were clear as far as the future welfare of the city was concerned. If elected, she promised a clean business administration, loyal support of the city's public utilities, the abolition of graft in every form, and "above all else, [to be] a mayor who not only knows but who will tell the truth about our city affairs."[20]

Landes was campaigning and speaking like a candidate who

believed she might actually become mayor, but she continued to profess the belief that the voters would adopt the city manager system she supported. However, antagonism to the idea grew, despite the middle-class endorsements of it as a forward-looking change both to professionalize and to sanitize city administration. In addition to the opposition of labor and veterans' organizations, others began questioning the wisdom of the city manager system as an erosion of direct control of city affairs. A few critics claimed it even smacked of Sovietism and socialist control.

The city manager plan would be a " 'Kaiser' with the people and a 'kitten' with the city council," the veterans group complained, adding that it was "colored with the burgomasterism of Germany." It would make nepotism possible by abrogating the rights of civil service employees and threatened to bring back a spoils system and nullify veterans' preference for city jobs.[21] Still, most predicted the city manager system would pass. The reformers' dedication to efficient, professionalized government had led 270 U. S. cities to try the city manager system by 1923, and 430 by 1930.[22]

The city manager system had been adopted in Cleveland and Kansas City, but without the civic purity results reformers hoped. Politics still entered into who was chosen city manager, and the city manager was indeed remote from concerns of disgruntled portions of the electorate. The professional manager generally failed at the political skills needed to build coalitions, reduce or accommodate conflict, and express the will of a motley citizenry. Cleveland finally rejected the form of government in 1931, and it failed miserably in Kansas City. However, in other cities that were smaller and more homogeneous, the experiment worked well.[23] Seattle voters, however, would once again decide, by the narrowest of margins, that this particular experiment in urban reform was not for them.

The day of the election was signaled by whistle blasts, and the *Times* reported that the women in particular were out early in force. By day's end Landes clearly had a lead at the polls, and so did the city manager system. She was pleased with the double victory and reportedly was pleased to be the center of congratulatory attention. Either way, she was a winner. The *Times* described the scene at her headquarters on the fifth floor of the Dexter Horton Building as a "center of jubilation and congratulation." Hundreds of people shook her hand, and numerous women embraced her. During the evening and far into the night, hundreds came, milled around the interlocking offices for a while, and then left. "Mrs. Landes, a dark-complexioned woman slightly less than the average height, in a one-piece blue satin dress trimmed in tan, was the center of it all. There were many women, but about as many men," the paper said. "There was an air of a public reception about it all, what with chatting, buzzing, handshaking and congratulation and Mrs. Landes was in somewhat the position of a hostess."[24]

The press was schizophrenic about her status as both female and candidate. With the details about the happy winning candidate and her hundreds of supporters came the details of what she wore and how her candidate role was analogous to that of the traditional feminine role of hostess. The press frequently employed such a pattern of wording in describing Landes as both the lady and the mayor. She went home, assuming she would not take the oath of office, only to be awakened with the news that the city manager plan failed by the slimmest of margins—103 votes, out of 73,315 cast (36,606 to 36,709). She had won the mayor's race, however, by a record 5,898 votes, in a record turnout. Landes garnered 48,700 votes to Brown's 42,802 votes.

Bertha Knight Landes, the first female mayor of a large city in the United States, was scheduled to take office on June 7, 1926. She was fifty-seven years old. Her yearly salary would go from $3,000 to $7,500. Landes had carried virtually all of the university and Green Lake precincts. Brown carried precincts downtown and south, and she carried most of the Queen Anne and Capitol Hill precincts. The districts she carried included Seattle's more stable and prosperous neighborhoods, a mixture of middle-class and working-class neighborhoods.[25]

She soon announced she would fire William B. Severyns, the police chief she had fired once before. Surprisingly, Severyns had only kind words for her, even as he drafted his resignation. He called her "a fine, good woman," saying that even his wife voted for her. He added he would hold no grudge. Elsewhere in the paper a small box touted her birthplace—Ware, Massachusetts—as a fount of female politicians. Besides Landes, the list included Ruth Baker Pratt, New York's first female alderman, and Rose Vasey Hayes, member of the Northampton City Council in Massachusetts.[26]

The Media on the Mayor-Elect

The *Times* editorial on her election interpreted the vote as a statement about women and women's vote—and as a dry vote by the populace. The Hearst paper, the *Post-Intelligencer,* called the results a vote for good government, and a test for women. Her election would demonstrate "the ability or inability of a woman to discharge the administrative duties of a city of 400,000."[27] The *Union-Record,* with its prolabor orientation, said that thousands of the votes she received were because the voters thought "she was the lesser of two evils," and they were tired of the mayor and city council constantly bickering. However, the paper gave her some credit as a reasonable reformer. "Mrs. Landes is an able woman, and her years of service as Council member have fitted her well for the more important office of Mayor. She is no fool, and realizes that a seaport cannot be run like a Sunday School."[28]

A letter from a former resident of Seattle to her on the news of her election distilled the feeling many held about her go-it-alone victory. "It seems too good to be true! And you didn't go in on your husband's achievements or to fill his unexpired term, nor because you're a woman. You went in because of your proved ability and because of your social purposes." The writer warned her, however, about what a woman in this position might face. "When a woman goes in, she is under the disadvantage of having a lot of old fogeys in the police, and other departments, who will sabotage her because it's a woman," he wrote. "But you will make up for it because of your civic consciousness and your political idealism and common sense, or rather uncommon sense."[29]

"Common sense," "practical," "intelligent" were words that frequently appeared in relation to Landes. Others remarked on her sincerity, which "almost reaches the point of bluntness, allied with sound, reliable common sense as the keynote of her character."[30] Not many descriptions of the mature Bertha Knight Landes survive, other than references to her intelligent, dark eyes, the smile that perennially played about her lips, and her easy-going, direct manner. She thought of herself as quiet and studious. Photographs show a matronly woman with an air of reserve and self-confidence, often with a small smile at the corners of her mouth. More revealing of what she was like are contemporary descriptions from journalists and one from the prince of Sweden. They are remarkably similar in some ways,

This official portrait of Mayor Landes was used in a variety of publications during and after her term in office. *Photo courtesy of the City of Seattle Engineering Department.*

revealing popular concepts of gender and statements recognizing her status as a metropolitan mayor.

Prince Wilhelm of Sweden made a speaking tour of the United States in 1927, lecturing about his hunts in Africa. He included a stop in Seattle, where he delivered a speech in English entitled "Hunting Big Game in Pygmy Land," accompanied by six thousand feet of film.[31] He later wrote a book about his travels, twelve pages of which were about Seattle. He described Landes as "a middle-aged, healthy and strong woman with graying hair, dark eyebrows and playful eyes. Her whole person sparkled with unusual liveliness and vitality," he wrote. "Snappy and awake is she, talking incessantly but always saying something worthwhile. It was not the usual light talk—there was a personality back of it with a temperament that shone through."[32]

He found her charming. "She also could laugh so catchingly and winsome that a man almost forgot that he had an official lady before him with such a warm ring to her laugh," he wrote, adding that the "simple, modest and somewhat old-fashioned dress she wore suited the whole situation excellently. . . . she impressed one as a feminine component of all that represents energy, liveliness and initiative." Once again she was compared favorably to men as the standard for public office. "When one everywhere hears how respected and appreciated she seems to be . . . one cannot fail to respect and wonder at the courage of such an undertaking by a woman." Being mayor "is, after all, quite a task for anyone to undertake. I have known lots of men with great ability who have refused such work and responsibility."[33]

A *Brooklyn Daily Eagle* reporter who interviewed her after she fired the police chief, but before she entered the mayor's race, described her as full of "pep and political sagacity," and "not at all the type that one would ordinarily consider such a precedent breaker should be. In her own words, she takes 'life as it comes and lets the future take care of itself.' " This was how "this matronly little woman, who for ten days kept one of the fifteen largest cities of the country in turmoil, is disposed to regard her work as anything but sensational."[34]

To observe "the quiet, self-contained woman" sitting at her desk, "with the merry twinkle in her eyes and a smile playing about her mouth at all times, one would imagine her discussing the problems of raising a family, or keeping a house," he wrote. "Anything but recounting how she had disposed of the head of the police force summarily when she did not approve of his actions." Yet underneath "there was a firmness that betokened little brooking of opposition when it promised no good to her way of thinking."[35] Another writer found similar qualities but described them a different way. She noted that Landes's fingers drummed restlessly on her desk, and she was clearly "an individual capable of playing a shrewd part in a political game."[36] Yet another journalist, writing for the *Minneapolis Tribune* about one of her speeches, was impressed with her "motherliness and femininity," and with her gown of soft black velvet. "She had a poise, a quiet dignity and spoke with a soft modulated voice," and her use of asides showed a sharp sense of humor.[37]

A few days after her election, the *New York Times,* in a lengthy, largely congratulatory analysis of her achievement, noted that the writer had expected to find in Landes "a too familiar type of the feminine hard hitter. She is not that or anything like it." The writer felt it important to define her difference from what he termed a certain, fashionable type. He said she was "neither a fashionable nor an unfashionable woman. She does not bob her hair. She has the looks and the quietude of wholesome breeding." She was not "tailored for exhibition; there are no waving plumes in her hat; there is no exhilaration either in her official or social attitude. She exhibits no trace of political ambition."[38]

On Landes's election, the media generally found it necessary to distinguish her from the prevailing construction of New Woman, a type that threatened serious departures from accepted standards of behavior for women. Control of the female body was fought out on the terrain of types. This New Woman type, in the popular mind, contrasted sharply with the nineteenth-century ideal woman. Definitions varied, but the New Woman of the 1920s was generally more individualistic, better educated, more liberated sexually and socially, and more skeptical about traditional roles for women than the generations that preceded her. Where the two opposing views of woman could find some common ground, exploited by Landes and other female politicians and activists who tried to work within the system to accomplish their goals, was in the ideology of civic service.

It was enfranchised woman's political responsibility to act, according to this ideology, if not out of any personal ambition then out of a sense of civic responsibility to improve conditions for residents of the city. "City governments exist largely because of the family and the home, and their first duty is to serve these two institutions," Landes wrote after her election. "There is nothing sentimental or womanish in this philosophy, I insist. It is hard common sense. No city is greater than its homes." She also criticized the indifference of men "on matters that seemed to me to be vital."[39]

It was also widely assumed that it was Landes's responsibility to prove women could handle an office as complex as the mayoralty of Seattle, despite any intrinsic weaknesses of the structure of the mayor's office. Her election was praised in editorials in papers as scattered as the *Chattanooga* (Tennessee) *News*, the *Indianapolis News*, the *San Antonio Express*, and the *Providence* (Rhode Island) *Journal*. However, the *Aberdeen* (Washington) *World* warned that "rightly or wrongly, more will be expected of her than of a man. Her sex is on trial through her. She will be watched to see whether women can be competent government administrators."[40] For her part, Landes tried to minimize her exceptionality and connect her achievement to that of other women. A few days after taking office she told the Business and Professional Women, "I am no superwoman—just an ordinary one going forward in the way my best judgment dictates."[41]

However, she had breached the norms that had previously excluded women from such a visible position. That fact needed to be explained, countered, redressed and rectified in the framework of the existing hierarchies of power and knowledge. Thus it became important to distinguish her from a more radical type of New Woman and to connect her to traditional structures, despite her obvious challenge to the structure as a female mayor. For example, the city's major newspaper (in terms of circulation and local coverage), the *Seattle Times*, handled the news of Landes's election as follows. The page 1 headline read: "Mayor-Elect Landes Not 'New Woman'; Studies Economic and Social Problems."[42]

The article summarized how the issues of gender definition were being argued in the 1920s. Even while recognizing that this woman was crossing a threshold by being the first woman to be elected to such a post, the writer was providing assurances that she was connected to husband, family, behavior codes, and beliefs in a way that grounded her in the social structure as it then existed. Despite her newfound power, she was not powerful enough (or radical enough) to reject her traditional roots and responsibilities. Even so, she was a different woman—she was mayor-elect Landes.

> Seattle's mayor-elect is not a "new woman."
>
> A "new woman," in the word of the modernists, ultramodernists, or whatever those enlightened up-to-the-minute thinkers choose to

call themselves, has certain well-defined characteristics that the mayor elect certainly has not.

For instance a "new woman," by the best informants, wears her skirts to her knees or almost, bobs her hair, smokes cigarettes (the grandmothers, too), uses a lipstick and reads Edna St. Vincent Millais' poems. A "new woman" does not have to do all of these to be "new," but she should make a showing in two or three of them, some folks believe.

Bertha K. Landes prefers to discuss economic and social problems. Ever since she was graduated from Indiana University, after completing a four-year course in three years, she has kept up an interest in matters of public importance.

Of course she had the doctor to talk things over with. Dr. Henry Landes, dean of geology at the University of Washington, theorizes and converses as professors will. Mrs. Landes' mind was well stocked with ideas on public welfare, politically, economically and socially, when she was elected to the City Council in 1922.

"The house seems lonesome now," she said to her husband after their daughter and son had married and moved away. "Why not move into an apartment?"

That was practical enough. An apartment meant less household cares and worries and kept old memories from intruding themselves too frequently.

First Woman Mayor

When the dean and Mrs. Landes moved into the Wilsonian Apartments she found much idle time on her hands. But Mrs. Landes merely redoubled her interest in public and community affairs. She increased her activity in the church and became more closely identified with club work in the University district.

Now she has the distinction of being the first woman elected mayor in a city of such size as Seattle.

"If the men will not show enough interest in their city government to get the right kind of candidates in the field, the women must," Mrs. Landes said when she entered the race.

Politicians assert she made an excellent candidate from various standpoints. For one thing, the usual assertion that a woman's place is in the home, not in public office, had no bearing on her. Mrs. Landes is 58 [she was actually 57] and has reared a family.

Husband Gets Along

"I suppose some of the politicians believe I should merely stay at home and darn my husband's socks," she laughed. "Darning socks for one's husband is a laudable occupation, no one will deny, but it certainly does not take all of a woman's time. I found that my husband got along very well after I became a member of the City Council."

"Darning socks" here and elsewhere became a symbol of domestic suitability and responsibility toward men, much as "smoking cigars" became a symbol for man's gendered suitability and responsibility for power and governance. Each symbol operated to exclude from the opposite sex the other's realm of activity.

Following a review of the family's history and her husband's career, the article continued with Dean Landes's reactions to his wife's success, to being outdone by his wife. He took the congratulations "good-naturedly, although protestingly," because he said he needed no congratulating, according to the article. It was "all in the family," Bertha Landes added. The reporter nevertheless added a quotation from Landes that suggested a bit of vanity. "But I do wish the newspapers would select good photographs of me," she said, calling the failure to do so an annoyance of public life. "Some of the pictures that were sent out over the country by syndicates were absolute monstrosities. One had my head as broad as a pumpkin," she said. "Another was so shadowed as to make me appear very shrewish, a rather bad advertisement for Seattle, don't you think?"[43] The reporter then shifted back to the issue at hand—her plans for Seattle and reports that she would name either Capt. William Searing or Capt. Claude G. Bannick as chief. "It is too early to talk of appointments. . . . I shall confer with various groups—but only confer with them: I shall be mayor."

The readers thus learned that her election was a family affair, that she was sufficiently "female" to be vain about photographs of her, and that she would claim the power of mayor for herself when it came to other advisers. The definition of "woman" in politics was indeed in transition. Even though she was acting like a man in entering a realm where no female had been before, she was still a traditional woman, many descriptions of her seemed to be saying. She said it herself, providing the expected reassurances about her status.

The *Times* article was nearly devoid of information about her plans and policies for Seattle, until the continuation of the article on page 12, which recounted some of her campaign statements. This issue of the newspaper did include other articles about her election, citing reactions by various regional and national sources. They praised her election for what it would mean for law enforcement in Seattle and reiterated her support for the city manager plan. Also on page 12, however, was an article about how the new mayor used to bake beans and bread every Saturday and serve them to hungry and homesick students working their way through college. It was used as an example of her service and devotion to motherhood, home, and social causes. The article also reviewed her rise through the service clubs of Seattle to the city council.

Outgoing Mayor Edwin Brown, with whom she had perennially battled as a member of the city council, was pictured in the paper performing a "gentlemanly" gesture toward Landes—he placed a basket of flowers on Landes's desk. "Don't worry; I'll be heard from in the future," he was quoted as saying. He gallantly added, "When these cheap politicians begin slandering Mrs. Landes as mayor, I'm going to be on them like a savage tiger. . . . I might be down, but never out." In an interesting twist, he blamed his defeat on closing "too many saloons on First Avenue, and it made the federal officers sore, that's what's back of it all."[44] Brown briefly retired from public service, but he was good on his word—he came back to the political scene both to challenge and then to lend support to his old city council nemesis.

Landes left for California for a rest and to visit governments in other cities, looking for ideas she might use in her administration. She also paid a happy visit to her sister Jessie and brother-in-law, former Stanford president David Starr Jordan, at Palo Alto.

Later in March, Landes accounted for her campaign expenses, which reflected the largest total spent to date in Seattle on any mayoral campaign. She noted for the *Times* that her statements were true, and she detailed every cent spent on her campaign to the best of her knowledge, unlike past campaigns, where candidates often disavowed knowledge of funds from other sources spent on their campaigns. The newspaper, in recounting the explanation of her campaign finances, labeled her with both her husband's name and her new office: "Mrs. Henry K. Landes, Seattle's first woman mayor-elect."[45] She had spent $8,145 after the primary.

"I did try to keep the total down to $6,000, but it got away from me," she said. Most of it was raised through the campaign, but "my personal expenditures reached a tidy sum," she said. The primary expenses were only $1,697. The largest single expenditure category was for printing, and among the bills was $120 spent on radio advertising.[46] The total expenditures belied to some extent the faith she and others professed in the passage of the city manager system.

Once in elected office, Bertha Knight Landes set her own course. She began work on an agenda that went beyond moral reform and exceeded the narrow goals of her predecessors, with considerable success. During her term as mayor she began to distance herself from the predominantly nineteenth-century constructions of gender that formed her. It was those nineteenth-century constructions about home, motherhood, and woman's special sensitivities that she had capitalized upon and manipulated—with the assent of Seattle's voters—in order to gain access to power when she was first elected to the city council in 1922.

Upon her return from California about ten days before taking office, she outlined her plans. The list included "a strict law enforcement campaign through an augmented staff of secret investigators," a move that brought her criticism in some quarters. Also on the list was (1) establishing more flexible control of traffic and efficient signals; (2) abolishing the "dance hall girl" in public dance halls, which referred to girls employed in halls as dancing partners (and often more) for male patrons, and surveying conditions in the dance halls; (3) reorganizing the Park Board, which had been operating in a deficit situation; (4) establishing an efficiency expert for the city departments; and (5) appointing a "city mother," outside the police department if possible, to counsel young people who lacked parental guidance, particularly young girls.[47]

Landes talked of her visit to San Francisco. "I observed in San Francisco all the dance halls are supervised by well-trained women. They even visit the homes occupied by the girls who patronize the halls and report promptly to the parents those girls of minor age who frequent the halls."[48] Apparently her earlier consideration of the women who worked in dance halls out of some economic necessity had evaporated in the face of ongoing problems with the dance halls.

The mayor was inaugurated into office June 6, 1926. The media paid great attention to the inaugural gown she wore, calling it a midnight blue crepe gown with panels "embroidered in harmonizing tones of rose, silver and soft blue . . . a string of sparkling crystal beads, trim tan and beige kidskin pumps and matching gloves completed the ensemble."[49] At least the coverage also included one story on her plans. The next day the Soroptimist Club, of which she was a charter member, sponsored an open reception for her at the Olympic Hotel. The newspaper claimed that five thousand people came, standing in line for a "handclasp and a word from the happy-looking woman in black and gold lace who stood at the far end." The paper also called her election "a triumph for feminism," even while describing at length her physical appearance.[50]

Landes Takes Charge

Her first appointments included William H. Searing, long perceived as an incorruptible police administrator, as police chief. Searing, no neophyte, had been chief of police under mayor Hugh Caldwell, Brown's predecessor. Searing stated his view on law enforcement and politicians in a speech he made to the Fifth International Police Convention at Victoria as chief. "We have so exalted the principle of personal liberty that we have actually made it difficult to punish the guilty," he said. In his view, America had the unfortunate reputation of being "the most lawless of civilized nations." Furthermore, this reputation was the result of "our insincere, unscrupulous, weak-kneed public officials who connive at the collection of corruption funds."[51]

Landes's other key appointment was actually the reappointment of the visionary, popular, and powerful J. D. Ross as superintendent of the Municipal Lighting Department. It was James Dalmage Ross, beginning in 1911, who envisioned and developed the extensive system of dams that would supply the metropolis of Seattle its electrical power, at cheap rates, then and well into the future. He masterminded a "City Building" concept, founded and sold on the premise that inexpensive public power would induce industry to locate in Seattle. He created it not for industry's sake, however, but to ensure better lives and electrical service for the city's disadvantaged residents, something he suspected private power companies would be slow to do. That idea drove his schemes; it also drove more than one elected official into oblivion when they thwarted Ross. First hired by the city in 1903 as chief electrical engineer, he became head of the year-old Department of Lighting in 1911.[52]

Ross was almost as skillful at public relations as he was at harnessing rivers. He gave talks boosting public power anywhere, anytime. Quite the showman, in 1924 he established a theatrical outing called later the Skagit Tour. Hundreds of area residents paid $7.50 for a day-long outing by train to Ladder Creek. Gradually orchids, colored floodlights, and piped-in music from hidden speakers were added to the tours of stairstep falls, creating quite a spectacle. In the 1930s the tours continued over Diablo Lake on tugboats to the Ruby Dam site (later called Ross Dam after its creator).[53]

Ross built a considerable following in the city and throughout the Pacific Northwest, becoming a pivotal figure in the debate over public versus private interests when it came to vital services in the Northwest. He promoted City Light across the nation as a model of municipal power success and often counseled other cities. He also figured into real and imagined disputes over the "power trust" and its impact on candidates like Landes, who backed public power.

Ross had not been reappointed by Mayor Brown, and he was one of Landes's short-term appointments when she seized control of the mayor's office while he was out of town.[54] By the 1920s, those groups that traditionally had been in Ross's public power pocket—the Municipal League and the Chamber of Commerce—found themselves in the impossible dilemma of arguing against private enterprise and private power interests in turf disputes with City Light. Ross fell out of favor, but not for long.

Ross was frequently at the center of the disputes between the mayor and council. He did not support the city manager plan proposed by the Municipal League for fear it would diminish his power-making authority over City Light, and he actively campaigned against it.[55] Candidates—and voters—used support for Ross and public power as a simple litmus test in campaigns. Most, including Landes, supported him, and he remained in his position throughout her term. As one writer of the time put it, he built up a $64 million business that paid him all of $7,500 a year.[56] His reputation was such that Franklin Roosevelt tapped him to head the Bonneville Power Administration in the 1930s.

Landes was sold on Ross's vision and City Light, as she made clear in one of her subsequent reports. City Light "stands on its own merits as a business institution. It has entered on one of the most ambitious power development programs, public or private, in the nation," and its financial condition "is such that bonds for its development are eagerly sought by investors, although they carry a net rate of less than 5 percent." She said Seattle was at the center of a region with the greatest "riches in water power resources in the entire nation." The development of water power by the municipal system guaranteed low rates for industries, "as evidenced in new factories in the city," and ensured "a great industrial future for Seattle as electrical processes become more and more important in our civilization."[57]

Landes, the Efficient Administrator

From the mayor's desk on June 7, 1926, Landes reiterated her administration's goals, stating that Seattle would not become a model city in sixty days, but its citizens could expect "honest and vigorous enforcement and raised standards in the police department." She added to the list her plan to reduce operating expenses in the Seattle street railway system and issued an appeal for more riders. The system was in serious trouble. She blamed the use of the auto, the growth of "community centers with stores and theatres" (what later city planners called malls), and "the home entertainment made possible by means of the radio." Her plans to fix the system included "efficiency economies" such as ending unprofitable routes (a decision that proved unpopular along those routes), making the system more comfortable and faster, and rewriting the purchase contract with reduced annual payments or reissuing the bonds with longer maturities (this decision, although it eventually saved the city from financial disaster, angered private utilities).[58]

She also said she wanted close cooperation with the city council in developing the city's 1927 budget.[59] She added that an increase in City Light business was encouraging but recognized that years of heavy expenditures were ahead on the upper Skagit River project being completed one hundred miles away from Seattle. "Business management and strict economy will have to be the slogan from now on," she said. In short order she also named engineer L. Murray Grant her water superintendent, and J. C. Dutton to the Park Board.[60]

Her initial views about the nature of the city, municipal administration, and women on the eve of her mayoralty were distilled in a speech she gave in July 1926 entitled "The Problem of the Large City." In it she said that governing a city comes closer to the people than did governance of any other political unit. "The farther away we get from the people in government, the less democratic it becomes, the less responsive to the voice and will of the people. Therefore the cities become the battleground of democracy and in them must be fought out the question of its preservation or its destruction for all future time."[61] She cited demographic figures. While in 1800 there were only five cities with over 10,000 population, containing 4 percent of the nation's population, by 1910 there were 603 such cities, containing 37 percent of the nation's population.

With larger cities came increases in poverty and disease, insanity and suicide, mental and moral deterioration, and vice and crime. So did class conflict: "The rich become richer; class hatred develops and labor troubles follow in the wake of industry," she said. "Increased and cheaper transportation brings the alien to our shores and pours them into our large cities, thus presenting us with an entirely new and different set of problems to be solved." The "melting pot" could not easily meld those inside it, which intensified problems. Yet, "most of us prefer the white lights of the city to the peacefulness of rural life."[62]

She also lamented the loss of *civitas* and democratic participation, a lament she voiced to the end of her life. "We prefer to belong to the governed class rather than the governing class because it is so much less trouble." She again linked the city to the home, drawing the private sphere into the public, not only as a metaphor, but also as an ideal. "The city is really only a larger household or family with its problems increased manyfold through its diversified interests and the cosmopolitan nature of its members, but the analogy is strong, just the same."[63]

Landes argued that cities have heavy responsibilities to provide residents with protection, transportation, education, recreation, and a moral and clean environment. "The waste of human life and human energy in our great city is appalling. . . . Let's get together, Men and Women—in working out our social and moral problems. . . . Men and Women must work together," she said. The social concerns were no longer women's alone, she argued, although she did envision an expanding role for women in working out the problems, drawing again on the exceptionality of woman: "I am inclined to the belief that woman is coming to do more than her half also. Women have always played the largest part in creating the proper spirit in the home. . . . She is a leader in all movements for social welfare legislation—she recognizes social waste more quickly than man."[64] She also made a plea for the election of additional qualified women to public office, and for making government a joint affair between men and women, joining the spirit of the home with political authority, "the virile strength of man and the idealism of woman." Her view of woman as exceptional and idealistic continued to fit nineteenth-century ideas about gender and the need to extend woman's separate sphere into the larger world.[65]

She continued with a personal message for "my own sex" that reiterated this definition of woman and her own connection to it:

> Let me tell you, for instance, that though I am a public official and a so-called politician—that I am first and always a woman, true to the highest ideals of womanhood as I know them; that I am a wife and mother but a mother whose children are grown and now in homes of their own; that I yield to no one my respect for wifehood and motherhood and regard those professions as the very highest ones which any woman can fulfill; that I am merely trying now to practice what I preach by giving whatever talents I may have or whatever wisdom the years may have brought me to the service of my community.[66]

But women can and must shoulder civic responsibility. "If woman is indifferent and fails to realize her responsibility—may I say her privilege and high calling—if she is unwilling to bear her part of the burden, then is the outlook gloomy and the future uncertain." Even a woman with small children "must pay some attention to what is going on outside the walls of her home," since her children go outside.[67]

However, she continued, good government can provide only superstructure—the citizens are the foundation, and they must have allegiance to the law, "not just when it's not contrary to pleasure or convenience"; otherwise the system, and democracy with it, will collapse. "The law is a rule of conduct decided upon, imposed by ourselves." She isolated two factors from the progressive tradition as vital to civic conditions: education and political action, "backed by public sentiment and tempered by mercy and justice."[68] She felt impelled to describe, once again, what city government should be. "City government looks after the welfare of the people, or should. It concerns itself with sanitation and public health, clean and safe streets, protection of the home, education, care of the poor and the sick," she said. These are "all problems which the mothers of the world have had to deal with in their homes and which, when presented on a municipal scale, are quite as much women's as men's problems."[69]

When she took office, she insisted on cooperation within her administration, moving to end divisive interagency squabbling wherever she found it. Getting diverse agencies to cooperate by bringing a "female" and nonconfrontational kind of orientation to her work became a hallmark of her years in office. Within two days of becoming mayor, she called together the heads of all agencies involved in law enforcement in and around Seattle, agencies locked in jurisdictional disputes and feuds for a decade. They included the chief of police, sheriff, the federal prohibition enforcement director, U.S. district attorney, captain of the Coast Guard, heads of the local secret service, immigration and customs offices, the county prosecutor, corporation counsel, and U.S. Department of Justice officials. All were summoned, constituting what came to be dubbed the Committee of 13. The press was barred from the meeting.[70]

She told the men that she expected cooperation and coordination from them and promised the same from her office. The men left three hours later, after electing Roy Lyle, the regional prohibition enforcement director, chairman and agreeing to work together in a centralized, coordinated effort to reduce Seattle's lawlessness in the new spirit of cooperation she sought. "I obtained the promise and, I believe, the performance of cooperation and coordination," she said later.[71] The warning was issued through the police department that even private clubs, with highly placed members, were now subject to liquor raids.[72]

Believing that all citizens shared responsibility for law enforcement and recognizing that police agencies were inadequate, given the extent of the problems, she asked for citizen help. That request did not sit well with all segments of Seattle's population, while others praised its bold intent. Residents were asked to report bootlegging and other lawbreaking, including any by the police officers themselves. Anonymity was assured by use of code numbers.

The response gratified her, even though the system was hardly foolproof. She liked to tell an anecdote about a respectable gentleman who had phoned in a report only to have the police mistakenly raid his home in confusion over the house numbers. He was giving a dinner for a bishop at the time, but he took the mistake with good humor.[73]

She applied a similar philosophy and solution to Seattle's burgeoning and sometimes lethal traffic problems. Seattle by 1930 had one car for every four residents, a volume that cluttered and clogged the streets. She reconvened the Public Safety Council she had formed during one of Brown's absences, with herself as president of its board of trustees. The council started a drive for five thousand citizen members, each of whom would be paid a dollar a year. Members were to report to the police all the reckless drivers and traffic violators they saw. Without divulging the source of the complaint, the police did not arrest but warned the violators by postcard, with the result, she felt, that violators were made more careful.

Although Landes saw this citizen involvement as a logical outgrowth of *civitas* and efficiency, not everybody was happy with her methods of using the citizenry or secret agents to support law enforcement. The class issue, which along with gender surfaced against her in her campaign for reelection two years hence, again appeared. Although the newspapers and business community generally approved and lauded her moves to foster law enforcement through individual vigilance, others disapproved of her vigilante approach and a secret fund the council authorized for hiring undercover agents.

In some labor circles, for instance, where spies and employer punishment had become a painful but effective means of undermining attempts to organize workers, her methods stirred criticism. Only three weeks after she took office, an editorial called "The Use of Stool Pigeons" appeared in the *Tacoma Labor Advocate*. It said that she, like any male or female mayor, rightly should undertake to enforce the law and "make the police walk the straight and narrow path of duty without graft or corruption." But the writer did not like her methodology. "She lays before the public a plan which is not so easy to commend. For she proposes to have stool pigeons stool upon the police and thus keep watch and ward on those who keep watch and ward upon the city." If there is reason to distrust police, "far more reason is there to suspect the stool pigeon."[74]

There is no end to spying, the editorial continued, and the spread of espionage was the "most dangerous form of parasitism that has ever been allowed to degrade private or public life." It criticized detective agencies' spies in particular, concluding that Landes should either purge her mind of distrust or discharge all police. "In these days of Volstead acts it seems quite the duty of all people who believe themselves custodians of other people's morals to suspect everyone but themselves."[75] The participants in this struggle also drew the battle lines over control of the body on the field of prohibition, setting civil rights against civic betterment. Like other public officials, Landes sometimes felt there was too much emphasis on individual rights and not enough on the collective good. In trying to protect the public good, individual rights sometimes suffered.

Nevertheless, Landes's initial plans on all fronts, and the actions she took to implement them early in her administration, generally garnered praise for being progressive, rational, and necessary. She proved herself a leader, and as a leader, she definitely undermined the prevailing view of females. She made sure she did whatever a male mayor would do in fulfilling the terms of the office, such as taking a hazardous eleven-mile hike from the tunnel intake of the Skagit River plant to the proposed site for a storage dam at Ruby Creek, in July.[76] As a member of the council, she had once walked a mile through enormous penstocks leading underground from the reservoir to the powerhouse at one of the dams. "Building dams and running electric light plants were normally a little out of my line," she said of her municipal power experiences, "but they were also a little out of the line of the average man on the Council."[77]

A National Reputation

Many times when Landes undertook one of these physical acts that were unusual for a female, newspaper photographers recorded the event and distributed the photos through the wire services. Photos such as Landes firing a gun at a rifle range or wearing a catcher's mask as she opened baseball games were deemed newsworthy and eyecatching by editors. Because of this and her "famous first" status, national attention came to Seattle. Many magazines featured her. To their female readers, feminist publications touted her as a model of what women could and should do. Mainstream publications touted her as an oddity who countered and changed the traditional notions of gender.

For instance, *Woman Citizen*, the publication of the National League of Women Voters,[78] featured Landes in a September 1926 article entitled "Well . . . Why Not?" Even this decidedly feminist publication felt it necessary to define traditional womanhood and how Landes fit and extended it. Landes, significantly, challenged some of the images and gender constructions the writer offered. The writer called Seattle a factory and mill and commercial city, with fisheries, lumber camps, and immigrant "flotsam" sometimes bringing "from the old world germs of turbulence and bolshevism and hate." Yet this city chose a woman as its mayor, knowing that bootleggers call her "Big Bertha."[79]

"She looks exactly like a Boston clubwoman and mother of a family, if you know the type," the writer stated. "The same calm and dignified bearing, the unrouged face and not overly-powdered nose, the intellectual forehead and alert, thoughtful eyes." She added that Landes did not look her age because she was too busy "to have time for elderliness." She was described as a "large woman, wholesomely good-looking, clad in attractive clothes that, like her age, have the air of being a secondary concern."[80]

The writer asked her what the special problems were for a woman mayor. Landes tried to neutralize the gender issue: "There are no special problems, I think, no problems that a man would not have. Being a good mayor isn't a matter of sex, but a matter of the enforcement of the law. It's absurd—isn't it?—to talk of petticoat rule?" Later in the article she seemed somewhat defensive about her family. "When my two children were small, they took most of my time," she remarked. "But now they are grown up and married. My husband's stockings are faithfully darned. The fact that I am Mayor of Seattle does not mean that my family are neglected, in the least."[81]

She once again turned aside the idea of political or personal ambition playing any role in her election. "How does it happen that I am Mayor? It is no accident, no sensational happening. It is just the logical outgrowth of other things that have come to me." Later, she added, "At first I hesitated to run for mayor . . . but finally decided to do so because it seemed very doubtful whether any of the men named as candidates would make it their first concern to see that Seattle was a law-abiding city."[82]

The writer brought up the classic issue of "cleaning house," and again Landes tried to neutralize the gendered expression. " 'Cleaning house? No, I don't like that way of putting it,' declared Mrs. Landes. It's old-fashioned, anyhow, she pointed out." Later in the interview, the writer mentioned that Landes offered her a chocolate from a five-pound box of bonbons "that she laughingly

The news media, intrigued by the novelty Landes presented in fulfilling ceremonial duties considered the province of male officials, frequently took photographs of her that were distributed by wire services. Here she takes aim at a shooting range. *Photo courtesy of Special Collections Division, University of Washington Libraries, neg. UW9162.*

called the substitute for the usual mayoral cigars, but did not take one herself; she doesn't seem the type of woman to care a lot for chocolates, somehow. 'No, I've never smoked a cigarette,' she answered, in an aside."[83]

In contrast, the *New York Times,* in an analysis that ran in July 1926, carried the following headline and lengthy subheads about her: "Seattle Ably Run by Woman Mayor; Mrs. B. K. Landes Auspiciously Starts Her Rule of Efficiency and Common Sense; Won't Please Reformers; New Executive Doesn't Expect to Revolutionize Either Human or Municipal Nature; Fit Men Had Refused Job, but She Stepped Out Boldly from an Academic Setting to Bring Order out of Civic Chaos."[84]

In the lead and throughout the article, the writer stressed the unusual nature of Landes's rise to office and how she countered the traditional ideas about women to establish a new paradigm for feminine behavior. This article was representative of much of the press she received immediately after her election to office and how the media framed and defined her election. It offered a clear description of the stereotypes and structures she challenged by her mere presence, and what reactions her status provoked. "Seattle is the first city of metropolitan pretensions to thrust aside the tradition that municipal administration is strictly a man's job. Here and there, as a concession to the 'Woman vote,' women have been brought into municipal councils, and here and there villages or small towns, more in the spirit of humor than of serious purpose, have placed their affairs in feminine hands." In this case, "whimsicality had nothing to do with this departure from precedent," and there were many questions about her suitability for the office, the *Times* said, with many feeling "Seattle would in some measure discredit itself by putting a woman at the head of her municipal affairs." There were many who said "that a woman, and a prominently womanly woman, might 'go too far and hurt business.' And business is the life of Seattle."

But finally the business community, according to the *Times,* "not without misgivings, got behind her and in combination with the more definitely humanistic element brought about her election." The writer defined the spirit of Seattle as "essentially masculine." Although Landes had concentrated "upon a kind of work that is presumed to be more fitting to masculine than to feminine hands," the nation was surprised that this "hustling, bustling and materialistic city should put into its Mayor's chair a woman," he wrote. Furthermore, she was "not only a woman, but a woman of academic associations," as "the wife of one college professor, the mother of another, the sister-in-law of still another."

The writer continued that Landes had fulfilled "woman's first obligation. Her children had grown up; she had taught them intelligently and wisely; their ways of life were established." At that point "among the women of the city there arose a demand for feminine representation in the Municipal Council," but Landes on the council was not "a wild-eyed crusader for superhuman virtues. . . . Industry and plain common sense marked her progress from a neophyte to the Acting Mayoralty." In fact, in city affairs she developed skills that "in another sphere would have made her a factor in the world of finance." Yet the writer felt it important to emphasize her adherence to feminine ideals and the crossing of class lines. "Through all she maintained the poise of one born and bred a lady, but one whose understanding and sympathies were without class limitation."

Landes had nevertheless frankly told him, he wrote, "that she had no illusions with regard to political, social or other phases of superhuman virtue. She has no program of sensational reforms other than that of establishing the public services under rules of efficiency." The writer tried to distinguish her from the bluenose stereotype with regard to prohibition and reform. "That the element once characterized by Mr. Roosevelt as the 'idiot fringe of reform' will be entirely satisfied with Mayor Landes's administration I seriously doubt."

Nearly all such articles about her—appearing in *Time, Literary Digest, Outlook, Sunset Magazine, Independent Woman,* and other media—contained similar analyses. They also found it necessary to indicate that her husband had a strong personality and professional role in his own right and that he was thoroughly supportive of his wife's active role in politics. "The mayor's husband is far from being the inconsequential person assigned by tradition to the woman of powerful personality," said *Sunset Magazine*.[85]

They also frequently found it necessary to indicate that she retained her feminine responsibilities to him, despite her newfound power and status as mayor of Seattle. The behavior codes about woman's proper role and concerns were in this way again being enforced and reinforced, even as Landes was being lauded for her exceptionality and common sense. Knowing and following the appropriate codes mediated potential alternative behaviors—such as being mayor.

For instance, the February 1927 issue of *Sunset* began its piece on her by making it clear that this new female mayor knew her place when it came to her responsibility to her husband. It opened with this statement:

> She starts it [the day] by cooking breakfast for her husband—this only woman in the United States who is mayor of a city of the first class.
>
> "Her place is in the home, not in politics," said opponents of Bertha Knight Landes throughout her campaign. . . . Public service has not usurped Mrs. Landes' home service. Throughout the two terms in the city council and in the months of her administration as mayor she has personally prepared the matutinal toast, eggs and coffee for two.
>
> "My husband did not suffer while I was a member of the council," she replied to a question, "and he has fared no worse since I was mayor. Children should have the first consideration," says this mother of two sons and a daughter, "but the woman who has raised her family should be free to undertake outside duties. My children are in homes of their own."
>
> Her husband states his attitude plainly: "There is nothing revolutionary about a woman in office. It is simply an enlargement of her sphere. Men are too busy to go into politics and women are better fitted temperamentally and by training."

The caption under the photograph of Landes at the office reinforced the point: "Mrs. Bertha Knight Landes, Mayor of Seattle, the only woman in the United States who is mayor of a city of the first class, stays on the job from early morning until midnight. But she is up at seven sharp to cook the matutinal meal for two, according to the best domestic tradition. Her husband is a noted scientist with the University of Washington."

The writer further explained that Landes had a mutual understanding with her husband that he should seldom take the time for functions where her official duties called her, other than for evening entertainments. Moreover, she did not occupy a big house and spend time entertaining. Indeed, she had moved to an apartment hotel (the Wilsonian Apartments near campus at 4710 University Way, built in 1923), with a choice of hotel dining room service and light housekeeping, "thus saving energy for the heavy burden of administering a budget of nine and a half millions."

The article presented quite a juxtaposition of images, which served to highlight her transitional nature. An undercurrent present in these articles was the need to sustain the traditional definitions of "woman" in the face of the possibility that a woman could effectively assume this powerful role from which she had previously been excluded. However, although the codes for feminine behavior were thus enforced, she also subverted them with her no-nonsense tone and approach to whatever she did, including her move to an apartment hotel where her domestic responsibilities were reduced. "How could I entertain when my duties keep me from eight-thirty in the morning to ten or twelve at night? The simpler my household arrangements, the easier disposed of," she said about her living arrangements to a California reporter who assumed she now did elaborate entertaining in a mayor's mansion.[86]

Such reactions in the media serve several purposes for famous firsts like Landes and for the culture. In her case they sanctioned her behavior in this social drama, while at the same time reintegrating and explaining her breach of the traditional norms. They and her reaction helped make a new paradigm not only possible but acceptable, because of its connections to existing conservative structures, but at the same time they reinforced the importance of those traditional constraints.

Landes herself made note of her unusual status more than once, and she more than once sought refuge in connecting it to the ideology of motherhood, hoping thereby to blunt its awkwardness. She gave a welcome address to the Eagles National Auxiliary a couple of months after she assumed office. "There may be some to whom a woman Mayor may seem *a little bit strange or freakish,* but even those will admit that it is *more or less appropriate for a mother,* and the present Mother of Seattle claims that proud distinction, to represent Seattle at this time" (emphasis added). She wished them a "pleasant sojourn here and best wishes and God speed from Mother Seattle."[87]

Landes's immediate responsibility, however, was to manage a complex enterprise, regardless of the stereotypes of her gender or responses to it. From an administrative standpoint, Landes immediately set about to do what in her campaign promises she had said she would do. She acted independently, refusing to make any partisan or political appointments to boards or commissions. The one exception was a Central Labor Council appointment to the Board of Public Works, succeeding a labor

As mayor of Seattle, Bertha Knight Landes frequently was the only female present at official functions. Here she is pictured with a trade delegation of foreign consuls meeting at Fisher Flour Mills in July 1926. *Photo by Walter P. Miller; courtesy of Henry Landes Papers, University of Washington Libraries*.

man, and she expressed concern over it.[88] She refused to play the political spoils system common to city politics, which was perhaps not the wisest move for a politician to make who hoped to be reelected. As her personal secretary wrote later of her administration, "She chose men of technical training for technical jobs without regard to friendship or politics."[89]

She told the writer of a management magazine what was wrong with politics and why she did what she did. "Men capable of conducting such a large business as that of a city are generally too busy with their own affairs and making too much money to be attracted by the salaries paid Mayors of American cities," she said. And those who are elected have few qualifications for the position and are "prone to appoint political and personal friends as heads of important departments who, likewise, have little or no experience, nor even ordinary ability." She said it was thus no surprise that there was more "inefficiency and extravagance" than would be tolerated in private business, nor any surprise that police departments suffered lax law enforcement and graft.[90]

She talked about Seattle and her vision of the ideal city in an article she wrote for *Woman Citizen* during her term of office. She said she had "fallen in love with my city," which she termed the largest municipality of its age in the world, "having multiplied its population by ten in less than forty years." She said it was "still in the formative period, young enough to have escaped the political pitfalls of municipal vice into which so many older cities fell, small enough to have an easily aroused civic consciousness, it is a place of infinite possibilities." In her opinion, "a woman unhampered by party politics, fairly experienced in municipal affairs, and filled with a real and intense desire to make Seattle a clean city was more likely to do it than any of the others slated as candidates."[91]

Landes's Agenda Broadens

Landes prided herself on making personnel decisions on the basis of merit alone, and she replaced members of the Civil Service Commission whom she felt had been unduly influenced by politics in their decisions. She removed Donna Baker and T. Harry Bolton from the commission, citing "greater efficiency" as the reason. Thomas Patterson stayed. She replaced one of the rejects with a woman she trusted—Harriet Elias, president of the Seward Park PTA and a member of the board of the Century Club.

Elias had also worked on Landes's campaign. The other appointment was David Beck, a bright young man who in a few years began a decades-long domination of Seattle city politics and labor circles.[92]

She also removed members from the Public Works Board, which she accused of conducting the business of the city "in an unbusinesslike way." She fired trade unionist G. W. Roberge from his job as city building inspector and installed Robert Proctor as a more objective official. She called together the Park Board and School Board to inventory the city's recreation sites and to establish new parks and supervised recreation programs for children, using school grounds and buildings. It embodied the idea that supervised play developed character and protected children from corruption. In July she named a special committee to work out plans for school gyms to be used in evenings by older children and adults.[93] In August, she left for California to do an extensive study of public health and hospital systems there, citing Seattle's public hospital situation as "one of the significant problems."[94]

Landes was on the move. In October, with the mayor of Tacoma, she proposed electrical lighting of the highway between Seattle and Tacoma, to help reduce crime, accidents, and rumrunning. In November, she left for Chicago to study traffic safety and address the Illinois League of Women Voters and to visit her brother Charles in Chicago and her son, Kenneth, at the University of Kansas. In Chicago, she criticized idle women. No woman whose family was reared "has any right to sit idle or to spend her time playing bridge," she said. She predicted that more and more women would become mayors, and that a woman would someday be president.[95] She also spoke to the Business and Professional Women at Evanston and to another club at Springfield. In Chicago she was particularly impressed by the training offered police officers, which included a month at a special school, and she decided to implement such training in Seattle, especially for the city's new officers.[96]

Landes prided herself on being able to work cooperatively with her old colleagues on the city council; the rancor that once existed between the two bodies had largely disappeared. For instance, on November 15 she asked the council for a new municipal court with two police judges, and the council quickly agreed.[97] However, they were not always of the same mind. That same month she vetoed one of the council's bills granting a dance hall license to a firm called the Bungalow Amusement Company, one that had come up before. She defended her veto with a short letter printed in the *Daily Journal of Commerce* on December 8, as was legally required at the time. "I consistently voted against this type of dance hall, while I was a member of the council, believing such to be detrimental to the public welfare. I see no reason for any change in this position now."[98] Unlike her predecessors' florid letters, Landes's letters tended to reflect her pragmatic, direct approach and her personality. They were short, clear, to the point, and without elaboration or sentimentality.

One letter that was more elaborate and sentimental was a note she wrote to accompany a gift to the man who served as her secretary, James Matthew O'Connor. Private secretaries to city officials then were usually male; later in the century, they enjoyed more inflated titles, such as administrative or executive assistants. They were responsible for scheduling, office management, appointments, and other myriad duties as needed. Frequently, press relations was also a responsibility of their office. O'Connor's predecessor in Edwin Brown's administration, Hugh Kelley, had been a former newspaperman.

At the time Landes appointed him, O'Connor was a journalism instructor at the University of Washington; he had received his master's degree from UW in June 1926.[99] Also on her staff as her "right hand lady" was Grace Marsden.[100] But it was O'Connor who would be her office confidante, her tireless supporter, and her frequent escort to functions where the mayor's presence was expected, solving one of the behavior code problems complicated by having a female in such an office. He also accompanied her on various official engagements during the day and represented her on less important matters.[101]

That their relationship was personal as well as professional was evident in a carbon copy of a note she saved in her papers that she had written to accompany a birthday gift to him one year into her term. The note also revealed something of her sense of irony and humor. It was addressed to Mr. Matthew O'Connor, "Generalissimo, Mayor's Office, Seattle":

> On this very auspicious occasion, marking as it does for you one more mile stone in life's journey, will you permit me, your slave driver and domineering superior, to wish you many more "quiet" returns of the day. May you attain in due course of time freedom from the serfdom under which you now labor. May your poet's brow

be crowned with laurels, your literary digestion maintain its present status quo. May filthy lucre never soil your hands nor cause you to lower your flag, and may long life and happiness attend your path.

Enclosed you will find, not filthy lucre, but a clean check which may be used for beauty or utility as you see fit. A treasured book, or a beautiful picture to adorn your room, or a bit of art work upon which to feast your eyes will satisfy the donor, or she will also agree to raiment of bright hue, or anything which your fancy may dictate.

Read between the foolish lines the words of friendship and appreciation of services rendered and pleasure in present association. May it long continue.[102]

Another side of Landes's personality, especially interesting given her reputation as a no-nonsense reformer, was reflected in the fact that she saved several satires written about her and her administration. Like other public officials, she was frequently "roasted" at social gatherings. For example, one 1927 song, a satire on "Oh Maryland, My Maryland," was titled "Mayorland, Dry Mayorland." The following song was to be sung to the tune of "When Johnny Comes Marching Home Again."

Oh, sing a song for Bertha's sake,
Hurrah, hurrah,
How Bertha used to scrub and bake,
Hurrah, hurrah,
But now she doesn't scrub at all
She's cleaning up the City Hall
And we all feel gay when
Bertha comes home again.

The Bertha that we used to know,
Hurrah, hurrah,
For church bazaars could sit and sew
Hurrah, hurrah,
But now she doesn't sew at all
She has to lead the Fireman's Ball
But we all feel gay when
Bertha comes home again.

To conventions far and near she goes,
Hurrah, hurrah,
And she even talks over radios,
Hurrah, hurrah,
But though she chums with Sweet Marie,
She smiles as sweet at you or me,
And we all feel gay when
Bertha comes home again.

We're glad to welcome her today,
  Hurrah, hurrah,
We want to hear what she will say
  Hurrah, hurrah
We'll do just what she tells us to
We'll back her up as we always do
  For we all feel gay
  When Bertha comes home again.[103]

She did not allow this side of her personality to surface often, at least publicly, lest it detract from the power and dignity of the office and the woman holding it. Sentimentality was expected of women, and it was also assumed that such emotions clouded their judgment.

Issues of Economic Development and Social Welfare

During her two-year term, her vision of Seattle's future and her agenda for its administration moved beyond law enforcement into social welfare and economic development. Her accomplishments reflected the shift. She managed to reduce expenses of the Parks Department and bring that agency out of a three-year deficit situation, while at the same time adding new parks to the system. She went ahead with visionary Skagit River development plans, citing lower power costs as vital to continued growth and industrial development of Seattle.

She noted that Seattle was committed to municipal ownership of public utilities. "I believe in this policy, but the utilities must be properly and economically managed if they are to be self-supporting and yet serve the people better and more cheaply than the private companies do."[104]

She placed a competent engineer at the head of the city water distribution system and increased receipts of the water department by $30,000 with low-cost water being delivered into Seattle homes at two cents a ton. She named Skagit project engineer W. Chester Morse to the position of city engineer. She held the line on city budgets through the power of persuasion, actually reducing the 1927 budget from the 1926 level by jawboning departments and the council. She even managed to make the doomed street railway system temporarily solvent, wiping out its deficit and creating a profit for 1927 of $300,000 and completing some needed reconstruction that had been delayed by the deficit.

Her agenda as mayor, as when she was on the city council, went far beyond prohibition.

Proud of her work in city planning and getting the code passed, she commented that city planning boards "are now regarded as an essential part of municipal administration." The Seattle Planning Commission was considering building an arterial system through the business district, a costly project but one she said was supported by private property and business owners alike. She also brought up the issue of rapid transit, noting that Seattle needed it, perhaps becoming the first in a long line of city officials who would make that observation. Although the city was not yet large enough she said to justify a total system, it could use part of it. In any case, Seattle needed a plan for the system.[105]

The shift in the area of social services was best revealed in Landes's annual report, submitted to the city council in June of 1927, midway through her administration. Although ostensibly a report from the mayor to the city council, such reports were really written and printed with the public in mind. The reports were also forwarded to mayors and libraries nationwide. They provided a personal blueprint of the Seattle these officials had in mind and an opportunity to review the past year's performance. As Edwin Brown's had, the reports typically talked about Seattle's sterling qualities, the development of its business and industry, the city's budget, its planned infrastructure projects, and changes in city services such as the police and fire departments.

Landes's 1927 report was different. It began with a history and description of Seattle and praise of its locks, shipping, and industry. It noted that building permits were up 11 percent in 1926 over 1925 levels. It described the street railway crisis and the measures she took to resolve it. Where it began to diverge from past reports was in addressing social problems such as hospitals and health care. First Landes criticized the public hospital situation in Seattle and King County. "We are not competently meeting the situation. We are failing to render service that humanity demands: First, by reason of the apathy and indifference of the public; second, because of the multiplicity of demands on the public treasury." Landes recommended a new city-county hospital to replace four existing, poor facilities. "The entire hospital program should be divorced from political manipulation. This end can be accomplished by a vote of the people." At the time, the "chronic, incurable sick are housed and cared for in the acute sick institutions," at high costs.[106]

This was an unusual concern for a mayor of Seattle. She reiterated the point in her report of the following year, saying that until the city (or city and county) had an up-to-date and properly equipped hospital, "we cannot call ourselves a really civilized or intelligent community." She added that the existing hospital, although well managed, was overcrowded, and "there are no special rooms for the seriously ill, noisy or dying patients, and it has no proper maternity department."[107] Eventually voters authorized the hospital.

She was also prescient in suggesting planning and legislative action for a city-county merger if voters approved it. "The automobile has to a large degree annihilated distance. These facts point to a very close relationship between city and county, and the feasibility of one political unit instead of two," she wrote.[108]

In 1927 she wrote that traffic safety remained a serious concern. "Lives are sacrificed to carelessness, to love of speed and love of that which befogs the mind and deadens muscular control." In addition to implementing the Public Safety Council, she suggested construction of pedestrian subways under heavily traveled streets and traffic signals.[109]

She talked about her proposed Municipal Recreation Committee and about plans to go forward with the civic auditorium project, which was "of the greatest significance to Seattle's community life." Voters had earlier authorized selling $900,000 in bonds to put a 7,500-seat center on the block bounded by Harrison, Mercer, and Third and Fourth avenues. It later became the city's opera house.

Environmental concerns also peppered the report. She said she would seek the development of the long-polluted Green Lake area as a recreational asset, with protection of its pure water. "A program of water sports should be worked out along with the other plans and our citizens should be enabled to derive full value from Nature's gifts," she wrote of Green Lake. She also proposed a Harbor View Park downtown and the gradual removal and consolidation of the unsightly poles proliferating in town. "In the U.S. we seem to have adopted the program of cutting down the trees in the rural districts and erecting them in the form of poles in our city streets. Such a program is both unsightly and dangerous," she wrote.[110]

She talked also about how less than half of those who took the Civil Service exam passed, indicating improved standards. In her report for the following year, she boasted that standards had improved to the point that only one-third who took the Civil Service exams passed them.[111]

She sought attention to the Child Welfare Division, an issue seldom addressed by former mayors other than as a budget line. "Few people realize the importance of the first few years of a child's life and their bearing on his adult life and health. Malnutrition, improper food, unsanitary surroundings in infancy, all act as feeders of the tax-supported charities for adults," she said. Children were all too frequently abandoned or orphaned, as indicated by the many children's homes existing in Seattle offering children varying standards of care. According to Landes:

> The boarding home is one of the big problems of child welfare. Broken homes, caused either by death or divorce, frequently necessitate the placing of helpless children in boarding homes. This division supervises these places and takes keen interest in the children and their surroundings. The department holds that all such children should be vaccinated, and should receive toxin antitoxin diphtheria, and keeps a close watch over the feeding and housing of these little ones. A new and better ordinance governing boarding homes for children is earnestly desired.[112]

The list of her concerns and proposals continued, including sanitation, the Tuberculosis Division, Health Department, Parks Department, and so on. Under the Food and Dairy Division for instance, she noted that the milk supply, "because of its universal use and the possibility of conveying disease, is an important factor in health work," and a target for inspection.

These issues and her stated goals indicated the creativity of her administration and the breadth of her concern as a female who was mayor, who made social and domestic concerns city policy priorities. They also indicated her support for an expansion of government to address social concerns, an expansion that in the 1930s would find full expression in the New Deal programs at the federal level. Landes represented a transitional mode of thinking about government's responsibilities to its citizens that included but went beyond "good government," to a redefinition of government's proper role.

Law enforcement remained a priority. While vice was still to be found in the city, "it is no longer open and flagrant," she wrote.

Seattle was full of children's homes, and Landes promoted social legislation that would make their lot easier through public health programs and regulations, foster home inspections, and joint school district and parks department recreation programs. Here she visits with residents of the Theodora Home. Landes herself bore three children, two of whom did not survive childhood, a great tragedy in her life. *Photo courtesy of the PEMCO–Webster & Stevens Collection, Museum of History and Industry, Seattle*.

"A large number of undesirables immediately left the city, but enough remained to give the police plenty to do, as the record of arrests shows." She added that conditions "are not ideal in Seattle, and probably never will be. I believe that as much progress has been made as could have been expected."[113]

In her agenda, she was like some of her male counterparts in other cities who held reform and efficiency as their ideals. Such mayors, dedicated to economy and efficiency, often imposed middle-class social values on others. They also recognized that new social programs to aid their cities required establishing a modern administrative system capable of providing such services to growing urban populations. Gradually services expanded to meet needs. Per capita expenditures for city services, to pay for charities, education, health, and recreation, rose sharply in most cities over 300,000 in population during the third decade of the twentieth century.[114] She was in the vanguard of this trend, although Seattle during her term spent about half what other cities paid for such services on a per capita basis.

The final pages of her report returned to law enforcement. She mentioned that she and Searing developed plans for a police training school in 1926 and put it into effect, and that all police records had been centralized and organized in one office.[115] At the end of the report, she asked for more staff for the Woman's Division of the Police Department. "In a seaport city there is a greater need for women officers than in an inland city. . . . The women officers have a necessary work to do in preventing delinquency and protecting women and children in this city." She asked for fifty new officers, men and women.[116]

There was even a prescient environmental plea for the purchase and reforestation of the Cedar River watershed, to regulate runoff, prevent excessive erosion, and help reseed the lower logged-off areas. Finally, she noted she had established central mailing and machine processing of the utility bills from all city departments, in the name of economy and efficiency.[117] In the scope of her program, her agenda far exceeded those of her predecessors in office. Many of her reports could have been written yesterday. Most of what she proposed came to pass—if not during her administration, then in subsequent years.

Economic hard times and intractable problems still plagued many residents of her city. As happened with the mothers in the dance hall, once again Landes confronted the economic realities that faced some women in Seattle, particularly in the seamy part of Seattle south of Yesler Way. Once again she bent to accommodate them. Landes, the mayor with the vision of what Seattle should be, encountered some unsavory aspects of the life some lived in Seattle. As the city's chief executive, she faced some hard choices that did not come up in Landes's usual conversations about policy or public affairs.

A man who worked at the Golden West Hotel in the 1920s, where gambling and other illegal activity had long been a tradition, said the houses of prostitution were concentrated on Yesler to Weller and Fifth to Twelfth in downtown Seattle. He recalled that Landes "enforced her campaign promises" by proceeding with plans to close them down upon her election as mayor. However, she found out by taking what he called a survey that there were hundreds of prostitutes working who had no other means of making a living. What's more, they were not prepared to make a living in any other way. As a result, he said that Landes herself agreed to back off. She supposedly agreed to let them work an eight-hour day plying their trade, under certain conditions. They could make no payoffs, and they had to keep to an 8:00 A.M. to 4:00 P.M. workday.

"If they wanted to work after 4 o'clock . . . they could be arrested," recalled Robert Wright.[118] Whether Landes directly authorized this arrangement was not clear from other records, but then such an action was not likely to appear in records. Based on her comments following her visit from the mothers who worked Seattle's dance halls, it was not inconceivable that Landes, with her penchant toward consensus and sensitivity to women's problems, would allow such an arrangement, at least temporarily.

The Municipal Railway Disaster

Besides prostitution, Landes inherited other persistent problems. One of the most difficult she (and previous mayors) faced was the Seattle Municipal Railway system. In 1899 the city of Seattle gave the Boston firm of Stone and Webster the franchise to consolidate street railway lines. Stone and Webster Management Corporation of Boston owned several transportation and electrical utilities in Washington, operated through municipal franchises. The company set the rates, and the parent corporation made money by charging subsidiaries for financial and engineering services. Stone and Webster frequently faced charges of stifling competition, buying off city officials, and charging excessive rates.[119]

By 1910 there was an organized movement for municipal ownership, and in 1911 Washington enacted a law regulating electrical utilities through an expansion of its railroad commission. Also in 1911, Seattle voters passed an $800,000 bond issue proposition to buy an ailing part of the system, thus creating the Seattle Municipal Railway with a total of four miles of track. In 1912 Stone and Webster combined Seattle Electric, Seattle-Tacoma Power Company, and the Pacific Coast Power Company into the formidable Puget Sound Traction, Power and Light Company. In 1913 the city accepted a gift of fourteen additional miles from the system's builders (a mile of it inoperable because of a landslide) and added electric lines and cable cars.[120] In the meantime, Puget Sound Traction, Power and Light Company continued to expand. A collision of interests was inevitable.

Finally, in 1918, under threat of losing federal wartime contracts to Seattle shipbuilders unless the city transportation system was improved, the city persuaded Stone and Webster to sell its entire system to the city and thus erase "Traction" from PP&L's name. Stone and Webster set an inflated price of $18 million. Mayor Ole Hanson offered an inflated $15 million, much more than the property was worth, but the four daily newspapers in Seattle trumpeted the purchase. Two years after the purchase, a special committee appointed by Mayor Hugh Caldwell to investigate details of the purchase found that all four newspapers had been influenced in some way by Stone and Webster interests.[121] Nevertheless, a November 5, 1918, election authorized making the $15 million purchase of a dilapidated 200-mile system worth less than half that amount, with the total amount to be paid off within only fifteen years and with a clause (later disputed) that forced the city to tap general tax revenues to make the payments if necessary.

By the time Landes took office, the debt load and system expenses could not be covered from the revenues, threatening the entire system. Everywhere, street railway systems were going into decline, after ridership peaked in 1926.[122] In the meantime, Seattle's rates had gone from the popular five-cent fare (a figure that helped elect Brown to office, which he promised but delivered for only one month in 1923) to eight and a half cents (a figure that brought Landes and the council criticism, although Brown's predecessor had raised the fare to ten cents). Landes distilled the problem this way: "It was a case of paying more than we should and in less time than we should."[123] More paranoid individuals believed that this decrepit white elephant was part of a contorted plot to force the city ultimately to abandon its Skagit River power development plan and make it possible for Puget Sound Power and Light—the successor to Puget Sound Traction—to take over City Light.

By 1926, the street railway system was in a crisis situation, and so was the city. Seattle by the end of the decade had one car for every four residents.[124] The ubiquitous automobile was taking more and more passengers away, the system had suffered a number of injury-causing accidents, maintenance of the routes was an increasing drain, and the extended routes were financial sinkholes.[125] Moreover, the courts had told the city of Seattle that it was prohibited by law from taking money from other city funding sources to offset the losses, which it had been doing. Christmas was coming, and the system's warrants to pay employees were bouncing. Banks were refusing to honor the system's vouchers, causing employees much hardship. One woman, whose husband worked for the streetcar lines for forty-five years, later recalled they had "an awful time getting them cashed."[126]

To head off the immediate problem, Landes, with others, organized an effort to back the warrants by using private capital through downtown businesses, sympathetic banks, and other sources.[127] It was a band-aid measure, however, and the systemic problems remained. To improve the system, she invested in improvements and cut costs by eliminating unprofitable routes and laying off one hundred men. The fare went to ten cents. Cutting routes and positions and raising fares temporarily turned the tide, but it also earned Landes the further enmity of the Civil Service League and those riders who used the outlying routes. Her decisions were made in the name of efficiency and solvency, and she made the system solvent while she was in office. But her decisions also had citizen and Civil Service impacts that were not politically expedient, as she would soon find out.

She also took matters into her own hands to reduce the principal and interest payments to the private utility holding the city in its grip. The situation was sufficiently serious to threaten the city's bond standing in the East, a calamity the growing city had to avoid. After negotiating with Stone and Webster, she traveled to Olympia to lobby for an enabling act that would allow the city to revise the street railway contract, arranging for an annual lower bond redemption payment and an extended payback period.[128] She clashed with private power interests over the bill's wording but succeeded in getting it passed. It held, despite a legal challenge, and the payments went from $850,000 a year to a more manageable $500,000.

Her position on public power did not endear her to the private utility interests, however, who were ill disposed toward her anyway. She had definitely impressed upon them her longstanding and active support of public ownership of utilities. This action too would prove to be not politically expedient for her reelection, but in her view there was no other course of rational action, given the situation she inherited with the street railway system. Despite her efforts and those of succeeding administrations, the Seattle Municipal Railway system did not survive. The last car of the system traveled its route on August 9, 1940.[129]

Landes also kept her campaign promises on the law enforcement front. From October of 1926 to October of 1927, the first year of her administration, a report showed that police court netted the city $301,693, or 36 percent more in fines than from the prior year's cases. Cases tried totaled 44,237, up 21 percent.[130]

However, the truce she negotiated among law enforcement agencies did not last throughout her administration. Disputes over jurisdiction arose between Sheriff Claude Bannick of King County, whom she had passed over for Seattle's police chief, and Police Chief William Searing of Seattle. By the second year of her administration, Bannick was repeating the familiar charge that there was either incompetency or graft within the Seattle Police Department.[131] He gave the city force an ultimatum to clean up Seattle or he would do it. Searing fumed but did not rise to the bait, and Landes said she would welcome the help. The press played the feud as a cops comedy.[132] It ended with Bannick somewhat the worse for wear when he was proved wrong in some of his specific accusations. Landes successfully prevented Searing (or herself) from making the situation worse, as her predecessor had done in his disputes with other agencies over law enforcement.

Success—and Dreams for the Future

The council, the group she worked with in harmony, finally overrode one of her infrequent vetoes at the end of 1927. Once again, dance halls were the issue. The council relicensed Columbus Public Dancehall, turning aside her veto 6-2. Supporting her were council members Campbell and Moore; opposing her were Tindall, Carroll, Cohen, Hesketh, Blaine, and Case.[133] The harmony may have been turning a bit discordant, although that was probably reading too much into this issue. Nevertheless, three of those who voted to overturn the veto a few months later decided to run against her for the office of mayor. The significance of their actions is uncertain, since there was a historic pattern in Seattle politics of a handful of present or former city council members running for mayor in every election.

In the meantime, Landes's personal stock with many constituents continued to rise, not all of them residents of Washington State. Midway through her term, the president of the National Council of Administrative Women in Education, after meeting her, suggested that Landes should run for the presidency of the United States and offered her support.[134] When she was a guest of the Minneapolis/St. Paul League of Women Voters, that possibility was again suggested to her.[135] She told a newspaper there that she would never become president of the United States, even if the opportunity arose, because she could never leave her husband. The idea that her husband might leave his job to accompany her in such an eventuality apparently never occurred to her.

Early in her term the *Seattle Times* quoted at length an article appearing in *Christian Advocate* magazine that further neutralized the issue of Landes's gender by describing her in masculine terms, calling her a "good sport . . . free from fads and silly sentimentalities, a real leader, of whom Seattle is justly proud." Furthermore, claimed the article, Seattle's mayor "does not fear to do what might be expected of a masculine mayor. She dons her old clothes and hikes into our Skagit hydroelectric project to study its needs first hand." Calling her successful at the polls on a "decency," not a "reform," program, the magazine termed her a sane, balanced, and progressive thinker, not governed by femininity. "A petticoat mayor? No! Never! This was one of the many ejaculations heard among the four hundred and more thousands of Seattlites in the mayoralty campaign last spring," the magazine said. But the voters decided "the woman was a far better man than her opponent." And she was "demonstrating to the world that a woman can have a balanced mind and be as capable, alert and efficient as a man."[136]

Her gender status in many quarters was becoming more and more ambiguous the longer she continued in office. Descriptions of her, however, often compared her favorably to a masculine standard in order to demonstrate her capabilities and prove she was not acting like a woman would be expected to act in the office. This became a theme in writing about Landes and reflected attempts to reconcile her gender to her newfound role and status, in effect demonstrating just how "masculine" political power was assumed to be.

Her name also began to surface as a potential gubernatorial candidate, as she traveled around the state and region on numerous speaking engagements. Papers as diverse as the *Portland Oregonian* and the *New York Times* discussed her potential candidacy, with the *New York Times* praising the idea, based on her administration of the mayor's office.[137]

If there was a subtle shift in the kind of coverage Bertha Knight Landes received as a result of her presence and efforts, there was also a subtle shift in her own attitude toward the position and the power and attention it brought her. There were small admissions of personal and professional ambition, and a further distancing of herself from essentialist gender constructions. She began to enjoy the office and her accomplishments. "Is there after all anything more wonderful, except life itself, than the building of a great city, physically, mentally and spiritually? It is romance itself, for it is life expressing itself in tangible ways," she said of her years in office.[138]

In a letter written to a supporter midway through her administration, Landes talked about her perceptions of her role as a model for the conduct of women in public affairs. The supporter had written Landes about how her election had caused a small but important gain for women. The writer said that she found that while men in various organizations were still not outspokenly supportive of treating women as equals, at least they were not actively opposed to including women in the decisions and activities of the group.

In response Landes set down her own vision of the future and her role in it. "One of my big desires in this work is to so conduct myself that women's interests will be forwarded, and women's ability to do things recognized by men as well as by her sister woman." So when the writer told her that men in organizations had moved, "if not from active opposition, at least to a feeling of lukewarmness concerning women's ability to carry on as men do in our workaday world," she was pleased. "You make me feel that I have accomplished something along those lines."[139]

It was significant that she saved in her papers a typescript carbon of a passage attributed to the *Brooklyn Daily Eagle,* describing her "unfeminine" operation of the mayor's office. It also hinted at her lack of time for and contempt of political gladhanding, which, if accurate, could also have served to erode the political base she might have built in office:

> Nothing of the flightiness, nothing of the tendency to turn a serious municipal adventure into a social spree which might be expected from a Mayor in skirts has developed since Mrs. Bertha Knight Landes took over city government reins.
>
> [She is] strictly a business type. . . . She declines invitations to tea. She excuses herself from social engagements which might interfere with the city's business. She has abolished the open door policy at city hall and it is more difficult for a political jobseeker or time-waster to obtain an audience with my lady Mayor than for the traditional camel to pass through the eye of the fabled needle.
>
> She is not of the gladhanding, backslapping tribe of politicians, and apparently takes no thought for her political future. Instead, she buries herself in the affairs of the city.
>
> [She has] shown a capacity to handle men, to get quarreling officials to agree and to cooperate, which her male predecessors have in years past altogether lacked.[140]

Landes herself complained that sometimes she had interviews every fifteen minutes all day long, and that citizens felt the mayor was their special property. "Often, if told the mayor was too busy, the reply would be 'I am a citizen and a taxpayer and demand to see the mayor.' " Landes said that despite campaign slogans that said, "We don't want a woman mayor," she noticed that "no citizen who had an axe to grind stayed away from the office because a woman sat in the mayor's chair."[141] She also found much unofficial business taking up time—a caller with "a wild or a constructive scheme, a mother asking the city to find her missing daughter, a crippled soldier looking for a job." She found that

When Charles Lindbergh came to Seattle, Landes spoke at a reception honoring him. In her remarks, she said that Seattle, like Lindbergh, had an interest in supporting commercial aviation. She aspired to Seattle's establishing a first-rate commercial airport. *Photo courtesy of the Museum of History and Industry, Seattle.*

"there's more to being a mayor than just playing around with Queen Marie and Lindbergh when they come to town," she said facetiously.[142]

Clearly she conducted herself, or was widely perceived as conducting herself, in a way that offered a sharp contrast to what were stereotypes of female behavior. This proper female, who came to office on the power of civic motherhood and separatist ideology, was acting in a radical, unprecedented way to prove herself a woman who was like a man in being able to manage the affairs of her office. It was a subtle but important difference, significant for the members of the patriarchal structures around her, which evaluated her as a representative of her gender as well as the mayor of Seattle.

Women also viewed her as representative of her gender, although with a different attitude than men displayed toward her unconventional identity. Where men typically saw a woman who thought like a man and was unlike a woman, women saw someone else. They typically saw her as a representative woman demonstrating women's unique nature and capabilities to carry out the duties of such an important office. Landes probably fell somewhere in the middle. She was a bright, savvy, powerful woman with woman's concerns who adopted the behavior patterns and methodologies of the men around her in order to be taken seriously and do the job as constructed. They, and Landes, were dealing with preconceptions about gender, and the struggle over proper female behavior continued.

In a magazine article she wrote a few months after her term as mayor ended, Landes described how she stretched the concept of gender to include all duties relating to the office of mayor. She spoke of the kind of duties that women normally would have been excluded from fulfilling, by their clothing, by behavior codes, by lack of required escorts, or by "breeding."

> An English woman mayor once asked me:
>
> "Whom do you have to do the things a woman cannot do and go to the places a woman cannot go?"
>
> There were no such things, or places, in Seattle when I was mayor.
>
> The fleet visited our harbor, and I found that the admiral had arranged for me to go down in a submarine and up in a naval hydroplane. I cheerfully went in each direction, and enjoyed myself immensely.
>
> I opened baseball games, rode in locomotive cabs and broke ground for innumerable buildings. When Seattle began the building of a huge dam, the Skagit hydroelectric development, a hundred miles from the city, I put on my oldest clothes and tramped with muddy shoes all about the site, to observe conditions at first hand.
>
> One of my pleasantest duties was welcoming and arranging for the reception of such distinguished visitors as Col. Lindbergh, Queen Marie of Roumania; Amundsen, Nobile and Lincoln Ellsworth, the returned polar explorers; Secretaries Hoover, Davis and Wilbur; and the British ambassador and his wife.[143]

She was dramatically extending the boundaries of what it was to be both female and powerful, and enjoying it. Although the acts she listed were standard ritual behavior when done by male officials, as they usually were, this was unexpected behavior when it came to female officials.

News photographs saved with her husband's papers demonstrate her singular transitional nature. One showed her sitting in the rear seat of the open cockpit plane, wearing the requisite

Lt. Howard Beswick piloted Landes from Seattle on the first passenger flight to Bremerton Naval Station, twenty miles away. The trip, which Landes insisted on making as part of her official duties, left Landes a little queasy upon arrival. *Photo by* Seattle Times; *courtesy of Henry Landes Papers, University of Washington Libraries.*

masculine leather helmet and goggles, for the first passenger ride to Bremerton's Ward Station twenty miles from Seattle. Another photograph showed her climbing aboard a navy ship for inspections. Yet another showed her playing engineer of a train, complete with a railroad engineer's cap on her head.

One photograph displayed her in a way that must have looked and felt awkward. In this one she is sitting amid foreign consuls at a luncheon at Fisher Flouring Mills. In the flag-draped hall, two lines of banquet tables stood parallel to one another, seating about sixty men per line of tables. Landes sits as the only woman amid the sea of male faces and suits, as she must have sat at dozens of official functions during her terms.[144]

Her political agenda for Seattle was broad and deep, compared with that of her predecessors, and only partially completed during her two-year term. She had more that she wanted to do for Seattle, and for herself. Rumors of a possible run for the governorship of the state still swirled around her. Although politically coy with reporters on that possibility, she undoubtedly realized that that was a political plum out of her reach. She probably was not much interested in it either, given her attitude toward politics and ambition. Nevertheless, she began hinting, as she entered the final year of her term in office, that she was not yet finished and might run again for mayor. Not unreasonably, she and those around her assumed that she had an unshakable hold on the office.

NO MORE PETTICOAT RULE

In 1927 Bertha Knight Landes was riding high. At the age of fifty-eight, she was in a position no woman had ever held before, leading a great city and seeing her goals, dreams, and ambitions realized. "Romance itself," is how she described these days in reflecting on her career. She had managed to break ground in a new age, where science and technology held promise for the future and the social sciences were unraveling the mysteries of irrational human behavior. She had earned for herself a considerable local and national reputation, to the point of hearing her name mentioned for the governor's race, and even higher. The future lay before her, rich with possibilities.

In August of that year, she made a ten-day trip to Alaska. While on the trip, she revealed something interesting, given her past views. She told the *Ketchikan Chronicle* she was "a suffragette" when it came to women in executive offices and politics. "I have helped convert a few men in Seattle to that belief and expect to educate a few more of them," she boasted. She added that "only those of very narrow vision or prejudiced minds can ignore the facts" on the clear ability of women to accept equal responsibility with men.[1] The rhetoric was quite different from what she had used in her first council campaign in talking to reporters.

She briefly spoke with other reporters on her return to Seattle. Pressed for a response about her future plans with the mayoral election seven months away, she indicated she probably would run for mayor again, but warned that anything could happen.[2] It did, in the form of a political unknown named Frank Edwards, in the form of a protracted and negative campaign on the part of an opponent who refused to discuss the issues, and in the form of a turning tide on both gender and class issues that swamped her small ship of state.

Her administration of the office of mayor disturbed many elements of the status quo sources of power—economic, social, and political. Although her supporters normally constituted a powerful group, they and Landes were not able to turn back the tide of these forces, once aroused. In fact, the tide had been building for some time, the result of her mere presence and her actions as mayor of Seattle. The more she did, the more she subverted her future. But that all seemed distant that day in August on her return to the Puget Sound.

She remained coy about her future or her political plans, telling reporters one Saturday when she was in her office, "Look at all this work piled here for me to do and you want to stop and talk politics." Nevertheless, the October headline read, "Mrs. Landes is Definitely in Mayorality [*sic*] Race."[3] In office, she continued along the course she had set for her administration, to clean up, modernize, make efficient, beautify, and generally better the mental and physical environment of Seattle.

The Theater Issue

One of the issues that had concerned her about Seattle's environment from her days on the city council was the operation of Seattle's movie houses. Some were open all night, sometimes showing films that were not suitable entertainment, particularly for children. The content of movies had been an issue for the Federation of Women's Clubs as well.

Long before Landes was ever on the political scene, Seattle had a Board of Theatre Censors. But under former mayor Edwin Brown, the city council and others viewed the board as ineffective, controlled by politics, and unresponsive to community needs. The council refused to appropriate even a pittance for its operating support, much to Brown's consternation. He called theater board members inspecting theaters and films "public spirited people" who "have to a degree at least been responsible [to see to it] that objectionable features have been eliminated. However, the powers of the board are so limited that much of the work that might be accomplished is not within the scope of the censors under existing ordinances."[4]

Landes planned to change the structure to make the board more effective. She fired those members she thought were ineffective—thirteen out of a membership of fifteen. Early in 1927 she revoked their appointments. The initial list of revocations included seven women and one man—a theater operator.[5] On the list, unnoticed heretofore, was the name Frank Edwards, the owner-operator of a small string of second-rate movie houses. Within a year, his name was known throughout Seattle.

The issue of control of leisure entertainments, as anthropologist Victor Turner predicted, is an area of endless confrontation for the existing power relationships in a social structure. Leisure entertainments, from carnivals to films, present alternative lifestyles, alternative visions of order (or disorder), alternative responses to existing conditions. They may threaten or undermine or reinforce existing standards and beliefs. Movies with their ability to put viewers into new situations had more power to do this than any other medium. Seattle's movie houses had presented problems in the past. In addition to ideas of antistructure, they may foster a sense of what Turner called *communitas,* or intense connections among disparate viewers, in ways that may either reinforce or undermine the existing status quo arrangements.

Seattle's first movie house, La Petite, opened on Pike Street in 1901. It was full of rows of chairs or benches and nickelodeon entertainment, generally short pieces on famous people or illustrated songs.[6] From that humble beginning to the release of the "talkie" *The Jazz Singer* less than three decades later, movies rapidly escalated in popularity. They offered low-cost, exciting, alternative forms of entertainment to so-called lower classes, although there were growing and widespread concerns about their social content and effects on education of the young. With the rapid spread of this technology, concerns about content burgeoned across the nation in cities like Seattle. As one film historian put it, "respectable people" quickly relegated movies to sideshow or underground status:

> Respectable people rejected the movies because they were thought to be trivial but also because they were thought to be corrupting and immoral. The whole atmosphere of the movies suggested "tumult and promiscuity." It was widely assumed that motion pictures would be sexually suggestive and probably explicit, the whole tone seemed secular and irresponsible, and few doubted that children and the weak-minded were being pointed towards crime and degeneracy.[7]

It was inevitable that political authorities began to take interest in the business of movies, despite the industry's efforts to gain respectability. In the 1920s, it became "intellectual orthodoxy"

When humorist Will Rogers came to Seattle, Mayor Landes served as his official host. She particularly enjoyed having the opportunity to meet the brave and famous, including figures such as Roald Amundsen, Queen Marie of Romania, and Rogers. (The significance of the anchor is not clear.) *Photo courtesy of the Museum of History and Industry, Seattle.*

to link movies with the mindlessness or immaturity of the masses.[8] To Landes and many others, the answer was not outright closure but licensing and review of the wares being sold in the theaters and of how they were being sold.

Landes was perhaps aware of something that had happened in nearby Tacoma a few years earlier, when a coalition of six black women appeared before the city council there. They spoke eloquently and with great pain about a theater's plans to show *The Birth of a Nation* by D. W. Griffiths, a film they found racist. They wanted the film suppressed by the council.

Arguing with them about the issue was a group of Tacoma clubwomen who defended the film. They felt the women overreacted. The black women persisted, with one saying the image left by the film was that their race was "immoral, beastly, socially degenerate and a race to be feared and shunned." The council, according to the news report, nevertheless took no action at the meeting.[9]

Landes's solution to potential theater problems in Seattle, after she made her own appointments to the newly constituted Board of Theatre Supervisors, was to have them function "with the idea of being helpful not only to the public, but also to the ethical theatre owners and managers." The board, with her endorsement, made two decisions on movie advertising, which also illustrated the unique problems the board faced: theaters could not advertise "by placing persons in glass cages in front of theatres," and "public theatres should open their entertainment to all the public at all times, not restricting attendance to only one sex at separate picture showings."[10]

The issue went beyond censorship of sexuality; intolerance, in the form of racism and sexism, was also the target. In her 1928 report to the city council, Landes outlined the criteria for the board's decisions. "In elimination of productions in their entirety the Board has attempted to eliminate only those based on sex degeneracy," she wrote, or as ordinances, such as business hours, required. However, the board also opposed the showing of films that treated irreverently "any creed, or held racial characteristics up to extreme ridicule or scorn." She added that "legitimate theatre entertainment" had been censored only on three occasions in the sixteen months of her term, once because of "exceedingly scant" attire of the participants.[11]

In supporting this action, Landes was a force of stability representing community standards, which often also coincided with women's interests. That she continued to be worried about children and the influences upon them, such as movies, was clear in a speech on delinquency she made in August 1927 to a group of social workers. Her view of home and city as the larger home had changed.

In it she said that the home was failing and losing its former place of influence and control. Now even the schools could sow seeds of delinquency, through exposure to truancy, lying, cheating, and vulgarity. "Can organized society do anything to reinstate the home in its former place of influence and control?" she asked. "Can it stem the tide of the onward sweep of so-called progress—of new inventions—of new interests—of new stimuli," she continued, "or must it make use of all these new movements and create an influence to offset this loss and thus bar the way to resultant delinquency?"[12]

Movies constituted one of the factors in this continuing erosion. The solution, she continued, went beyond control. It was a matter of humanizing social services and educating the citizenry about the bad conditions facing many young people, such as the privations of improper housing and cruel and abusive treatment, and how to effect reforms. "We need a socialized police force, both men and women, especially more and more of the latter."[13]

She continued to worry about moral conditions in Seattle, and she resolved to remedy them in some creative ways. For instance, she named a Municipal Recreation Committee, which surveyed facilities and needs. She helped establish five community centers in Seattle offering joint recreation programs, where activities included "group games, singing classes, athletic contests, story telling, parties, athletic leagues, tournaments, splash parties, sailboat races, hikes and final community night,"[14] to give participants something to do.

The 1928 Primary

In October of 1927, Landes finally declared her candidacy for reelection but declined to get involved in any campaigning at that point, saying it was much too early. She again professed that her political interests were limited to the mayor's office, and again set aside the issue of gender as not germane to the election. "I haven't seen any reason, since taking office, why a woman can't fill it as well as a man," she said. Yet she said she also hoped to prove that a woman could gain the endorsement of voters for a second term.[15]

Seemingly out of nowhere, the challenger appeared, long before the campaign officially opened. He announced his candidacy in November, well before the filing period even opened for the March election. On November 26, 1927, Frank Edwards, a political neophyte, said he too was running for mayor. He said that the city could lower its taxes and encourage new industry to locate there. He promised a financial survey of Seattle's publicly owned utilities and improvements to the water system and street railway services.[16] By all accounts, he was a longshot in the race that was not even a race yet.

Landes kicked off her own campaign on New Year's Day, with the endorsements of 350 individuals belonging to a variety of business groups, women's clubs, community organizations, and professional associations. The names were listed in a long newspaper column. Immediately below it—perhaps by chance—was a two-inch display ad promoting "Cut-Rate Dentistry" at the Brown Dentist Offices, with a picture of the former mayor.[17] Brown and his former police chief William Severyns remained visible in Seattle affairs during Landes's term, through appearances before service clubs. They expected to see public service again.

Accompanying the news of Landes's campaign endorsements was a lengthy article in the *Times* noting Seattle's phenomenal growth and national attention. Landes clearly had a role in both. The growth came in part from increases in conventions and an improved business climate. The National Education Association convention and National Association of Real Estate Boards each brought thousands of visitors when they met in Seattle, and the Investment Bankers of America were meeting there later in 1928. The $900,000 civic auditorium bond issue had passed in March, and the city's fire insurance rates were down.[18]

Building was booming. Boeing had orders for ten transcontinental planes, and 1928 promised to be even better. Landes had already broken ground for the new civic auditorium (remodeled in 1961 into the city's opera house), and the Denny Hill regrade was going forward. Over $1 million a month was being invested in industries in the Seattle area, according to the head of the Manufacturers' Association.[19] This article on Seattle's growth offered quite a contrast to the articles that appeared the morning she won the election.

If she had disappeared the morning after entering the race for mayor in 1928, she would have accomplished one of her most important goals—demonstrating that a woman could handle this complex administrative job and keep the city both flourishing and solvent. She had empowered women to participate in local government and the direct management of civic affairs instead of the more indirect route through the vote or club campaigns. Thousands of women later in the twentieth century cut their political teeth in local government, in elected and appointed positions, from zoning commissions to city councils to mayoralties. Women generally found more receptivity to their political involvement in their home communities than they did in state and national elected positions. Activism at home reflected the acceptable extension of women's sphere that Landes and others called for in 1922.

By the end of the January 1928 filing period, Landes and

Much of a mayor's time is spent in ceremonial functions, and Landes consciously made sure she did whatever was expected of all the men who had held the office before her. Here she breaks ground for the new civic auditorium (another source identifies it as a University of Washington building). The bond issue for the civic auditorium, a project she supported, passed during her administration and was completed after she left office. The auditorium later became the city's opera house. *Photo courtesy of the Museum of History and Industry, Seattle.*

Edwards were part of a crowded field that had grown to ten candidates, all vying to be Seattle's next mayor. The field, which must have brought a smile to Landes's lips, included two women, a former mayor, and three members of the city council. On the list running against her were her old colleagues Kathryn Miracle and Edwin Brown, and all the candidates seemed to be trying to out-Landes Landes in the framing of the campaign issues. Maybe that was predictable, since she was the incumbent.

Whatever alliance there had been between Miracle and Landes had broken apart. Miracle, who had been elected on the strength of Landes's landslide, had lost her bid for reelection to the city council in 1925 when Landes was reelected. There apparently were some lingering resentments. In the final hours of the filing period, Miracle had decided against running again for a council seat, as she had previously declared her intention to do, but decided to run for mayor instead. In a campaign statement, she said she decided to run for mayor after a "certain, capable experienced businessman" declined to run himself because he could not leave his business affairs.[20]

Miracle was critical of Landes and, ironically, of female mayors, despite the fact that she was running for the office. "I believe the office of mayor is primarily a place for a capable man, but I believe also that an experienced business woman fits into it." She said that she had been a Seattle taxpayer for twenty-five years and had earned her own way. For the past sixteen years she had been handling properties out of her own home real estate office and had run a boardinghouse.

Attacking Landes on class and business background became a theme in the election campaign. "A business woman's viewpoint is similar to that of a business man. She has a very much keener conception of life than has the woman who has been wholly or partially protected from the economic stresses of life," Miracle said.[21] However, Miracle herself also sounded the motherhood analogy, the theme that helped put Landes into office. "I know that Seattle is a sick child. It needs nursing back to normal and my experience in the city council from 1922 to 1925 qualifies me to fill the position of nurse." She added that while she was on the council she "worked diligently for the homeowners and spent much time participating in the work of industrial development."[22]

Also running for mayor were three sitting council members,

although one—Robert Hesketh, the labor leader—quickly withdrew his name from the field. The other two were Philip Tindall, who had run for mayor in 1926, and A. Lou Cohen. Other candidates to file included W. T. Christensen, port commissioner; Clifford Clark, a businessman; Joseph Greenwell; and Edwards, who was the fifth individual to file formally for office.[23] On the list of candidates running for council was one woman—Margaret Griffin.

Landes had clashed with one of her opponents, councilman Cohen, a few months earlier. Cohen, a merchant who had lived in Seattle thirty-five years, was elected to the council the same year she was. As councilman, he drafted an ordinance that provided for thirty-day publication of calls for bids on sale of city bonds and the ordinance that submitted the auditorium bond issue to the voters. He held that city utilities should confine their services to city limits, a position that favored private power interests.[24]

Cohen had criticized Landes publicly for influencing the department heads she named, and he was particularly incensed over a recommendation by Superintendent J. D. Ross of City Light that the retail sales division of the light department alter its policies. At the time City Light also sold electrical appliances, such as electric heaters and ranges, not an uncommon practice for utilities. City crews installed and maintained them. Ross had recommended, for efficiency reasons, that the selling of electrical appliances cease, except for ranges and heaters. Ross had earlier supported the sales, and Cohen blamed Landes for pressuring for the change.[25]

A few years earlier, Cohen also blamed her for stealing the limelight on moral reform. As chairman of the council's License Committee, she had refused to renew the licenses to certain cabarets, and eight thousand signatures had been collected and forwarded to the council in support of her position. "Lou Cohen objected to the singling out of Mrs. Landes as the only committee member standing for a higher standard of morality and social decency in cabarets," a reporter wrote. He had that standard too, he said.[26]

Critics perceived Landes as being at best impatient and at worst high-handed with her ideas and recommendations to improve public institutions and city efficiency, although she and the council had cut the city's expenditures for 1927 by 5 percent, saving taxpayers hundreds of thousands of dollars. For instance, only two months into her administration, in looking for ways to cut the city budget, she suggested lowering the salaries of those city employees who had lighter duties as the result of advanced years, or who had been partially incapacitated. The idea was not exactly well received by civil service employees.

As objections mounted, Landes backed down, quickly assuring the Board of Public Works that she "would maintain a 'hands-off' policy concerning the operation of their departments."[27] This short-sighted idea, combined with her subsequent layoffs of one hundred street railway workers to keep the system solvent, her stated preference for making layoffs by both efficiency and seniority rather than seniority alone, and her "clean-up" of the Civil Service Commission created some powerful enemies in the Civil Service League. League leaders reportedly campaigned actively against Landes during her reelection campaign, on the job and off. The league may also have played a role in recruiting Edwards, the stealth candidate, to run against her for office.[28]

Such criticisms were relatively trivial, however, compared with the scandals in, and criticisms of, past administrations. Nobody questioned Landes's motives or intelligence, or the progress Seattle had made under her administration. Landes's grasp on the position of mayor seemed to be firm. As the *Seattle Times* wrote in the headline above an article about the other candidates in the campaign, "Mrs. Landes is Conceded Edge in Mayor Race; Even Other Candidates Are Convinced Woman Has Best Chance to Lead in Voting."[29] She named Arthur Anderson to head her reelection campaign and set up her headquarters at the McDowall Building at Third and Union in downtown Seattle.[30]

Landes's goals for her next administration were not much different from what they had been before. She said she had unfinished business, although much had been accomplished.[31] Her goals included continuing the development of the Diablo Dam on the Skagit River, constructing a commercial airport, salvaging the street railway system, building a city-county public hospital, improving recreational programs and health standards, increasing police efficiency, and providing more efficient, effective government. "My promise is to continue to conduct my office in a dignified, sane and reasonable manner, bending all my efforts, as in the past, to promoting public good and public ser-

This photograph was taken for a campaign brochure when Landes ran for reelection as mayor. Its purpose was to show a busy mayor at work in the office, but the rubber band holding down the receiver cradle belied the image. In the meantime, her opponent Frank Edwards promoted himself as a businessman and family man who loved the out-of-doors, characteristics Landes could not match. *Photo courtesy of the Museum of History and Industry, Seattle.*

vice," she said in a statement.[32] She did not, however, promise that all her goals could be accomplished with lower taxes.

For his part, Edwards did not promise either improved social services or police efficiency. Edwards did, however, promise to use his skills as a businessman, which he said the present leadership of the city did not possess. Business acumen was a central tenet of Edwards's campaign. He campaigned on administering government like a business in order to reduce costs, lower taxes, and encourage industry. In actuality, Seattle's bonded indebtedness, at $16.6 million at the end of 1927, was at its lowest point since 1912, although the utility bond debt had increased $2.55

million during 1927, to a sizable $39.5 million, as a result of continued development of city-owned power. In fact, the burgeoning plant expansion for City Light meant that it was not until after World War II, with the final completion of the Skagit development, that ratepayers would see a significant reduction in their power rates.[33] However, Seattle homeowners in the 1920s paid 2.73 cents per kilowatt hour, compared to a national average of 6.6 cents. In the city budget overall, gross revenue for 1927 was $22.8 million with expenses of $20.9 million.[34]

The extensive infrastructure improvements of the city and passage of all the bonds came at a price, however. Concern about taxes was growing. In February 1928 an editorial in the *Seattle Star*—which endorsed Landes— said working people in Seattle who had their tax statements in front of them would not be pleased to learn that the combined city, school, county, and state rates had given Seattle residents the third highest combined tax rate in the nation. It said Seattle's combined adjusted tax rate was $34.60 per $1,000 valuation, compared with rates of $19.15 in New York City, $23.23 in Chicago, and $23.07 in Minneapolis. The editorial said that only Newark, New Jersey, and Fall River, Massachusetts, had higher combined rates.[35] It was silent, however, on whether assessments were equivalent. The Edwards campaign reprinted the editorial and distributed it widely.

In fact, by 1930 Seattle's bonded indebtedness, on a per capita basis, was one of the highest in the country as the result of purchase and development of its municipally owned utilities, concluded a 1930 Municipal League report. And the city, by past practice, had been lax about creating a sinking fund for bond redemption, or for allowing the life of the bond to exceed the life of the improvement. If a city owned its own water, light, and sewer systems, its council, by Washington law, could increase bonded indebtedness to 5 percent of the taxable property without voter approval. By 1930, that limit had been reached in Seattle, and the 5 percent on taxable property that had to be authorized by voters for bonds had an available margin of less than $3 million.[36] Besides funding the construction of city-owned power plants, bond issues in Seattle had provided a telephone system and additions to the street railway system as well as other projects.

However, Seattle city expenditures were not out of line. A 1930 analysis, using 1928 city financial statistics, compared Seattle with cities nationally. It found tax rates for city services in Seattle well below national figures. In virtually every expenditure category—except those of protection (police and fire) and general government—Seattle was spending less per capita, often substantially less, than other cities. For all departments, Seattle spent $38.68 per capita compared with $43.01 nationally.[37]

Taxes remained an issue in the contest. So did Edwards's background. Generally, Edwards was an unknown quantity in the election campaign, with a mysterious background about which he seemed reluctant to reveal details. Well before he entered the campaign, the *Seattle Star* carried a story on his business enterprises. In it he claimed he had turned $250 in cash and four years of fourteen-hour days into a string of theaters, which he was then able to sell for $250,000.[38]

However, because Edwards was not active in either civic or political affairs, he had little visibility before the campaign. But his early efforts at organization and his extensive expenditures on advertising his nascent campaign quickly gave him visibility. He had actually worked on his campaign since May 1925, and had established six district campaign offices around Seattle by January 1926. They were staffed by women in what one newspaper termed a "drive for the support of the Seattle women."[39] Perhaps more significantly, he began capitalizing on the very image technology that Landes and others had long worried about—the movies.

Edwards's supporters—whoever they were—recognized the potential of media campaigns and candidate image-making. They had tapped into the movie house network to make arrangements, as one newspaper reported, "for the showing of prepared pictures, in which the candidate appears as the principal figure." The films included an inspection tour of the Skagit power project and visits "to other scenes of municipal activity," where the candidate looked the part of the businessman,[40] a part Landes could not play. He also made extensive use of another relatively new form of communications technology that Landes used—radio broadcasts. His efforts to distinguish himself from the herd running behind Landes paid off.

There was an unusual level of interest in this campaign, despite a complaint in the *Times* that all the challengers sounded alike. The February 28 primary election saw a remarkable 91,879 voters of a total 114,272 registered show up at the polls, indicating a high level of interest in the campaign. The 80 percent turnout in this presidential election year set a Seattle record. The vote was 28,183 votes for Landes, 25,034 votes for Edwards, and 22,515 votes for Brown.[41] The next nearest candidate was councilman Philip Tindall, far behind with 8,966 votes, with Miracle trailing him with only a few thousand votes.[42] Clearly either dark horse Edwards or mayor emeritus Brown might be able to topple Landes, depending on the course of the remainder of the short campaign before the mid-March general election. Yet she still appeared to most observers to have a lock on the election. They saw Edwards as an irrational presence not to be taken too seriously—at least not before the primary election votes were counted.

Finalists Landes, Edwards, and Brown

Reporters—and Landes—soon began to press Edwards for details about his past history and his campaign, particularly as evidence mounted that considerable sums were being spent on his campaign in the form of a paid publicist, billboards, newspaper ads, extensive radio time, and large mailings. The *Times* studied past city directories, only to find that in 1912 the directory had no occupation listed for Edwards, and that in several subsequent years he was not listed at all.[43]

In the closing weeks of the campaign, Edwards finally released details of his background as the rumors about him grew more and more negative. His prior political experience was running unsuccessfully for the legislature in 1916 on the Progressive party ticket. His only portfolio of civic interest or activity had been, in his own words, "paying taxes."[44] He told reporters that he was fifty-four years old and had been born in Summersetshire, England. He had immigrated to the United States at age eighteen, first to California, then Montana, before coming to Seattle in 1900. From 1900 to 1908 he worked for the American District Telegraph Company, first as a clerk and then as a superintendent. He became a U.S. citizen in 1906 and married in 1907. He had a son at the University of Washington, one in high school, and a five-year-old daughter. From 1909 to 1910 he worked for Morrison's Cafe as a buyer and accountant. Although Morrison had a saloon, Edwards denied one of the more persistent rumors—that he had been a bartender.

He briefly ran a real estate and insurance business and then in 1912 became an examiner for the state insurance commissioner, moving in 1913–14 to the position of auditor for the Issaquah and Superior Mining Company. For the next four years he worked as an auditor for the Washington Industrial Insurance Commission. In 1918 he went to work for John Danz, Seattle theater operator, leaving him in 1922. Then he took over the failing Winter Garden Theatre, selling it in 1927. He claimed to be a graduate of Weston College, specializing in business training. He said he was spending his own money on his campaign; he said he knew that others had spent money on his behalf but claimed to know nothing about it.[45]

Landes continued to go on the offensive against Edwards, sensing that he was close behind her. Her response to his promise to boost industry through tax reductions was that industry was attracted more by low power rates, good schools, and a good moral, social and civic environment. "Any voter, well informed on municipal government principles, will realize that the empty boast of building industrial payrolls as if they were temporary garages is not to be expected," she said in a speech. "Industry is attracted to a city where power is economical, and where social, moral, civic and business affairs are desirable from the standpoint of workers and their families."[46]

She also chided him for his lack of specificity about where the money would come from to cut taxes and pointed out that only the city council—not the mayor—had the power to cut taxes.[47] The day that he spoke to the Swedish Businessmen's Association, telling members the key to industrial development was low taxes, she gained the endorsement of the Women's Commercial Club, one of the first in a long series of endorsements she received.[48]

The third candidate, former mayor Edwin Brown, vowed to stay in the race as a write-in candidate, despite losing the primary. In his view, Seattle under Landes was no longer any fun but a police regime like the one he had cured in 1921 when he was first elected mayor. "Do you know that Seattle has lost the patronage of the workers—that Alaskans, loggers, millmen, fishermen, sailors, miners and even many of the patrons from suburban towns do not come to Seattle to buy and trade now?" he asked "Mr. and Mrs. Voter" in a pamphlet called "What Price Harmony."[49]

He said while such people needed to be assured that "blind pigs, gambling dens and vice will not be tolerated," they should be promised "that there will be no unjust infringement upon the enjoyment of life and liberty, or the invasion and violation of the privacy of their homes." Furthermore, if Seattle was to become a "world city," it should "stop its child play, leave off its baby and juvenile clothing, and dress up in adult garb," a reference to Landes's "womanish" efforts.[50]

When he entered the campaign, he said he would "restore Seattle's confidence, patronage, prestige and business, [and] push forward the public enterprises that have been neglected for the past two years." He also vowed to see that "the Seattle Police Department functions with the other law enforcement agencies in the apprehension of murderers, robbers and other law violators."[51]

Brown criticized Landes for failing to stimulate Seattle's economy sufficiently, claiming that during 1927 there had actually been decreases in building permits and exports and imports, as well as an increase in downtown business closures. However, Brown did not offer complicated economic reasons for the downturn, saying simplistically that miners, loggers, Alaskans, and sailors no longer felt welcome in Seattle and did not come there for their "recreation" anymore. He also said Seattle was "losing ground because of a lack of aggressive executive leadership since June, 1926." He used the masculine adjective "aggressive" repeatedly and claimed to be a law-and-order candidate.[52]

Landes's response to charges about a downturn in building was that in February alone the city's building permits exceeded the combined value of those in Portland and San Francisco. She said that although the number of permits appeared to decline in 1927, actual construction increased, based on an unusually large number of permits awarded in 1926.[53] She did not respond directly to the "recreation" issue that Brown raised.

Meanwhile, candidate Edwards continued to stress his business background and its importance to the city, which had the effect of highlighting his gender as well, since women generally were excluded from the management of business and industry. "My object is action," he said early in the campaign.[54] More than one newspaper questioned the validity of his claims to have a business background, given the lack of details about his life before the campaign. His reputation had been built over the course of only a few weeks, "like a house of cards, and no one can say that it is any more substantial, for no one knows," the *Seattle Times* editorialized.[55]

Edwards's strategy in the campaign was simple but effective. He refused to discuss the issues, instead holding to safe platitudes such as "lower taxes" and "more business." He refused to debate Landes or to respond to her programs or remarks, pointed to her gender and class status directly and indirectly, and spent comparatively huge sums in blanket advertising focusing on his "family man" and "business man" image. He also campaigned for nine months, an unprecedented length of time in Seattle city politics, while she continued to manage Seattle and campaigned vigorously only during the last few months.

Landes, no political neophyte, did what she could to capitalize on his no-show status, his evasion, and his attempt to make gender an issue in the election. She demanded that he come out from behind his cloak of mystery to reveal who he was and who was backing his campaign financially. Landes said that Edwards was "known only through his high-powered paid publicist . . . [he has purchased] acres of billboards, column upon column of newspaper space, hours of radio time, [and] paid hundreds of people, who up to that time never heard of him."[56] She noted he had accused her of mudslinging. "There is a difference between mud-slinging and fact-finding and it is the latter in which I am interested."[57]

In an editorial, the *Seattle Star* questioned who would really be mayor if Edwards won and listed a number of his boosters. They included several police officers who had not fared as well under Landes as they had under Brown, and a number of former and current city employees and old "pols" who the paper said would be pulling Edwards's strings. They hailed primarily from the south and west sides of the city. The list included George Reynolds, a former candidate for sheriff and supposedly expert collector of campaign funds, eight men who at one time or another had been part of the police department, and four police administrators—including Capt. Joe Mason—who the paper said had left soft downtown offices for stations in the "sticks" under Landes. The newspaper concluded that Edwards's campaign had deceived those citizens who supported him.[58]

Landes left an intriguing fragmentary message related to the campaign in her papers. A March 3, 1928, memo to her described a visit to her office from someone named Susan Clark. Clark had picked up her party line phone while it was ringing at 1:40 A.M. the night after the primary election. She overheard the name

"Edwards" and then heard someone say, "I have just taken Edwards home and put him to bed. He feels pretty cocky." She said she overheard the other man on the line respond, "We'll take that out of him. Don't let him go downtown, or out of your sight. If he doesn't mind, turn him over to me." Clark said the name sounded like Shurburne or Shirley. What Landes or others made of Clark's information remained a mystery, but clearly Landes and the *Star* were not the only ones who felt that outside forces controlled Edwards's candidacy.

Edwards, meanwhile, told the press he planned no mass rallies, preferring instead to campaign hand-to-hand with industrial workers.[59] He promoted development of an industrial foundation fund that would solicit private contributions to support industry. He professed support of city-owned utilities and denied that any power trust was backing him. His campaign slogan was "Elect Frank Edwards, the Man You'll Be Proud to Call Mayor."[60] The slogan itself carried overtones of sexism and shame.

Landes used a certain campaign theatricality to challenge his lack of responsiveness and refusal to debate her. This was the point at which she began calling her opponent Mr. Blank, and addressed her remarks at speeches to an empty chair on the speaker's platforms.[61] She continued to challenge him to debate her on the issues, herself trying to blunt the issue of gender and transform it into something positive for her campaign.

"What is he afraid of? Can it be true that a man is afraid of a woman?" she asked rhetorically. "If we need a man for mayor of Seattle, why is it that the man nominated for this office is afraid to debate with me at the Metropolitan Theatre tomorrow at noon?"[62] She used the issue of gender roles to challenge his manhood, in a sense, in an effort to turn her gender into a weapon instead of a deficiency.

She added that voters should know who was financing all his advertising publicity and organization expenses. "What is the sum total of this fund that brought him from an almost unknown citizen to the nomination for mayor? . . . Does it ($20,000, $30,000, $50,000) represent some special interest? What are his qualifications?"[63] She alluded to the presence of a power trust backing him to discredit public ownership of utilities.[64] City Light Superintendent Ross, among others, firmly believed there was a widespread conspiracy by private power interests to destroy him and municipal ownership.[65]

"Petticoat" Politics

Edwards, finally forced into explaining why he refused to debate Landes, had this response: "Any married man knows better than that."[66] In those seven words he had managed again to point to her gender, to the power relationships her gender implied, and to trivialize her complaints. He dismissed her, with a smirk. He then reiterated his campaign goals: to foster public utilities, prevent a summer water shortage, put a firm hand on the police department, and give the street railway system proper supervision. He added himself to Landes's opponents who felt Seattle was not represented well nationally and internationally with a woman as mayor.[67] Petticoat rule was unacceptable.

The petticoat rule metaphor appeared many times regarding Landes, either to discredit her or the narrow-sightedness of her opponents. It is a venerable metaphor for rule of men by women, taking as its root image a unique item of feminine apparel. Long after the garment itself had gone out of use, the metaphor remained, as Landes once pointed out in an interview after she was elected mayor. "When my opponent made remarks about petticoat rule during the recent campaign, I was tempted to say in public that women don't wear them any more. . . . But then I felt that wouldn't be—wouldn't quite—oh, you know."[68] In another interview, she commented that "petticoat government" turned out to be "without the hysterical feminine frills that were feared. Now the citizens gallantly admit that a man-size job may be woman-size as well," she added, trying to remove gender from the idea.[69]

A woman's petticoat, an underskirt often decorated with lace, in the nineteenth and twentieth centuries came to represent anything feminine, long after women generally stopped wearing the undergarment. To deconstruct the phrase "petticoat rule," one has to recognize that the petticoat, as a private piece of attire seldom seen anywhere outside the privacy of the bedroom, is a term with sexual overtones. To refer to a woman's petticoat represented an invasion of privacy, leaving a vague sense of embarrassment, as the preceding quotation from Landes demonstrated.

The petticoat was designed to increase the volume of the skirt, further hiding the legs of a woman and objectifying her as something distinct from men. The layered petticoats also hampered free movement, imposing a psychological and physiological behavior code that distinguished women, especially upper-class women, from others. The petticoat was emblematic of the gendered differences in clothing. Petticoats represented one level of power and differentiation; "wearing the pants" represented quite another level. The differentiation itself could have been accomplished by using skirt as a metaphor, but the use of the private woman's garment "petticoat" became the dominant metaphor and afforded an easy target to satirize.

In the South, women supposedly would pick up and swish their crinoline petticoats and skirts as a gesture of disdain or defiance toward men, which adds another dimension to "petticoat rule." Such women were at that moment not under control.[70] With their hoopskirts, they also represented an elite class of women condescending to comment, in that gesture, on behavior beneath their codes of what was acceptable in male behavior. Gendered metaphors such as "petticoat rule" are common in political discourse as a means of signifying seemingly legitimate and natural hierarchies of power, and challenges to that hierarchy.[71]

The term "petticoat rule" has a long history. Its verbal symbolism held throughout the nineteenth and twentieth centuries, and the phrase came up frequently in reference to Landes. So did the imagery of Seattle as a "he-man" town that supposedly balked under "petticoat rule." The *Oxford English Dictionary* dates the term "petticoat government" from 1702. It is defined as "(undue) rule or predominance of women in the home or in politics. So petticoat-governed, adjective, [is] ruled by a woman, hen-pecked."[72] "Petticoat," used as a synonym for a woman, or something "executed, performed, wielded by a woman," or "to be a woman, to behave as befits a woman," was also "applied humorously or contemptuously to the skirts of a scholar's or clergyman's gown."[73]

In 1896, the year after Landes came to Seattle, *Godey's Magazine* of guidance for women outlined the proper behavior codes by warning women: "Men declare that the petticoatless female has unsexed herself and left her modesty behind."[74] Petticoat rule was a powerful image to use against Landes and other female politicians, in more than one connotation. Such women, those who had rejected the gender definitions connected to petticoats, had "unsexed" themselves, left proper modesty behind, made themselves something to be treated humorously or contemptuously, and, by their behavior, threatened the natural hierarchy of power by governing, influencing, or controlling men. In challenging her challenger, Landes committed all these sins.

Landes's Campaign

The Landes-Edwards campaign was distilled in two mock newspapers printed and distributed by the two candidates. Landes's campaign newspaper pulled no punches about Edwards, calling him a movie prince who had a distorted view of reality.[75] "So far in life he has been an understudy, an employe accustomed to taking orders from some one higher up. The name 'Frank Edwards' has never appeared over the door of a factory or a business house in Seattle or elsewhere; in theatrical parlance he has always been the 'supernumerary.' "

Landes's newspaper included statements from a variety of businessmen and politicians who praised her leadership of Seattle and her business acumen. The paper also noted the favorable attention and fame in newspapers and magazines she and Seattle had received since her election and focused on the stability and honesty of her administration. It quoted praise for her and her administration of Seattle in newspapers from the *Los Angeles Examiner* to the *Chicago News* to the *New York Times*.

It also addressed the concept of "petticoat rule," under "Man and the Mayoralty:"

> Why so much emphasis on the statement, a Man for Mayor? Aren't half the citizens women? Is the age-old prejudice against the sex—which classed them with Indians and Idiots—to sway the voters who have only to select the Best Equipped Candidate to perform service?
>
> Look back twenty-five years over the Man-Mayors—mostly Man-Made Mayors, too! Candidly how do their administrations compare in real public service and community progress with these first two years of Mrs. Landes?

Her campaign newspaper also recounted her responsibility for the development of city utilities and the resultant savings on users' light and power bills. It described the threat to municipal utilities from "nationally allied, super-power corporations, seeking with a million dollar publicity fund annually, in self-interest to discredit Municipal Ownership in their field of profit-taking."

Landes's campaign materials complained about Edwards's extensive use of the radio and "clever writers," while he refused to discuss the issues in person. They also questioned his claims to special business qualifications for mayor, noting that he earned $140 a month for several years checking industrial payrolls for the State Industrial Commission. They also claimed that Edwards's work as a bookkeeper for theater owner John Danz hardly qualified him to administer a $100 million utility investment or manage a city of 400,000 people.[76]

A long list of citations of support included the names of three hundred Seattle businessmen. It also included an important statement of labor support from David Levine, president of the Seattle Central Labor Council. He said Landes should be re-elected "because she has been foremost in promoting harmony between the various industrial groups of Seattle, and has given each a square deal."[77]

Her campaign slogans were "Don't Rock the Boat," "Re-elect Landes, an Honest Capable Common Sense Mayor," and "Keep a Safe 'Skipper' at the Helm."[78] They contrasted sharply with Edwards's slogan, "The Man You Would Be Proud to Call Mayor."

Landes no longer classified herself as "the woman's candidate" and made no special appeal for the woman's vote. Nor did she draw herself as the exceptional domestic heroine out to finish her municipal housekeeping. Her use of gender in these materials was simply to counter existing negative images, in contrast to her past campaigns, where she capitalized on gender and woman's exceptionality. Her materials in this campaign generally focused less on the social and moral issues and instead followed Edwards's lead in addressing business and utility conditions and economic development, citing her accomplishments in those areas. She fell into a defensive pattern of describing city progress as financial development and administration and left behind the broader issues of social, environmental, reform and other civic causes.

Landes had the declared support of the three major dailies in Seattle, of the Central Labor Council, and of the Seattle Building Trades Council and Teaming Trades in Joint Council. Levine, the president of the Labor Council, also said that she represented all citizens of Seattle "in a fair and impartial manner" and that she had "always given Labor very fair consideration," and the city "a fair and harmonious administration."[79] In fact, both the president and the secretary of the Central Labor Council spoke on the radio and made speeches on her behalf. She was also supported by the influential Seattle Municipal League, which studied and reported to the voters on each candidate for office. "The Committee found that Mrs. Landes had a keen insight into civic affairs and believes that she has made a very capable and dignified Mayor . . . well qualified for the office she seeks."[80]

Edwards's Campaign

Her opponent, Frank Edwards, had no such endorsements. He tried to turn that into an asset for his campaign. In his own campaign newspaper, he attacked Landes's administration and the newspapers, which were unified in their endorsement of her. He turned the unity into a conspiracy against him to protect privilege and position. "I take this method of introduction to the voters of Seattle owing to the fact that the newspapers—with the exception of their advertising columns—are closed to any one who would endanger the group special interests and privilege seekers."[81]

Edwards's own newspaper was distributed through the mails throughout Seattle in the final few days of the campaign, without enough time for Landes to respond. In it Edwards talked about his own business plans for the office and his ability to deal with figures. He was careful not to attack Landes as a woman directly but did so indirectly over and over. He also attacked her on a class basis. And he lashed back at Landes for her challenges to appear at forums with her. Under "A Message for Her Honor, the Mayor" on page 1, he wrote: "You assume that the office of Mayor of Seattle was created especially for you and you for the office; maybe it was and maybe you are the only one who can fill it. You have invited me to appear with you on theatre stages to answer the question[s] that are encased in your pent up bosom. . . . It is manifestly hard for any man to make debate with a hostile or infuriated woman."[82] The use of gendered reductions such as "pent up bosom," and "hostile or infuriated woman" both trivialized and objectified her by gender and body parts.

He refuted what she claimed as accomplishments and inflated class differences. He argued that despite her best efforts, Seattle "is one of the most deplorably wet cities on the American continent." He asserted that she did not work harmoniously with city officials, as she claimed, or three of the councilmen would not be running against her. Furthermore, he said, she was wealthy, was not a supporter of municipal ownership, and had not invested her own money in Seattle, as he had. "How much of your own money—for you are admittedly wealthy, with a big salary—have you actually invested in Seattle property?"[83]

He continued to hammer at the class issue, sometimes mixing it with additional denigration of her gender, as in this satire putting words in her mouth under the headline, "The Mayor—and the 'Blank' Candidate," written as an imaginary conversation between Landes and Edwards.[84] "Pardon me please if I occasionally revert to slang phrase but I am getting so used to talking 'down' to people that it is awfully hard to talk 'up,' if you know what I mean," said the article, supposedly quoting Landes. "I hope you'll know what I mean when I use an occasional big word—most voters do not—but I know you'll understand me for you've made a lot of money so I know you must be intelligent," the article said.

"If I had been just an ordinary uneducated person like you, Mr. Blank, the people would surely have called me a grafter like they did my predecessor in office." He made of her a wealthy caricature. "You surely would not accuse a lady, even though she stooped to accept the office of Mayor, of taking money from crooked cardrooms, Chinese gamblers, dance halls, cribs and houses of prostitution, now would you Mr. Blank?" the mayor said in this paper. "My darling Dean brings home enough for his own keep, which added to my $7,500 a year, puts us beyond the need of such pelf."

Elsewhere, in his criticism of her management of the police, Edwards continued these themes. "If you were a man, Mayor Landes, and were aware as you should be, of the awful crime-ridden condition of the City over which you rule, I would get up from the chair you have assigned 'Mr. Blank' and tell you if your [*sic*] were a man—that if you were ignorant of the vice conditions you were worse than a dolt; if you admitted your knowledge—that you were unfit to occupy the chair for which you think you have divine franchise."

He denigrated her ability to manage Seattle's financial affairs and blamed her for the council's budgets. "Seriously, Mayor Landes, could you read and understand the mass of columns handed you for the pruning knife? A knowledge of poetry and rhetoric is fine, but in the management of a $150,000,000 corporation a knowledge of figures, I think, is the more important." He also trivialized her ability to make sound decisions on power projects and sarcastically pointed to her wearing men's apparel in an inspection of a Skagit River dam site. "[The Skagit River power project] is so vast and important that any one person, even a wonderfully intelligent woman official, encased for the visit in kahki [*sic*] breeches, is hardly competent to lay out the development of the big power scheme. Personally, I would get the best professional advice that America can produce before I would hazard an opinion that opposed that of men who had spent years in its study."[85]

Edwards claimed that she had been silent on the city manager idea during this campaign. "Some of your speeches were filled with an almost religious frenzy over this City Manager fetish. . . . but I know that if you are defeated, Mayor Landes, the City Manager Plan will become a very live issue with you—'the people must be protected from the proletariat.' "[86]

He claimed that she charged $25 to take on speaking engagements. He said that even area high schools had paid the charge, even though she supposedly traveled to the engagements in "municipally-owned limousines, with city-paid drivers. . . . Frank Edwards thinks it rather cheapens an executive to ask pay for such kindly recognition."[87]

Brown, in the meantime, despite losing the primary election, vowed that he was still in the race. Soon, however, he threw his support to his old nemesis, Landes, rather than support Edwards. He said he did this out of suspicions about the amount of money from unknown sources spent on Edwards's campaign—and perhaps because of his regard for Landes and her administration, despite their differences. Ultimately, the *Star* pointed out, Landes gained the endorsement of every candidate for mayor who did not survive the 1928 primary, and of every living former mayor. She even gained the endorsement of the conservative United Veterans Clubs, long suspicious about the city manager idea, although individual clubs split on her candidacy.[88]

Edwards had his own explanations for Brown's endorsement of Landes and the endorsements of virtually all other civic groups and the media. He claimed that the reason Brown had thrown his support to Landes was not out of any preference for her as mayor but merely to bolster his own political chances. "He knows Mrs. Landes could never again be re-elected, that her defective administration would thoroughly ruin her chances in another two years." Frank Edwards, however, "would prove such an excellent business-like and capable mayor that Seattle voters would not consider losing him."[89]

Similarly, Edwards assailed the endorsements of Landes by the city's three major newspapers. First of all, he complained that to put the content of his campaign newspaper in their advertising columns, which combined reached between 70 and 75 percent of the voters, would have cost him $8,628—if the press had accepted his ads. By using the mails, he could reach 100 percent of the voters at a fraction of that cost. He sidestepped, again, the issue of his campaign funding. He said the cost of these materials was footed entirely "by friends and associates who know him and esteem him so highly that they are spending their own money in his behalf and in behalf of better government for the City of Seattle."[90]

The reason all three dailies endorsed Landes, he claimed, was so they could control the mayor's office. He was implying again that a woman in such a post could not be an independent, self-directed official. In a box in bold-faced type in his newspaper, he asked, "Who will be mayor if Landes is re-elected? Will it be Ritchie of The *Star*? Will it be King Dykeman of the *P-I*? Will it be Col. Blethen of the *Times*? Will it be Honest Doc Brown? Or, will they fight it out for the spoils?"[91]

In another section, he accused Landes of promising one of the editors that she would appoint his brother-in-law as her chief of police. He also accused her backers of corruption. Supposedly, one of Landes's former workers had offered to work for Edwards, if he would pay. The worker did not ask for cash, Edwards said, but for political favors. "I could not accept favors that are offered with vicious strings tied to them," he wrote. In this way Edwards obliquely attacked a tenet of her administration—that she was not beholden to any group and would not make any political appointments. He said elsewhere in the publication that he "would go in clean and come out clean." Moreover, he said he would remove the "756 political-incurables" presently on city payrolls in her administration.[92]

Elsewhere, he linked the newspapers to wealthy businessmen and corporations. Although he himself ran as a businessman, he also attacked big business. Big business and the media supposedly had put together a "huge slush fund . . . in a desperate attempt to draw the voters of Seattle into a blind alley of misinformation" about Edwards and his supposed lack of support for municipal utilities, which he called ridiculous. Instead of their complaining about the scandalous amount he was spending, they should look to themselves. "We are witnessing the fact of wealthy Seattle men, clubmen, and big stores, digging up a huge slush fund for Mrs. Landes. Frank Edwards has accepted no such support. *Every dollar spent is his own*" (emphasis added).[93]

The fact that his statement about financial support of his campaign contradicted statements found elsewhere in his newspaper hardly mattered. He had made his point. He connected Landes and the newspapers to secret slush funds and to Seattle fatcats, while discrediting their statements of support for Landes and city-owned utilities.

Edwards also took from the three newspapers endorsing Landes a montage of crime-related headlines from March 6, 1928—only one week before the election—and reprinted them. They reportedly had all appeared in that one day's issue, a day after a drunken driver caused a spectacular fatal accident. The display was designed to discredit Landes's claim that law enforcement conditions had improved in Seattle under her administration. He said that these crimes were going on and that police were in "intern[e]cine warfare, while you are filling theatres and radio plants with eloquence." He added that there were "many more police records I assume are being covered up, while you are campaigning in genteel elegance."[94]

He picked the day after two school girls had been struck by a car as they stood on a street corner, so there was plenty of material for the headline montage. The headline montage appeared under its own headline, "Just One Day's Crime Record! Mayor Landes has ample Evidence That Seattle—'The Seaport of Success'—is Not a Pink Tea Village."[95] The references to "pink tea" were again designed to discredit her on the basis of gender as much as whether Seattle's crime rates had actually gone up or down.

He hinted that Seattle was a laughingstock as a result of having its aberrant mayor, implying that those who endorsed Landes were somehow connected to the inflated $15 million street railway system contract signed a decade earlier. The endorsements she received were satirized:

> It is to laugh! The Times, The Star, The Post-Intelligencer, and Good Old Honest "Doc" are all on the side of Righteousness. . . . I have not seen the three coupled together heretofore since the

> $15,000,000 street car deal. This time The Star has the main part of the kite for it discovered first that Mayor Landes was a woman paragon, or something like that, and then the Times, recognizing the infallible judgment of the Star's "furrin' " owners, picked up the kite's tail.[96]

This unlikely group supposedly found that they needed Brown to get their kite into the air. "And Mayor Landes, looking on at the innocent pastime, could only say, 'Ye Gods; Shakespeare was right, city politics do make Strange bedfellows!' Only said in an educated way." And finally, Brown supposedly replies, "I am always willing to help poor little girls fly their kites free but I betcha I won't help any Big Boys fly theirs unless they pay me lots of money, ten thousand dollars, you betcha."[97] The passage supposedly came from something called the "Seattle Daily Wireless." In it, Edwards turned the words "educated" and "little girl" into pejoratives.

Edwards also heaped satire and scorn on Landes's other endorsements. If Brown was a somewhat surprising member of the Landes camp, so was another—Edwards's former boss, John Danz, who also gave Landes his endorsement. He had even sent out a postal card attacking Edwards and supporting Landes. Edwards explained that problem away by discrediting Danz as a theater owner who was always "notoriously unfair to, and a bitter enemy of organized labor, [who] has joined the political camp of Mayor Bertha K. Landes." Edwards, in contrast, said he had "always been friendly to and given union labor a square deal." He said leading members of organized labor who had dealt with Edwards "as a business man . . . had issued a warning to all union labor and union labor sympathizers to beware of John Danz's 'unfair' propaganda."[98]

As for labor's endorsement of Landes's candidacy, Edwards said that although official channels might endorse her, the rank and file membership did not. He cited William Molyneux, business representative of the Amalgamated Association of Street and Electric Railway Employees, as denouncing "as false and misleading the statements in the public press claiming that organized labor stood solidly behind Mayor Bertha K. Landes." Instead, it was the "arbitrary action of a willful few."[99]

In addition, Edwards made extravagant, impossible-to-keep political promises. He vowed not to reduce wages of any city employees and find jobs for all jobless citizens. Work in this country "must be provided for every man or woman who will accept it. . . . When there are thousands of idle men on the 'skid-road' there's something the matter with the system."[100]

Although Edwards had raised the gender issue throughout his publication, he claimed that he had not. "Mayor Landes, during my whole campaign I have not raised the sex question; I realize that you were directed—a clean, fine woman,—to mop up a most deplorably dirty mess, wished on Seattle by an executive who had none of your finer sensibilities." He said that "some little part of the mess" had been cleaned up by her, but "the great part—the real stench still remains, that part that you are cognizant of and for which cleansing you are asking the people of Seattle to retain you in office." But she had made hardly "a dent in the vice armor" in six years. "Mayor Landes, you have not been kept informed of the awful conditions in the underworld; a good woman may not enter these dens of iniquity; many good women hold their noses and look away from the cesspools."[101]

Edwards's campaign messages continually pointed to and sneered at her gender, both in how descriptions were constructed and in their comments on various aspects of her administration. However, the coup de grace, if there was one, came in yet another last-minute publication full of additional attacks on her class. This time the copy also attacked her husband. It came in a small, four-page brochure titled "Facts—A Newspaper of Plain Truths—Clean House Now," distributed citywide only the day before the election.

On its front page was a forceful picture of Edwards shaking his fist at his off-camera foes. Next to it was a statement that he had received no money or other consideration from Puget Sound Power and Light, or any other public service corporation. Underneath that was a statement that he was "not now, and have never been, a member of the Ku Klux Klan. I have not sought nor desired the endorsement of that organization."[102] Apparently someone had connected him to the KKK during his campaign. The wording may also have been an attempt to imply that he was not in the pocket of the company or the Klan but that Landes was, although that was not very likely. In fact, the Klan had played an ugly role in the 1924 elections in Seattle and Washington, heightening fears and spreading hatred of Catholics, Jews, immigrants, and blacks.[103]

On page 2 he claimed a "big majority" of the street car men

union supported him, as did members of the carpenters union, the motion picture operators union, and the musicians union. He again denied that he was an "unknown adventurer." In a box, in boldfaced type, was an attack on Landes and her husband:

> For years Dean Henry Landes has been on the public payroll. His salary is $5,200 a year.
>
> Mayor Bertha K. Landes, his wife, served four years on the city council at $3,000 a year, and has now served two years as mayor at $7,500 a year.
>
> The combined salaries [are] . . . now $12,700 a year, or $1,058 per month, from the public funds, more than some families that pay taxes have to live on in a year. Every two months their combined salaries, paid by the taxpayers, amounts to $2,116, or more money than a very large percentage of the taxpayers of Seattle are able to earn to support and educate large families.

Furthermore, when she was a member of the city council, "her husband was drawing a salary from the public treasury and at the same time he was employed as an expert witness by the Chicago, Milwaukee & St. Paul Railroad." He was paid $50 a day, Edwards said, to testify in the railroad's suit against the city, litigation that cost the city of Seattle nearly $200,000.[104]

In fact, Henry Landes did have a longstanding consulting geology firm, in partnership with S. L. Glover, at 375 Colman Building in Seattle.[105] It was Landes and another UW geologist who told power magnate Ross and city officials that to construct a Cedar River masonry dam over glacial bedrock that tilted to Snoqualmie Falls would result in seepage. Unfortunately, advocates pushed ahead with the costly project, and Landes was proved right. It did not hold water.[106]

Edwards drove the point home about Henry Landes and his consulting. "The public was then treated to a spectacle of a wife publicly employed to save the city money while her husband, also publicly employed, was trying to gouge the public's bank roll."[107] He continued, "When the voters go to the polls next Tuesday let them remember that Dean and Bertha Landes are getting rich at the public expense. What is the public getting?"[108]

He again attacked her gender and lack of business experience. "Where did she get the experience and training to qualify as an expert executive of a $40,000,000 corporation? What business did she ever build up from bankruptcy to success?" He also focused on her lack of outside employment, the very lack that made her middle-class nature acceptable to voters when she first entered politics. "What money did she ever *earn* except that paid by the taxpayers of Seattle? If she leaves the mayor's office can she step into another job and *earn* $7,500 a year?"[109]

The back of the fact sheet contained a picture of the candidate Edwards with his wife and three children. The copy with the photo described him as "a happy and contented husband and father," and a member of the Episcopal church. "He is a lover of the outdoors, [and] takes keen delight in long hikes through the woods. He is an enthusiastic supporter of athletic sports, football, baseball and golf."[110] Again, it offered a sharp contrast, emphasizing Edwards's family and participation in masculine activities, while Landes's campaign materials mentioned nothing of her hobbies (which would have seemed frivolous) and pictured the candidate only at work or in official duties.

The fact sheet closed with a reprint of the *Star's* February 29 editorial criticizing the size of Seattle's combined city, county, school, and state tax rates and comparing those taxes with those of other cities. Also included in the publication were specific instructions to the voter on what to do. "Pull Down Trigger 4-A" in order to elect Edwards, it said.

Meanwhile, Landes and others continued to try to force him into appearances before the voters. At one point they attacked him for sending in a substitute for a radio broadcast without informing listeners that it was not Edwards who was speaking. He later said that he had developed laryngitis and could not finish the appearance.[111] The Saturday before the election he finally agreed to appear with Landes as a speaker but again claimed to have come down with laryngitis, refusing to appear at the last minute.[112]

Edwards had dozens of billboards, hundreds of precinct workers, and thousands of handbills circulating throughout the city, as well as the movie footage showing in many theaters. Suspicions and questions about his funding snowballed as the campaign came to a close. The *Seattle Times* in particular aggressively pursued the issue of where Edwards's money came from and the fact that his campaign finance reports first were slow, then were incomplete. There were hints from the prosecuting attorney's office that, if he won the election, his victory could be challenged on financial grounds.

In the last days of the campaign, the *Times* began an unprecedented series of page 1 editorials promoting Landes, arguing that the only reason she might lose would be her gender, and that would be unfair. On Monday, March 5, 1928, under the headline "Seattle Knows Mrs. Landes; Why Try an Unknown Man?" the editorial stated that "the only issue to be determined is whether Seattle shall have a woman or a man for mayor." It added that her administration had been tested and found trustworthy and competent, with a "well-charted course," while there was "no least shred of proof that Mr. Edwards is qualified to be mayor of Seattle." It concluded that Seattle should not give up "a meritorious administration, known, proved, progressive and satisfactory, to take a chance in the dark with the unknown and unproved. . . . Seattle should know when it is well off. Mayor Landes should be reelected."[113]

Again, the next day: "Not even the political strikers and payroll supporters of Mr. Edwards can say anything more than she is a woman." That her administration had been "clean, constructive, capable and altogether admirable is nowhere disputed." She deserved reelection. "Her defeat at this time is urged solely on the grounds that here is an unknown man with plenty of money who is personally eager to take her place."[114] Similar editorials appeared every day during the remainder of the week. Toward the end of the week, the newspaper called upon Landes's old allies—the women of Seattle—to make sure she won.

In the meantime, Seattle's women's clubs, with the support of the *Times* news columns, as of January had turned their collective efforts to a drive for new voter registration. Week after week before and after the primary, the campaign results of individual clubs were tallied in the newspaper, indicating progress toward a goal of 100 percent registration of qualified voters, all in the name of democracy. Even with the drive, voters registered totaled only about 100,000 out of a city population of almost 400,000. The Seattle club efforts along these lines reflected a national pattern, a shift in women's activism from direct political action to voter education.

The *Times* put the Landes-Edwards election in the context of women's participation in politics. "The one issue in this campaign that stands foremost in all discussions is the very simple issue of a woman against a man," said the newspaper two days before the election, again on the front page. "Every vote that might be cast against Mrs. Landes next Tuesday would be derogatory to all the claims that women have made with respect to the desirability, propriety and happy influence of their participation in public affairs," it said. "The defeat of Mrs. Landes, for no other or better reason than that some man wants her place, should be viewed by every public-spirited citizen as a calamitous affront to womankind that must be averted."[115]

The *Times*, which was looking for a weapon to use against Edwards, made gender a kind of weapon, as did other newspapers. The more sensational *Star* ran its own series of editorials in her support, also revolving around gender. "If you believe in sex equity then sex should have nothing to do with your vote at the election," it said. "And if you don't, then a vote for Mrs. Landes will be a courteous gesture to womanhood." It threw in a dose of motherhood, too. "If a woman was good enough to be your mother, surely a woman is good enough to be mayor of Seattle."[116] In another editorial, the paper also provided some criticism of her administration. It called her sometimes not forceful enough and too hesitant, perhaps inclined to shift responsibility to the people too much, but said she had given the city two years of harmony and honesty and deserved reelection.[117]

Finally, the day before the election, the *Times* campaign reached its zenith. In an effort to get women out to vote, the *Times* ran a banner across the top of page 1 that proclaimed, "The Women Will Decide Tomorrow's Election."[118] Whatever happened with Landes's candidacy would be blamed on the women. The *Times*, along with most analysts then and in the decades after, put the election in simple male-female terms. Most analysts completely ignored the issue of class, which Edwards had used so effectively against her. As it turned out, there was no woman's bloc voting in the mayoral election in Seattle in 1928, as nationally there was no woman's bloc deciding other issues on gender alone.

Just as there was a formal system of political power in Seattle with its own authority codes, there was an informal system of power. It was a network into which Edwards apparently tapped. It provided him support, funding, campaign help, and a strategy. It built his candidacy and helped manipulate the voters through a negative campaign. Landes blamed the power trust; there were other economic forces in Seattle that stood to benefit from Edwards's election (or Landes's defeat) as well.

Landes's strengths in 1926 included being the right kind of middle-class woman to rise through the ranks of Seattle's thousands of clubwomen to become their favored candidate. She carried forward feminism, enacting a reform agenda through social programs and government intervention, and backing the enforcement of prohibition laws. These strengths became deficiencies to her candidacy in 1928, the year millionaire engineer Herbert Hoover gained the presidency on a "New Day" campaign by a landslide, and Amelia Earhart crossed the Pacific.

Landes had played her role well, however. She entered office as a kind of freak, arousing concern, adulation, and ridicule for the mere fact that she was female. By the end of her term, many parts of her agenda had been accomplished, and she had put her imprint on Seattle. She went from freak to favored candidate. She won over the usual power brokers to her side, in the media, in business and industry, and in labor, perhaps as much for her programs and vision of Seattle and her ability to get cooperation out of diverse city elements as for her own abilities and competence. Forces that frequently clashed, such as organized labor and business, were able to agree and coalesce behind her, particularly in the face of her opponent and his secret supporters.

Right or wrong, her support and her background linked her to a powerful elite in the eyes of many voters. Despite her unique status, she had become an insider, a career politician, at a time when voters were perhaps looking for outsiders. This perception was heightened by two visionary aspects of Edwards's campaign, the deployment of two techniques that became ever more important in twentieth-century politics: a successful media image campaign, and a last-minute, negative ad campaign with insufficient time for the victim to respond.

For an underdog candidate like Frank Edwards, the strategy was brilliant.

VI

"ADVENTURES IN MUNICIPAL HOUSEKEEPING"

A record proportion of Seattle's men and women made it to the polls on Tuesday, March 13, 1928, to decide the fate of Bertha Knight Landes and Frank Edwards, opposing candidates for mayor of Seattle. A remarkable 88 percent of the registered voters picked their preference on their ballots. The voters' preference was clearly challenger Frank Edwards. He pulled in 58,873 votes to Landes's 39,819—a difference of some 19,000 votes and a new record. The election was not even close.

The Landes era in Seattle city politics was at an end. She went on to other interests. Edwards went on to take over what had been her office, only to lose it himself to a disgruntled electorate in a recall election a few years later. However, Landes and her legacy, largely unrecognized at the time, continued to affect city administration, city politics, the status of women in politics in the region, popular images of activist women, and the development of Seattle, for years to come. Through her speaking tours, she became a symbol both of what exemplary women could do in public office and what they could not do in changing fundamental constructions of gender and power.

Landes's Loss and Questions About Edwards

When she lost in 1928, women got the credit for her defeat just as they got the credit for her election two years earlier, both of which were considerable exaggerations. Nor was her defeat only about women in politics; other issues related to class, economics, and her administrative policies. Nevertheless, the Times, in a front-page editorial the day after the election, bitterly blamed her loss on the women of Seattle. It said women failed to come to her aid in the election, thereby forfeiting their claims to either political equity or participation in government. "Seattle has shelved all claims of women to higher places in local government; and this shelving, it must be remembered, has been done by the women themselves."[1]

For years afterward, stories circulated that Edwards, in addition to his extensive campaign materials and expensive media advertising, had hired fifty people to do nothing more than spread "have-you-heard" rumors about Landes. Her daughter Viola referred to the rumors in an interview. "You can't *believe* some of the things that were said about my mother. . . . None of them were true."[2]

True or not, whatever was said or believed about Landes counted more than the many rumors that had been circulating about Edwards as a result of his secretiveness. While Landes credited the "power trust" for his campaign funding, others claimed his funding came from criminal elements in the city that would profit from Seattle's returning to more lax law enforcement than had existed before it had been under Landes. Questions about his funding continued to surface long after the election. His initial campaign report showed total expenditures of $12,477, an amount former mayor Edwin Brown, for one, said could reflect only one-fifth of the total amount spent on his campaign.[3] Even at $12,477—soon amended to $15,300—the total was an astronomical sum to be spent on a mayoral campaign, almost double the record sum Landes had spent in 1926. The prosecuting attorney threatened a probe of Edwards's funding, finding it odd that Edwards knew nothing about the hundreds of paid precinct workers who supported his campaign, or who was paying for his dozens of billboards.[4]

The sworn itemized statement Edwards signed contained a phrase requiring the candidate to set forth "each sum of money and thing of value, or any consideration whatever, contributed, paid or promised by him, *or any one for him,* with his knowledge or acquiescence, for the purpose of securing or influencing in any way, affecting his nomination or election to said office" (emphasis added).[5] But by law only the losing candidate could challenge the election, and Landes, for whatever reasons, declined to pursue it. The issue of who financed his campaign faded, but it was not forgotten. It remained a sore spot and a source of criticism during his two terms in office and resurfaced with vehemence during the election to remove him from the office he wrested from Landes.

Edwards's final 1928 campaign report accounted for spending of $27,800, compared to Landes's total less than half that amount—$12,853. He had spent almost half his money—$12,477—in the few weeks between the primary and the general elections, with printing being the largest single expenditure.[6] Numerous irregularities remained. Throughout the closing weeks of the campaign, there were news reports about Edwards's not knowing who donated his motion picture advertising, about supposed donors of his billboards being surprised to find they were listed as donors, and about his continuing claim of ignorance of any outside support. He said in his final report that he had been told there was some donations of motion picture advertising, precinct workers, and billboard space, but he did not know by whom or how much they invested.

Many continued to be perplexed about how Landes could have lost the election, especially to an opponent like Frank Edwards. The discussion at the time centered on two issues—his money and her gender. Landes herself said she was defeated for three reasons: his nine-month-long campaign, his "excessive expenditures," and "sex prejudice," combined in a well-organized political machine.[7]

Whether or not private power interests had helped fund Edwards's campaign was never resolved. However, political scientist Florence Deacon analyzed Landes's defeat and found company fingers fiddling in the campaign. She found that the private utility Puget Sound Power and Light Company had authorized expenditures of up to $160,000 in 1927 to publicize the deficiencies of the Seattle municipal power plant. The money was given to the supposedly nonpartisan Voter's Information League for an "objective" study. It gave $24,000 to the league's president and, between 1923 and 1928, contributed $30,300 to the independent taxpayers study group.[8] The league's study and report, not surprisingly, did not favor municipal power and Seattle City Light. The report also indirectly favored Edwards.

A writer of the time found that one of the directors of the Voter's Information League was the same man Edwards later appointed to succeed Ross as head of City Light.[9] Furthermore, Edwards, in the middle of his campaign, traveled to Boston to the offices of Stone and Webster which owned Puget Sound Power and Light.[10] The substance of that meeting was secret, but Edwards would hardly have undertaken such a journey across the country if it had not had some significance for his campaign.

A writer for *Harper's Magazine* said in 1930, after Edwards visited Boston, that Puget Sound Power and Light president A. W. Leonard wrote to George Clifford of Stone and Webster. Leonard said that Edwards "was very well pleased with the attention shown him while there." He supposedly added that he hoped Edwards "will feel that he is justified in carrying out some of the suggestions that he has previously made relative to personnel, etc., of the lighting department."[11]

The veiled reference was apparently to the popular power promoter J. D. Ross, whom Edwards fired after promising throughout his campaign to keep him as head of City Light. His promise to keep Ross was used to symbolize his support for city-owned utilities despite suspicions to the contrary.[12] The firing then seemed to constitute proof of Edwards's link with private utility firms and "the interests," particularly distasteful to the electorate at a time when breadlines were growing every day. Talk of the "power trust" emerged again, coming from Ross and others, although only a year before he was fired Ross in a letter had praised Edwards for cooperating with City Light.[13]

Edwards fired Ross on March 9, 1931, after a series of conflicts with the single-minded and sometimes obstinate builder and promoter of City Light. Edwards supposedly fired Ross after being taunted by some businessmen that he was less popular with the people than was Ross, although the situation was more complicated than that. Ross had set a course that forced a collision—through purchase or condemnation, he planned to take over Puget Sound Power and Light. He also sought increased power for his office to make engineering decisions.

Ross was fired only a day before a vote on an issue that would have strengthened public power. Edwards took this ill-advised action at a time when Seattle's electric rates were still one-half the national average, due in large measure, many believed, to the competition Ross gave private utilities. Decreasing demand for power because of the Depression had spurred Ross to seek customers outside the city. Through a petition drive, he and City Light backers had forced a vote on a charter amendment giving more engineering authority to Ross's office, to the consternation of Edwards and some council members who earlier refused his request.

The same day Edwards fired Ross, the Star editorialized that Edwards by this action had classified himself "as a one-night stand politician."[14] Ross supporters soon filed petitions to recall Edwards, and the impeachment charges included his refusal to enforce the laws against prostitution, gambling, liquor, and narcotics.[15] In 1931 a new group called the Citizens's Municipal Utilities Protective League led the drive to his impeachment. However, the recall vote was framed even as far away as New York as a referendum on municipal ownership versus the "power trust."[16]

Edwards called the signers of the recall petition Communists out to destroy government and its institutions. Marion Zioncheck, who in 1932 was elected to Congress, spearheaded the recall drive, which ended in a July 13, 1931, vote of 35,659 to 21,839 in favor of throwing Edwards out of office.[17] The first official act of Robert Harlin, the city council president and thus acting mayor after Edwards was recalled, was to rehire Ross. His second act was to request the resignation of every other city department head under Edwards.[18] The mayor's political star had risen—and fallen—very quickly.

Edwards's candidacy against Landes may have begun with the Civil Service League. One researcher, writing in 1928, concluded on the basis of interviews that the city employees' Civil Service League leadership was irritated by Landes and her get-tough attitude toward some groups of city employees. They supposedly induced Edwards to run and helped him plan his campaign four months before he announced. The league counted four thousand municipal employees on its membership rolls. However, it had been denied the protection of membership in the Central Labor Council, the city's coalition of trade unions.

The researcher, using anonymous sources, found not only that league leaders worked for Edwards but also that city firemen and policemen campaigned for him while on duty. This was partly the result of Landes's method of encouraging layoffs on the basis of efficiency and seniority, rather than just seniority.[19] Municipal employees supposedly found Landes too vacillating, too willing to follow the council, and too evasive when they went to her asking for salary increases.[20] She had made note in her 1928 mayoral message that Seattle's trainmen were paid higher wages than any in the country except perhaps for three U.S. cities,[21] and she resisted any proposed salary increases for them, given the system's failing financial situation.

Perhaps another factor in Landes's defeat was Seattle's persistent pattern of one-term mayors, although some mayors were out of office a few years and then reelected. In the forty–four years between 1885 and 1928, only four people served as Seattle's mayor for more than one two-year term.[22] Outsiders quickly become insiders. Incumbency—usually an election campaign advantage—was apparently not much of an advantage in Seattle city politics. However, newspaper endorsements usually were. A 1924 study of newspaper endorsements found that in the years 1911 to 1923, the voters followed the *Star's* endorsements 84 percent of the time on forty-four candidates, the *Times* endorsements 67 percent of the time on forty-seven recommendations, and the *Post-Intelligencer* on 73 percent of its fifty-two recommendations.[23]

Class, which most analysts have disregarded as a factor in the outcome, was significant in Landes's loss, which happened despite the endorsements of all the usual Seattle power brokers. Political scientist Deacon did a rough analysis of some of the voting patterns in the 1928 election, although its statistical significance and methodology are somewhat suspect. She took the results in 20 important Seattle precincts (out of 295) and performed a random sample analysis of the voters in them, comparing Landes's votes in 1926 and 1928. Her findings disputed the claim that women were to blame for her defeat.

Despite the widespread assertion that women failed to support Landes and turned against her, Deacon found that in 1928, in the five precincts giving her the strongest showing, 56 percent of the registered voters were female. In the five precincts where Landes had the poorest showing, only 34 percent of the registered voters were female. But she did find an erosion of working-class support. Those precincts where Landes had the poorest showing also were more generally "lower class and blue collar, and have more immigrants than the others," with about 25 percent of the registered voters being immigrants.[24] Comparatively, the five precincts where she did best were about 5 percent foreign born and had 53 percent of their registered voters in what Deacon termed the "five highest prestige occupations" and 11.6 percent in the "ten lowest prestige occupations." In precincts where Landes did worst, only 1.3 percent of the registered voters held the highest-prestige occupations and 53 percent held the lowest-prestige occupations.

Another analyst found that Edwards picked up votes in South Seattle and the Georgetown districts as well as in West Seattle, which were predominantly labor and lower-income working classes. The University District again supported Landes, while the upper-class Capitol Hill divided its vote, and the Queen Anne and downtown business districts, with the middle-class and more prosperous workers, generally supported Edwards.[25]

Clearly class played some role in the outcome of the election. Indeed, the very voter registration drive that the women's clubs organized—focused as it was on new immigrants and the politically inactive—might have inadvertently hurt Landes's chances. Presumably much of that registration came from previously unregistered populations in working-class and immigrant neighborhoods, comparatively naive groups of voters, the very groups to which a last-minute class approach and negative campaign like Edwards used would appeal. As new voters exercising their election prerogatives for the first time, they also might have boosted the remarkable 88 percent voter turnout for this municipal election.

Another potential factor was Landes's support among working women. Deacon, in her admittedly limited sample, found that in precincts where Landes prevailed, 40 percent of the female registered voters had jobs outside the home, compared with 20 percent in the low-support precincts.[26] Of newly added registrants voting in 1928 alone, Deacon found that more men voted in the precincts where Landes did worst and more females voted in precincts where she did best. Although it is difficult to pin down the statistical significance of these precincts in the total picture, Deacon concluded that at the least it was not "petty spite of women," as some writers claimed, that took Landes out of office.[27]

Most election analysts at the time completely ignored the issue of class or the possibility that an informal (as opposed to a conspiratorial) network of powerful interests had helped fund her defeat. They attributed her defeat primarily to the fact that she was a woman. A variety of sources cited and reprinted the *Portland Oregonian*'s editorial analyzing her loss as a rejection of petticoat government.

It attributed her defeat, given her abilities and experience compared with those of Edwards, to Seattle's wish "to be known as a he-man's town," which had the misfortune to be governed by a woman. It added that on inauguration day, perhaps a pair of breeches would fly from the city hall flagpole. "[Seattle] wants for its official greeter a man who smells strongly of tobacco smoke and who can exchange the kind of stories that the Order of Howling Bears loves to tell and hear," it said. "[Seattle] wants a mayor's office where one can put one's feet on the desk . . . a mayor whose presence does not call also for letting everyone's wife in to the festivities. . . . Many a bearded cheek in Seattle has blushed in the past two years over this imagined shame upon a he-man's town."[28] Once again, curling smoke invoked masculine political power, and a woman in power was shameful.

Landes's own personality probably also played a role. She had become, despite her gender, a powerful insider used to imposing her will and her ideas of civic betterment on the city and the electorate. She took action on issues that other council members complacently accepted. Many of her achievements were accomplished through increased regulation, and even her friends noted that with her vision came impatience. "She saw problems and the solutions in a large way, but was often impatient of details," said one.[29] The fact that she was saddled with trying to enforce the laws connected with prohibition at a time when the country began questioning prohibition as impossible to enforce exacerbated her reputation, despite her efforts to avoid categorization as a frenzied reformer. In 1926 alone eight states held referenda either modifying or repealing some aspect of prohibition, three states passed them.[30]

Time magazine blamed her loss as a failure of what it termed "the better element" to ensure her reelection. It was this better element, which, once aroused, "lifts politics right out of Politics," the magazine said. Saying that she had as acting mayor "closed the town" when it needed it badly, the magazine complained that the "Better Element" forgot the importance of politics and let her be defeated by Edwards, whom it termed a "retired Seattle showman."[31]

Landes's private secretary, Matthew O'Connor, ever her ardent supporter, credited the petticoat rule line of thinking. "Seattle must have a man for mayor to uphold her dignity and her place among the cities of the country." He also credited the fact that Edwards campaigned the better part of a year and outspent her.[32] The issue of gender was framed as dignity versus shame and ridicule.

Writing for the *Nation,* Julia Budlong echoed his sentiment, referring obliquely to the perceived problems of petticoat rule.

"Seattle is sensitive to its reputation as a he-man city. It did not like to be teased about its mayor." The city was irritated by taunts such as, "The great open spaces [of the West], where men are men and women are mayors," or "What's the matter with you folks out there; haven't you got any men in Seattle that you have to have a woman for mayor?" Budlong added that no one, "not even a city, not even an honorable woman, can stand up against a campaign of ridicule."[33]

Ridicule and trivialization are important weapons in power's arsenal. Landes had stepped out of line—out of a long line of masculine mayors and a tradition of male leadership in politics. This breach of the norms, along with her concerted efforts at reform, made her an anomaly to some voters and a threat or irritation to others, despite her winning endorsements from the usual power brokers. At another level, Landes had come up against an informal network of power that wanted her out of office, probably for economic reasons that were only peripherally related to her gender. The underground political forces that opposed her skillfully used traditional norms about women's behavior (and about men's expected roles) to help defeat her, capitalizing upon both class and gender divisions. It was not the first time Landes and other politically active women faced ridicule and trivialization in the election process, nor would it be the last.

Another factor in her defeat was her stand against traditional machine politics and against the concept of political privilege in favor of untainted professionalism. The *Nation* noted that Landes was unwilling to build any kind of a political machine or make political appointments, thus contributing to her failure to win political office again. Such behavior "built up no political machine for the Mayor with which she could counteract the *sub rosa* campaign waged against her from the start by the old and well-entrenched political ring." This was a serious flaw, despite her endorsements from virtually all civic organizations and the daily newspapers. "That is not political backing, and in American cities today good-housekeeping is not good politics, shameful as it is to admit it."[34]

Edwards's last-minute negative campaign also played a significant part, as one of Landes's supporters noted privately. She credited the campaign materials that Edwards distributed for bringing about Landes's downfall, or at least influencing its magnitude, and for raising the class issues. On behalf of the Women's Christian Temperance Union, Alfa Freeman wrote Landes a letter "of love and appreciation" from the local chapter of the organization. She also criticized voters' judgment in this democratic process. "It is so crushing that the 'rabble' should choose our Mayor for us. Perhaps that is an unkind expression to use and 'unthinking masses' would be better. They are intelligent enough if they would but use their intelligence," she wrote. She lamented that many people do not read newspapers but instead form their opinions on civic matters and public affairs "from the talk they hear about them." She too asserted there were paid rumormongers. "To crowds of such, paid workers went in and out among them with their misleading information." The crux of the effort, in her view, was the final four-page "fact-sheet" Edwards distributed the day before the vote: "The four-page letter that was delivered at every house the day before the election did a big work. It influenced those who never think for themselves. The pleasing picture of the family group and matters so plausibly put won them," she wrote. "If we had sent out a companion sheet it would have saved us many thousand voters."[35]

She added that those who knew Edwards had told her he was a "very ordinary man in intelligence, . . . not one of brains or insight and honest efficiency." The persistence and vehemence of sex prejudice continued to surprise Freeman. "I am astonished, too, to find how many men and women do not believe in a woman being in a place of power. . . . They refuse to see that there is no sex in intellect, in talent, in genius or powers to achieve."[36]

Edwards continued to maintain publicly that he was beholden to no one. Following the election he left for a supposed fact-finding trip before he took office, promising an upheaval at city hall when he returned. "I am going to shake up City Hall; it needs it badly," he said, ten days before leaving for a five-week tour of southern and eastern cities.[37] When he took office he fired all the department heads Landes had named except for the fire chief.

Landes meanwhile prepared to leave the mayor's office and made one last attempt to keep the ideals of her administration in power. She supported a move to establish a shadow government to keep tabs on Edwards's administration. She was one of several civic leaders pushing for a Seattle Social Senate, to be a watchdog in Seattle civic affairs, organized "to unify community opinions

Frank Edwards, an unknown theater operator who reveled in his lack of civic involvements, connections, or endorsements, refused to debate Landes or discuss the issues she raised. He promised lower taxes, more business development, and jobs for everyone. He was also the beneficiary of record amounts spent on his campaign, of which he claimed to have no knowledge. Here he greets a supporter shortly after taking office. *Photo courtesy of the PEMCO–Webster & Stevens Collection, Museum of History and Industry, Seattle.*

on matters of city-wide importance." Nothing would be left out—all city policies would be probed and evaluated by the group. Landes presided over its initial May meeting attended by a wide variety of Seattle's community leaders. The idea had been proposed by Dr. Howard Woolston, the head of sociology at UW, and other leaders included a judge, the *Post-Intelligencer*'s "King" Dykeman, and Landes campaign leader Ethel Utter.[38]

On May 24, 1928, she wrote a letter to Edwards, suggesting he come to the office and setting a tentative appointment for May 28. She explained to him that she had arranged to have the office and rugs thoroughly cleaned and inquired if he wanted any special changes in the arrangements, so everything would be in order for him when he took office June 4.

She also wanted him to meet the office staff (perhaps to help protect their jobs). She concluded by saying that she would be happy "to give you any desired information or assist you in any way possible."[39] It was a gracious gesture on her part. Whether he kept the appointment with her is not clear. She added that she would be leaving Seattle on May 30 for a convention in Washington, D.C., "and personal business." Presiding at the actual transfer of power was something she missed—or avoided. At the end of March she had been elected a delegate to the June meeting of the Soroptimist Federation meeting in Washington, D.C.[40]

Landes met her defeat stoically, gracefully, with some bitterness, but ready to go forward with her life. She also retained her sense of humor. At a speech delivered the day following the election, she told the Citizenship Day attendees they were imposing a "severe test" on her to expect her to "laud voters for 'intelligent citizenship' in view of their decision of the previous day."[41] In response to a letter from a loyal supporter angry about her loss, she described how she dealt with her defeat. "I am glad to say that both my training and I suppose my ancestry bred in me the attitude of mind which leads one to be a 'good sport' even under adverse circumstances."[42] Her administration garnered praise in papers as distant as Nashville, Honolulu, Providence, and Springfield. The *Nashville Banner* contrasted her—again—with "Ma" Ferguson, saying she had an "administration beyond reproach."[43]

She was now fifty-nine years old and could have retired completely from public life. She had had six years of difficult and contentious public service as an elected official, full of evening hearings, quarrelsome meetings, and insoluble problems. Although some suggested she remain in politics and stand waiting in the wings to run again, she was cool to the idea, feeling the voters had spoken their piece on what kind of government they wanted.

Ten years after she left office, she wrote about her exit. "I could never count on my days or my evenings, and six years in public life were fully sufficient for me. I have never had any yearning for more, but am more than glad to have had that much."[44] However, Landes was not the sort of woman to retire easily from either the public eye or public service. In her sixties she continued to champion causes and interests important to her.

Regrets and condolences flowed to Landes after she lost the election. The president of the Chamber of Commerce wrote Landes one such letter, indicating that he himself voted for her, praising her work with the chamber and her development of the city.[45] The Seattle Park Board of Commissioners sent her flowers her last week in office.[46] Her famous brother-in-law, Stanford president emeritus David Starr Jordan, wrote her that he was proud of what she had achieved and not really surprised that she was defeated. "When were the good and true ever in the majority," he wrote, quoting Thoreau.[47] She saved these communications and a number of others, letters that were both consoling and congratulatory about her years of service and contributions while in office. She had many supporters.

Upon reflection, Landes herself attributed her loss also to her years on the city council and the enemies her efforts toward civic betterment had accrued, along with her not holding the women's vote. "I felt like a lamb going to be slaughtered, but the slaughter was postponed for two years." People got comfortable that all was going well, "and they could rest upon their oars. . . . So two years later they left their woman mayor to the wolves—an unguarded sheep, for the 'lamb' had become a sheep by that time," she wrote for her university alumni magazine. "Then the wolves came down *en masse* and, to all practical purposes, devoured her."[48]

Nevertheless, she was proud of what she perceived she had accomplished for women in public office, and of what she had done to improve Seattle's civic life, environment, and future development. Her subsequent words and deeds reflected a changing philosophy and an evolving attitude toward herself, other women, and the exercise of power and politics. In her appearances, she tried to diminish the issue of gender as a measure of suitability for public life. The national media carried her views far and wide. So did her speeches and tours.

Speaking Out on Women and Politics

For instance, while in office she spoke in Portland to a group of advertising executives. The speech, about what women really want, was reprinted in *Printers' Ink* and *Reader's Digest* and was cited widely.[49] In that speech, she tried again to reduce the social and political constraints of gender. Advertisers (and others) "have carried in their minds wrong conceptions of woman and her mental reactions. . . . Woman is a reasoning, intelligent human being, capable of assimilating and correlating facts, able to arrive at sound conclusions." Advertising, then, should appeal to that.

"Why feel that the appeal to the woman buyer must be made from the sentimental, the emotional or the subtle standpoint?" she asked. "Why not approach her as you would approach a man if conditions were reversed?" If a man were to use a household labor-saving device, advertisers would induce him to buy it by showing him "its practicability and convenience, . . . [and] need of the article. Women are no more likely than men to be hoodwinked by spacious words."

Landes also argued that there was no "average woman," only individual ones, and that each woman should be treated "as having at least a medium amount of intelligence." The appeal to a woman should be the same as to a man, except perhaps "along the line of beauty and color. Even this is not certain. Some women appear to be deficient in artistic sense, and some men are impressed by the artistic far more than by the practical."

Along with this message of equality, Landes promoted individual differences as opposed to stereotypes. "Don't group us like so many cattle in a herd or sheep in a flock ready to follow the leader." If necessary, she suggested grouping women along "social lines." The woman with servants, "a decreasing tribe by the way," was not subject to the same inducements as a woman without servants, "and legion is her name." Luxuries and needs were not the same, she noted. This popular speech contained little of the separatist vision, the vision that glorified motherhood and woman's sphere.

The popular "housecleaning" metaphors connected to civic

betterment remained prevalent, nevertheless, in another of her bylined articles, appearing in *Collier's* in 1929.[50] In it Landes promoted a role for women in government, thus improving politics, but not out of a sense of female superiority. "This feeling is not based on a smug sex superiority complex," she wrote, adopting the imagery of Freudian language then gaining currency. "I am not one of those who go around saying—or thinking—that women are better than men. Only, at present, most women, in order to be elected to office, have to be better than their men opponents." It was not equal pay for equal work, she noted, but equal pay for better work that currently ruled social practices. "In politics it commonly takes a superior woman to overcome the handicap of traditional prejudice." When a woman becomes mayor, legislator, county treasurer, or governor, her constituents will benefit from her realization that, "because of her sex—she is on trial and must make a record." She recognized that a few women, "as men are quick to remind us," failed to meet this high standard. "These failures are a great pity, although they have been exaggerated out of all just proportion," she wrote. A few will fail, just as men sometimes fail.

Yet women were much less susceptible to corruption because they were more aware of the consequences, she said. "Can anybody imagine large numbers of women calmly collecting graft from speakeasies, gambling houses and red-light districts? Women have too much moral imagination. It is too easy for them to visualize how these social evils may affect the individual home." She said women see husbands blinded by poisoned whiskey, or fathers losing money that should have gone into their child's college fund, or worse. "Men smile because women 'make everything personal,' but making a thing personal sometimes makes it intolerable!"

She outlined some of the structural reasons why she felt municipal corruption existed, starting with the fact that men capable of effectively running a large city "are generally too busy with their own affairs and are making too much money to be attracted by the salaries paid mayors of American cities." And to be reelected, such a man necessarily became "one of the gang, a part of the machine." As "one of the boys," he must depend "on the favor of 'the boys' when, in a year or two, he again runs for office."

Other negative influences were "antique and disorderly" methods for conducting public affairs—methods embedded in "charter and law," and the machine's sentimental misuse of public jobs "to aid its faithful and humble supporters." Added to that were the low pay and the strain "upon an undeveloped personality of loyalty to something as intangible as the community or the state." It is little wonder that politicians and politics have a bad name, and having a bad name keeps good people out of it, she wrote. "The low general opinion of politics and politicians helps keep both debased, on the principle of 'give a dog a bad name and hang him.' "[51]

As a result, Landes argued, an elected female official is likely to be superior to her male opponents, and the "odium still attached in many quarters to the male politician does not cling to the female of the species," she said. "She is probably an educated woman, financially solvent, with a highly developed sense of community service." She is like the type of man who should be in government but cannot afford it. "This woman is going into politics as she used to go into philanthropy and club work—for what she can give, rather than what she can get." Landes was describing herself and the avenue she took to public office. She was also describing a relatively elite group.

Politics will come slowly to women's lives, she continued. School and college and "perhaps a few years of ambitious, arduous self-support" follows, then marriage and children. She still held to the ideal of women's staying at home with small children. "I do not want to regulate other women's lives, but to me children and home seem a full-time job." A mother has heavy responsibilities, "with the most searching demands upon her intelligence, her self-control and her conscience." Yet it is in the nursery as a proving place where a woman's heart and brain learn "judgement, poise, compromise, patience, resolution, tact, self-forgetfulness, tolerance, common sense. There are no qualities which we need more in our public life."[52]

In another of her speeches she credited women for passage of what she called social legislation. Women are innately more radical than men, she said, and cannot view social legislation coldly. In fact, most social legislation "passed by public bodies for years now has been through the indirect work of a woman."[53] In a reminiscence she wrote for *Survey* magazine, she outlined the personal qualities she felt she had that were necessary for effective public service, and for getting along in male-dominated fields of politics and administration. To get along, women had to be unemotional, able to give and take, and tenacious. "Above all, one should be a good sport, able to take the hard knocks that are inevitable. No tears and no showing of the white feather must be the rule," she said. "If you cannot get a whole loaf take a half, or even a quarter and come back later for more. Do not fail to come back. Neglect in this regard is fatal." She explained her own success at working with men with a touch of humor. "A woman must be able to work with men on an equal basis. Don't try to coerce or dominate, and above all, don't try to reform them. Women often feel called upon to make men over. Don't try it. It cannot be done. Their vices and their virtues are their own. Let them keep them."[54]

She was also sensitive to the power of language in defining women's roles and to the limits language placed upon what women could or could not accomplish. She said she always preferred the word "councilman" to "councilwoman." "And I threaten to shoot on sight, without benefit of clergy, anyone calling me the mayoress instead of the mayor." She was serious about what was implied in these names. "Joking aside, I am fighting for a principle in taking that stand. Let women who go into politics be the real thing or nothing!"[55] Despite her efforts, she was often labeled mayoress by the press when she spoke outside the Puget Sound area.

She called again for making public service gender-neutral. "Let us, while never forgetting our womanhood, drop all emphasis on sex, and put it on being public servants." She said that a leading banker who once opposed her election for fear of business effects had since declared in a public statement that her "sane and sensible administration has entirely altered his view of women as civic heads." Her main point was clear: "Petticoat government has turned out to be without the hysterical feminine frills that were feared."[56] These words were published only a few months before her 1928 defeat.

She reveled in the experience of having been council member and mayor, which she said had meant "adventure and romance and accomplishment to me." To be in some degree "a guiding force in the destiny of a city, to help lay the foundation stones for making it good and great, to aid in advancing the political position of women," to be the person to whom men and women and children look "for protection against lawlessness, to spread the political philosophy that the city is only a larger home—I find it richly worthwhile!"[57]

Powerful social forces had built the stage upon which Landes performed in the 1920s. But the stage started to creak and groan. Not surprisingly, paranoia about some of those divisive forces, such as "radical feminism" and "sex neurosis"—increasingly the same—spread by the end of the 1920s, despite the inroads of a few exceptional women like Landes.[58]

Backlash and Retrenchment

The pattern of activism, conflict, controversy, conservatism, and withdrawal in the late 1920s and 1930s was reflected in the changing priorities of the Seattle and Washington Federation of Women's Clubs. The federation gradually moved away from the direct political action for women's interests evident in federation resolutions of the 1910s and early 1920s. By the end of the decade, the federation's priorities had turned more toward concerns of literary, social, and personal improvement. Its resolutions focused on illiteracy, community improvement projects, literature, and art projects; its membership dropped.

At the end of the decade the Century Club, League of Women Voters, and the Women's City Club (which Landes founded) were no longer members of the Seattle federation.[59] In 1929–31 the state federation focused on beautification and historical projects and on an "author's day." In 1931–33 the federation sponsored essay contests and focused on the home. It also deplored the "frequency of drinking scenes in the depiction of American life" and supported the League of Nations. Federation leaders continued to complain that there were fewer attendees. In 1933–35 the focus was a "Know Your State Government" survey and campaign and a suggestion that the state group copy the general federation's new policy of having both sides of controversial issues represented on the platform at the national meeting. At that particular meeting opponents as well as proponents spoke on birth control, the Equal Rights Amendment, old age pensions, and unemployment insurance.[60]

By World War II, the Washington federation was actually arguing against women's employment in the name of children. Concerned about juvenile problems and mothers' being out of the home, it went on record opposing employment of women by Seattle's major industries. That included industries such as shipyards, which were gearing up for the war effort. The federation said that its opposition applied to women who had children of junior high age or younger, "unless and until such mothers shall have arranged for and provided adequate and responsible supervision and companionship for their children during the hours of the mother's employment."[61]

The wording shifted responsibility for the arrangements completely to the women involved. It also reflected a dramatic shift in the nature of the federation from the time Landes headed the Seattle federation in 1920, when it and the state group were lobbying for equal pay for women, equal opportunity for advancement, and for women to be able to choose their occupations without restriction "through custom or prejudice."

Another aspect of this conservative shift was the paranoia about change and Communism, embodied in the Spider Web controversy that began in 1924 with the circulation of a chart linking leaders of feminist, peace, and socialist movements together in a subversive, conspiratorial, interlocking directorate.[62] Critics of the Child Labor Amendment claimed that Communists had written the amendment as part of a conspiracy to destroy American institutions, including the family. This "nationalization of youth" promised harassment of parents, critics charged. Governor Roland Hartley of Washington equated it to coddling children and corrupting their minds with ideas of social reform, and the state failed to ratify the amendment.[63]

The Sheppard-Towner Act disappeared when Congress cut its funding in 1927 and terminated it in 1929; the federal Child Labor Amendment failed to get state ratification, and supporters gave up the effort in 1925; and the Equal Rights Amendment never made it out of Congress. Although the ERA had been introduced in the House and Senate in 1924, 1925, and 1929, it was never favorably reported out of committee.[64]

Added to this political retrenchment and the new social science interpretations of gender was a growing conservative reaction to the perceived dissolution and rebellion of the Roaring Twenties, symbolized by booze and the uninhibited flapper—concerns that the economic disaster of the Depression would only intensify.

By the end of the 1920s, policymakers and the press deemed the reformist triumph of prohibition a failure that fostered lawlessness and economic privation. Although moral support remained for the law, other forces, largely economic, caused widespread questioning. Questions arose about the legitimacy of the law and about the meddlesome motives of those who saw their mission to enforce this impossible-to-enforce amendment.

Despite the conservative shift, women continued to move in ever larger numbers into the workplace and the professions, but they were generally trapped in low-pay, low-power, low-status jobs. In 1920, fully 86 percent of the 8.3 million working women were concentrated in only ten occupations. In the factories they worked predominantly in industries that were extensions of the domestic functions, such as clothing, textiles, shoemaking, and food processing, and they worked at those jobs for 52 to 55 percent of what male workers were paid. Only one working woman in thirty-four was a member of a union, and not all unions welcomed women as members.[65] The career woman of the 1920s was exceptional, despite spread of women like Landes into many heretofore closed fields.[66]

Where new office technologies and operations opened job opportunities, women filled them quickly. Employers perceived women as having high manual dexterity and a tolerance for routine motions. Women filled 52 percent of all the clerical positions by 1930. Work was and continued to be segregated by gender in the professions as well. Even in 1930, women still constituted 81 percent of the teachers, 79 percent of the social workers, and 98 percent of the nurses. Women in medicine, science, or law ended up in gendered areas, such as pediatrics or home economics.[67] Women had the most difficulty making gains where their employment involved reversing the established hierarchies of gender. Changes, when they came, often came as expansions of existing categories.

By 1930, when the country fell into the economic maelstrom of the Depression, the drive to transform many of the social welfare concerns important to women into city and state priorities faltered, in a grim acceptance of present problems and fear of future conditions. Economic privation led to acceptance and accommodation, at least for a time. In the face of hard times, moral debates on all sides were set aside in the rush to meet physical survival needs, and escapism became even more important to people. Feminism faded, and its proponents divided over its direction. Economic indicators sounded impending doom.

Washington State was hit hard between 1929 and 1932, when

farm income dropped from $7 billion to $2 billion, corporate income from $11 billion to $2 billion, and national income from $88 billion to $40 billion. Industrial production by 1932 was off 50 percent; state unemployment reached 25 percent and was even higher in Seattle because of the depressed agriculture and logging industries and the cyclic nature of shipbuilding and other manufacturing.

Gains women made in the 1920s disappeared in the 1930s, as movements to keep women out of the workplace grew under the guise of protecting jobs and self-respect for family breadwinners. Landes came to the defense of Seattle women faced with these hard times. Despite turmoil about women's employment in men's jobs and about women's political rights, women slowly continued to make employment gains throughout the century, even in the 1930s. Social legislation for the protection of mothers and children resurfaced in the New Deal and later in the War on Poverty. Aid to Families with Dependent Children, the Women and Infants program, a host of child labor laws, Social Security retirement and survivors' benefits—a long list of social welfare measures—became an entrenched part of the modern American state, thanks in no small way to the efforts of clubwomen like Landes.

Through the political process, activists—even those women whom some feminists deemed at best marginal to the cause of women's equality—helped accomplish broad social goals relating to social welfare and traditional women's concerns.[68] Their achievement carried a certain irony. The gains for women, unlike the expansion of government to provide for the social welfare of all its citizens, did not become a permanent part of American politics. No legislation can make women full partners in government and politics. That requires a change in the consciousness of both men and women about gender itself, a change that has been slow in coming.

Landes's Legacy to Seattle

The civic betterment and social legislation agenda that Landes in Seattle and others elsewhere forwarded put changes in motion. In Seattle as elsewhere, cities increasingly turned to professional expertise, hired on the basis of civil service and merit rather than politics, but operating under citizen control to balance the rise of a technocracy. Public administration and personnel management became thoroughly professionalized, as did merit systems for city employment. City planning and zoning laws became routine in the management of cities and their industries and landscapes. These ideas for civic betterment were not Bertha Knight Landes's invention, nor was she the sole agent making all of them a reality in Seattle. But she played a key role in the process of making the city "a larger home."

Specifically, the Landes legacy filled a long list: the Seattle City Planning Commission, the city's initial traffic law code, revision of the building code, comprehensive planning and zoning codes, strengthened municipal licensing of entertainment establishments, hiring by merit through a strengthened Civil Service Commission, city-county coordination for provision of decent public hospital services, setting aside areas for parks and recreation downtown and around natural features such as Green Lake, coordination of schools and parks in supervised recreation programs, development of and efficient management for city utility services with centralized billing, Seattle's first rapid transit committee, and so on. The list of her goals and achievements reads like a textbook on city management. The list also fostered the expansion and use of government to impose civic betterment on citizens and the city's economy, despite Landes's nominal Republican affiliation in the age of Warren Harding and Calvin Coolidge.[69]

After Landes left office, in 1931 King County opened the first unit of a modern hospital on the old county courthouse site, with 425 beds.[70] Diablo Dam on the Skagit River was finally turned over to the city by the contractors in August 1930, with the power tunnel and powerhouse foundations completed the following year. The entire project was finished in 1934, including a transmission line from Diablo to the Gorge Power Plant.[71] Also realized after she left office were the opening of the Stone Way (Aurora) Bridge and the civic auditorium, projects begun on her watch. A Women's Division of the Police Department, headed by its own superintendent, finally became a reality in 1933. A Seattle Junior Safety Patrol to protect pedestrians began operations in 1928. The Traffic Code was finished in 1934.[72] The City Planning Commission and its code, largely her creation in 1924, were reorganized in 1930 and 1932 but survived. In later years the commission included the city engineer, president of the Park Board, superintendent of buildings, and six mayoral appointees.[73]

The comprehensive zoning ordinance, which went into effect in 1923 through the efforts of Landes and others, likewise survived attacks by subsequent mayors and councils.[74]

In addition, despite her 1928 defeat, Landes's six years in city office opened the door on powerful positions in local government for other women by the way she conducted herself. The door she and Miracle left ajar on the Seattle City Council subsequently admitted Mildred Powell, who held her council seat for two decades, from 1935 to 1955. Powell, like Landes, was called "Seattle's Woman Nominee for the City Council." In fact, Landes had encouraged Powell to run and took some credit for her victory.[75] Other women followed Powell on the council, creating a tradition.[76] Women, who had difficulty successfully entering state and national politics, had more success when they turned to local politics and community activism, continuing a trend that Landes and her club cohorts had started.

Lectures, Tours, and More Presidencies

After Landes left office in 1928, she continued to make herself useful in community activism, in Seattle and in a national arena as well. She had earned a national reputation and did not readily relinquish the limelight and the influence it gave her. Landes out of office at age sixty was nearly as active as Landes in office. Her life after public office led her to national speaking tours, to more club and campaign directorships, to work on improving conditions for women and children during the Depression, and to leading educational tours with her husband to exotic parts of the world, from Pago Pago to Hong Kong.

In May 1928, shortly before she left the mayor's quarters in the Municipal Building, University of Washington president Lyle Spencer wrote a supposedly unsolicited letter on her behalf. He corresponded with a New York agent responsible for arranging speaking tours about how wonderful Landes would be on the national circuit. Many writers had commented about her speaking ability, wit, and presence of mind on the podium. Spencer wrote J. B. Pond that he had heard she might deliver a series of lectures through the Pond's Bureau during the upcoming season. He said he had watched her in public speaking engagements throughout her six years in office. Her poise, ease of speaking, and choice of words, delivered in a "good voice" even to a large audience, had always impressed him.[77]

He also admired the "genuine intellectual ability shown in her lectures and addresses." In his opinion, she was "not only a deep student of the social side of our relations" but also someone with "keen insight into the human problems of our cities." Aware of the anomaly of a woman speaking from the podium as a main attraction, he added that she was a womanly woman. "She has no mannerisms on the platform that offend audiences in any way. Her commonsense speeches, her gracious manner, her splendid diction, and her ability as a speaker, all tend to conquer her audience at once." What's more, she was popular. "It is not surprising that we have no one else in the Northwest who is in more demand than is Mrs. Landes for all varieties of public addresses."[78]

Pond apparently concurred. She did go on a speaking tour for Pond's Lecture Bureau called "Adventures in Municipal Housekeeping," the first of several national tours. In the years following her election, she appeared in places ranging from St. Louis and Wheeling, West Virginia, to Boston, where she gave a speech entitled "The Challenge of the City."[79] In June 1930 she was on the cabin program of Cunard Lines RMS *Caronia,* speaking to the guests aboard ship on women in politics.[80]

When she spoke in New York City in 1928, she said her experience led her to believe in what she termed increased socialization of government, pointing to Seattle's municipal ownership of water, light, and transportation facilities. She also said that prohibition had "not yet had a fair trial."[81] Interviews with reporters resulted from many of her lecture stops, and the questions were more often about being female than about politics. In St. Louis, she was asked if women in politics were generally more honest than men. "Can you imagine a woman grafting by adulterating milk to children?" she responded tartly. The writer described her as "not of the masculine type, nor is she worldly wise in the manner of some business women."[82] Gender remained the primary unspoken issue.

Landes stayed active in civic and social circles as well. In December 1928 the Women's City Club of New York invited her to sit at the speaker's table during a lunch with Eleanor Roosevelt at New York's City's Biltmore.[83] She accepted. In 1930 she attended the Pan-Pacific Women's Conference in Honolulu. The paper there called her "a woman of unusual mental attainments and executive ability."[84]

From 1930 to 1932 she was national president of the new

American Federation of Soroptimist Clubs. Nationally the group had thirty-six clubs. The Soroptimists consisted of female executives from various businesses who worked to raise standards and help women in business. Under her presidency, Soroptimist clubs studied the problems of job discrimination and unemployment for women over thirty-five, hit particularly hard by the Depression, and the problems of women in business.[85] The objective was to develop a plan for relief for older women who had suffered disproportionate job loss because younger women—and men—got employment preference.[86] Also while she was president, the Soroptimists in Seattle led the way in ending a "whites only" membership policy, a restriction dropped by the national federation while she was president.[87]

Another priority of the American Federation of Soroptimist Clubs while she was president was world peace and disarmament. "We believe Americans should disarm as rapidly as is compatible with national safety," she told the Salt Lake City club.[88] In fact, in this regard her path would once again cross that of Seattle Century Club founder Carrie Chapman Catt. In 1925 Catt organized a series of national conferences on the causes and cure of war.[89] Landes spoke at the Oregon meeting on agencies for peace, regarding resolutions to be presented for a multilateral disarmament treaty.[90] As federation president, she also traveled to England to help found the European Federation of Soroptomists.[91]

While president of the Soroptimist clubs, she also made another of her national speaking tours. At one stop she said with some surprise, "Of course women make as good mayors as men. A woman is a human being. She has the right to work out her destiny."[92] The stump speech she gave on this tour, entitled "Woman's Place in the Sun," was delivered at the Woman's City Club in Kansas City, at San Antonio, at Meadville, Pennsylvania, and other places. In it she said women had an inferiority complex, which explains why they were not advancing to the goal of equality with men faster. Once again women were blaming women for perceived inadequacies, and the social science vocabulary provided the explanation. Landes said that women should "be proud of their sex" and that they had important contributions to make other than as mothers and "household drudges." That remark offered a significant contrast to the "motherhood" rhetoric of ten years earlier.[93]

In the speech she traced the history of women, beginning in the time (not so long ago) when women were not persons but chattel belonging to men. "It has been a slow growth through which woman has escaped the status of drudge and slave," she said. In the nineteenth century American man learned his wife was a person. After that followed education of women, and then women's suffrage. It was not until 1869, with Ann Arbor's lead, that universities and colleges began to open their doors to women; women could not even make their own wills until fairly recently in their history.[94]

Landes complained about the direction women's clubs had taken by the 1930s. "If women's clubs would pay more attention to civic needs instead of literary pursuits . . . much could be accomplished," she said. Women's place now "is in the sun, right beside the men." In fact, woman's place "is wherever she is needed." In 1929 she made a speaking tour of the Southwest, giving a speech entitled "Delinquency and Recreation" at El Paso and Dallas. In 1929 and 1930 she delivered "The Challenge of the City" in Boston, spoke to the Women's Chamber of Commerce at Kansas City, and lectured in Lewiston, Idaho, on the home and family.[95]

At New York City, she advocated the "back to the soil" movement to relieve serious overcrowding in cities, which were now housing more than 60 percent of the nation's population as small towns and rural areas were being drained. She said cites had outgrown old methods of government, and they were too slow to change to new and more efficient methods. She cited as typical a problem in Chicago. There the police force had been headed by twenty-five men in forty-eight years. In contrast, there had been only six changes in the leadership of Scotland Yard in fifty years.[96]

Also in 1930, Landes made a speaking tour through Florida with her lecture "Adventures in Municipal Housekeeping." She spoke at Orlando, Jacksonville, and other sites.[97] She continued to take her speeches on the road, even going overseas. She made a 1930 tour alone to England and Germany. Her passport listed her occupation as lecturer.[98] Some of her public addresses were more and more critical of citizens who did not get involved in civic affairs, and she pointed out the resulting danger to democracy. At Wilmington, Delaware, she complained to the New Century Club that cities were increasingly ruled by the 50 percent

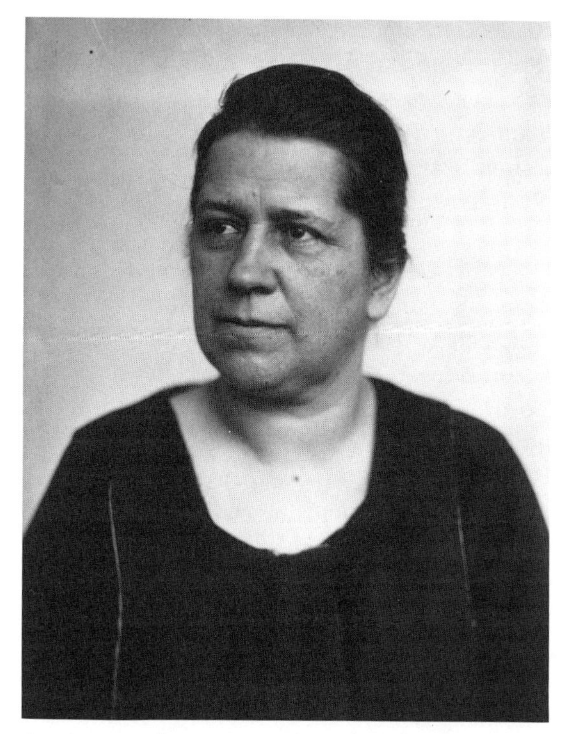

Landes was almost sixty when she left public office. Although encouraged to run again, she declined. Instead she took up other pursuits, including lecture tours and international travel. This photograph, presumably for a passport, shows an older and sadder Landes. Although she took her defeat gracefully, she was disheartened by the direction she saw her Seattle taking, especially during the Depression years, which hit Seattle particularly hard. *Photo courtesy of the PEMCO–Webster & Stevens Collection, Museum of History and Industry, Seattle.*

(or less) who voted in municipal elections, and other elections as well.[99] She lamented the loss of *civitas,* that sense of obligatory civic involvement by women and men.

Despite her national travels, she retained her interest and involvement in Seattle city affairs. In 1930 she requested a report on Seattle police activities from 1924 to 1928 on liquor arrests. The number of arrests in 1924 had been 635 and had netted $165,364 in fines. In 1926 the figures had jumped to 1,147 and

$257,819 collected, and in 1927, her final full year in office, to a high of 1,386 arrests and $274,647 in fines. However, in 1928—the year she left office—the arrests dropped to 727, with fines of $177,150, almost a 50 percent decline.[100] The fact that she had requested such a report and saved it indicates her continuing interest in city law enforcement.

Local and National Causes

In 1930, Landes's name appeared on a list of workers for a $1.15 million campaign to build Seattle General Hospital.[101] Also in 1930 President Herbert Hoover appointed her to the White House Conference on Child Health and Protection, one of the early forums that discussed the federal government's role in protecting children through the Child Labor Amendment and other issues. She accepted that assignment, attending the Washington, D.C., conference as a delegate, from November 19 to 22.[102] The conference attendees, to Hoover's surprise, declined to back his side in a showdown between the women running the Children's Bureau and the professional men in medicine.

Hoover planned to transfer the Children's Bureau and its programs to the male-dominated U.S. Public Health Service. Child welfare policies, expressed in the threatened Sheppard-Towner Maternity and Infancy Act and the Child Labor Amendment, were under attack as costly, meddlesome, and invasive. They were also programs female professionals ran. Important programs that clubwomen had fostered and promoted, embodying their ideas about policy priorities, suddenly were caught in the mainstream of public policy and its attendant professionalization. Many male politicians and the American Medical Association began belittling the female professionals involved in the bureau's work, such as health clinics and the work itself, in part because it threatened AMA members' income and physicians' professional codes. The conference participants were supposed to rubber-stamp Hoover's trade-off of support for federal maternal and infant health programs as long as they were administered by the Public Health Service.[103] Conference attendees refused, forcing the recommendation to be withdrawn.

Back in Seattle in 1931, she came to the defense of her "larger home" and its women. She was again listed as a member of the Board of Directors of the Seattle Community Fund, a precursor to the United Way.[104] That same year, in December, she defended women working in city government as the principal speaker against a proposed city council charter amendment that would have prohibited women from being employed by the city. As unemployment worsened, married women who were employed saw their job rights threatened. Early in 1932 the *Seattle Times* ran an article describing how the *New York Daily News* had fired four married women "whose husbands are making a living wage," following the example of Mayor Roland Marvin of Syracuse, who had discharged 165 working wives and filled their places with unmarried women.[105]

Working women became targets. Not only did they endure efforts to restrict their employment—such as the amendment proffered in Seattle—but they also saw their wages and hours cut, or took on piecework at low rates in order to stay employed at all. Working women were scapegoated when the economy could not provide men with jobs.[106] Wage differentials based on sex were so accepted as to be built into the National Recovery Administration codes, despite objections from the General Federation of Women's Clubs, the National Women's Party, the Women's Trade Union League, and other women's organizations. The Civilian Conservation Corps camps paid women 50 cents a day, versus the $1 a day men received, and CCC slots available to women totaled 6,400 out of an estimated 3.5 million women who were unemployed by 1937.[107]

The Seattle lobbying effort that drafted Landes, organized through a newly formed group called the Women's Protective Association, with Landes as its chief advocate, succeeded in defeating the restriction on married women's employment. The United Veterans of King County had sponsored the bill, and some, irritated by the group's proposed amendment, suggested an amendment to end veterans' preference in city hiring.

Landes received praise for "convincing the members of the city council that the proposed amendment was unjust and un-American."[108] Opponents of this and other restrictions on women's employment put together an organization for all married and unmarried women in the city's service. Landes was singled out and asked to continue to help them in "defeating any legislation which will discriminate against us."[109]

In 1931, as the Depression's social ravages worsened, Landes was named by the mayor to head the women's division of Seattle's Commission for Improved Employment to organize relief efforts during the early years of the Depression. She organized sewing rooms and arranged city employment for destitute women. The sewing rooms repaired and constructed clothing primarily for needy children.

The work of her division centered on reconstructing old clothes, sewing new clothes (such as pajamas for patients at Firland Sanatorium), and making rugs, layettes, and handicrafts to be sold through stores and elsewhere. Landes and others arranged for donations of the needed raw materials and office space. The city and clubs donated funds, and the women involved were paid work-relief wages. The commission additionally arranged work in library and city departments, also paid from work-relief funds. Women also made new clothes for children, which were sold through Rhodes Department Store and a shop in the University District.[110]

The magnitude of the need was enormous. In December of 1931, some 255 Seattle women had been given work. By May 1932, the figure was 744. By June, the commission had 3,388 women registered for whatever aid they could get, including 639 widows, 982 with families of one to twelve children, 235 single women, 77 on mother's pensions, 80 with permanently disabled husbands, and 37 whose husbands had disappeared.[111] It was a litany of need and privation, which Landes's commission did what it could to relieve. A summary report said that 3,615 women were registered, of whom 1,658 were given work for a combined total of 14,679 days.[112]

Landes felt it was important that these women see themselves as gainfully employed and in useful service, rather than as objects of charity. "The bigger problem is to avoid the dole. . . . We are making every effort to provide work and see that work is paid for so that there is no feeling of accepting charity," she said about the program in a Portland speech. She said that all women could help other women in dire need. Those who could afford to do so should provide one job a week to an unemployed person to help relieve unemployment.[113] In a speech she made in Salt Lake City, she argued that women also should patronize home industries across the nation to benefit other women. She said she hoped the tide had turned, but improvement would be slow.[114]

As conditions worsened in Seattle, these massive community volunteer efforts proved to be insufficient, although they helped tide many families and individuals through the first few bad winters of the Depression. The head of the commission, telephone company executive I. F. Dix, praised Landes in 1932 for her efforts "extended to women of our city in dire need of sympathy and understanding assistance. . . . With the limited resources and the magnitude of the problem, you have done a remarkable piece of work."[115] She subsequently put her organizational skills to work again in chairing the advisory committee for King County relief work.

Sometimes those hit with privation questioned where the aid actually went and whether the decisions made allocating scarce resources were fair. Perhaps such accusations circled around Landes as well, or maybe she wanted to head them off. H. W. Carroll, longtime city comptroller, thus wrote Landes in 1932, apparently at her request, to certify that none of the 4,100 checks run through the women's division of the Commission for Improved Employment had been written to her.[116]

In 1932, when money ran out for the sewing rooms, Landes turned her attention to campaigns to get clothing for schoolchildren. Some were in such dire need of decent clothes that they were not attending school. She and five other women, via the Children's Bureau of County Welfare, managed an effort that collected 40,000 pieces of clothing for 14,000 children. In her speeches about the effort, she asked that people bring old clothes, scraps, buttons, razor blades, and so on to the city's police and fire stations for collection.[117] The community-wide response to the effort gratified her.

After Landes left office she also testified before various legislative bodies. One was the House Judiciary Committee in 1930, which at the time was considering arguments for and against the repeal of prohibition.[118] She was one of twenty women who testified at the long hearing. Another was the Commission on Public Service Personnel, in 1934.[119] In a release of her statement from the Woman's National Committee for Law Enforcement about her congressional testimony, Landes praised the results of prohibition, despite its inadequate law enforcement: "Women and children everywhere there [in Washington State], but particularly in the mining towns and the families of our men in lumber camps, have gained much."

Prohibition's credits, she said, included better housing conditions; more and better food, clothes, and shoes; more schooling; and money in the bank. She warned that women and children were the usual victims of what followed intemperance. The main business of government, she testified, "should be to protect the welfare of its people," especially those who need it most "and who have nowhere else to turn for the same."[120] The government turned the other way on the issue of prohibition, as production and consumption of alcohol became legal again in 1933.

In 1933 Landes was a guest of honor at a League of Women Voters meeting where Jeannette Rankin spoke on antiwar and activism in an address titled, "How Public Opinion Can Promote Peace." If women could win suffrage, they could also win a permanent peace, Rankin said. The group also discussed Landes's long-sought ideal—the city manager form of government.[121] In 1935 Landes helped host a Washington LWV fundraising tea, when the Seattle LWV's program included the slogan "Every Woman an Intelligent Voter" on the cover. The group's departments included International Cooperation to Prevent War, Child Welfare, Professions Branch, and the Legal Status of Women.[122] She continued to be active in the Woman's City Club, the group she founded, as its honorary president and spokesperson.

Overseas Tour Guide

Finally, Bertha, in her sixties, and Henry took up a recreational pursuit—conducting University of Washington extension tours to the Orient and other exotic locales. They also took groups, often made up of schoolteachers from all over the United States, to sites in Alaska, Yellowstone and Glacier national parks, or the Pacific Northwest. In 1933 the University of Washington Dragonland Cruise guest list included twenty-two names. In all, they went five times to the Orient and took one trip through the Hawaiian Islands.[123]

Henry conducted the tours as study groups, holding sessions on board on the geographic, climatic, and physical features of their destinations, which the group would then visit. Unfortunately, hosting one of these educational cruises cost Landes her greatest ally—her lifelong partner, Henry.

During a summer tour aboard the *Jackson* in 1936, Henry, according to friends, had insisted on looking after all the details on side trips to Nanking and Shanghai, despite his bronchitis and his wife's entreaties.[124] Their passports for June and July of that year contained many stamps. Unfortunately, Henry's bronchitis became pneumonia. Shortly after returning to Seattle, Henry

Bertha and Henry Landes conducted a number of study tours for University of Washington alumni to exotic parts of the world, including China, where they are pictured here. One of these trips, which they both enjoyed, cost Bertha her lifelong ally: Henry died following one of their journeys abroad. Bertha continued to host the tours alone while in her mid-sixties until her own health began to deteriorate. *Photo courtesy of Special Collections Division, University of Washington Libraries, neg. UW7334.*

Landes died, on August 23, 1936. He was sixty-eight years old, and she was sixty-five.

Landes lauded him and their life together. He was "pleased and willing to have me try my wings" and was her "tower of strength in times of stress, and made many sacrifices without complaint that I might give my time and strength to my civic service." His death was a terrible loss. "Life was to be lived to the fullest, always on a partnership basis and a definite sharing of different special interests," she wrote of their relationship. "It was so lived for 40 years until the summons came for one of us, and now I have to face life and its problems alone."[125]

A few months later his peers erected a memorial to him in Seattle's Evergreen Memorial Park. It was made from a glacial boulder taken from the Cascade Mountains he trekked so often.

Letters of condolence flooded in from across the country to Bertha, recalling fondly Henry's strength, his generous spirit, his sense of humor, and the mark he had left on Seattle, the University of Washington, his colleagues, and hundreds of students. She saved many of these letters in her papers, including one that came from her old nemesis, Mayor Edwin Brown.

By the time of his death Henry Landes had led a half-dozen of the University of Washington trips, and Bertha decided to continue the tradition. The University of Washington asked her to conduct another tour in 1937, and she wrote the U.S. ambassador in China to make arrangements.[126] She continued her travels in 1938, listed aboard the SS *Monterey,* bound for Honolulu, Pago Pago, Auckland, Sydney, and Melbourne.[127]

On that trip she made particular note to a reporter that a woman—Belle Reeves—had been elected secretary of state for Washington, that Frances Perkins had been named to Roosevelt's cabinet, and that Roosevelt had named two female ambassadors.[128] Only five people accompanied her on this trip, and her passport this time shows a woman whose eyes were puffy, who looked a good deal older than the woman in the passport photo taken eight years earlier. She still called herself lecturer by profession.[129]

Final Years

By this time, Bertha Knight Landes was almost seventy years old. She continued to live at the Wilsonian, the U-shaped apartment building near campus where she and Henry had lived while she was in office to make the burdens of her housekeeping a little lighter. She also continued her speaking engagements. In 1937 she was an "unprecedented" speaker—called that because she was female—to the Topeka, Kansas, Real Estate Board. She talked about her experiences in public life.[130] In Topeka she also spoke to the Soroptimist Club, noting that friends had pressed her to run either for governor or Congress, but that she had declined.[131] That was one of her last speaking engagements. Although she was still a strong speaker, the nature and the size of her audiences was changing. They were smaller, less important groups.

The community causes she pursued reflected a lower level of activism by the end of the 1930s, as she approached seventy years. She made appearances at social functions and lent her name and assistance to community causes such as the Women's City Club Chorus and the Seattle symphony drive, or fundraising socials for the League of Women Voters. Her own health began to deteriorate. After living forty-six years in Seattle, she moved in 1941 to Pacific Palisades, California, at the age of seventy-two. She hoped that the change in climate would improve her health. While in California, she taught civic and legislative affairs.[132]

In the final years of her life, she turned from church to a self-help sect, the Unity School of Christianity, and its Society of Silent Unity, based then at Kansas City, Missouri. It was founded in that city in 1887 by Charles Fillmore, a real estate agent, and his wife, Myrtle, after her spiritual healing. Its emphasis was and is upon spiritual healing and practical Christianity and prosperity. It operated through "silent unity," or prayer and counseling through telephone and mail, using widely distributed pamphlets and books.

It was not a denominational organization. Those in need sent in requests for prayer and counseling service to a central staff. The Unity School held that rebirths led to regeneration of the body and that the Bible was allegorical. Unity encouraged abstention from meat, tobacco, drugs, and intoxicants and from sex except for purposes of procreation. Its emphasis was upon the positive influence of religion as a factor in daily life, and salvation through the recognition of personal sinlessness and incorruptibility. It had no clergy until the Unity School for Ministers was established in 1930.[133] The group, which also believed that the spirit of God was expressed in each individual, held that God was not masculine and patriarchal but both feminine and masculine in nature. And individuals—not God—were responsible for the quality of their lives.

The Unity School of Christianity was one of the largest and most influential of the New Thought groups, which generally believed in the creative power of thought and spiritual healing, holding that both mental and physical strength derived from an inner source. Sin, evil, and suffering were illusory, and Jesus Christ was a symbol of a divine spark in every person. His purpose was not to reconcile or redeem but to point out that every individual was an incarnation of God. New Thought first arose in the decades after the Civil War, when ideas of evolution and material progress unsettled faith in Christianity. Initial leaders of the movement came from the Methodist church.[134]

In the early 1940s the Unity church's publications promoted prayer, sanctioning even prayers for money and prosperity. It also promoted healing without medicines, a positive outlook, and divine guidance.[135] One of its publications said that the way to prosperity could be found through attention to a particular drill, which would build up a prosperity "bank." The way consisted of being faithful to practicing the drill and remaining positive, singleminded, alert (especially to the intrusion of negative thoughts), consistent, faithful, and righteous.

The appeal of this organization to Landes was consistent with her nature and had some connections to the Congregational church. In addition to poems about faith, Landes saved a number of the small publications of the Unity church. Except for these and her public comments to the media, Landes left little in the way of a written record that elucidated her thoughts in the closing years of her life. The 1939 article she wrote for her alumni magazine was perhaps her last major statement on her career. In it she talked about the changes in her own perceptions over time. "One sees life from many different angles, meets all kinds of people and gets more than a liberal education and a very much broader outlook on life," she wrote.[136]

She reflected on what she found when she got into Seattle politics and why she stayed in it, despite the many trials and tribulations that six years of public service and decades of club service brought her. "Here was a city of about 350,000 population at that time, a seaport town with all that signifies—ships bearing cargo, good and bad entering its harbor. Drugs, liquor, stowaways, and sailors from many places come to us," she wrote, but the city also contained fine citizens who needed protection. "Could I or anyone else bring order out of the chaos which had been created by lax law enforcement?" She felt that she had succeeded in putting life in Seattle "on a very different plane than before."

Looking back on her years as city council member, Landes remembered as chief among her achievements the Planning Commission, the zoning laws, the revision of the building ordinance, and the traffic code, as well as improving the standards of Seattle's night life, "along with such cheerful items as barking dogs and crowing roosters." She believed that, as mayor, her most important task had been to name capable and qualified people to administrative positions. "No questions were asked as to past political support to the incumbent of the office of mayor, nothing in regard to religion or political party. The questions were, What have you done? What can you do?" She noted that this had not built her a political base. "I was there to serve the city, not myself."[137]

Landes welcomed the insights and opportunities of public office. "So I left the work gladly in the end; thankful for my many experiences, a wiser but not a sadder woman, and returned to home and husband with full appreciation of what I had been given and to what I was returning."[138]

Her last cross-country trip came two years after her move to California, to her son's home in Ann Arbor, Michigan, in September 1943. Her son, Kenneth Knight Landes, was head of geology at the University of Michigan. She died at his home at 10:30 A.M. on November 29, 1943, one month after her seventy-fifth birthday. Her *Times* obituary called her an "ardent feminist" and a "well-known writer and political lecturer."[139] Her two children and three grandchildren survived her.

At the city council's next meeting, Mildred Powell, the woman who filled the council seat Landes once held, delivered a eulogy at the meeting, and the council passed a resolution honoring her. The University Congregational Church held a memorial service for her on December 5. Her ashes were brought back to Seattle and interred.

The day after she died, the *Times* editorialized that her death concluded "a long lifetime of sincere devotion to public service." It said that "there will be general agreement that she gave the city a prudent administration. Her integrity as a public official was never questioned." The newspaper said Landes firmly believed "that women can make a significant contribution to political affairs," and that conviction brought her a national reputation. "But those who worked closely with her will think more especially of her gentle sense of humor and ready wit, her generous impulses and her kindness and loyalty to old friends."[140]

There was symbolic significance in two small items she saved in her papers about women in politics. One was a brief letter written to her in 1929. In its entirety, it said: "Women owe you a debt which we can never repay. You have lifted our standards higher and we are rising to them. Always the brightest and best are chosen for martyrdom, but for you lasting defeat is not possible."[141] The second item was an undated clipping from 1942, shortly before she died. Its headline read, "Six Women Victorious in Campaigns for Congress," including Clare Booth Luce.[142]

For Landes, the clipping offered a tangible link to the future, from her post–Civil War past to the raising of the curtain on a new age for women in the twentieth century. Bertha Knight Landes had helped pull the cord that drew the curtain.

VII POWER AND POLITICS POSTSCRIPT

Bertha Knight Landes's life and achievements stand on their own. But her life also serves as a metaphor for an era when women began working together to gain education and awareness, then social change, then the vote—a metaphor for the resulting euphoria about the potential for social change, as well as the disappointments over the persistence of gender, class, and political divisions despite the vote. Landes prefigured debates that continued throughout the twentieth century about the barriers to woman's participation in the systems and hierarchies of power and prestige that men dominated, such as politics and government. Many of the issues she faced, from sexist labels to negative media campaigns, remained issues for candidates for the remainder of the century. Although she came out of one side of the Progressive tradition, she fell somewhere on the continuum between that era and the New Deal and the Great Society. She also rode upon the twentieth century's relentless drive toward professionalization, bureaucratization, and its perennial concern about the effects of leisure pursuits and new mass entertainments.

At the beginning of her civic career, Bertha Knight Landes did not present herself, and did not see herself, as a radical infiltrating the dominant structures in politics and social life. She presented herself rather as a natural adjunct to those institutions to represent the woman's viewpoint, with a right to sit at the table in one of the seats of power. She demanded consideration for the woman's viewpoint, particularly regarding issues of special interest to women. In contrast to the prevailing business-oriented viewpoint, she and her backers held that the city's moral, social, and physical environment, like the environment in a home, was as important to nurturing, comforting, and protecting its inhabitants as was the city's efficient management as a business corporation ever-mindful of its investors' dollars.

Later in her political career, she moved away from the limitations of gender-specific concerns and began to redefine gender and its relationship to politics and civic life. As a result, her idea of representation of the woman's viewpoint also changed. The woman's viewpoint gradually embraced the idea that women's concerns were rightfully the concerns of both men and women and that, in managing a city, a woman could address the concerns of both sexes as well as a man could. She also worked against traditional views of the city and urban management, changing city priorities from their focus on economic development alone to include meeting social needs.

In any social movement intended to rearrange the hierarchies of power and change the definitions of what is important, there is a dividing line separating leaders. On one side of the line there are those who work like gadflies from outside the system to force it to change, by collecting adherents and redefining the status quo, through the media, the courts, or other institutions. On the other side are those who work from within a system, acquiescing to the system's structures in order to gain acceptance and validation, but with an ongoing effort to force the system to change—or at least to open up to the idea of change—through accommodating their new ideas or to meet previously unrecognized needs.

Bertha Knight Landes certainly worked from within the system throughout her professional life. In this way she fit anthropologist Victor Turner's definition of "marginal," someone who subscribed to the rules and roles of one system yet who hailed originally from a group very much outside the power structure and called upon that experience. As Turner noted, such individuals aspire to the rewards and power of the dominant structure, yet they look to their group of origin for *communitas* values that transcend individuals and their usual status roles. Landes did this with the clubwomen of Seattle, borrowing their visions and models for alternative structures and testing them in the larger arena through social legislation and city regulation.

To enter and remain in the dominant system and impact the larger political arena, she subscribed to the roles and rules of the system in power. In some ways, she gradually moved away from her group of origin as a result, although she remained devoted to women's causes and women's organizations all her life. As Turner noted, individuals with one foot in each camp often have unique opportunities—as Landes had—to evaluate the dominant system and offer important critiques of it and to see those critiques given consideration because of their membership in that dominant system.

Landes's Resistance to the Status Quo

One of the fundamental questions to ask about a figure such as Landes is, What counts as resistance or acquiescence to the status quo? Where were the limits challenged, and how?[1] Landes, like most women of her time, did not promote the more radical view of feminism that the National Women's Party backed in the Equal Rights Amendment. Like other women, she supported the contradictory ideas of equal pay for equal work and protectionist legislation for women and children. She did not participate in actions of civil disobedience to bring attention to the cause of women's inequality. She did not adopt radical changes in behavior codes—what Foucault called imprints on the body—as some New Women did in the 1920s, despite her awareness that restrictions on clothing and etiquette controlled women through control of their bodies and the nature of their activities. However, she did offer resistance to traditional "imprints" when she decided to do whatever was expected of male mayors, such as hiking to dam sites and opening ball games.

When Landes was in power, she did not try to eradicate all illicit behavior or behavior of which she disapproved in favor of the efficient intrusions of a police state, despite her efforts to enlist citizen aid in reducing police corruption and traffic crimes. She did not criticize, denigrate, or counterattack men who chose unfair methods of dealing with women, despite her opponents' personal and sexist attacks to denigrate and trivialize her and her candidacy. She did not become more radicalized by her experiences in politics. Instead, she remained generally within the security and stability of the system throughout her life in order to accomplish whatever goals she had. What, then, counted as resistance for Bertha Knight Landes?

Movement leaders, both insiders and outsiders, change cultural norms and social systems. While revolution-focused radicals usually have more visibility and attention, they also arouse more fear and anger and thus risk retribution and correction as responses from the power structure, even as such leaders gain converts (or perhaps because of their power to create converts). Those reformers who work from within the system to change it also play a vital role, particularly where change with stability, not disruptive chaos, is the long-range goal. Some agents of change begin with one orientation and are able to move to another according to the momentary needs of the movement and their personal proclivities. The success of either type depends upon the legitimacy of their demands and their acceptance in the larger community constituted as the body politic or the standard-bearers of the cultural norms. The relative importance and success of these two sorts of change agents also depend in large measure on the ability of the system to accommodate shifts and changes, or at least its apparent flexibility in the short and long term. Women, after all, did finally get the right to vote and run for office.

Once the avenue of women's clubwork opened up to Landes and gave her a power base, she never really considered going outside the system to accomplish her goals. Instead, she tried to make her goals for Seattle the city's own goals. The clubwork gave her and many women a professional life and a network of support. It also gave her a way to define herself to herself. That definition as a civic reformer and, in her case, as a leader of women enabled her to act out her vision in city politics.

Of the many editorials that praised her administration, one in particular related to her self-definition. On this clipping, she had written a note, asking that it be saved. It said that Landes had proved that "*sex* has little to do with *ability* to *think,* to *reason* temperately and to *discover causes* rather than effects."[2] She had underlined words that related directly to *Isaac Watts' Improvement of the Mind,* the book that she had used for guidance—with the addition of the gender factor. This was how she defined herself and her accomplishments to herself. She was conscious of her role representing all women, unfair as that burden might have been, even before she, with Kathryn Miracle, broke the gender barrier in Seattle city politics. She remarked repeatedly on that role and knew what it meant to the women who might follow her.

In Landes's case, what counted as resistance to the status quo were her attempts to overcome the prevailing ideas about women and narrow gender roles to enter political power structures and then to make those structures bend to her will through her ability to build consensus, to make her priorities and solutions theirs, and to provide leadership. Through persistence and argumentation she succeeded more often than not in making her vision their vision, which is a mark of leadership. Another aspect of her resistance was something she agonized about, namely, the blatant act of seeking power and authority, which she did by running for office, by seizing the power of the mayor's office when the opportunity arose, and finally by running for the highly visible post of mayor. To do so, she resisted powerful status quo forces, including her own perceptions of woman's reserve and selflessness. Furthermore, she resisted the status quo in her repeated attempts to expand the concept of women's sphere to include public affairs, and of public affairs to include women's concerns by remaking the city into the home, making sure these interests were protected through women's votes, just as she used her vote on the city council.

Her resistance appears in several other aspects of her life. She overcame her nineteenth-century past to take on a public career, looking forward to the opportunities that would follow for women if she and other pioneering women acquitted themselves well. Later in her public service, she attempted to deflect attention from gender in the management of public affairs. Even after she left public office at the age of almost sixty, she determined to continue to be of service to her community, region, and nation on behalf of an expanded role for government, but especially for women and their interests. Opposing the selflessness of the "ideal woman" was her own rise to power itself, even though she, like other women, was reluctant to call that personal desire for power by name.

The Power/Knowledge Link

According to Michel Foucault, French historian and critical theorist, power is expressed through a society's practices and structures. Participants accept and internalize such practices and structures, or else they resist and modify them. Power is codified in the accepted regularities and standards of a discourse, such as science or politics, and thus is fundamentally connected to "knowledge" and "discipline." To use power/knowledge links implies also the use of exclusion, rejection, repression, and prohibition to control behavior and patrol the borders.

Until 1920 and the passage of the Nineteenth Amendment,

accepted rationales of power/knowledge regarding women, involving for example assumptions about women's emotional nature, excluded most women in the United States from many legal rights, including voting and real political power. Women eventually won the battle about who had a right to vote, state by state initially, winning the West first. Women's suffrage threatened a major disruption of the existing order. Thus new rationales arose to limit women's access to power, just as "property" and "literacy" suddenly became standards that kept enfranchised blacks from voting in the South. In the 1920s—and, for that matter, by the end of the twentieth century—only handfuls of women were able to ascend through the "authority code" to elected seats of power.

In the 1920s, fields such as the social sciences used power/knowledge links to professionalize and "objectify" management of government and services, at the same time labeling as neurotic those women who worked for equality in the professional, political, economic, and social arena. Power/knowledge, bound together, continued to lead to subjection, not only of women, but of classes. To understand and use the proper codes represented the power to subject others to that knowledge and thus retain power over them. Each realm of human behavior has its own codes, from the arcane mechanisms of a city council to the elaborate etiquette of the domestic sphere, and practitioners enforce the codes. Informal networks of power and behavior codes exist also around economic relationships of all kinds, including those governing speakeasies and dance halls, where women were frequently exploited for gratification and profit.

Accepted codes, standards, or practices can, however, be modified or overthrown by new power/knowledge links that challenge the accepted beliefs and structures. Legal and professional codes can "outlaw" previously accepted codes, as physicians outlawed midwives and justices outlawed segregation. The struggles, strategies, and tactics used in the process of change constitute the process of history, according to Foucault. According to that definition, history can be found in several places and times in Landes's life: her campaigns, and the rhetoric she and opponents used; the hearings the city council and council committees held on issues of social control; the arguments in the media over policies, candidates, and personalities; and the disputes over what is proper and right for women, and for the men who would be men by rejecting so-called petticoat rule.

Landes, like Jane Addams, Frances Willard, and others before her, initially accepted the prevailing power/knowledge links that attached not only value but even superiority to women's so-called true nature and separate sphere. They tactically altered its elements to justify and then demand a role for women in public service and government. Landes utilized several ideas from that tradition, including the "municipal housecleaning" idea. The ideal home needed sanitation, morality, recreation, aesthetics, economic support, and protection from corruption. She used the idea that women needed representation in decisions affecting that larger home as reinforcement of women's unique role as mothers in creating new citizens who would be educated, ethical, and ready to assume the responsibilities of citizenship. Capitalizing upon these ideas, she applied them to the struggles over professionalization of city management and municipal control of utilities; over improvement of city health and environment; over dance hall, pool hall, and cabaret licensing; and over prohibition. She also applied them in the long struggle over control of the leisure behavior of the body—the bodies of the residents of Seattle, whether tangled up by traffic or corrupted by bawdy movies.

The media response mirrored forces for tradition during times of change. In their language they dealt with Landes first by treating her as an anomaly, then by echoing the power/knowledge "rightness" of the prevailing behavior codes, and then by demonstrating how she was not really a New Woman rebelling against those prevailing codes but in fact a woman with a "judicious mind"—a mind like a man's. In her campaigns she used her own symbols to counteract the symbols of male-dominated politics, from smoking cigars (men's role) to darning socks (women's role). The political struggle she lived concerned more than women and their empowerment; it also set the forces of civic and behavioral reform, law enforcement, and professional administration against the forces of dissolution, backroom politics, and political favoritism. Informal networks of power, fueled by economic interests, existed alongside and either competed against or colluded with the networks of legitimate political power. If history is indeed found in what Foucault labels the discontinuities and disjunctions of social practices, Landes was in the middle of several of those in Seattle. Suffrage, prohibition, the social welfare state, and feminism all eventually came to represent sharp divisions from past practices.

Landes's loss in her second mayoral election brought an apparent return to the status quo patriarchy. Even in defeat, however, Landes had altered the status quo, for now the idea of women in public office, even at the helm of a large American city, would never again be so odd as to be unimaginable in Seattle or elsewhere. The strands of reform and feminism that she and others fostered helped form the modern American federal welfare state, with all its programs bestowing benefits and protections upon its citizens through health, food, shelter, and education services and through building the state and national infrastructure to supply those services and environmental protections. Standards for city administration, including those for police training and other emergency services, eventually became thoroughly professionalized. Education and training requirements superseded political connections, as did personnel decisions made on merit rather than politics.

In this way Landes and others challenged, modified, or overturned existing power/knowledge assumptions and systems that grew out of laissez-faire capitalism, party politics, and social Darwinism. Landes indeed left her mark in several areas of Seattle's governance. This unique mayor also left her mark through her personal interactions with men on the council, in the Seattle business community, and in a larger audience. Her speeches and media coverage gave her a regional and national reputation. Women lauded and looked to her achievements, as reflected in the national media coverage from *Woman Citizen* to *Reader's Digest*. Men were surprised. In Landes's case, the social change she promoted did not involve the overthrow of existing structures but was realized slowly, as implanted ideas bore fruit even decades after they were planted.

Although Frank Edwards defeated Bertha Landes in 1928, his campaign had sown the seeds of his own destruction. An influential part of the electorate remained suspicious about his relationship to Seattle's private power interests. Landes was ultimately vindicated when Edwards was recalled from office. She saved in her papers not the article but the inch-high headline that trumpeted his ouster.[3]

Landes was the subject of many articles, most of them focusing on two narrow aspects of life—her gender and her efforts to enforce prohibition.[4] Gender, an obvious and exhaustive basis of demarcation between human beings, has significant intersections with class and race. And culture and class fused in many ways for the women who were active in clubs and social welfare. "Culture" came to mean the apex of civilization and social relations, and it was generally the property of the white middle class. Although it certainly contained elements of social control, it was also viewed as the highest achievement of the species and was deemed something that all races, classes, and other cultures could both aspire to and benefit from.[5]

During Landes's life, there was ample evidence of divisions among women (and men) over issues of class. Indeed, to women in the working class, class was a more important dividing line than gender. Women often were more accepting of gender roles and their restrictions than of class differences, perhaps because gender—unlike class—was immutable. Class affiliations, within families and within jobs, linked participants in a way that seemed more tangible and obvious than the transsocial and transhistorical divisions around gender. However, while class appears clearly to have been a significant factor in Landes's defeat, it is not true that women, both middle and working class, turned against her. Nor is it true, as some writers claimed, that her defeat was a simple referendum on prohibition and reform. And although gender certainly was not the only factor in her defeat, as some writers claimed, it was a significant factor.

One of the most important components of the forces stemming from the power/knowledge link described by Foucault is the ability to impose its standards upon others without their even being conscious of the process. Power/knowledge is enforced not only through the mechanisms of direct control, such as repression and prohibition, but also through stereotyping, trivializing, ridicule, and sarcasm. Women who push against the boundaries of what is deemed appropriate behavior do not necessarily encounter head-on opposition. Instead of dealing directly with the ideas they broach, opponents may attack obliquely. Opponents (and they are not always male) use the process of trivializing such women or their concerns through labeling, stereotyping them or their backers with such terms as blue-nose and petticoat government. Or they treat them with scorn and humiliation through sarcasm or by calling attention to their bodies or sexuality. A small example was one of Landes's campaign appearances at which some criticized her not for her ideas but for wearing rubber overshoes at the podium. These emblematic attacks on Landes served to deflect attention away from issues at hand and turn the debate into confrontations between stereotypical images. They frequently fit into repetitive images and patterns, into "cultural scripts" that work to enforce an existing network of relations.

Power/knowledge also commands by controlling the definitions, possibilities, alternatives, taboos, or forums for discussion of new ideas, even the very language in which the new ideas have to be expressed to be understood or recognized. For instance, how could women enter the smoke-filled rooms of politics when tradition deemed it bad behavior for women to smoke? How could they talk about equality in the legal codes when the generic words for human were forms of "he" and "mankind"? How could women become politically active when politics was part of a corrupt world outside the ken of women in their private, home spheres? How could women be police officers—or tough managers—if they were the delicate, emotional creatures in mind and body that they were supposed to be? How could the state be allowed to intervene in family affairs if the patriarchal family by natural rights was guaranteed protection from onerous state interference?

Language is a powerful instrument for exercising the linkage between power and knowledge. Metaphors such as "petticoat rule," for example, are means of controlling definitions and behavior. Because language patterns structure thought, such constructions are significant expressions of power and control. They also limit consideration of alternative structures and systems.

If the power/knowledge codes remain strong enough, contradictory or alternative ideas cannot even enter discussion without risking labels and interpretations such as "abhorrent," "radical," "extreme," "weird," or "seditious." Such ideas may even be completely prohibited as taboo or as treasonous. As a contract governing exchange, power is not static but governs relations in constant tension, with disciplinary codes meant to enforce and aggregate power. It is interesting that "discipline" refers both to a body of knowledge and to enforcement of a code of behavior expectations, including policing one's own behavior and actions.

There are many layers, dimensions, and systems in power/knowledge, with complex interactions among these elements.

Many voices vie for control in a field like politics, in which minor shifts and new alliances are continually being born. Whatever the skirmishes, however, there is an overarching complex of systems, discourses, codes, norms, and values, as well as accepted practices, that evolve to tie cultural and societal systems together, connecting what happened to Landes to what happened before and after her. Theories from Foucault and Turner offer models that explain that overarching complex and perhaps how changes occur within it across time.

In the view of Michel Foucault, power begins in small interactions and ends in institutionalized power. Power is expressed in many voices, arguing and struggling over the terrain that language controls and defines. The languages of gender (such as the rhetoric of domesticity) and the discourses of power (such as legal codes) constitute fields where battles for control are fought.[6] Languages and discourses determine the possibilities open to all, but most particularly to those individuals and groups who have the least power. An individual's or group's desire for power—their will to power—must first find expression. The parameters, limitations, metaphors, constructs, and concepts embodied in language shape the expression of power (or the desire for it) in myriad ways. Discourses—special languages connected to disciplines and to knowledge—determine constructions of reality, and in turn control human behavior. The professions, with their operational codes, jargon and training/licensing requirements, provide concrete examples of such discourses.

Gender is one of the many reference points through which political power has been conceived and legitimated. Although it is a fundamental category, gender is not a simple binary opposition of men and women, or of victimizers and victims. It is a complex system, with many hotly disputed ideas of "woman" and "man." As historian Joan Scott has written, "Political history has, in a sense, been enacted on the field of gender. It is a field that seems fixed yet whose meaning is contested and in flux." Gender is contextually defined and repeatedly constructed, and "we must constantly ask not only what is at stake in proclamations or debates that invoke gender to explain or justify their positions but also how implicit understandings of gender are being invoked and reinscribed."[7] Meaning lies with the individual subject and the social organization, in what Foucault describes as "fields of force," with unequal relationships and shifting alliances that constitute power. As was evident in Seattle, there can also be informal networks of power born of those shifting alliances that shadow recognized sources of power such as the political authority of the city or of the state.

In this analysis of power relationships and the role of language and practices in the expression of power, Foucault's work is particularly insightful. He wrote little about feminism or women's history, but had much to say about power relationships and our definition and control of discourses. According to Foucault, power comes from below, through "the manifold relationships of force that take shape and come into play in the machinery of production, in families, limited groups, and institutions." They are the bases for power relationships and divisions that run through the social body as a whole.[8]

For Foucault, historical method is not finding causes, describing great men (or women) and great events, or mining a meaningful continuity of progress. Rather, history is found through uncovering the process that transformed certain "documents" into "monuments." Documents themselves do not offer up secrets of human intentions, but they do supply discourses that must be related to other texts.[9] The result is a rejection of totalization (or univocal analysis) and periodization in history, in favor of tracing the jerky and scattered movements within and among the fields. For instance, the term "Progressive," used by historians to describe an era and an attitude, becomes conflated in common usage to embrace many different kinds of acts for many purposes in many places. This simplifies events in a historical time frame in a way that distorts as much as it clarifies.

To Foucault, power is relational. Law and prohibition are a means to control knowledge and social action, as well as individual behavior.[10] Women who gained positions of power at the turn of the century frequently did so by invoking the accepted values of motherhood and the home, tacitly recognizing the taboo against women's political involvement even as they worked against it. And when women of the nineteenth century spoke exclusively and intently about home and family, about the tangible expressions of domestic life in the needle arts and etiquette of sitting parlors, they were engaging in a discourse designed (although not necessarily consciously) to control and empower the domestic sphere.

Foucault's view means not taking practices encoded in discourse or in language at face value but looking behind and beyond a practice to find out why it is structured the way it is. What series of conflicts gave rise to it, and what power relationships does it express? For instance, what gives gendered political symbols, such as cigars and petticoats, their power? Thus history's meaning is found not necessarily in the "document" but in its "margins," although documents are generally what historians have to work with. They can be used, Foucault says, as long as they too are viewed as part of a discursive practice, a clue to reconstructing the regulating forces that produce them. The question must always be asked, Why was this said but not this?

Further, the fundamental conflicts of history are detected not simply in dramatic or unique events, but throughout the levels of a social formation. One such level is "woman's proper sphere" and its interaction with legal structures, political structures, child-rearing ideas, economic patterns, and so on. Conflicts about a social formation are conveyed in conversation, messages, reports, resistance, and rumors, such as those carried in the media.[11]

In Landes's time, discursive formations governing women placed controls on their behavior through clothing, etiquette, employment, and other phases of their lives. Where power/knowledge effectively constrains the body—as with these controls on women—historical forces are apparent. Feminist critical theory intersects with Foucault's ideas in the historical time and space of the body, where relations of power point to the body as object, with the emergence of practices that define and control the body and thus behavior and identity.

To Foucault, events are inscribed on the body, and the body is imprinted by history and the play of forces.[12] The confinement and isolation of women's bodies, perpetuated more by accepted practices and codes than force, illustrate Foucault's meaning. For example, the cumbersome clothing worn by nineteenth-century women significantly limited their movement. At least initially, what Bertha Knight Landes wore and the novelty of her performing the masculine "game-opening" and "ground-breaking" ceremonies of public office were given almost as much media attention as her policies and plans for Seattle. It is interesting that women who become active in politics frequently are their most productive at age fifty and beyond. (Landes was fifty-three when she was elected to the Seattle city council.) Women of this age, freed of constraints such as family responsibilities, or perhaps the constraints of appearances and restrictions on behavior, are no longer afraid of "making a spectacle of themselves" to accomplish their goals.[13]

Foucault's model of power depicts a network of relations in constant tension. Power is not a privilege to be defended, but a contract governing exchange. Disciplinary codes originate not at one point but at different points in society.[14] Foucault, however, is not clear about the role of the subject—the actor—caught in the discursive formations that discipline behavior. What in human agency reverses, shifts, conspires, or revolts? Landes called upon particular resources she wanted from past formations, from the theories of self-development and education in Isaac Watts's work to the tenets of municipal reform and efficiency to the exploration of social issues in her clubs. They enabled her to create a political philosophy and act upon her vision of the future.

Because men traditionally have filled positions of power, women, in the view of one writer, "regularly surrender the validity of their own truth in the face of challenges by men and by others perceived to be in power" and build individual theories to explain women's inadequacies.[15] This process occurred at the end of the 1920s, when many writers blamed women themselves for an inability to capitalize on women's suffrage to gain political power. Women repeatedly witness their apparent inability to fill decision-making and status-holding positions and blame themselves.

This failure to maintain positions of power, combined with the general devaluation of women's work and culture, leads to the inevitable conclusion, as psychologist Polly Young-Eisendrath puts it, that "something is wrong with me." Assumptions of male superiority are present everywhere in American culture. Male standards "for health, mental health, leadership, culture, competence, judgment, relationships, and personal freedom constitute our recorded and received social reality."[16] The double bind occurs when democratic ideals of personal responsibility and self-determination conflict with ideals and accepted practices for womanly behavior. If a woman behaves as a mature, authoritative, competent adult, she will be criticized for being unwomanly; conversely, if she behaves as a "feminine" woman, she may be considered childlike or even neurotic. Often at issue in the descriptions and media coverage of Landes was how feminine she was. And when she was found to be feminine, some critics accused her of petticoat government, or of not being assertive enough. But when she was aggressive, she was "Big Bertha, the frenzied reformer."

Women who identify themselves with competence and authority and who oppose female inferiority find themselves with conflicting emotions and having what they say questioned because they assume the posture or manner of authority or competence. To violate the code of expected behaviors is to risk becoming labeled a freak, nonperson, outsider, or neurotic.

Turner and Social Change

How does change emerge, then, out of conflict? Anthropologist Victor Turner has developed a theory of change that reflects some continuity from one culture or social unit to the next, large or small, and one span of time to another. In his view, society repeats a specific process in creating, confronting, and testing change and ultimately accommodating it. He terms the process "social drama." The changes can be brought about either by personal or factional dissensions over conflicting norms, or even by technical or organizational innovations. The phases lead to social and political realignments and the acceptance of change. This dynamic process is full of social and cultural symbols and systems that shed and gather meaning over time and are altered in form. Through the conflicts, society grows and develops, even though certain social patterns persist and strive to enforce regularization and order.[17]

Central to Turner's theory is the idea of "liminality" (from the Latin *limen,* or threshold). It is a transitional phase, in which the subjects pass through a time and space of ambiguity. It is a kind of social limbo that has few of the characteristics of either the preceding or the subsequent social or cultural states.[18] When persons, groups, or even sets of ideas move from level or style of organization to another, there is an interface, Turner says, an interval "when the past is momentarily negated, suspended, or abrogated, and the future has not yet begun."[19] The factors or elements of culture may be recombined in varied—sometimes even grotesque—ways. Liminality is connected to the concept "anti-structure," which Turner defines as a latent system of potential alternatives from which new structures—such as women in political office—will arise when contingencies in the normative system, such as perceived need for municipal reform, necessitate it. It is a hallmark of antistructure that the normative social structure, with its defined roles, statuses, rights, and duties, is set aside, at least for a time, as in clubs or at exhibits.[20]

Turner sees this process as the seedbed for new symbols, models, and paradigms, which may then feed back into the structures of power, revising their goals, incentives, and direction. They are a means to critique and reformulate the existing structures. They can also serve as ways of examining order and disorder, testing boundaries without turning the order upside down permanently. Fiestas, Halloween games, and charivaries are examples of these. It was a show in an arena, the display of goods in an experimental setting, that brought Landes to the attention of the power structure.[21]

In a modernist society, individuals may offer their rational critique of the established order through what Turner terms liminoid genre, such as novels, drama, or other media, exposing the "injustices, inefficiencies, immoralities, alienations, and the like, held to be generated by mainstream modern economic and political structures and processes."[22] He might also include the formal presentation of research papers on social problems and issues, as occurred in thousands of clubs preceding their social and political activism.

Antistructure can provide a storehouse for alternative models for living, from utopias to programs, and influence the behavior of those in dominant social and political roles for or against radical change. An example from Landes's era and the years following was the extensive social welfare legislation that she and other women pushed through their clubs and political activism. Liminoid activities also often take place in neutral spaces or privileged areas, such as laboratories and studios—or club meetings—which are outside the mainstream of productive or political events. Liminoid phenomena tend to develop apart from central political and economic processes, "alone the margins, in the interstices, on the interfaces of central and servicing institutions."[23]

A central element of antistructure is *communitas,* a merging of individuals focused on the project at hand. In Turner's view, people anywhere can be subverted—if only briefly—from their duties and rights into an atmosphere of *communitas,* a timeless, egalitarian sense of experimentation and potential. While individual identity is retained in *communitas,* the roles, statuses, classes, cultural sexroles, age-divisions, and ethnic affiliations—all the divisions we create for ourselves—are temporarily suspended in a collective experience of unity, fleeting though it may be. Individuals are at least momentarily freed from the culturally defined encumbrances of role.[24] Women's clubs at the turn of the century, to women who were formerly isolated and restricted, offered *communitas* experiences and the benefits of new allegiances and the exploration of new ideas.

Communitas tends to generate its own metaphors and symbols, often in reaction to the structure to which it is connected. The various images of women from the 1910s and 1920s—as "municipal housekeepers," as new voters who would save society, as liberated and androgynous "flappers"—are metaphors from which new cultural values evolved. *Communitas* also tends to touch off repressive campaigns by the structurally entrenched elements of society. Structure is conservative and practical; *communitas* is speculative, imagistic, even apocalyptic, and thus threatening.

Leisure offers time and space away from institutional obligations and for liminal experimentation. "Leisure thus became potentially capable of releasing creative powers, individual or communal, either to criticize or buttress the dominant social structural values."[25] Turner thus finds it no accident that various genres of leisure entertainment, including theatrical productions and carnivals, have frequently been targets of legislation.

Certainly reformers' efforts to regulate drinking, dance halls, and movie theaters in the 1920s and subsequent decades would seem to bear out his analysis. These liminoid activities of leisure time persist, however, in artistic and popular entertainments, and they often criticize the status quo in some way, even as they offer opportunities for play and creativity. Hollywood treatments of law enforcement authorities or of career women in the 1920s, and after, offer further examples.

Turner seems to agree with Foucault that history's meaning is found in the process of conflict and change and the struggle between them. "Conflict seems to bring fundamental aspects of society, normally overlaid by the customs and habits of daily intercourse, into frightening prominence. People have to take sides in terms of deeply entrenched moral imperatives and constraints, often against their own personal preferences. Choice is overborne by duty."[26]

Duty is one of those concepts that guide behavior. People are governed by a set of ideas, images, concepts, and so on that assist with the processing of an endless stream of social interactions and that impose on them whatever degree of order they possess.[27] However, alternative visions, which are always tentative, incomplete, and open-ended, carry with them alternative goals and alternative means of attaining them. To study them, Turner says, involves studying the communication process, the sources of pressures to communicate, and the "symbols, signs, signals and tokens, verbal and non-verbal, that people employ in order to attain personal and group goals."[28] That includes the use of certain political symbols, such as cigars, petticoats, and the epithet "wimp."

In the field of politics, public goals and mechanisms are at the center. Power, in this sense, may be thought of as the capacity to secure compliance with binding decisions. Priorities are sorted out by a hierarchy of power, and the system of assignment Turner calls the authority code.[29] Social dramas occur within groups who share values and interests and have a common history. Briefly the phases of social drama are breach, crisis, redress, and either reintegration or recognition of schism.[30] The phases can be discerned, for instance, in the crisis Landes created when she seized the mayor's office and fired the police chief. From a political standpoint, the process includes:

1. Mobilization of political capital—using internal techniques (such as influence, threats of force, and rewards for support) and external techniques (such as lobbying, infiltration, conspiracy), building toward a confrontation if needs or demands cannot be met.
2. Breach of the peace—violating the norms or standards, with one or more members of the community producing tensions. It may consist simply of putting a rival in an embarrassing position or oneself in a favorable light at the rival's expense.
3. Crisis—breaching a significant norm considered binding on all members of the political field. It may be a basic political, legal, or ethical norm, or an unauthorized trespass on another's territory, or failure to observe critical caste or kinship rules. "Whatever the nature of the breach, it may serve as a pretext—at a given level of tension in a political field—to initiate an encounter between rival power seekers."[31] Turner has said

elsewhere that all public crises have liminal characteristics, since they are thresholds between more or less stable phases of the social process.

4. Countervailing tendencies—trying to maintain social cohesion so that a breach does not divide the community as a whole and threaten its past relationships. A break may be restrained by appealing to past relationships and perhaps stopped before it reaches a crisis point.
5. Adjustive or redressive mechanisms—turning to arbitration, formal legal machinery, or the performance of public ritual to end the breach. Judicial mechanisms can sometimes be used to resolve the conflict. If the conflict is over social norms or values, judicial decisions cannot relieve the quarrels in a way that preserves the threatened relationships. Intermediaries or arbitrators may be more successful. If not, a pervasive factionalism may remain, or the conflict may escalate to a complete break.
6. Restoration of peace (elsewhere termed reintegration by Turner)—if redressive mechanisms work, they lead to reestablishing relations among the contending parties, or else to a recognition of irreparable schism.

But even when peace is restored, changes remain. Some components will have less support, others more, and some none. The distribution of the factors of legitimacy will have changed, and perhaps as well the techniques used for gaining compliance. High status may now be low status. New norms will have been created, and some old norms will have been abandoned. The bases of support will have changed. Closeness will have become distance, and vice versa. New power will have been channeled into new authority. Yet through all these phases and changes, certain norms and relationships will persist. The stages of this political process reflect both constancy and change.[32] Turner himself says that his analysis may be weighted toward the view of community as governed by discrete situations and their imprint on subsequent behavior. "Situations that involve groups of large span and great range and scope are relatively few."[33]

Turner, like Foucault, is not specific about the role of human agency, of individuals in this process. He also does not write about feminism per se, although feminist criticism can make use of his theories and his ideas of liminality and how the process of change of status and structure occurs. He does state that a feature of many liminal rituals is the reversal of sex roles for participants.

According to Turner, in major social movements and revolutions the process of change erupts from the cumulative experience of a whole population whose "deepest material and spiritual needs and wants have for long been denied any legitimate expression by power-holding elites." The concept of suffrage comes to mind here. Turner adds that there may be violence, creativity, or a whole hidden cultural structure, richly clothed in symbols, "suddenly revealed and become itself both model and stimulus for new fruitful developments—in law and in administration, as well as arts and sciences." Civic maternalism and club activism are examples of symbolic structures that became both models and stimuli for changed political relations that were important to reform efforts. One of the characteristics of the process of large-scale societal social drama is its seeming inevitability of development, the rise of deep human needs "for more direct and egalitarian ways of knowing and experiencing relationships, needs which have been frustrated or perverted by . . . institutionalized social structure."[34]

Furthermore, the process uses certain change agents who are sacrificed or sacrifice themselves to their cause. They take on a tendency to speak in a representative way. "Collective representation" displaces "individual representation."[35] From the time she ran for her first office, Landes was conscious of her role as representative of her gender and woman's place in politics. She and others saw her administration as a test of all women's ability to manage the complexities of city government. Her rhetoric took on that representative tone, and she saw her political defeat as a sacrifice to sexism and to the criminal element in Seattle that stood to profit from her defeat.

Other factors that Turner cites as important for placing social change and movement leaders in context include class structure, category, church, state, sect, and party (he omits gender). At a more local level, the list includes business alliances, patterns of religious and governmental hierarchies, and local factions. He is critical, however, of theorists who treat politics either as a game or a rational process governed solely by interests. "People will die for values that oppose their interests and promote interests that oppose their values. And it is this practical result in behavior that we are interested in here."[36]

The politics of class struggle does not go according to commonly accepted rules, particularly the rules associated with gentlemanly conduct, as in games, Turner notes. With regard to Landes, this is particularly relevant to her campaign for reelection as mayor of Seattle. In that campaign her opponent used dirty politics, attacking her on the basis of both her sex and her class, as he refused her attempts to force him to debate her on the issues important to Seattle's future.

Turner notes that participants in a struggle for social changes are of two types—outsiders and marginals. The outsiders are people in a semipermanent state of liminality existing outside the structural arrangements of a given social system. They voluntarily set themselves apart from the behavior of "status-occupying, role-playing members" who are part of that system. An example of an outsider might be counterculture rebels, or artists and writers who withdraw from active participation in society but still offer a critique of its structures.

These he distinguishes from the marginals, who are members of two or more groups whose social definitions and cultural norms are different from, and often opposed to, one another. In that list he includes immigrants, second-generation Americans, upwardly or downwardly mobile members, migrants from country to city, and, relevant to this book, "women in a changed, nontraditional role."[37] Landes certainly acted in this way, in her use of clubs as the genesis for her activism and women's interests as a wedge for political control and critique of government. Yet she remained steadfast in her allegiance to women's causes.

Landes's Life as a Recurring Story

No life can be summed up in a few models. Both Turner and Foucault offer demonstrable theories and valuable insights for the retelling of history in a way that connects to present conflicts. They help explain where Bertha Knight Landes found herself and why, and how Landes as historical agent was able to accomplish both as much and as little as she did, given the context of her times. Their models and theories offer useful reference points for how paradigms are created, how societal reorderings come about, how forces interact, and how power is created and used particularly with regard to gender. What Landes faced and what happened to her became a common pattern in the twentieth century.

In 1984, for example, when Geraldine Ferraro became the first female vice-presidential nominee of a major American political party, the media's coverage of her was different from their coverage of other national candidates. For instance, much—again—was made of her gender, of her liminal "first" status, of her family, of her emotional fitness, and so on. Early in the campaign the networks ran newsclips of Ferraro buying her own groceries. When she debated George Bush, then Ronald Reagan's running mate, his offhand remark after the debate that he had "kicked a little ass" was taken as a crude, physical, sexist put-down of her, despite his protestations. Some election analysts claimed that even the dogged tracking of her husband's troubled finances was not what the spouse of any male candidate would have received, a claim that others disputed. In any case, the response to her candidacy was not like that elicited by other national candidates. The fact that although women had the vote since 1920, yet not until 1984 was a woman nominated by either the Democratic or Republican party for national office was in itself indicative of how gender-sensitive politics has remained.

In 1990, in a bitter election fight for the position of governor of Texas, state treasurer Ann Richards won the primary and general elections against her male opponents. Hal Bruno, ABC television's political director, commented without much sense of history that it was "the first time we've seen such a negative campaign against a woman." He added that a negative campaign against a woman was also being waged in California, where former San Francisco Mayor Dianne Feinstein was running unsuccessfully for governor. One of the ads in that campaign ended, "Dianne Feinstein—if she couldn't manage a city, how could she manage California?" As happened with another media analyst writing in 1928 about Landes, Bruno credited the women's vote as the key factor in Richards's victory.[38] Richards was the first woman in a half century to hold statewide office in Texas when she was elected state treasurer in 1982.

New York Times writer Robin Toner also recounted the negative personal attacks on Richards in the governor's race, and her counterattacks. One of the attack ads, for television, asked, "Did she use marijuana, or something worse like cocaine, not as a college kid but as a 47-year-old elected official sworn to uphold the law?" Toner also included the following sentence analyzing Richards's victory: "Richards' victory was hailed by the National Women's Political Caucus as emblematic of the political progress of women and inspirational to other female candidates around the country."[39]

The year 1992 was labeled the Year of the Woman because of a comparative surge in raw numbers of women running for national office, combined with the fact that several women were successful at raising requisite funds for campaigns of that scope. At the state level, women continued to make slow but steady inroads into legislatures. As of the 1992 elections, women held 20 percent of the legislative seats, up from 18 percent the year before. Total proportions ranged from a low in Kentucky (4.3 percent of the seats) to a high—Landes would have been pleased—in Washington State (38 percent).[40] Once again, regional differences were apparent. The states with the highest female representation were mostly in the West; those with the lowest were in the South.

As of the November 1992 election, the number of women in the U.S. Senate tripled, but it was to a still disproportionate six out of one hundred seats. In a symbolic move, the Senate leadership decided it was finally time the women senators had their own bathroom near the Senate floor, authorizing construction of one near the one men have always had. The year 1992 was deemed by pundits a successful one for women, who were said at last to be joining the men in the halls of political power and inspiring other women. Virtually the same words, however, had appeared about Landes in the 1920s. Women still saw their achievements labeled as exceptional for their gender, or as not wholly their own, for good or ill, but claimed by others as inspiration for women who will surely follow.

An Associated Press reporter wrote that a male candidate running against a woman was nowadays in a difficult spot. "The political landscape is strewn with faux pas by men—mostly older ones—more accustomed to thinking of women in the kitchen than on the campaign trail," the piece said. The reporter quoted Celinda Lake, a Democratic pollster, as saying, "Women running is just plain different and men sense it." The Associated Press writer noted that in 1988 male candidates told female opponents in both Wisconsin and New Hampshire races that they should not run for Congress because they had young children.[41]

In 1988 the major negative factor that presidential candidate George Bush had to overcome, at least initially in his campaign, was not the Iran-Contra "arms for hostages" scandal but the label "wimp." The so-called wimp factor haunted him during his campaign until his contentious confrontation with CBS Evening News anchorman Dan Rather. The coaching he received and the aggressive, counterattack stance he took with Rather's probing questions caused the wimp factor to evaporate as an issue in the campaign.[42]

"Wimp," like "petticoat," apparently takes its strength by referring to and denigrating a piece of female attire that is transformed into a symbol for female (i.e., weak and ineffectual) behavior. "Wimp" may have derived from "wimple," a woman's headcloth circling the face and drawn in folds under the chin, usually worn out of doors. Some authorities say the word may also have come from a corruption of the word "women."[43] The New Dictionary of American Slang defines "wimp" as an ineffectual, "soft, silly person; a weakling." It traces the word to the early twentieth century and use at Cambridge University as a word for "young woman."[44] The 1989 *Thesaurus of American Slang* lists these synonyms for "wimp": baby, Ethel, flower, goody-goody, limp dishrag, mama's boy, nervous Nellie, nobody, nothing, pantywaist, weak sister, sissy.[45] They provide a cogent commentary on the devaluation and denigration of the female gender through language.

In the traditional seat of power—politics—women continued to fare poorly worldwide despite highly visible (and powerful) firsts such as Britain's Margaret Thatcher. As of 1984, the percentage of female members in Congress and other national legislatures ranged from 4.5 percent in the United States and Australia to a high of 28 percent in Sweden and 32.5 percent in the former Union of Soviet Socialist Republics. The United States and Australia were tied for second lowest, right above Britain at 3.6 percent, in terms of female participation.[46] Women had never held more than 4.5 percent of all seats in the U.S. Congress, nor held more than two governorships simultaneously out of all fifty states, well into the sixth decade after women gained the vote.[47]

Social scientists have continued to debate what would make the difference, from childhood on, in empowering women. Instead of the psychoanalytical constructs of the 1920s, concluding that women's real route to happiness and satisfaction was through home, husband, and children, the end of the century saw scientific explanations arise for gender differences through biochemistry and the effects of hormones, before and after birth. These explanations acted in much the same way as the psychological explanations did to enforce existing gender relations in the early decades of the century, by denying women their will to power (often termed "aggression" in reference to female behavior). They also tended to reinforce female separateness through highlighting qualities such as empathy and noncompetitiveness, thus bolstering arguments against equality. Their reliance on purported scientific objectivity gave these studies similar credibility as "truth," just as sociology and psychoanalytic theory had obtained that credibility in earlier decades.

Sociologist Sally Helgesen's popular study of 1990, *The Female Advantage: Women's Ways of Leadership,* concluded that female leaders in the business world had different values from men. These values included listening, teaching, favoring cooperation with colleagues over competition, and encouraging subordinates rather than dominating them—fundamentally the classic nurturing behavior. Women, Helgesen concluded after observing the work habits of women at senior levels in corporations, encourage creativity, downplay hierarchy, and stress human development rather than subordination to a chain of command, in contrast to traditional corporate leaders.[48] In fact, she argued that women in the corporate jungle should no longer try to think and act like men in the workplace, counter to advice provided in other self-help books in the popular press. Over a half-century earlier in 1927, Landes had offered women similar advice: "Don't emulate men. Take into business your womanly characteristics and be yourself. By that road only can woman arrive, be it in business, in politics, or in the professions."[49]

Helgesen, like many suffragists at the turn of the century, accepted the concept that women are fundamentally different from men and thus act in ways counter to the ways men act. *Time* magazine in 1990 said surveys showed women were perceived to be better than men on dealing with issues such as the young, the aged, the sick, and the environment. Furthermore, they were perceived to have higher ethical standards and greater honesty.[50] Nevertheless, discourses and practices governing those professions where men predominated required women to respond according to the standards established by the dominant gender, if women chose to participate.

A few women in the twentieth century did attain positions of real power. Feminist Rosalind Powell studied the lives of forty powerful and influential women worldwide, trying to discern what made the difference in their lives. She isolated a half-dozen commonalties that she said made these women different, which both pointed them toward, and made it possible for them to attain, positions of power in government, in corporations, and elsewhere. The factors she isolated included having an empowering family with high expectations; a degree of early insecurity, of feeling "out of phase" with one's peers; a growing sense of one's own ability to cope and of being stronger than others, including men; some early concrete outside success as a proof of worth; academic achievement and validation as further proof of worth; and last, a sense of "personal autonomy, self-reliance, and ability to take on responsibility."[51]

What makes one person—one woman—succeed dramatically where others have not cannot be reduced to a list and is often dependent on external factors. However, Powell's list of common characteristics provides an interesting commentary on gender roles and relations, and on expectations of children who are female. The list seems to fit several aspects of Bertha Knight Landes's life.

For instance, her family contained several high achievers, and she herself wrote about high family expectations. Others have written at length about the high achievement standards held by many such New England families. Landes, who admittedly played with boys as well as girls, was "out of phase" with other New England girls. In getting a high school and college education, she was again unusual when compared with other young women of her time. How much she felt out of phase with them is not evident in the record Landes left, but attending Indiana University, where, before the turn of the century, only one of every ten students was female, must have made her feel, at the least, unusual. That she developed a sense of her own ability to cope and to lead others who were not as strong—including men, eventually—was indisputable, given her record of achievement through club elections and city elections. She had an initial validation in her academic success and years of teaching, and later in her elections to dozens of club offices. Although they came later in her life, she had many other validating experiences, through her active and public role in civic affairs. And from her early years on, she had a sense of what Powell called "personal autonomy, self-reliance, and ability to take on responsibility," reflected in her comments on duty and her explanations of why she did what she did.

It has been many decades since women earned the right to vote. The paradigm Landes helped create for feminine behavior has not yet been fully realized, although a little more progress toward equality is made with every passing decade, at least in the United States. Social welfare, civic responsibility, and concerns about crime still dominate much public discourse. Economic, technological, and even territorial factors, as well as the ability of the political system to accommodate pressures, have generally reinforced the hegemony of traditional patterns and hierarchies.

Women's clubs, the fount of much education, activism, and social welfare, in general continued to see a membership slide that started in the 1920s. In 1988 one news magazine called women's clubs an endangered species with an aging membership. Members fell to below 500,000, as more jobs, other organizations and opportunities, and increasing demands on time made the clubs less attractive. "We're in steady decline," Leigh Wintz, then executive director of the General Federation, told the magazine, "and it's a difficult process to reverse."[52] Clubs, although still important to individual communities and members, no longer provided the broad opportunities for social reform and leadership development that they offered in Landes's time.

Public policy analysts tried to calculate the cost of the loss of volunteer time to community institutions, losses that all institutions found difficulty replacing. The magazine noted that from their beginning, clubs gave women opportunities to reform not only themselves but also society. "Over the years they provided the leadership for the suffragist movement, child-labor reform, conservation, temperance and civil rights." Clubs also fell victim to their successes. As women gained access to government, the courts, and the workplace, "women's clubs are no longer the primary path to fulfillment or power."[53] Now clubs had to compete with professional associations, single-issue groups, and even men's clubs suddenly open to women. The magazine advocated a return to an activist past and adapting programs and schedules to potential members' needs as the way to save the women's clubs for future generations.

Bertha Knight Landes's call for civic involvement as women's right and responsibility, and the example she provided, helped pave the way for those women who did follow, on the Seattle City Council and elsewhere in local government. She saw herself, and others measured her, as an anomaly, but by the end of the twentieth century women almost routinely became council members, mayors of cities large and small, and even occasionally governors of states. Landes's civic reform ideals continued to find expression in a host of social welfare programs and environmental measures, from zoning to health regulations.

She had helped shape the city's landscape, policies, and personality, even though her time in elected public office totaled only six years. National publicity made her one of those "first woman who" figures used to show that the limits on women's participation had truly been lifted or that women could handle jobs traditionally done by men.

Landes was born only three years after the Civil War ended. She died during World War II. She saw tumultuous changes in the intervening decades and, empowered by the women's club movement, became active in politics out of a sense of civic duty. Her college education, rare for a woman of her generation, served her well in the development of a political philosophy and a role that citizens—including female ones—could play in improving their communities. Always the leader, Landes may have positioned herself as the reluctant candidate, but she wrested power where possible and campaigned hard and long for her idealistic vision of what government should be and should do.

Bertha Knight Landes was a significant figure in western history and women's history in the 1920s for what she embodied as well as what she accomplished. She was caught in the cross currents of prohibition, feminism, urban growth, professionalization, and bureaucratization as they ran through the city of Seattle and the Pacific Northwest. She was also caught up in a conservative, anti-New Woman shift by the end of the decade, and soon after, the social stresses of the Depression. During the down years of the Depression, her national speaking tours continued to carve out a place for women in the management of city affairs and improvement of the lives of city residents.

When Landes is remembered in the future, it should not be as a female anomaly or a bluenose but for what she was—a powerful woman responding creatively to the needs, pressures, and opportunities of her time and the strictures of her culture. In developing her political philosophy, acting on her vision of the future, and retelling her own story, Bertha Knight Landes outlined an itinerary for those women and men who traveled behind, following her ideals of civic betterment.

NOTES

PREFACE

1. For instance, Nard Jones (in his *Seattle*) dismissed her as someone who "goaded the police into a closed-town policy," of whom "Seattle quickly grew tired." James Warren dismissed her as a "prohibitionist and strict moralist" (*King County and Its Queen City: Seattle,* 126). There was no mention at all of her in Murray Morgan's popular *Skid Road: An Informal Portrait of Seattle,* or in Roger Sale's more recent *Seattle, Past to Present*. She was also omitted from Melvin Holli and Peter Jones, *Biographical Dictionary of American Mayors, 1820–1980*. There are many other examples.

2. *Seattle Times,* March 10, 1926.

I. THE CITY IS BUT "THE LARGER HOME"

1. *Seattle Times,* March 10, 1928.

2. *Harper's Weekly,* May 16, 1868, 320, cited in Sara Evans, *Born for Liberty,* no page no.

3. Karen Blair, *The Clubwoman as Feminist: True Womanhood Redefined, 1868–1914,* 15.

4. Cornelius H. Hanford, ed., *Seattle and Environs, 1852–1924,* 3:435–36.

5. Julia Budlong, "What Happened in Seattle," *Nation,* August 29, 1928, 197.

6. Erma Conkling Lee, ed., *The Biographical Cyclopaedia of American Women,* 2:148.

7. Louis Tracy, Genealogy for "Mr. Knight," 1897, Bertha Knight Landes Papers, box 1, Manuscripts Collection, University of Washington, Seattle (hereafter cited as Landes Papers). The line continues through David Knight, who married Sarah Bachus on March 17, 1691, in Norwich, Connecticut. They had seven children, and he died at age fifty-three.

8. David Starr Jordan, *The Days of a Man: Being Memories of a Naturalist, Teacher, and Minor Prophet of Democracy,* 1:530.

9. L. Brent Vaughan, ed., *Hill's Practical Reference Library of General Knowledge,* "Massachusetts."

10. Ibid., "Ware."

11. Robert Burke, "Bertha Ethel Knight Landes," in *Notable American Women, 1607–1950,* ed. Edward James and Janet James, 2:362–63.

12. Vaughan, *Hill's Library,* "Worcester."

13. Jennie Cunningham Croly, *The History of the Woman's Club Movement in America,* 666.

14. Ibid., 667–68.

15. "Statements" on Landes City Council Campaign letterhead, 1922, Landes Papers, box 1.

16. Bertha Knight Landes, "Reminiscence," written for *Survey Graphic,* n.d., Landes Papers, box 1.

17. Matthew O'Connor, "Biography of Bertha Knight Landes," Landes Papers, box 1.

18. Certificate, Dix Street School, June 28, 1884, Landes Papers, box 1.

19. Lee, *Biographical Cyclopaedia,* 148; and Hanford, *Seattle and Environs,* 3:435–36.

20. Capt. E. L. Balch, "Admiral A. M. Knight," *Palo Alto Times,* March 4, 1897.

21. Jordan, *Days of a Man,* 326.

22. *New York Times,* February 27, 1927.

23. "Woman Mayor Launches Manager Plan," *American Public Official Magazine,* July 1926, no page no.

24. Jordan, *Days of a Man,* 301–2, 325–26.

25. Ibid., 530.

26. Ibid., 293.

27. G. M. Miller, Head of English at the University of Idaho, letter to editor of *Spokesman-Review,* n.d.

28. Ibid.

29. Jordan, *Days of a Man,* 299.

30. In the Civil War Jordan had lost an older brother whom he worshiped, leading him to argue against the slaughter of young men in warfare. Richard Hofstadter credited Jordan more than any other individual for establishing in the American mind the concept of war as a biological evil that kills off the physically and mentally fit, leading to degeneration (*Social Darwinism in American Thought,* 195–96).

31. Thomas Clark, *Indiana University: Midwestern Pioneer,* 1:235–37.

32. Lynn Gordon, *Gender and Higher Education in the Progressive Era,* 2.

33. *Isaac Watts' Improvement of the Mind,* rev. Joseph Emerson, principal of the Female Seminary, Wethersfield, Conn.

34. Ibid., vi.

35. Ibid., 35–48.

36. Ibid., 30–33.

37. "The Landis or Landes Family and Its Name," n.d., Henry Landes Papers, University Archives, University of Washington, Seattle.

38. Lee, *Biographical Cyclopaedia,* 150.

39. G. E. Goodspeed, "Memorial of Henry Landes," *Proceedings of the Geological Society of America for 1936,* June 1937, 207.

40. Ibid.

41. Henry Landes to Bertha Knight, July 9, 1893, Landes Papers, box 1.

42. Alice Kessler-Harris, *Women Have Always Worked: A Historical Overview,* 109.

43. Goodspeed, "Memorial of Henry Landes," 207–13.

44. Arthur H. Allen, *Who's Who in Washington State: A Compilation of Biographical Sketches of Men and Women Prominent in the Affairs of Washington State,* 1:139.

45. Jordan, *Days of a Man,* 223–24.

46. Janice Reiff, "Urbanization and the Social Structure: Seattle, Washington, 1852–1910" (Ph.D. diss., University of Washington, 1981), 75.

47. Paul Dorpat, *Seattle: Now and Then,* no. 36.

48. Goodspeed, "Memorial of Henry Landes," 208.

49. *Seattle Post-Intelligencer,* October 2, 1897.

50. Hanford, *Seattle and Environs,* 1:253.

51. Jones, *Seattle,* 20; and Warren, *King County and Its Queen City,* 98–99.

52. Frederick M. Padelford, "The Community," in *University Congregational Church Fiftieth Anniversary Program* (1941), cited in Doris Pieroth, "Bertha Knight Landes: The Woman Who Was Mayor," in *Women in Pacific Northwest History,* ed. Karen Blair, 89.

53. Warren, *King County and Its Queen City,* 178.

54. Pieroth, "Bertha Knight Landes," 88–89.

55. *El Paso Times,* March 2, 1929.

56. Pieroth, "Bertha Knight Landes," 88.

57. Edwin S. Gaustad, *A Religious History of America,* 122.

58. Ibid., 188.

59. Ibid., 145.

60. "The Insanity of Surgery," editorial in the *Seattle Mail and Herald,* April 1, 1905. The weekly newspaper was sharply critical of the physician and the pro-

cedure because the girl had been in good health and the need for the surgery did not justify the risk if the girl had a weak heart. "The only incentive on the part of her parents to have the operation performed was the fear, inspired by some doctor, that in case she were to be attacked by some throat malady the condition of her tonsils would make the disease more difficult to cure."

61. [T. P.?] Graves to Henry Landes, n.d., Henry Landes Papers, box 1.

62. *Polk's Seattle City Directory,* 1940.

63. Rillmond Schear, "Our One and Only Madame Mayor," *Seattle Magazine,* February 1965, 21.

64. They include *Geology and Man,* with Russell Hussey; *Petroleum Geology;* and *Petroleum Geology of the United States.*

65. Biography, no title or date, in Henry Landes Papers, box 1.

66. *Seattle Times,* April 19, 1922.

67. Ibid.

68. Goodspeed, "Memorial of Henry Landes," 208.

69. Superior Court Judge James Ronald to Washington governor Ernest Lister, May 21, 1915, Henry Landes Papers. Hanford, in *Seattle and Environs,* wrote that Landes had served the university well but that the regents felt they needed a "man trained and experienced in different fields" (1:555).

70. William Markham, Board of Regents Secretary, to Henry Landes, May 19, 1915, Henry Landes Papers.

71. Goodspeed, "Memorial of Henry Landes," 209.

72. Ibid., 210

73. *University of Washington Daily,* April 6, 1920.

74. Goodspeed, "Memorial of Henry Landes," 209. The document states that Landes was named state geologist in 1901; however, his papers contain a certificate signed by Governor J. H. McGraw appointing him state geologist as of January 1897, noting also that the state "shall not be liable for any salary or expenses herein."

75. "Writings," Henry Landes Papers, box 1.

76. Goodspeed, "Memorial of Henry Landes," 210.

77. Allen, *Who's Who,* 139.

78. Newspaper clipping, Cincinnati paper, February 9, 1927, Landes Papers, box 2.

79. Nancy Cott, in *The Bonds of Womanhood: "Woman's Sphere" in New England, 1780–1835,* as well as other writers, holds that the rise of domesticity, of language describing men's and women's spheres as separate but equal, was an advance for women in that it heightened the woman's influence within families and fostered a gender-linked consciousness among women. This step in turn gave rise to the development of feminism. However, "in opening certain avenues to women because of their sex, it barricaded all others" (201).

80. The metaphor of woman's separate sphere needs to be analyzed, instead of being offered as a restrictive duality, in order to recover how it was socially constructed both for and by women and to discern what role men played and how they too were constricted by it. Historian Linda Kerber also notes that the concept was not a nineteenth-century phenomenon but one that extends far back into history, as part of a pattern of subordination of women ("Separate Spheres, Female Worlds, Woman's Place: The Rhetoric of Women's History," *Journal of American History* 75 [June 1988]: 9–39). The same process needs to be applied to the metaphor "municipal housekeeping." See also Rosalind Rosenberg, *Beyond Separate Spheres: Intellectual Roots of Modern Feminism,* which traces how a shift in attitude toward gender, as being socially constructed rather than a biological given, began with the social scientists of the early part of the twentieth century.

81. Croly, *History of the Woman's Club Movement,* 666.

82. Mrs. A. W. Comins, quoted in ibid., 668.

83. John Buenker described the function of such organic networks in describing ethnic coalitions during the Progressive Era in "Sovereign Individuals

and Organic Networks: Political Cultures in Conflict during the Progressive Era," *American Quarterly* 40 (June 1988): 187–204. Although Buenker refers specifically to the function of such networks in ethnic neighborhoods, the same principles can be recognized in women's clubwork.

84. Carolyn Heilbrun, in *Writing a Woman's Life,* notes that women traditionally refuse to recognize and write about women's desire for power. "We must stop reinscribing male words, and rewrite our ideas about what Nancy Miller calls a female impulse to power as opposed to the erotic impulse which alone is supposed to impel women. We know we are without a text, and must discover one" (44).

85. Landes, "Reminiscence."

86. *Spokane Spokesman-Review,* n.d., Landes Papers, box 2.

87. "Woman's Mission and Women's Clubs," *Ladies Home Journal* 22 (May 1905): 3–4, cited in Blair, *Clubwoman as Feminist,* 144.

88. The General Federation of Women's Clubs, organized in 1890 by Jane Cunningham Croly, was formed to bring literary clubs together in a national association. Once formed, however, the cultural programs turned toward municipal housekeeping and applying women's sensitivities to the problems of the community. Croly borrowed from the "army of women" techniques of the Women's Christian Temperance Union, founded in 1873 (Blair, *Clubwoman as Feminist,* 93, 98).

89. Edith H. Altbach, *Women in America,* 115–17.

90. At national meetings the federation heard clamorous arguments for and against women's suffrage, including an address from Carrie Chapman Catt in 1906. At the 1910 General Federation meeting at Cincinnati, Alice Hill Chittenden of Brooklyn delivered an address that typified the argument against giving women the vote. According to Chittenden,"The whole social structure of the State would be weakened by attempting to equalize . . . the practical activities of the sexes, and the basic principles of our government shattered by making possible a majority which could not enforce its own rules." Doubling the electorate would not assure a "higher standard of intelligence in the votes cast." Furthermore, woman might lose man's protection, and gaining the vote would mean an unhealthy diffusion of women's energies if political life were added to her responsibilities (H. H. Dawson, ed., *General Federation of Women's Clubs' Tenth Biennial Convention Official Report,* 243–44, 248, 252). Also see Nancy Cott, *The Grounding of Modern Feminism,* 32–33.

91. In 1911 those clubs included the Alpha Club, Classic Culture Club, Clionian Club, Coterie Club, Green Lake Home Economics, Ladies' Literary and Musical Club, King County Graduate Nurses' Club, Medical Women's Club, Queen Anne Fortnightly Club, Lake Wood Civic Improvement, Progressive Thought, Seattle Women's Club, Sorosis Club, Sunset Heights Literary Club, Women's Century Club, Women's Tuesday Club, Schubert Club, Women's Educational Club, Political Equality Club, West Seattle Art Club, Ladies of the Round Table, Pennsylvania Study Club, and the Emerson Club (*Seattle Society Blue Book,* 64).

92. Cott, *Grounding of Modern Feminism,* 57.

93. Ibid., 258

94. Century Club History, Washington State Federation of Women's Clubs, box 2, Manuscripts Collection, University of Washington (hereafter cited as WSFWC).

95. Jacqueline Van Voris, *Carrie Chapman Catt: A Public Life,* 11–15.

96. New Century Clubs and Woman's Century Clubs were founded in several places across the United States as part of the larger club movement, such as New Century Club founded by 1880 in Philadelphia by Lucretia Longshore Blankenburg, the daughter of Philadelphia's first female physician (Catherine Clinton, *The Other Civil War: Women in the Nineteenth Century,* 174).

97. *History of the Woman's Century Club,* n.d. (1942 photostat), Pacific Northwest Collection, University of Washington.

98. *Votes for Women,* ed. Mrs. M. T. B. Hanna, August–September 1910, 6.

99. Croly, *History of the Woman's Club Movement,* 1143–44, 1149.

100. Carkeek Scrapbooks, Seattle History, 1884–1917, vol. 1, Museum of History and Industry, Seattle.

101. *Transactions of the National Council of Women,* 119.

102. Century Club History, WSFWC, box 1.

103. Margaret Knowles, ed., *The Seattle Woman—the Club Woman's Annual,* December 1924, 47.

104. *Constitution of the Woman's Century Club,* n.d. (1942 photostat), Pacific Northwest Collection, University of Washington.

105. The Olympia Club encouraged discussion of all questions except "religion, temperance and politics." Despite its high cost, it claimed that all classes and opinions were represented, with character and intelligence being the only qualification for membership (Croly, *History of the Woman's Club Movement,* 1133).

106. Woman's Century Club was one of eight Seattle clubs meeting in Olympia in 1897 to found the Washington Federation. The others from Seattle were Classic Culture Club, Nineteenth Century Literary Club, P.E.O. Club, Woman's Industrial Club (representing working women), Kindergarten Club, Fortnightly Club, and Advance Club, according to "Classified List of Delegates to First Convention," June 22–23, 1897, Olympia, WSFWC, box 1.

107. Croly, *History of the Woman's Club Movement,* 1139.

108. Century Club Yearbooks, Women's Clubs Files, Washington History Files, box 5, Northwest Room, Washington State Library.

109. Ibid.

110. "Washington State Federation of Women's Clubs Register, 1896–1923," and WSFWC, box 2.

111. WSFWC, box 1.

112. Amy Stacy, as quoted in Croly, *History of the Woman's Club Movement,* 1148.

113. Resolutions for 1907, "Minutes of the Washington State Federation of Women's Clubs, 1900–1908," WSFWC, box 2.

114. Richard Berner, *Seattle, 1900–1920: From Boomtown, Urban Turbulence, to Restoration,* 51, 54.

115. WSFWC, box 1.

116. Carkeek Scrapbooks, vol. 4.

117. Serena Mathews, "History of the Washington State Federation of Women's Clubs," WSFWC, box 2. Turner was president from 1899 to 1901 and remained active in federation leadership.

118. Karen Blair, "The Limits of Sisterhood: The Woman's Building in Seattle, 1908–1921," in *Women in Pacific Northwest History,* ed. Blair, 67.

119. Mildred Andrews, *Washington Women as Pathbreakers,* 99.

120. Berner, *Seattle, 1900–1920,* 205, 236.

121. Mathews, "History of the Washington State Federation of Women's Clubs," 55.

122. *Seattle Times,* February 26, 1926.

123. "Statements" on Landes City Council Campaign letterhead, 1922, Landes Papers, box 1.

124. Mildred Andrews, *Seattle Women: A Legacy of Community Development,* 36–37.

125. Hanford, *Seattle and Environs,* 1:351–52.

126. Ibid., 231.

127. Berner, *Seattle, 1900–1920,* 229.

128. Mathews, "History of the Washington State Federation of Women's Clubs," 61–63.

129. Ibid., 70.

130. Andrew W. Lind, *A Study of Mobility of Population in Seattle,* 12, 14. In descending order, the foreign-born population came primarily from Sweden, Norway, England, Japan, and Germany.

131. Seattle for a time also had its own settlement house working with immigrants, established in 1906 by Babette Gatzert. It offered classes in Ameri-

canization, English, sewing, and religion. Later it expanded to include help with employment, baby health, legal advice, and clubs (Andrews, *Washington Women as Pathbreakers,* 69).

132. The General Federation, like most of the state federations, remained silent on the question of woman's suffrage during this period. Suffrage for clubwomen had taken a back seat to obtaining influence "through invocation of women's traditional domestic qualities." It took a concerted and repeated effort by suffrage supporters to win the General Federation's endorsement of the idea (Blair, *Clubwoman as Feminist,* 111–12).

133. Mrs. H. O. Stone, "Mrs. Landes, Why We Loved Her," Memorial to Bertha Landes by Women's City Club, February 8, 1944, t.s., Carkeek Scrapbooks, vol. 3.

134. Berner, *Seattle, 1900–1920,* 79.

135. *Twenty-third Annual Report,* Washington State Federation of Women's Clubs, Yearbook for 1919–20, 119–20, Pacific Northwest Collection, University of Washington; and Mathews, "History of the Washington State Federation of Women's Clubs," 71.

136. WSFWC, box 1.

137. Andrews, *Seattle Women,* 45.

138. Andrews, *Washington Women as Pathbreakers,* 28.

139. Hanford, *Seattle and Environs,* 1:397.

140. *American Soroptimist,* October 1940; and *Seattle Times,* November 30, 1942.

141. "Historical Highlights, Women's University Club of Seattle, 1914–1980," 3–16, Pacific Northwest Collection, University of Washington.

142. Schear, "Our One and Only Madame Mayor," 20.

143. Ibid., 19.

144. Newspaper clipping, no date or title, Landes Papers, box 1. In this clipping, published probably at the outset of her 1922 campaign for city council, someone—presumably Landes—underlined the sentence quoted. The clipping also credited her for organizing excursions to factories, for being a director of the YWCA, and for organizing a club of parents and teachers in her school district, before parent-teacher clubs were common.

145. Helen L. Webster, "Transactions of the National Council of Women," 181.

146. Clinton, *Other Civil War,* 128.

147. Sandra L. Myres, *Westering Women and the Frontier Experience, 1800–1915,* 225–26.

148. The linkage in the West is discussed at length by G. Thomas Edwards in *Sowing Good Seeds*. Also see Ross Evans Paulson, *Women's Suffrage and Prohibition: A Comparative Study of Equality and Social Control.* Paulson concludes that in some ways, the granting of women's suffrage—as an effort to address social disorder through women's moral superiority—was a conservative rather than a liberal move.

Jed Dannenbaum, in "The Origins of Temperance Activism and Militancy among American Women," *Journal of Social History* 15 (Winter 1981): 235–52, traces the roots of the temperance and prohibition movement leading to the formation of the Women's Christian Temperance Union. Dannenbaum argues that the religious and class lines around Irish and German immigrants and the moral education of children were the particular concerns leading to the movement in the decades before 1870. Those concerns in turn led to demands for power from the women involved, from the right to speak from public platforms to saloon-smashing.

149. Mary W. Avery, *History and Government of the State of Washington,* 320–21.

150. Harold Barton and Catharine Bullard, *History of the State of Washington,* 260–61.

151. Ibid., 140.

152. *Seattle Post-Intelligencer* and *Seattle Times,* July 5, 1909.

153. Ida Hustad Harper, ed., *History of Woman Suffrage,* 5:264.

154. Andrews, *Washington Women as Pathbreakers,* 101.

155. *New York Suffrage Newsletter,* December 1910, 198–99; *International Woman Suffrage Alliance Report,* 1911, 63, cited in Van Voris, *Carrie Chapman Catt,* 81.

156. William Kerr, Jr., "The Progressives of Washington, 1910–1912," *Pacific Northwest Quarterly 55* (January 1964): 17.

157. For an extensive explanation of how women in the nineteenth century expanded their sphere into community service and care of dependents, "areas not fully within men's or women's politics" that combined "public roles and administration with nurturance and compassion," see Paula Baker, "The Domestication of Politics: Women and American Political Society, 1780–1920," *American Historical Review 89* (June 1984): 620–47.

158. Abigail Scott Duniway, speech before the National American Woman Suffrage Association convention, Grand Rapids, May 2, 1899, as quoted in Lauren Kessler, "A Siege of the Citadels: Access of Woman Suffrage Ideas to the Oregon Press, 1884–1912" (Ph.D. diss., University of Washington, 1980), 44.

159. This position is explored at length by Barbara Leslie Epstein in *The Politics of Domesticity: Women, Evangelism, and Temperance in Nineteenth-Century America.* She notes in particular that nineteenth-century domestic culture and feminism were shaped within the interests of the urban middle class, which looked antagonistically at working-class cultures, particularly immigrant cultures. The only organization of the time that was working consistently to confront issues of both sex and class and to bring middle-class and working women together was the Women's Trade Union League, and it was not very successful.

160. The consequences of capitalism were different for working-class women than they were for middle-class women. Where middle-class women found themselves cut off from production and economically dependent on men, working-class women were forced into the factory to become wage-laborers. This arrangement served to strengthen patriarchy in the upper classes but fundamentally changed it for the working class (Sheila Rowbotham, *Hidden from History: Three Hundred Years of Women's Oppression and the Fight against It,* 53).

161. *Directory and Handbook, King County Women's Christian Temperance Union,* 1923, 65, 71, Pacific Northwest Collection, University of Washington.

162. Ibid., 47.

163. Well into this century, as Heilbrun writes in *Writing a Woman's Life,* it was impossible "for women to admit into their autobiographical narratives the claim of achievement, the admission of ambition, the recognition that accomplishment was neither luck nor the result of the efforts or generosity of others" (24). She adds that a study by Jill Conway of the autobiographies of five influential women of the Progressive Era found a "narrative flatness" toward their own exciting lives. "They portray themselves as intuitive, nurturing, passive, but never—in spite of the contrary evidence of their accomplishments—managerial" (24). Landes's own words on her life fit this pattern. For instance, even as late as 1939, she described her entry into politics this way: "After many years of Church work, club activities, and service on boards of social agencies as well as homemaking, the call came to enlarge my sphere of influence and go into public service" ("An Alumna in Politics," *Indiana Alumni Magazine,* April 1939, 13).

164. Bertha Knight Landes, "Women in Government," *Seattle Star,* April 4, 1922.

165. Alice Kessler-Harris, *Out to Work: A History of Wage-Earning Women in the United States,* viii–xi.

166. Daniel Scott Smith, "Family Limitation, Sexual Control, and Domestic Feminism in Victorian America," *Feminist Studies* 1 (1973): 41. This ratio, however, does not address the single or widowed or divorced women, who were part of the labor force in more significant numbers.

167. Kessler-Harris, *Women Have Always Worked,* 80.

168. U.S. Bureau of the Census, *Special Reports: Occupations at the Twelfth Census; Fourteenth Census of the United States; Population, 1920: Occupations;*

and *Historical Statistics of the United States: Colonial Times to 1975,* cited in Maurine Weiner Greenwald, "Working-Class Feminism and the Family Wage Ideal: The Seattle Debate on Married Women's Right to Work, 1914–1920," *Journal of American History* 76, no. 1 (June 1989): 124–25.

169. Ibid., 125–26. Also see Kessler-Harris, *Out to Work,* 171–72. She adds that women nationally were rarely admitted to required apprenticeships to learn skilled trades, and where they did gain the necessary skills, craft unions "sometimes grudgingly helped women to form separate, affiliated unions." To allow such training for women "posed an unending threat."

170. In analyzing how Hull House leader Florence Kelley managed to gain 1893 passage of antisweatshop legislation mandating an eight-hour workday for women and children in Illinois manufacturing, Kathryn Kish Sklar found women had to have both sources of support (i.e., their own female institutions, culture, and consciousness) and the determination to reach outside those boundaries to work with male-dominated institutions in order to accomplish their goals ("Hull House in the 1890s: A Community of Women Reformers," *Signs* 10 [Summer 1985]: 658–77). See also Estelle Freedman, "Separatism as Strategy: Female Institution Building and American Feminism, 1870–1930," *Feminist Studies* 5, no. 3 (Fall 1979): 512–29.

171. See Nancy Cott, "What's in a Name? The Limits of 'Social Feminism'; or, Expanding the Vocabulary of Women's History," *Journal of American History* 76, no. 3 (December 1989): 826.

172. This shift in focus, viewed variously as consciously manipulative or as an outgrowth of the domestic ideology of the nineteenth century, is advanced by Epstein in *Politics of Domesticity* and by Aileen Kraditor, *The Ideas of the Woman Suffrage Movement, 1890–1920.* See also Cott, *Grounding of Modern Feminism,* 29–32, for discussion of how the two views were used simultaneously in the final years of the suffrage campaign to suit the purposes of campaign leaders.

173. *Votes for Women,* official paper of the Washington Equal Suffrage Association, ed. Mrs. M. T. B. Hanna, August–September 1910. In February 1911 the paper became the *New Citizen,* listing Abigail Scott Duniway as its Oregon editor.

174. In 1906 Adella Parker, a Seattle high school teacher and clubwoman who graduated from the University of Washington law school, organized a successful campaign to amend the city charter to provide for the recall of public officials, prior to state authorization of the process (Warren B. Johnson, "Muckraking in the Northwest: Joe Smith and Seattle Reform," *Pacific Historical Review* 40 [November 1971]: 481–87).

175. Ibid., 488.

176. "The Recall in Seattle," *Outlook,* February 25, 1911, 376.

177. Bertha Knight Landes, "The Problem of the Large City," speech delivered in Willamette Valley, July 11, 1926, Landes Papers, box 1.

178. Bertha Knight Landes, "On Being Mayor," n.d., article for Delta Zeta Lamp, Landes Papers, box 1.

179. The language of maternalism was a malleable vehicle used by men and women of widely differing political ideologies to justify the social and welfare policies they supported. See a report by Seth Koven and Sonya Michel, "Gender and the Origins of the Welfare State," *Radical History Review* 43 (1989): 112–19.

180. Blair, *Clubwoman as Feminist,* 93, 102. Blair points out that clubwomen creatively applied the idea of municipal housekeeping to almost any issue in finding solutions to problems. Textbooks link Upton Sinclair's work *The Jungle* to passage of a Pure Food and Drug Law, and Theodore Roosevelt to conservation. "In fact," Blair notes, "these measures, and others like them, were supported by the hundreds of thousands of active clubwomen who made it their business to transform America and the notion of what a responsible government should provide" (102).

181. Bertha K. Landes, "Does Politics Make Women Crooked?" *Collier's,* March 16, 1929, 24.

182. *Official Register and Directory of Women's Clubs in America,* 21.

183. While one could not discuss the industrial revolution and capitalism

without considering the ramifications of technology, the advent of home technology has been little studied for its social and economic effects. Similarly, housework, and its role in the political economy, needs more analysis. In the past it has gone unrecognized, often trivialized. See Nona Glazer-Malbin, "Housework," *Signs* 1, no. 4 (1976): 905–22. For an analysis of housework as a point of struggle on the contested terrain of "family," see Heidi Hartmann, "The Family as the Locus of Gender, Class, and Political Struggle: The Example of Housework," in *Feminism and Methodology: Social Science Issues*, ed. Sandra Harding, 109–34. The history of housework and technology's relationship to consumerism and women is found in Susan Strasser, *Never Done: A History of American Housework*, esp. 180–262; and Ruth S. Cowan, *More Work for Mother: The Ironies of Household Technology, from the Open Hearth to the Microwave*.

184. Bertha Knight Landes, "Women in Government," *Seattle Star*, April 4, 1922.

185. Bertha Knight Landes, "A Woman—on Women," *Printers' Ink*, July 7, 1927, 159.

186. The idea of separate displays recognizing the growing influence and power of women was gaining popularity, partly as an outgrowth of the Women's Exhibit at the World's Columbian Exposition in Chicago in 1893. The exposition showcased women's artistic and literary talents as well as women's clubs—including a display sent from the Seattle Woman's Century Club—and women in unusual jobs. Landes's skills in organizing this exhibit can be appreciated from reading about the difficulties and disputes Bertha Palmer and her Board of Lady Managers faced in deciding upon and enforcing the structure and contents of the exhibits at the 1893 exposition. Much of the debate centered on suffrage and temperance. The enormously popular exhibit carried a self-effacing slogan in its emblem: "Not for Herself but for Humanity" (Jeanne M. Weimann, *The Fair Women*).

187. *Seattle Post-Intelligencer* clipping, April 1921, Landes Papers, box 2.

188. Robert Boyns to Bertha Landes, April 19, 1921, Landes Papers, box 1.

189. E. J. Gunther, sales manager of General Manufacturing Co., Inc., to Bertha Knight Landes, April 24, 1921, Landes Papers, box 1.

190. W. C. Hutchinson, Secretary-Treasurer, to Bertha Landes, April 27, 1921, Landes Papers, box 1.

191. Mayor Hugh M. Caldwell to Bertha Landes, May 3, 1922, Landes Papers, box 1.

192. George R. Leighton, "Seattle, Washington: The Edge of the Last Frontier," *Harper's Magazine*, March 1939, 427.

II. THE WOMEN'S PSYCHOLOGICAL HOUR

1. *Official Register and Directory of Women's Clubs in America*, vol. 22.
2. Ibid.
3. Ibid., vols. 22–26.
4. Dorothy Brown, *Setting a Course: American Women in the 1920s*, 52.
5. Cott, *Grounding of Modern Feminism*, 97–99, 122; and Lemons, *Woman Citizen*, 56–57.
6. In *Grounding of Modern Feminism*, 229–65, Nancy Cott argues that women tried to have it both ways but that the positions were irreconcilable. Women wanted both to be treated as if gender did not matter and to have the protective legislation and separate spheres that reflected existing divisions by gender.
7. The latter situation was remedied with passage of the Married Women's Independent Citizenship Act (the Cable Act) on September 22, 1922. The issue of allowing women on juries had to be resolved on a state-by-state basis through the courts or legislation because so many state constitutions restricted jury service to men. It was not resolved in Connecticut until 1937 and in Oklahoma until 1942.
8. *Seattle Post-Intelligencer*, August 31, 1919; Carkeek Scrapbooks, vol 4.
9. Berner, *Seattle, 1900–1920*, 61.
10. Blair, *Clubwoman as Feminist*, 109.

11. Ibid., 140, 148.

12. Ruth Howe, *New York World,* January 16, 1929.

13. Fierce opposition to the Equal Rights Amendment arose quickly, despite NWP's assurances that it too wanted to safeguard protective legislation, although its leaders also recognized the threat the amendment proposed to that legislation. See Kessler-Harris, *Out to Work,* 207–9.

14. Neither side of this debate acknowledged the ambiguities and complexities that made both sides partially correct. On the one hand, those favoring protective legislation did not see how their gender-biased expectations of women confirmed women's second-class status in the economy. On the other, advocates of the ERA likewise discounted how much protective legislation had improved the conditions for women working in industry and did not recognize that the ERA itself would not alone free women from the limitations on their economic opportunities stemming from the domestic stereotype (Nancy Cott, "Feminist Politics in the 1920s: The National Women's Party," *Journal of American History* 71, no. 1 [June 1984]: 43–68).

15. Joseph F. Tripp, "Progressive Labor Laws in Washington State (1900–1925)" (Ph.D. diss., University of Washington, 1973). Tripp notes that one of the issues the minimum wage commissions faced was whether employers had a right to check on employed women's after-work morals in the name of efficiency. Some employers felt obligated to ensure that the women they hired were of good moral character, assuming that those who were found wanting would not be good employees or would be taking jobs away from more deserving women.

16. Landes, "Reminiscence," 9.

17. "Woman's sphere" was initially a powerful cultural matrix for Victorian professional women. Its demise began when scientific and bureaucratic ideals began to crowd out "the altruistic, heroic model of nineteenth-century professionalism." In Ellen S. More's study of female physicians, "'A Certain Restless Ambition': Women Physicians and World War I," *American Quarterly* 41 (December 1989): 636–60, the author points out that the transition to the culture of modern professionalism for female physicians was largely the result of their wishing to be identified with the rising prestige of modern medicine, although there was considerable ambivalence and tension about abandoning the woman's claim to a natural feminine proclivity for healing and the care of women and children.

18. Freedman, "Separatism as Strategy," 512–29; and Sara Evans, "Toward a Usable Past: Feminism as History and Politics," *Minnesota History* 48 (Summer 1983): 230–35, develop this argument. Another view is provided by Blanche W. Cook, "Female Support Networks and Political Activism," in *A Heritage of Her Own: Toward a New Social History of American Women,* ed. Nancy Cott and Elizabeth Pleck, 412–44.

19. The unique discourse that women lost with one another in the rise of the new New Woman is described in Carroll Smith-Rosenberg, "The Body Politic," in *Coming to Terms: Feminism, Theory, and Politics,* ed. Elizabeth Weed, esp. 116–21.

20. *Chicago Daily Tribune,* November 10, 1926.

21. The declaration of principles of the Anti-Saloon League summarized the prevailing anti-alcohol attitude: Liquor traffic "beggars the individual, burdens the State and impoverishes the Nation. It commercializes vice and capitalizes human weakness. It impairs the public health; breaks the public peace, and debauches the public morals. It intimidates and makes cowards of public men. It dominates parties and conventions. It cajoles, bribes or badgers the makers, interpreters and administrators of law, and suborns the public press" (Ernest H. Cherrington, ed., *The Anti-Saloon League Yearbook, 1915: An Encyclopedia of Facts and Figures Dealing with the Liquor Traffic and the Temperance Reform,* 82).

22. John Burnham argues that social and intellectual developments led to Progressive reform ideas and commitments, not for the reformers to claim power so much as to gain a means of social control in order to promote "correct" think-

ing that would solve social problems. Such problems could be solved through the sciences and reduction of life phenomena into pliable "biological units" (*Paths into American Culture: Psychology, Medicine, and Morals*).

23. Norman H. Clark, *The Dry Years: Prohibition and Social Change in Washington,* viii, 122.

24. The Anti-Saloon League, influential in Washington State, was a pioneer in political organizing around a single issue, using managerial skills to advance the cause, according to K. Austin Kerr, *Organized for Prohibition: A New History of the Anti-Saloon League,* 282–83. Kerr argues that it was forty years before consumption of alcohol went back up to preprohibition levels on a per capita adult basis (283). After prohibition, the league divided and fell apart over what course to pursue (279) and offered only scattered resistance to the antiprohibition forces seeking repeal.

25. Prohibition actually began nationally well before 1920 with the restrictions on drinking and production of alcohol for military reasons. Citing the somewhat conflicting statistics available, John Burnham argues that the prohibition "experiment" actually enjoyed modest success during its early years and improved conditions among low-income Americans, despite its growing reputation then and later as a failure. He cites growing concerns about crime and hysterical journalism about gangsters as giving it the image of having failed, which brought about its subsequent repeal. This was fueled both by reformers' exaggerated claims about prohibition's success and by the need to find a Depression era scapegoat ("New Perspectives on the Prohibition Experiment of the 1920s," *Journal of Social History* 2 [1968]: 457–65).

26. Cherrington, *Anti-Saloon League Yearbook, 1915,* 208.

27. Newell, *Rogues, Buffoons, and Statesmen,* 275; and Clark, *Dry Years,* 130.

28. Newell, *Rogues, Buffoons, and Statesmen,* 275.

29. Ibid., 276; and Clark, *Dry Years,* 131–33.

30. Clark, *Dry Years,* 141.

31. Ibid., 146.

32. Newell, *Rogues, Buffoons, and Statesmen,* 308.

33. Clark, *Dry Years,* 153.

34. Ibid.

35. Ibid., 154–55.

36. Hartley pushed for lowered education appropriations, persuaded the legislature not to ratify the federal Child Labor Amendment, vetoed a personal income tax bill and corporate income tax bill, and ultimately through his Board of Regents forced the resignation of Henry Suzzallo, the popular president of the University of Washington. Despite the controversy, Hartley was reelected by a sizable majority (Cecil Dryden, *History of Washington,* 269–70).

37. Clark, *Dry Years,* 155.

38. Gaustad, *Religious History of America,* 200–201.

39. Robert D. Saltvig, "The Progressive Movement in Washington," 87, 112–13. Saltvig's analysis indicated that after 1910, liberal Republicans aligned with the upper middle class, often called the better class, to promote reforms that promised honest, efficient, economical government, but they were not so enthusiastic about expansion of government functions. Liberal Democrats, in contrast, identified "the people" with labor and the lower middle class and pushed reforms to promote their economic and political interests. They were more likely to support public ownership of utilities to attack the "interests." They also promoted use of direct legislation for greater voice and control by the voter and linked Populism and Progressivism in Washington (112–14).

40. Lind, *Study of Mobility of Population in Seattle,* 12, 14. The other cities were Long Beach, San Diego, and Tulsa. The study cites U.S. Census Data.

41. R. D. McKenzie, "Community Forces: A Study of the Non-Partisan Municipal Elections in Seattle," *Journal of Social Forces* 2 (January 1924): 266–70.

42. This line of thought and the emergence of the American middle class as

an egalitarian concept and ideal are argued in Burton Bledstein, *The Culture of Professionalism: The Middle Class and the Development of Higher Education in America,* esp. 89–127.

43. Albert A. Acena, "The Washington Commonwealth Federation: Reform Politics and the Popular Front" (Ph.D. diss., University of Washington, 1975), 29–32, 35–40.

44. The striving for a sense of community and nation in the face of rampant individualism and distinct communities has existed throughout American history. See Robert Wiebe, *The Segmented Society: An Introduction to the Meaning of America.*

45. Blackford, "Reform Politics in Seattle during the Progressive Era," 181–82.

46. *Seattle Times,* February 28, 1922.

47. Andrews, *Washington Women as Pathbreakers,* 18.

48. Voters Information League Bulletin no. 44, February 20, 1925, 2.

49. *Seattle Times,* February 28, 1922.

50. Ibid., March 2, 1922.

51. Ibid., March 5, 1922.

52. Anne Steese Richardson, "My Trip across the Continent, Where I Learned Many Interesting Things about Good Citizenship," *Woman's Home Companion,* October 1922, 141.

53. Declaration of Candidacy, Bertha Knight Landes, March 2, 1922, file no. 84185, City Archives, Seattle Municipal Building.

54. *Seattle Times,* March 2, 1922.

55. Ibid.

56. *Pigott's Political Reference Book for King County,* 32.

57. Andrews, *Seattle Women,* 42.

58. David Brewster and David Buerge, eds., *The Washingtonians: A Biographical Portrait of the State,* 88.

59. Rosalind Urbach Moss, "The 'Girls' from Syracuse: Sex Role Negotiation of Kansas Women in Politics, 1887–1890," in *The Women's West,* ed. Susan Armitage and Elizabeth Jameson, 253–62.

60. Susan Armitage, "The Challenge of Women's History," in *Women in Pacific Northwest History: An Anthology,* ed. Karen J. Blair, 239.

61. Andrews, *Washington Women as Pathbreakers,* 12.

62. Lemons, *Woman Citizen,* 104.

63. Andrews, *Washington Women as Pathbreakers,* 9.

64. Newell, *Rogues, Buffoons, and Statesmen,* 255, 257.

65. Barbara Gooding, "Women in the Washington State Legislature" (Senior thesis, Evergreen College, 1983), 12–13.

66. Newell, *Rogues, Buffoons, and Statesmen,* 315, 333, 343.

67. *Polk's Seattle City Directory,* 1921; and "Washington Federation of Women's Clubs Register, 1897–1923."

68. *Seattle Times,* May 13, 1934.

69. *Polk's Seattle City Directory,* 1921, 1926.

70. *Seattle Times,* February 26, 1922.

71. *Seattle Star,* n.d., Landes Papers, box 2.

72. *Seattle Times,* April 19, 1922.

73. Undated clipping, Landes Papers, box 2.

74. *Seattle Times* and *Star,* March 7, 1922.

75. Undated clipping, Landes Papers, box 2.

76. Ibid.

77. *Seattle Post-Intelligencer,* April 25, 1922; and *Seattle Star,* April 26, 1922.

78. "Chance for Women," undated clipping from 1922, Landes Papers, box 2.

79. "Mrs. Landes in Busy Campaign," undated clipping from 1922, Landes Papers, box 2.

80. *Union Record* clipping, n.d., Landes Papers, box 2.

81. "Busy Day Faced by Mrs. Landes," undated clipping from 1922, Landes Papers, box 2.
82. Clipping, no title, 1922, Landes Papers, box 2.
83. *Seattle Star,* April 19, 1922.
84. *Seattle Times,* April 19, 1922.
85. Ibid.
86. Ibid.
87. Bertha Knight Landes, no title, April 12, 1922, Landes Papers, box 2.
88. *Seattle Star,* April 21, 1922.
89. Budlong, "What Happened in Seattle," 197–98.
90. Clipping, no title, April 18, 1922, Landes Papers, box 2.
91. Landes, "Does Politics Make Women Crooked?" 36, 38.
92. Lee, *Biographical Cyclopaedia,* 149.
93. Statement of Expenses, Bertha Knight Landes campaign, filed April 28, 1922, file no. 84764, and filed May 8, 1922, file no. 84908, City Archives.
94. File no. 84902, City Archives.
95. Landes, "Alumna in Politics," 13.

III. RACING A FAST TRAIN

1. Edmond Meany, "Living Pioneers of Washington," n.d., Carkeek Scrapbooks, vol. 4.
2. *Seattle Star,* April 11, 1922.
3. Ibid.
4. Ibid., April 4, 1922.
5. *Seattle Post-Intelligencer,* March 10, 1922.
6. Lee, *Biographical Cyclopedia,* 150.
7. *Seattle Times,* January 1, 1928.
8. Journal of the Proceedings of the City Council of the City of Seattle, June 5, 1922, Comptroller's Office, Seattle Municipal Building (hereafter referred to as City Council Minutes).
9. William John Dickson, "Labor in Municipal Politics: A Study of Labor's Political Policies and Activities in Seattle" (Master's thesis, University of Washington, 1928), 38.
10. *Pigott's Political Reference Book,* 83; Dickson, "Labor in Municipal Politics," 88; and Allen, *Who's Who,* 112.
11. *Pigott's Political Reference Book,* 59–60; Allen, *Who's Who,* 83–84; and Saltvig, "Progressive Movement in Washington," 379.
12. *Pigott's Political Reference Book,* 78.
13. Allen, *Who's Who,* 168.
14. Ibid., 88.
15. Ibid., 54.
16. Review of City Council Minutes.
17. The city council had established a zoning commission in 1920. By the end of 1922 it had nearly completed a zoning plan for the entire city, which then was carried forward and eventually codified by the council.
18. Jon C. Teaford, *The Twentieth-Century American City,* 40. The leading practitioner of the city-beautiful planning concept was Daniel Burnham, who went from overseeing the construction of the Chicago World's Fair of 1893, with its dazzling neoclassical structures and statuary, to drafting comprehensive plans for San Francisco, Cleveland, and Chicago.
19. Lee, *Biographical Cyclopedia,* 150.
20. City Council Minutes, September 25, 1922.
21. Ibid., September 5, 1922.
22. Fears of radicalism and union activity in Washington during and following World War I affected past alliances and created a conservative climate. See Jonathan Dembo, *Unions and Politics in Washington State, 1885–1935;* Albert Gunns, *Civil Liberties in Crisis: The Pacific Northwest,* 1917–1940; and Robert L. Friedheim, "The Seattle General Strike of 1919," *Pacific Northwest Quarterly* 52, no. 3 (July 1961): 81–98. The history of organized labor in Washington at the

turn of the century was unique. See Carlos Schwantes, "Leftward Tilt on the Pacific Slope," *Pacific Northwest Quarterly* 70 (January 1979): 24–34.

23. Dickson, "Labor in Municipal Politics," 1.

24. In his extensive analysis of the general strike, historian Paul Friedheim concluded that organized labor in Seattle paid heavily for it, seeing a business-backed coalition called Associated Industries push for the open shop, with some success. It also flooded the labor movement with spies. The general strike was a disorganized movement with no clear goals other than sympathy for striking shipyard workers and a display of power. Sensing public revulsion, forces of moderation within organized labor itself kept the strike from escalating to violence and minimized the deleterious effects ("The Seattle General Strike of 1919," 81–98).

25. Dickson, "Labor in Municipal Politics," 53–54.

26. Ibid., 132.

27. Lee Forrest Pendergrass, "Urban Reform and Voluntary Association: A Case Study of the Seattle Municipal League, 1910–1929," 2.

28. A study of seventy of Seattle's business leaders 1880 to 1910 found them also predominantly Republican and Protestant, with the Congregationalist denomination being the single largest group. In background and training, they were similar to their national counterparts, except that Seattle's leaders were somewhat more likely to be sons of farmers (Norbert MacDonald, "The Business Leaders of Seattle, 1880–1910," *Pacific Northwest Quarterly* 50 [January 1959]: 1–13).

29. Ibid., 13.

30. Dickson, "Labor in Municipal Politics," 123.

31. Ibid., 53.

32. Ibid., 75–76, 93.

33. See Irene Somerville Durham, "Community Clubs in Seattle" (Master's thesis, University of Washington, 1929). She surveyed Seattle and found 107 community clubs, 18 community commercial clubs, and 4 federations, with a total membership equal to 7 percent of the registered voters.

34. Ibid., 11.

35. Ibid., 13–14.

36. Dana Mills Barbour, "Measuring City Government—the Munroe Criteria Applied to Seattle" (Master's thesis, University of Washington, 1930), 50.

37. Clipping, no title or date, speech at Oregon City to Willamette Valley Chautauqua, Landes Papers, box 2.

38. Durham, "Community Clubs in Seattle," 38.

39. *Seattle Municipal News,* October 30, 1926.

40. Lillian L. Waldron to Mrs. C. H. Lester, El Paso, December 30, 1926, Manuscripts Collection, folder 106, Museum of History and Industry, Seattle.

41. *Seattle Times,* May 13, 1934.

42. Schear, "Our One and Only Madame Mayor," 21.

43. Ibid.

44. *Seattle Times,* March 14, 1922.

45. Landes, "Alumna in Politics," 13.

46. Bertha Knight Landes, untitled speech, n.d., Landes Papers, box 1.

47. Bertha Knight Landes, "Steering a Big City Straight," *Woman Citizen,* December 1927, 7.

48. City Council Minutes, June 12, 1922.

49. *Seattle Times,* April 19, 1922. He defeated corporate counsel Walter Meier but came in behind former senator Dan Landon by 1,600 votes. He defeated Landon in the general election easily, however, by almost 12,000 votes, despite Landon's attacks accusing Brown of being red.

50. City Council Minutes, July 24, 1922.

51. Ibid., November 11 and December 4, 1922.

52. *Seattle Post-Intelligencer,* October 16, 1922.

53. City Council Minutes, January 28, April 28, May 19 and 26, 1924.

54. Ibid., June 2, 1924.
55. Ibid., June 9, 1924.
56. Ibid., August 4, 1924.
57. Sale, *Seattle, Past to Present,* 83, 95–100; and Berner, *Seattle, 1900–1920,* 103–6.
58. *Seattle Times,* October 4, 1924.
59. Backman, "Organization of Municipal Government in Seattle," 23.
60. Bertha Knight Landes, untitled speech, n.d., Landes Papers, box 1.
61. City Council Minutes, September 10, 1924.
62. Ibid., September 19, 1924.
63. Dickson, "Labor in Municipal Politics," 59.
64. *Polk's Seattle City Directory,* 373.
65. *Seattle Times,* May 3, 1922; and Hanford, *Seattle and Environs,* 2:236–40.
66. Dickson, "Labor in Municipal Politics," 29.
67. *Seattle Socialist,* January 11, 1908, cited in Dickson, "Labor in Municipal Politics," 30.
68. Clark, *Dry Years,* 159–60.
69. Hanford, *Seattle and Environs,* 2:236–40.
70. *Seattle Post-Intelligencer,* October 15, 1922.
71. Ibid., October 12, 1922.
72. Ibid., October 13, 1922.
73. Ibid.
74. Ibid., October 21, 1922.
75. Berner, *Seattle, 1900–1920,* 115.
76. Kathy Peiss, *Cheap Amusements: Working Women and Leisure in Turn-of-the-Century New York,* 98.
77. Ibid., 99, 101–5.
78. Landes, "Does Politics Make Women Crooked?" 38.
79. Superior Court Judge James Ronald to Bertha Knight Landes, January 15, 1923, Landes Papers, box 1. Ronald, as a deputy prosecutor for King County before the turn of the century, had warred on vice in the city. He won election as district attorney in 1884 and 1886 and was elected mayor of Seattle in 1892. He ran for Congress and lost in 1900. Later he was a member of the Seattle School Board and a regent for the University of Washington, a post he resigned when he became a judge in 1909 (Hanford, *Seattle and Environs,* 2:153–55).
80. Landes, "Reminiscence," 9.
81. *Seattle Post-Intelligencer,* January 3, 1923.
82. Landes, "Reminiscence," 9.
83. Bertha Knight Landes, untitled speech, n.d., Landes Papers, box 1.
84. *Seattle Times,* October 24, 1922.
85. Barbour, "Measuring City Government," 30–31.
86. Ibid., 45.
87. Ibid., 33–34.
88. Ibid., 54.
89. *Seattle Times,* March 16, 1923.
90. Ibid., March 7, 1923.
91. Ibid., December 19, 1923.
92. Ibid., March 20, 1923.
93. Ibid., October 23, 1922. In a dramatic confrontation on the courthouse steps, Brown was denied the opportunity to testify on Nellie Hartford's behalf before a grand jury. He accused Revelle of using her to attack his administration.
94. Ibid., December 21, 1922.
95. Ibid., November 19 and 25, 1923.
96. Ibid., June 3, 1924.
97. Ibid.
98. Ibid., June 10, 1924.
99. *Seattle Star,* June 25, 1924.

100. U.S. Federal Trade Commission, *Utility Corporations,* cited in Florence Deacon, "Why Wasn't Bertha Knight Landes Re-elected?" (Master's thesis, University of Washington, 1978), 14.
101. Bertha Knight Landes to Police Chief William B. Severyns, June 23, 1924, Landes Papers, box 1.
102. Ibid., draft copy, Landes Papers, box 1.
103. *Pigott's Political Reference Book,* 54; and Hanford, *Seattle and Environs,* 3:97–98.
104. G. O. Williams, "History of the Seattle Police Department: The Prohibition Era in Seattle," *Sheriff & Police Reporter,* February 1951, 8.
105. William B. Severyns to Bertha Knight Landes, June 24, 1924, Landes Papers, box 1.
106. Ibid.
107. Landes, "Does Politics Make Women Crooked?" 36.
108. Bertha Knight Landes to William B. Severyns, June 25, 1924, City Archives.
109. Kenneth Rose, "Booze and News in 1924: Prohibition in Seattle," *Portage,* Winter 1984, 20.
110. Proclamation, Mrs. Henry Landes, Acting Mayor, Assuming Charge of the Police Department, June 26, 1924, file no. 95242, City Archives.
111. *Brooklyn Daily Eagle,* as cited in "The Temporary Lady Mayor Who Fired Seattle's Chief of Police," *Literary Digest,* August 9, 1924, 43.
112. *Seattle Times,* June 23, 1924.
113. *Seattle Union Record,* June 26, 1924.
114. *Seattle Times,* July 1, 1924.
115. Ibid., June 28 and 29, 1924.
116. Schear, "Our One and Only Madame Mayor," 19.
117. David Suffia, "When Doc Brown's Cigar Thwarted a Reform Move," *Seattle Times,* January 7, 1974.
118. Ross Cunningham, "Seattle's First and Only Woman Mayor," *Seattle Times,* December 20, 1972.
119. *Los Angeles Times,* June 30, 1924.
120. Bertha Knight Landes, "Conditions to Be Corrected at Beginning of Term," Landes Papers, box 1.
121. "What Variety of City Government Do You Want?" *Sunset Magazine,* September 1924, 47–48.
122. *Seattle Argus,* July 5, 1924.
123. *Brooklyn Daily Eagle,* cited in "Temporary Lady Mayor," 44.
124. Ibid., 45.
125. Ibid.
126. Ruth Howe, *New York World,* January 16, 1929.
127. *Seattle Times,* August 28, 1924.
128. Ibid., December 27, 1924.
129. Request of C. L. Maxfield, December 27, 1924, file no. 97830, City Archives.
130. Ibid.
131. Text of petitions, n.d., file no. 102930, City Archives.
132. *Seattle Times,* May 17, 1925.
133. Ibid., February 19, 1925.
134. Ibid., February 21, 1925.
135. Ibid., February 26, 27 and 28, 1925.
136. Ibid., February 22, 1925.
137. Ibid., February 1, 1925.
138. Ibid., February 11, 1925.
139. "Landes for Mayor" brochure, 1926, Municipal Elections File, Archives, Seattle Public Library.
140. Deacon, "Why Wasn't Bertha Knight Landes Re-elected?" 24–25.
141. *Seattle Times,* June 2, 1925.
142. Ibid., August 29, 1925.

143. Ibid., October 12, 1925.
144. Ibid., December 4, 5, 7, 14, and 15, 1925.
145. Ibid., January 22, 1926.
146. Warren, *Seattle,* 125; and Clark, *Dry Years,* 162–64.
147. This is disputed by Clark, *Dry Years,* 171. The station was KFOX, which later became KOMO.
148. Ibid., 126.
149. "Submission of Proposed New Charter by Municipal League," September 21 and 28, 1925, file no. 101892, City Archives.
150. *Seattle Times,* January 23, 1926.
151. "Woman Mayor Launches Manager Plan," no page no.
152. Landes, "Alumna in Politics," 13.
153. *Seattle Times,* February 9, 1926.
154 Allen, *Who's Who,* 203.
155. Ibid., 133; and Hanford, *Seattle and Environs,* 2:335–36.
156. Allen, *Who's Who,* 56.
157. *Seattle Times,* May 13, 1934.
158. Ibid., February 2, 1926. None of her managers, or their husbands, are listed in the 1927 edition of *Who's Who in Washington State.*
159. *Polk's Seattle City Directory,* 1921.
160. "Washington Federation of Women's Clubs History," box 1, 134; and *Seattle Times,* March 27, 1938.
161. *Seattle Times,* February 13, 1926.
162. Ibid., February 5, 1926.
163. *Seattle Post-Intelligencer,* January 29, 1926.
164. Ibid., January 30, 1926.
165. This is based on a review of campaign coverage before the primary in Seattle's two newspapers with the largest circulation, the *Post-Intelligencer* and the *Times.* The coverage generally consisted of reports on the candidates and their various appearances as a group rather than as stories on individual candidates per se.
166. *Seattle Times,* February 24, 1926.

IV. THE "FREAKISH" MAYOR

1. Photographs, no title, inscriptions on back, Henry Landes Papers, box 1.
2. *Seattle Union-Record,* March 6, 1926.
3. *Seattle Times,* March 1, 1926.
4. Revelle had been an unsuccessful candidate for the Republican gubernatorial nomination in 1924. A former Methodist minister, Revelle later said he had been told to convict Roy Olmstead and his codefendants or face losing his job (Clark, *Dry Years,* 171).
5. *Seattle Times,* March 5, 1926.
6. Six of the initial nine candidates for the office came to the contest. Landes was not among the tournament leaders (*Seattle Star,* n.d., Landes Papers, box 2).
7. Ibid.
8. "Landes for Mayor" brochure.
9. Ibid.
10. Ibid.
11. Ibid.
12. *Seattle Times,* March 10, 1926.
13. Horace Chapin Henry is identified in the 1927 *Who's Who in Washington State* as a Civil War veteran who became a railroad contractor, building the railway between Minneapolis and St. Louis. In 1890–91 he built the Great Northern Railway in Washington west of the Cascades. In 1906 he contracted to build seven hundred miles of railroad through Montana, Idaho, and Washington for $20 million, a project employing ten thousand men. He also built two iron ore docks in the Midwest and other railroads and, after having amassed a considerable fortune, was president of several financial institutions. Following World War I he

supported 1,800 fatherless children in France, for which he was awarded the Legion of Honor from the French government. He donated land and money for Firland Sanitarium in Seattle, gave valuable paintings to the University of Washington and built the gallery to display them that bears his name, and matched Seattle newsboys' deposits in savings accounts (111). See also Hanford, *Seattle and Environs,* 2:5–8.

14. *Seattle Times,* March 5, 1926.
15. *Seattle Argus,* February 20, 1926.
16. Ibid., March 6, 1926.
17. Declaration of Candidacy, February 23, 1926, file no. 103660, City Archives.
18. *Seattle Times,* March 7, 1926.
19. *Seattle Times* and *Post-Intelligencer,* March 8, 1926.
20. *Seattle Times,* March 8, 1926.
21. Ibid, March 5, 1925.
22. Schiesl, *Politics of Efficiency,* 188. Schiesl traces the history of several city government reforms, such as the city manager system and civil service, as part of a national movement. See also Teaford, *Twentieth-Century American City*.
23. Teaford, *Twentieth-Century American City,* 53–55.
24. *Seattle Times,* March 10, 1926.
25. Ibid.
26. Ibid., March 11, 1926.
27. *Seattle Post-Intelligencer,* March 11, 1926.
28. *Seattle Union-Record,* n.d., cited in "Municipal Housekeeper," *Literary Digest,* March 27, 1926, 13.
29. Tam Deering, Superintendent of Recreation for San Diego, to Bertha Knight Landes, April 11, 1926, Landes Papers, box 1.
30. "Dealing in Personalities," *Independent Woman,* June 1926, 10–11.
31. *Seattle Times,* October 23, 1927.
32. Prince Wilhelm of Sweden, n.d., Landes Papers, box 1.
33. Ibid.
34. *Brooklyn Daily Eagle,* n.d., cited in *"Temporary Lady Mayor,"* 42, 44.
35. Ibid.
36. Ruth Howe, *New York World,* January 16, 1929.
37. Lillian Taaffe, *Minneapolis Tribune,* November 23, 1926.
38. Alfred Holman, *New York Times,* July 4, 1926.
39. Bertha Knight Landes, "A Woman Mayor's Observations," *Alameda* (California) *Times Star,* n.d., Landes Papers, box 2.
40. "Editorial Digest," 1926 clipping, Landes Papers, box 2.
41. *Seattle Times,* June 8, 1926.
42. Ibid., March 10, 1926.
43. Despite the seeming vanity of her complaint, Landes had a point. The photograph the Newspaper Enterprise Association distributed, used in *Time* magazine, displayed her as ugly and unkempt, so much so compared with other photographs of Landes that it appeared to have been chosen for that purpose.
44. *Seattle Times,* March 10, 1926.
45. Ibid., March 19, 1926.
46. Ibid.
47. *Seattle Times,* May 28, 1926.
48. Ibid.
49. Ibid., June 7, 1926.
50. *Seattle Post-Intelligencer,* June 8, 1928.
51. *Seattle Star,* n.d., Landes Papers, box 2.
52. William O'Dell Sparks, "J. D. Ross and Seattle City Light, 1917–1932" (Master's thesis, University of Washington, 1964), 4–6.
53. Paul C. Pitzer, "J. D. Ross and the Old Skagit Tour," (Paper presented at Pacific Northwest History Conference, Walla Walla, Washington, February 27, 1990). Ross died in 1939, but the successful tours continued for decades after.

They also included slides, movies, an elaborate dinner, and even a dance at the camp. Reportedly 100,000 people in fourteen years took the tours. In the last half of the twentieth century, the North Cascades Park and Ross Recreation Area were added.

54. *Seattle Times,* March 11, 1926.

55. Sparks, "J. D. Ross and Seattle City Light, 1917–1932," 144–46.

56. Carl Dreher, "J. D. Ross, Public Power Magnate," *Harper's Magazine,* June 1940, 46.

57. Seattle Year Book, Annual Report of Mayor Bertha Knight Landes, June 4, 1928, Landes Papers, box 1.

58. Seattle Year Book, June 6, 1927.

59. *Seattle Times,* June 7, 1926.

60. Ibid., June 8, 1926.

61. Bertha K. Landes, "The Problem of the Large City," speech delivered in Willamette Valley, July 11, 1926, Landes Papers, box 1.

62. Ibid., 2–5.

63. Ibid.

64. Ibid., 6–7.

65. Ibid.

66. Ibid., 12–13.

67. Ibid., 13–14.

68. Ibid., 8, 10, 12.

69. "Municipal Housekeeper," *Literary Digest,* March 27, 1926, 13.

70. *Seattle Star,* June 8, 1926.

71. Landes, "Does Politics Make Women Crooked?" 24.

72. Ibid.; *Seattle Union-Record* and *Seattle Post-Intelligencer,* June 9, 1926; and other sources.

73. Landes, "Does Politics Make Women Crooked?" 36; and Debra Dragovich, "Government Was 'But a Larger Housekeeping,'" Northwest Magazine, *Seattle Post-Intelligencer,* December 9, 1979, 2.

74. *Tacoma Labor Advocate,* June 25, 1926.

75. Ibid.

76. *Seattle Times,* July 26, 1926.

77. Bertha Knight Landes, "Alumna in Politics," 27.

78. *Woman's Journal* was the official publication of the National American Woman Suffrage Association from 1890 to 1917. Between 1917 and 1931, it was published as the *Woman Citizen* as a result of a bequest to Carrie Chapman Catt from Mrs. Frank Leslie.

79. Blanche Brace, "Well . . . Why Not?" *Woman Citizen,* September 1926, 9.

80. Ibid., 9–10.

81. Ibid., 10.

82. Ibid., 10–11.

83. Ibid., 11, 38.

84. Alfred Holman, *New York Times,* July 4, 1926.

85. Louise F. Shields, "The Woman Mayor Calls It a Day," *Sunset Magazine,* February 1927, 46.

86. Ibid.

87. "Welcome Address to Eagles National Auxiliary," August 1926, Landes Papers, box 1.

88. Budlong, "What Happened in Seattle?" 198.

89. J. Matthew O'Connor, "Biography of Bertha Knight Landes," n.d., Landes Papers, box 1.

90. "Woman Mayor Launches Manager Plan," no page given.

91. Bertha Knight Landes, "Steering a Big City Straight," *Woman Citizen,* December 1927, 7.

92. Dave Beck, a truck driver, angered by the 1919 general strike, which he said won nothing and brought disrepute to labor, organized the laundry teamsters. He ultimately became president of the Teamsters Union, a member of the Seattle First National Bank board, a regent of the University of Washington, and

one of Seattle's most influential residents. In 1925 he had been hired by the Teamsters Union as a full-time organizer. In that position he soon displayed a knack for also working well with businessmen, often brokering deals, using force if necessary with competing unions. In 1959 he was convicted of income tax evasion and served thirty months in prison. See Robert E. Ficken and Charles P. LeWarne, *Washington: A Centennial History,* 167–169.

93. *Seattle Union-Record,* July 2, 1926.

94. *Seattle Post-Intelligencer,* August 25, 1926.

95. *Chicago Daily Tribune,* November 10, 1926.

96. *Seattle Post-Intelligencer,* November 26, 1926.

97. November 15, 1926, file no. 107972, City Archives.

98. "Mayor's Veto of C.B. 42088," November 29, 1926, file no. 108161, City Archives.

99. *Seattle Times,* May 1, 1926.

100. *Seattle Star,* June 8, 1926.

101. Shields, "Woman Mayor Calls It a Day," 46.

102. Note to Matthew O'Connor, t.s., July 13, 1927, Landes Papers, box 1.

103. Landes Papers, box 1, 22. The reference to Sweet Marie was to Queen Marie of Romania, whom Landes once hosted at Seattle.

104. Landes, "Does Politics Make Women Crooked?" 36.

105. Seattle Year Book, Annual Report of Mayor Bertha Knight Landes, June 6, 1927, 15, file no. 11173, City Archives.

106. Ibid., 13.

107. Seattle Year Book, Annual Report of Mayor Bertha Knight Landes, June 4, 1928, Landes Papers, box 1, 21.

108. Seattle Year Book, Annual Report of Mayor Bertha Knight Landes, 1927, 20.

109. Ibid., 14.

110. Ibid., 16, 19, 21.

111. Seattle Year Book, Annual Report of Mayor Bertha Knight Landes, 1928, 27.

112. Seattle Year Book, Annual Report of Mayor Bertha Knight Landes, 1927, 24, 26, 34.

113. Ibid., 40–41.

114. Schiesl, *Politics of Efficiency,* 169.

115. Seattle Year Book, Annual Report of Mayor Bertha Knight Landes, 1927, 41–42.

116. Ibid., 42.

117. Ibid., 49.

118. Robert Wright, Washington State Oral/Aural History Program, 5–7, microfiche. The interview was conducted in 1975.

119. Berner, *Seattle, 1900–1920,* 39.

120. Leslie Blanchard, *The Street Railway Era in Seattle: A Chronicle of Six Decades,* 77, 81.

121. Ibid., 94.

122. Ridership went from 17.2 billion total rides in 1926 to 15.6 billion by 1930, and the worst decline occurred in cities between 100,000 and 250,000 in population. "As urban Americans forsook the streetcar, transit revenues plummeted and operating deficits became commonplace." Fares in most cities rose from five cents to seven or eight cents in the decade after World War I (Teaford, *Twentieth-Century American City,* 66).

123. Clipping, "Woman Mayor Here for Church Meeting," Omaha speech at national Congregational Church meeting, Landes Papers, box 2.

124. Teaford, *Twentieth-Century American City,* 62.

125. Blanchard, *Street Railway Era in Seattle,* 98–109.

126. Inez Bell Chapman, Washington State Oral/Aural History Program, 14, microfiche.

127. For instance, a statement dated January 26, 1927, reads, "Received from R. T. Reid, of Seattle, the sum of $5,700 cash, to be used for the purpose of

buying Feb. 25, 1927 warrants issued for the purpose of paying the wages of employees of the Municipal Street Railway System. It being understood that the Municipality of Seattle will turn over to said R. T. Reid warrants as above mentioned in the sum of $5,700." Signed, Bertha K. Landes (Landes Papers, box 1).

128. *Seattle Star,* March 1, 4, 8, 1927.

129. Blanchard, *Street Railway Era in Seattle,* 132.

130. "Remarks," n.d., Landes Papers, box 1.

131. *Seattle Star,* April 12, 1927.

132. *Seattle Star, Times,* and *Post-Intelligencer,* April 23–26, 1927.

133. *Seattle Post-Intelligencer,* December 28, 1927.

134. President, National Council of Administrative Women in Education, to Bertha K. Landes, July 7, 1927, Landes Papers, box 1.

135. Clipping, n.d., St. Paul, Landes Papers, box 2.

136. *Christian Advocate Magazine,* no date or title, cited in *Seattle Times,* June 24, 1927.

137. *New York Times,* April 17, 1927.

138. Landes, "Reminiscence," 5.

139. Bertha K. Landes to Stella Warner, April 27, 1927, Landes Papers, box 1.

140. Attributed to *Brooklyn Eagle,* n.d., Landes Papers, box 1.

141. Landes, "Alumna in Politics," 28.

142. Landes, "Steering a Big City Straight," 37.

143. Landes, "Does Politics Make Women Crooked?" 36.

144. Photographs, no title, inscriptions on back, Henry Landes Papers, box 1.

V. NO MORE PETTICOAT RULE

1. *Ketchikan Chronicle,* August 25, 1927.

2. *Seattle Post-Intelligencer,* August 30, 1927.

3. *Seattle Times,* October 30, 1927.

4. Mayor Edwin J. Brown, Third Annual Message to City Council, June 1, 1925, file no. 100236, City Archives, 41.

5. "Revocations of Appointments of Theatre Censors by Mayor," March 3, 1927, file no. 109474, City Archives.

6. Morgan, *Skid Road,* 147.

7. Peter Stead, *Film and the Working Class: The Feature Film in British and American Society,* 14.

8. Ibid., 37.

9. "Women Lock on Fight over Film," clipping, [1919?], in Earl W. Shimmons Scrapbook, in possession of Roy Atwood, University of Idaho. A handwritten note under the article said that the black women clearly won the debate and that the article about the meeting was suppressed by other area newspapers.

10. Seattle Year Book, Annual Report of Bertha Knight Landes, June 4, 1928, 23–24, Landes Papers, box 1.

11. Ibid., 24.

12. Speech on delinquency to conference of social workers, no title, August 17, 1927, 6, Landes Papers, box 1.

13. Ibid., 10.

14. Seattle Year Book, Annual Report of Bertha Knight Landes, 1928, 19, 42.

15. *Seattle Post-Intelligencer* and *Times,* October 30, 1927.

16. *Seattle Post-Intelligencer,* November 27, 1927.

17. *Seattle Times,* January 1, 1928.

18. Ibid.

19. Ibid.

20. Ibid., January 29, 1928.

21. Ibid.

22. Ibid.

23. Ibid., January 3–4, 1928.

24. Voters Information League, Bulletin no. 44 (February 20, 1925), Seattle Campaign Literature, 2 (1925), Northwest Collection, Seattle Public Library.

25. *Seattle Times,* October 31, 1927.
26. Clipping, no title or date, Landes Papers, box 2.
27. *Seattle Times,* June 11, 1926.
28. A 1928 political study based on interviews found that Edwards was induced to run by the Civil Service League, with a membership of four thousand municipal employees (Dickson, "Labor in Municipal Politics," 68–72).
29. *Seattle Times,* January 8, 1928.
30. Ibid., January 9 and 17, 1928.
31. Ibid., January 29, 1928.
32. Ibid.
33. Sparks, "J. D. Ross and Seattle City Light," 136.
34. Seattle Year Book, Annual Report of Bertha Knight Landes, 1928, 10.
35. *Seattle Star,* February 29, 1928.
36. Barbour, "Measuring City Government," 84–89.
37. Ibid., 94–96. For general government it spent $4.48 compared with $4.27; for fire and police protection it spent $8.99 per capita compared with $8.47; notably, for the combined category of charities, hospital, relief, and corrections, Seattle spent only $1.51 per capita compared with $3.23 nationally. "Seattle compares very favorably with cities of her size," Barbour concluded, in its expenditures on city services.
38. *Seattle Star,* n.d., cited in Deacon, "Why Wasn't Bertha Knight Landes Re-elected?" 66.
39. *Seattle Times,* January 24, 1928.
40. Ibid., January 8, 1928.
41. Municipal, School, and Port Elections, 1928, Seattle Campaign Literature, 2 (1928).
42. *Seattle Times,* March 1, 1928.
43. Ibid.
44. Ibid., March 2 and 4, 1928.
45. Ibid., March 4, 1928.
46. Ibid., January 20, 1928.
47. Ibid.
48. Ibid., January 18, 1928.
49. Edwin Brown, "What Price Harmony," Seattle Campaign Literature, 2 (1928).
50. Ibid.
51. *Seattle Times,* January 25, 1928.
52. Ibid., January 29, 1928.
53. Seattle Year Book, Annual Report of Bertha Knight Landes, 1927, 3.
54. *Seattle Times,* January 29, 1928.
55. Ibid., March 4, 1928.
56. Ibid., March 2, 1928.
57. Ibid.
58. *Seattle Star,* March 5, 1928.
59. *Seattle Times,* March 4, 1928.
60. Edwards' Mayoralty Message, Seattle Campaign Literature, 2 (1928).
61. *Seattle Star* and *Times,* March 1, 1928.
62. *Seattle Times,* March 1, 1928.
63. Ibid.
64. Ibid., March 2, 1928.
65. Sparks, "J. D. Ross and Seattle City Light," 140. Landes and Ross were right to be concerned, if not about the turn-of-the-century trusts, then about the holding companies, which represented the industrial consolidation of the 1920s. By 1920, only ten companies controlled 72 percent of the nation's electric power. Holding companies controlled much of the nation's total capital and production. In banking, only 1 percent of the banks controlled almost half the nation's banking resources, and four meatpackers controlled 70 percent of production (Brown, *Setting a Course,* 9).
66. *Seattle Times,* March 11, 1928.

67. Ibid.
68. "Seattle's Municipal Housekeeper," *Literary Digest,* March 27, 1927, 13.
69. Landes, "Woman Mayor's Observations."
70. A fascinating analysis of the gendered imagery of Jefferson Davis trying to escape his northern captors by dressing in petticoats and skirt, and the role the image played in the power relations between North and South after the Civil War, is found in Nina Silber, "Intemperate Men, Spiteful Women, and Jefferson Davis: Northern Views of the Defeated South," *American Quarterly* 41, no. 4 (December 1989): 614–35.
71. See Smith-Rosenberg, *Disorderly Conduct;* and Joan Scott, "Gender: A Useful Category of Historical Analysis," in *Coming to Terms: Feminism, Theory, Politics,* ed. Elizabeth Weed.
72. *Oxford English Dictionary,* 2d ed., 11:642.
73. Ibid.
74. *Godey's Magazine,* April 1896, cited in *Oxford English Dictionary,* 11:643.
75. Seattle Campaign Literature, 2 (1928).
76. Ibid.
77. Ibid.
78. Ibid.
79. "Re-elect Mayor Bertha K. Landes" brochure, Seattle Campaign Literature, 2 (1928).
80. Ibid.
81. Edwards' Mayoralty Message.
82. Ibid.
83. Ibid.
84. "The Mayor and the 'Blank' Candidate," Edwards' Mayoralty Message.
85. Edwards' Mayoralty Message.
86. Ibid.
87. Ibid.
88. *Seattle Post-Intelligencer,* March 6, 1928.
89. Edwards' Mayoralty Message.
90. "To the Public," Edwards' Mayoralty Message.
91. Edwards' Mayoralty Message.
92. Ibid.
93. "Interesting Reasons Why Certain 'Interest' Support Has Gone to Mrs. Landes," Edwards' Mayoralty Message.
94. "And an Open Letter to Mrs. Landes," Edwards' Mayoralty Message.
95. "Just One Day's Crime Record!" Edwards' Mayoralty Message.
96. "Yes, the World Laughs with Us!" Edwards' Mayoralty Message.
97. Ibid.
98. "Notoriously Unfair, John Danz Denounces Edwards Who Always Gave Union Labor Square Deal," Edwards' Mayoralty Message.
99. Edwards' Mayoralty Message.
100. Ibid.
101. "And an Open Letter to Mrs. Landes," Edwards' Mayoralty Message.
102. "Facts—a Newspaper of Plain Truths—Clean House Now," Seattle Campaign Literature, 2 (1928).
103. Brewster and Buerge, *Washingtonians,* 174.
104. "Facts."
105. *Polk's Seattle City Directory,* 1921.
106. Berner, *Seattle, 1900–1920,* 192–95.
107. "Facts."
108. Ibid.
109. Ibid., 3.
110. Ibid., 4.
111. *Seattle Times,* March 8 and 9, 1928.
112. *Seattle Times* and *Star,* March 10, 1928.
113. *Seattle Times,* March 5, 1928.

114. Ibid., March 6, 1928.
115. Ibid., March 11, 1928.
116. *Seattle Star,* March 5, 1928.
117. Ibid., n.d.; Landes Papers, box 2.
118. *Seattle Times,* March 12, 1928.

VI. "ADVENTURES IN MUNICIPAL HOUSEKEEPING"

1. *Seattle Times,* March 14, 1928.
2. Schear, "Our One and Only Madame Mayor," 21.
3. *Seattle Times,* March 10 and 13, 1928.
4. Ibid., March 11, 1928.
5. Frank Edwards, Statement of Expenses for Office, March 13, 1928, file no. 115326, City Archives.
6. *Seattle Times* and *Post-Intelligencer,* March 24, 25, and 27, 1928.
7. Clipping, n.d., Landes Papers, box 2.
8. Deacon, "Why Wasn't Bertha Knight Landes Re-elected?" 89–90. See also Sparks, "J. D. Ross and Seattle City Light," 140–41.
9. Robert L. Hill, "Power and Politics in Seattle," *Nation,* March 2, 1932, 254.
10. Deacon, "Why Wasn't Bertha Knight Landes Re-elected?" 91.
11. Dreher, "J. D. Ross, Public Power Magnate," 52–53.
12. Sparks, "J. D. Ross and Seattle City Light," 165–66.
13. Ibid., 170–71.
14. *Seattle Star,* March 9, 1931.
15. *Seattle Post-Intelligencer,* March 17, 1931.
16. *New York Times,* July 15, 1931.
17. *Seattle Times,* April 4 and May 29, 1931.
18. Hill, "Power and Politics in Seattle," 254.
19. Dickson, "Labor in Municipal Politics," 68–71.
20. Ibid., 71.
21. Barbour, "Measuring City Government," 64. Barbour also concluded that in its desire to protect civil service employees, Seattle had made it too difficult to remove poor employees except for the "most gross failings" (61).
22. Deacon, "Why Wasn't Bertha Knight Landes Re-elected?" 96.
23. R. D. McKenzie, "Community Forces: A Study of the Non-Partisan Elections in Seattle," *Journal of Social Forces* 2 (May 1924): 568.
24. Deacon, "Why Wasn't Bertha Knight Landes Re-elected?" 107–9.
25. Dickson, "Labor in Municipal Politics," 71.
26. Deacon, "Why Wasn't Bertha Knight Landes Re-elected?" 108–10.
27. Ibid., 112.
28. *Portland Oregonian,* March 15, 1928; and *Seattle Times,* March 16, 1928.
29. Stone, "Mrs. Landes and Why We Loved Her."
30. David Kyvig, *Repealing National Prohibition,* 68.
31. *Time,* March 26, 1928, 13–14.
32. O'Connor, "Biography of Bertha Knight Landes," Landes Papers, box 1.
33. Budlong, "What Happened in Seattle," 198.
34. Ibid.
35. Alfa Freeman to Bertha Knight Landes, March 24, 1928, Landes Papers, box 1.
36. Ibid.
37. *Seattle Times,* March 14, 1928.
38. *Seattle Star,* May 3, 1928.
39. Bertha Knight Landes to Frank Edwards, May 24, 1928, Landes Papers, box 1.
40. *Seattle Times,* March 30, 1928.
41. *Seattle Post-Intelligencer,* March 15, 1928.
42. Bertha Knight Landes to University of Washington Librarian Henry, n.d., Landes Papers, box 1.
43. *Nashville Banner,* n.d., Landes Papers, box 2.

44. Landes, "Alumna in Politics," 28.

45. E. H. Hatch to Bertha Knight Landes, March 14, 1928, Landes Papers, box 1.

46. Seattle Park Board of Commissioners, note to Bertha Knight Landes, May 30, 1928, Landes Papers, box 1.

47. David Starr Jordan to Bertha Knight Landes, March 14, 1928, Landes Papers, box 1.

48. Landes, "Alumna in Politics," 27.

49. Landes, "A Woman—on Women," 156–60.

50. Landes, "Does Politics Make Women Crooked?" 36–38.

51. Ibid.

52. Ibid.

53. Howe, *New York World*, January 16, 1929.

54. Landes, "Reminiscence," 3.

55. Landes, "Steering a Big City Straight," 7.

56. Ibid.

57. Ibid., 37.

58. The explicit feminism of the National Women's Party was anathema to most women's organizations. Despite the celebratory comments about women's emancipation in the media, the debate became more strident about where women's true satisfaction and happiness could be found, and the answer often given was that it was not to be found in careers and activism, but in the home. Feminism was under heavy fire by 1930 as too futuristic and sexless, with feminist women being portrayed either as turning into men or as set against men in a sex war (Cott, *Grounding of Modern Feminism*, 243, 271–79).

59. "Seattle Federation of Women's Clubs" directory, 1928–1929, WSFWC, box 1.

60. Mathews, "History of the Washington State Federation of Women's Clubs," 97–116.

61. "Resolutions Adopted by the Washington Federation," *Washington Clubwomen* 27 (June 1944): 6.

62. Robyn Muncy, *Creating a Female Dominion in American Reform, 1890–1935*, 128–30; and Lemons, *Woman Citizen*, 214–16, offer detailed explanations of the Spider Web controversy and its significance to the cause of feminism.

63. Tripp, "Progressive Labor Laws in Washington State," 278, 281.

64. Ibid., 54, 58, 63. David Kyvig, in *Repealing National Prohibition*, argues the interesting position that when prohibition was repealed in 1933, only fourteen years after its ratification, it was the final measure of growing disfavor and disillusionment with the constitutional process. That disfavor also affected the fate of the ERA and the Child Labor Amendment. Policymakers then turned to institutional arrangements to deal with social issues, such as the New Deal programs, and sought to reverse the erosion of support for government caused by prohibition enforcement hypocrisy. In Washington and four other states, the GOP platform in 1930 endorsed repeal, and a referendum on prohibition issues in 1932 in Washington saw the "wets" win.

65. Brown, *Setting a Course*, 246.

66. Cott, *Grounding of Modern Feminism*, 225–29.

67. Brown, *Setting a Course*, 247.

68. Women active in politics and government in the 1930s frequently identified themselves as social reformers rather than as feminists, although they promoted the advancement of women as well. The programs they pursued benefited both men and women and created a network of women emerging with political power (Susan Ware, *Beyond Suffrage: Women in the New Deal*, 6–8).

69. Since the turn of the century, Washington had been thoroughly dominated by the Republican party, with the state's voters supporting Hoover two to one in 1928 (Ficken and LeWarne, *Washington: A Centennial History*, 113).

70. Samuel Fleming and Noah Davenport, *Government in Seattle: City, County, State, National*, 88.

71. Ibid., 65.
72. Ibid., 42.
73. Ibid., 31–32.
74. Ibid., 31.
75. *Oregon Journal,* October 21, 1938, Landes Papers, box 2.
76. Schear, "Our One and Only Madame Mayor," 20–21.
77. M. Lyle Spencer, University of Washington President, to J. B. Pond, May 7, 1928, Landes Papers, box 1.
78. Ibid.
79. Clippings, no title or date, Landes Papers, box 2.
80. Cabin Program, Cunard Lines RMS *Caronia,* June 12, 1930, Landes Papers, box 1.
81. *New York Times,* November 29, 1928.
82. *St. Louis Star,* n.d. 1929, Landes Papers, box 2.
83. Mrs. H. Edward Dreier to Bertha Knight Landes, December 21, 1928 and January 4, 1929, Landes Papers, box 1.
84. *Honolulu Star-Bulletin,* n.d., Landes Papers, box 2.
85. *Portland Oregonian,* n.d. 1931, Landes Papers, box 2; and *American Soroptimist,* September 1962, 10.
86. International News Service, clipping, Sacramento, n.d. 1931, Landes Papers, box 2.
87. Pieroth, "Bertha Knight Landes," 125.
88. *Deseret News,* November 18, no year, Landes Papers, box 2.
89. Catt's group united the League of Women Voters, the General Federation of Women's Clubs, the YWCA, the WCTU, and various women's religious groups behind one cause, at least temporarily. However, as happened in the Spider Web controversy, despite Catt's efforts, conservative women's groups such as the Daughters of the American Revolution accused Catt's followers and the other organizations of Communism, Sovietism, and radical feminism, which they said was subversive and destructive to moral order and the nation (Cott, *Grounding of Modern Feminism,* 257–60). See also Joan Jensen, "All Pink Sisters: The War Department and the Feminist Movement in the 1920s," in *Decades of Discontent: The Women's Movement, 1920–40,* ed. Lois Scharf and Joan M. Jensen, 199–222.
90. *Portland Oregonian,* n.d., Landes Papers, box 2.
91. Stone, "Mrs. Landes, Why We Loved Her."
92. Clipping, n.d., Salt Lake City, Landes Papers, box 2.
93. *Meadville* (Pennsylvania) *Republican,* March 6, 193?, and clipping, Wheeling, West Virginia, n.d., Landes Papers, box 2.
94. *Meadville* (Pennsylvania) *Republican,* March 6, 193?, and clipping, Wheeling, West Virginia, n.d., Landes Papers, box 2.
95. *Dallas Morning News,* February 24, 1929; *El Paso Times,* February 28, 1929; *Boston Globe Democrat,* February 9, 1929; *Boston Transcript,* March 5, 1930; *Lewiston Morning Tribune,* October 20, 1929; *Kansas City Star,* February 22, 1929, Landes Papers, box 2.
96. *New York Times,* February 24, 1930.
97. Clippings, Jacksonville, Florida, February 10, 1930; and *Orlando Morning Sentinel,* January 30, 1930, Landes Papers, box 2.
98. Passport, Bertha Knight Landes, issued May 12, 1930, Henry Landes Papers, box 1.
99. *Wilmington Evening,* February 18, 1931, Landes Papers, box 2.
100. Unsigned letter on police activities, March 5, 1930, Landes Papers, box 1.
101. *Seattle Post-Intelligencer,* March 10, 1930.
102. The White House to Bertha Knight Landes, n.d., and acceptance letter from Landes, November 4, 1930, Landes Papers, box 1.
103. Muncy, *Creating a Female Dominion in American Reform, 1890–1935,* 124–25, 144–50.
104. Chas. P. Morrill to Bertha Knight Landes, October 12, 1931, Landes

Papers, box 1. In the letter Morrill, the publicity chairman, praises Landes for her outstanding help with fundraising through the churches of Seattle.

105. *Seattle Times,* January 4, 1932.

106. "Family" was invoked by sociologists, unionists, moviemakers, and magazines as a weapon against working women during the years leading to World War II (Kessler-Harris, *Out to Work,* 250–61).

107. Lois Scharf, " 'The Forgotten Woman': Working Women, the New Deal, and Women's Organizations," in *Decades of Discontent: The Women's Movement, 1920–40,* 245–46. Scharf argues that the threats to married women's employment united previously divided women's organizations, who later gained repeal of the provisions of section 13 of the 1932 Economy Act that prohibited federal employment of female spouses (249). The groups also fought individual state efforts to pass the same kinds of restrictions on women's employment.

108. Lois Jermin, secretary, Women's Protective Association, to Bertha Knight Landes, December 3, 1928, Landes Papers, box 1.

109. Ibid.

110. "Review of Work of Mrs. Landes' Committee, November 1, 1931, to June 30, 1932," Landes Papers, box 1.

111. Reports, Women's Division of Commission for Improved Employment, December 1931 and January, May, June 1932, Landes Papers, box 1.

112. "Review of Work of Mrs. Landes' Committee."

113. *Portland Oregonian,* n.d. 1931, Landes Papers, box 2.

114. *Deseret News,* November 18, no year, Landes Papers, box 2.

115. I. F. Dix, Pacific Telephone and Telegraph Co. vice president and general manager, to Bertha Knight Landes, February 19, 1932, Landes Papers, box 1.

116. H. W. Carroll to Bertha Landes, May 17, 1932, Landes Papers, box 1.

117. Bertha Landes, speech on child welfare, no title or date, Landes Papers, box 1.

118. The House Judiciary Committee held three months of hearings in 1930 on modification of the Eighteenth Amendment. The highly publicized hearings saw a parade of representatives from various organizations arguing their positions on enforcement and other issues (Kyvig, *Repealing National Prohibition,* 112).

119. Russell Barthell, executive secretary of the University of Washington Bureau of Government Research, to Bertha Knight Landes, November 14, 1934, Landes Papers, box 1.

120. "Statement by Bertha Knight Landes, Former Mayor of Seattle," testimony before Judiciary Committee, March 12, 1930, Landes Papers, box 1.

121. League of Women Voters Work, 1933, Susan B. Cooper Papers, box 3, Manuscripts Collection, University of Washington; and *Seattle Post-Intelligencer,* November 19, 1933. Carrie Chapman Catt also visited and addressed the Washington LWV in 1937 (Catt to Susan Cooper, letter of thanks, April 28, 1937), Susan B. Cooper Papers, box 3.

122. "Seattle League of Women Voters Program, 1934–5," Susan B. Cooper Papers, box 3.

123. Goodspeed, "Memorial of Henry Landes," 209.

124. May and Frank Cashman, *Vicksburg Evening Post* publisher, to Bertha Knight Landes, n.d., Landes Papers, box 1.

125. Landes, "Alumna in Politics," 13.

126. Bertha Knight Landes to Nelson Trusler Johnson, U.S. Ambassador to China, May 14, 1937, Landes Papers, box 1.

127. Ship's passenger list, *S.S. Monterey,* June 22, 1938, Landes Papers, box 1.

128. Clipping, no title or date, Landes Papers, box 2.

129. Passport, Bertha Knight Landes, June 1, 1938, Henry Landes Papers, box 1.

130. *Topeka Daily Capital,* n.d., Landes Papers, box 2.

131. *Kansas City Times,* December 2, 1937, Landes Papers, box 2.

132. *Seattle Times,* May 14, 1941.

133. R. K. MacMaster, "Unity School of Christianity," in *Encyclopedic Dictionary of Religion*, ed. Paul Meagher, Thomas O'Brien, and Consuelo Maria Aherne, 3:3613.

134. R. K. MacMaster, "New Thought," in *Encyclopedic Dictionary of Religion*, 2:2523.

135. Instruction pamphlet, Unity School of Christianity, Landes Papers, box 1.

136. Landes, "Alumna in Politics," 13.

137. Ibid., 26, 28.

138. Ibid., 28.

139. *Seattle Times*, November 29, 1943.

140. Ibid., November 30, 1943.

141. Delphine Bell to Bertha Knight Landes, March 20, 1929, Landes Papers, box 1.

142. "Six Women Victorious in Campaigns for Congress," clipping, n.d., Landes Papers, box 2.

VII. POWER AND POLITICS POSTSCRIPT

1. Kathleen Barry argues that analyzing women's lives requires looking at patterns of resistance in context, with reference to the status quo of the day. Barry, "Biography and the Search for Women's Subjectivity," *Women's Studies International Forum* 12 (1990): 561–77. See also Carolyn Heilbrun, *Writing a Woman's Life;* and Ann Gordon, "Writing the Lives of Women," *NWSA Journal* 1 (Winter 1988–89): 221–37.

2. *Honolulu Advertiser*, August 8, 1930, Landes Papers, box 2.

3. Ibid., July 14, 1931.

4. The best work on Landes was written by Doris Pieroth, "Bertha Knight Landes: The Woman Who Was Mayor," in *Women in Pacific Northwest History*, 83–106 (first appeared in *Pacific Northwest Quarterly* in 1984).

5. At the turn of the century, race and culture were synonymous ideas, not to suggest equality as much as a hierarchy of racial development ranging from primitive to civilized, and women, protected from the rigors of economic competition and struggle (at least in the ideal), were assumed to be both the protectors and conveyors of the culture of civilization. In the same fashion, it was assumed that the mere presence of white women in the West "civilized" it when women entered it in numbers (Peggy Pascoe, *Relations of Rescue: The Search for Female Moral Authority in the American West, 1874–1939*, xvii, 114–15).

6. The family is another site of the long-range struggle over production and values. See Heidi Hartmann, "The Family as the Locus of Gender, Class, and Political Struggle: The Example of Housework," in *Feminism and Methodology*, ed. Sandra Harding, 109–34.

7. Scott, "Gender," 100. Also see Gisela Bock, "Women's History and Gender History: Aspects of an International Debate," *Gender and History* 1 (Spring 1989): 7–30, for a useful discussion of the treatment of gender in historiography.

8. Michel Foucault, *History of Sexuality*, trans. Robert Hurley, 1:94.

9. Foucault, *Archaeology of Knowledge*, trans. A. M. Sheridan Smith, 2–12. The "great texts" of history need to be reexamined in light of developments in literary theory (Susanne Gearhart, "History as Criticism: The Dialogue of History and Literature," *Diacritics* 17 [1987]: 56–65).

10. See Foucault's *Discourse on Language*, trans. Rupert Swyer, printed as an appendix to *Archaeology of Knowledge*.

11. Foucault, "History of Systems of Thought," in *Language, Counter-memory, and Practice: Selected Essays and Interviews*, ed. Donald Bouchard, 200.

12. Foucault, "Nietzsche, Genealogy, History," in *Language, Counter-Memory, and Practice: Selected Essays and Interviews*, 148.

13. While men tend to become more conservative as they age, women may feel freed from family and societal restraints. "It is perhaps only in old age, certainly past fifty, that women can stop being female impersonators, can grasp the

opportunity to reverse their most cherished principles of 'femininity' " (Heilbrun, *Writing a Woman's Life,* 126). Historian Susan Henry concluded that women have different life cycles than men. Women's opportunities, far more than men's, have been influenced by age-related factors, with the result that because male patterns are the norm, women's life patterns "are ignored or misunderstood" ("Nearsightedness and Blind Spots in Studying the History of Women in Journalism" [Paper presented at the annual meeting of American Journalism Historians Association, Coeur d'Alene, Idaho, October 4–6, 1990]).

14. Foucault, *Discipline and Punish: The Birth of the Prison,* trans. Allan Sheridan, 24–25.

15. Polly Young-Eisendrath, "The Female Person and How We Talk about Her," in *Feminist Thought and the Structure of Knowledge,* ed. Mary McCanney Gergen, 158.

16. Ibid., 160.

17. Victor Turner, *Process, Performance, and Pilgrimage: A Study in Comparative Symbology,* 13, 62.

18. Ibid., 20.

19. Victor Turner, *From Ritual to Theatre: The Human Seriousness of Play,* 44.

20. Turner, *Process, Performance, and Pilgrimage,* 13.

21. Ibid., 21.

22. Victor Turner, "Frame, Flow, and Reflection," in *Performance in Postmodern Culture,* ed. Michel Benamou and Charles Caramello, 49–51.

23. Ibid., 51.

24. Turner, *Process, Performance, and Pilgrimage,* 43–45.

25. Ibid., 32.

26. Victor Turner, *Dramas, Fields, and Metaphors: Symbolic Action in Human Society,* 35.

27. Ibid., 36.

28. Ibid., 37.

29. Victor Turner, Marc Swartz, and Arthur Tuden, "Introduction," in *Political Anthropology,* ed. Turner, Swartz, and Tuden, 7–17.

30. Turner, *From Ritual to Theatre,* 69.

31. Ibid., 35.

32. Ibid., 32–37.

33. Victor Turner, "Ritual Aspects of Conflict Control in African Micropolitics," in *Political Anthropology,* ed. Turner, Swartz, and Tuden, 240–41.

34. Turner, *Dramas, Fields, and Metaphors,* 110–11.

35. Ibid., 122–23.

36. Ibid., 140–41.

37. Ibid., 233.

38. Hal Bruno, ABC News political director, on ABC's "Good Morning America," April 11, 1990.

39. Robin Toner, *New York Times,* reprinted in *Lewiston Tribune,* April 11, 1990.

40. Meg Dennison, "Washington, Idaho Among Top Women's Legislatures," Associated Press report and graphic, *Moscow-Pullman Daily News,* November 12, 1992.

41. Associated Press Wire Service, "Running against Women Gives Some Men the Blues," in *Moscow Idahonian,* April 7, 1990.

42. See Bruce Curtis, "The Wimp Factor," *American Heritage,* November 1989, 40–50.

43. *Old English Dictionary,* 20:368.

44. Robert L. Chapman, ed., *New Dictionary of American Slang,* 468.

45. Robert L. Chapman, ed., *Thesaurus of American Slang,* 248.

46. Rosalind Powell, *Women and Power,* 22.

47. Susan Carroll, *Women as Candidates in American Politics,* 121.

48. Sally Helgesen, quoted in "Author Advises Corporate Women to Be More Like Women," Associated Press, in *Lewiston Tribune,* July 23, 1990.

49. Bertha Knight Landes, "What the Housewife Demands of Advertising," speech to Pacific Coast Advertising Association, Portland, June 27, 1927, Landes Papers, box 1.

50. Margaret Carlson, "It's Our Turn," *Time* special issue, Fall 1990, 16.

51. Powell, *Women and Power,* 59.

52. Nancy R. Gibbs, "High Noon for Women's Clubs," *Time,* May 30, 1988, 72.

53. Ibid.

BIBLIOGRAPHY

PRIMARY SOURCES

Published Works

Allen, Arthur H. *Who's Who in Washington State: A Compilation of Biographical Sketches of Men and Women Prominent in the Affairs of Washington State.* Seattle: Privately printed, 1927.

"Bertha K. Landes, Past President of the American Federation of Soroptimist Clubs, and Honorary Member of the Seattle Club." *American Soroptimist,* October 1940, 10.

Brace, Blanche. "Well . . . Why Not?" *Woman Citizen,* September 1926, 8.

Brown, Edwin. "What Price Harmony?" Seattle Campaign Literature 2, 1928. Northwest Collection, Seattle Public Library.

Budlong, Julia. "What Happened in Seattle," *Nation,* August 29, 1928, 197–98.

Cherrington, Ernest H., ed. *The Anti-Saloon League Yearbook, 1915: An Encyclopedia of Facts and Figures Dealing with the Liquor Traffic and the Temperance Reform.* Westerville, Ohio: Anti-Saloon League of America, 1915.

Croly, Jennie Cunningham. *The History of the Woman's Club Movement in America.* New York: Henry G. Allen, 1898.

Directory and Handbook, King County Women's Christian Temperance Union. Seattle: WCTU, 1923. Pacific Northwest Collection, University of Washington, Seattle.

Dreher, Carl. "J. D. Ross, Public Power Magnate." *Harper's Magazine,* June 1940, 46–60.

Fleming, Samuel, and Noah Davenport. *Government in Seattle: City, County, State, National.* Seattle: Seattle Public Schools, 1935.

General Federation of Women's Clubs. *Tenth Biennial Convention Official Report.* Edited by H. H. Dawson. Newark, N.J.: General Federation of Women's Clubs, 1910.

Goodspeed, G. E. "Memorial of Henry Landes." *Proceedings of the Geological Society of America for 1936,* June 1937, 207–13.

Hanford, Cornelius, ed. *Seattle and Environs, 1852–1924.* 3 vols. Chicago and Seattle: Pioneer Historical Publishing, 1924.

Hanna, Mrs. M. T. B., ed. *Votes for Women,* August–September 1910.

Hill, Robert L. "Power and Politics in Seattle." *Nation,* March 2, 1932, 253–54.

"How It Would Be If Some Ladies Had Their Own Way." *Harper's Weekly,* May 16, 1868, 320.

Jordan, David Starr. *The Days of a Man: Being Memories of a Naturalist, Teacher, and Minor Prophet of Democracy.* 2 vols. New York: World Book, 1922.

Knowles, Margaret, ed. *The Seattle Woman—The Club Woman's Annual,* Seattle Federation of Women's Clubs, December 1924.

Landes, Bertha Knight. "An Alumna in Politics." *Indiana Alumni Magazine,* April 1939, 13.

———. "Does Politics Make Women Crooked?" *Collier's,* March 16, 1929, 24.

———. "Steering a Big City Straight." *Woman Citizen,* December 1927, 6.

———. "A Woman—On Women." *Printer's Ink,* July 7, 1927, 156.

Lee, Erma Conkling, ed. *The Biographical Cyclopaedia of American Women.* Vol. 2. New York: Franklin W. Lee Publishing, 1925. S.v. "Bertha E. Knight Landes," 148–51.

Leighton, George R. "Seattle, Washington: The Edge of the Last Frontier." *Harper's Magazine,* March 1939, 422–40.
Lind, Andrew W. *A Study of Mobility of Population in Seattle.* Seattle: University of Washington Press, 1925.
McKenzie, R. D. "Community Forces: A Study of the Non-Partisan Municipal Elections in Seattle." *Journal of Social Forces* 2 (January 1924): 266–73; (May 1924): 568–69.
Meany, Edmond. "Living Pioneers of Washington." Vol. 4. Carkeek Scrapbooks. Museum of History and Industry, Seattle.
Municipal Elections File, 1926. Archives, Seattle Public Library.
"National Affairs—Women." *Time,* March 22, 1926, 9.
Pigott's Political Reference Book for King County. Seattle: H. C. Pigott, 1928.
"Political Notes—Landes Out." *Time,* March 26, 1928, 12.
Polk's Seattle City Directory. Seattle: R. L. Polk, 1921, 1926, 1940.
"Resolutions Adopted by the Washington Federation." *Washington Clubwomen,* June 1944, 6.
Richardson, Anne Steese. "My Trip across the Continent, Where I Learned Many Interesting Things about Good Citizenship." *Woman's Home Companion,* October 1922, 29.
Seattle Society Blue Book. Seattle: Blue Book Publishing, 1911.
"Seattle's Municipal Housekeeper." *Literary Digest,* March 27, 1927, 13.
Shields, Louise F. "The Woman Mayor Calls It a Day." *Sunset Magazine,* February 1927, 46.
"The Temporary Lady Mayor Who Fired Seattle's Chief of Police." *Literary Digest,* August 9, 1924, 41–43.
Transactions of the National Council of Women. Washington, D.C.: National Council of Women, 1891.
Twenty-third Annual Report, Yearbook for 1919–20. Seattle: Washington State Federation of Women's Clubs, 1919–20. Pacific Northwest Collection, University of Washington, Seattle.
Vaughan, L. Brent, ed. *Hill's Practical Reference Library of General Knowledge.* 5 vols. Chicago: Dixon, Hanson, 1906. S.v. "Massachusetts," "Ware," and "Worcester."
"Voters Information League Bulletin no. 44." Seattle: Voters Information League, February 20, 1925.
Watts, Isaac. *Isaac Watts' Improvement of the Mind.* Revised by Joseph Emerson. Boston: James Loring's General Sabbath School Depository, 1833.
"What Variety of City Government Do You Want?" *Sunset Magazine,* September 1924, 47–48.
"Woman Mayor Launches Manager Plan." *American Public Official Magazine,* July 1926.
"Woman's Mission and Women's Clubs." *Ladies Home Journal,* May 1905, 3–4.

Seattle Newspapers Consulted

Argus. 1922–26.
Post-Intelligencer. 1897–1931.
Star. 1922–38.
Times. 1920–74.
Union-Record. 1920–27.

Unpublished Works

Backman, Paul S. "The Organization of Municipal Government in Seattle." Master's thesis, University of Washington, 1925.
Barbour, Dana Mills. "Measuring City Government—the Munroe Criteria Applied to Seattle." Master's thesis, University of Washington, 1930.
Carkeek Scrapbooks, Seattle History, 1884–1917. 4 vols. Museum of History and Industry, Seattle.
Chapman, Inez Bell. Interview, Washington State Oral/Aural History Program. Olympia: Washington State Archives, 14. Microfiche.

City Archives, Seattle Municipal Building, 1922–28.
"Classified List of Delegates to First Convention," June 22–23, 1897, Olympia. Washington State Federation of Women's Clubs, box 1. Manuscripts Collection, University of Washington, Seattle.
Susan B. Cooper Papers, box 3. Manuscripts Collection, University of Washington, Seattle.
Dickson, William John. "Labor in Municipal Politics: A Study of Labor's Political Policies and Activities in Seattle." Master's thesis, University of Washington, 1928.
Durham, Irene Somerville. "Community Clubs in Seattle." Master's thesis, University of Washington, 1929.
"Historical Highlights, Women's University Club of Seattle, 1914–1980." Pacific Northwest Collection, University of Washington.
"History of the Woman's Century Club." Pacific Northwest Collection, University of Washington, Seattle, 1942. Photostat.
Journal of the Proceedings of the City Council of the City of Seattle, 1922–1928, referred to as City Council Minutes. Comptroller's Office, Seattle Municipal Building. Microfiche.
Bertha Knight Landes Papers, boxes 1–2. Manuscripts Collection, University of Washington, Seattle.
Henry Landes Papers. University Archives, University of Washington, Seattle.
Mathews, Serena. "History of the Washington State Federation of Women's Clubs." Washington State Federation of Women's Clubs, box 2. Manuscripts Collection, University of Washington, Seattle.
"Minutes of the Washington State Federation of Women's Clubs, 1900–1908." Washington State Federation of Women's Clubs, box 2. Manuscripts Collection, University of Washington, Seattle.
"Official Register and Directory of Women's Clubs in America." Vols. 21–26. Shirley, Mass: Federated Women's Clubs, 1921–25.
"Register, 1896–1923." Washington State Federation of Women's Clubs, box 2. Manuscripts Collection, University of Washington, Seattle.
Seattle Campaign Literature, 2 vols., 1925–28. Northwest Collection, Seattle Public Library.
"Seattle Federation of Women's Clubs" Directory. Washington Federation of Women's Clubs, 1928–29. Manuscripts Collection, University of Washington, Seattle.
Stone, Mrs. H. O. "Mrs. Landes, Why We Loved Her." Memorial to Bertha Landes by Women's City Club, February 8, 1944. Vol. 3. Women's City Club Scrapbooks, Museum of History and Industry, Seattle.
Washington State Federation of Women's Clubs. Century Club History, box 2. Manuscripts Collection, University of Washington, Seattle.
Washington State Federation of Women's Clubs Records, boxes 1–2. Manuscripts Collection, University of Washington, Seattle.
Woman's Century Club Constitution. Pacific Northwest Collection, University of Washington, Seattle, 1942. Photostat.
Wright, Robert. Interview, Washington State Oral/Aural History Program. Olympia: Washington State Archives, 5–7. Microfiche.

SECONDARY SOURCES

Published Works

Alcoff, Linda. "Cultural Feminism versus Poststructuralism." *Signs* 13 (Spring 1988): 405–36.
Altbach, Edith H. *Women in America.* Lexington, Mass.: D. C. Heath, 1974.
Andrews, Mildred. *Seattle Women: A Legacy of Community Development.* Seattle: YWCA of Seattle–King County, 1984.
———. *Washington Women as Pathbreakers.* Dubuque, Iowa: Kendall/Hunt Publishing, 1989.
Armitage, Susan. "The Challenge of Women's History." In *Women in Pacific*

Northwest History: An Anthology, ed. Karen Blair. Seattle: University of Washington Press, 1988.

Avery, Mary W. *History and Government of the State of Washington.* Seattle: University of Washington Press, 1961.

Baker, Paula. "The Domestication of Politics: Women and American Political Society, 1780–1920." *American Historical Review* 89 (June 1984): 620–47.

Barker-Benfield, G. J. " 'Mother Emancipator': The Meaning of Jane Addams' Sickness and Cure." *Journal of Family History,* Winter 1979: 395–420.

Barry, Kathleen. "Biography and the Search for Women's Subjectivity." *Women's Studies International Forum* 12 (1990): 561–77.

Barton, Harold, and Catharine Bullard. *History of the State of Washington.* Boston: D. C. Heath, 1953.

Bennett, Judith. "Feminism and History." *Gender and History* 1 (Autumn 1989): 251–72.

Blackford, Mansel. "Reform Politics in Seattle during the Progressive Era." *Pacific Northwest Quarterly* 59 (October 1968): 177–85.

Blair, Karen. *The Clubwoman as Feminist: True Womanhood Redefined, 1868–1914.* New York: Holmes and Meier, 1980.

———. "The Limits of Sisterhood: The Woman's Building in Seattle, 1908–1921." In *Women in Pacific Northwest History,* ed. Karen Blair. Seattle: University of Washington Press, 1988.

Blanchard, Leslie. *The Street Railway Era in Seattle: A Chronicle of Six Decades.* Forty Fort, Penn.: Harold E. Cox, Publisher, 1968.

Bledstein, Burton. *The Culture of Professionalism: The Middle Class and the Development of Higher Education in America.* New York: W. W. Norton, 1976.

Bock, Gisela. "Women's History and Gender History: Aspects of an International Debate." *Gender and History* 1 (Spring 1989): 7–30.

Brown, Dorothy. *Setting a Course: American Women in the 1920s.* Boston: Twayne Publishers, 1987.

Buenker, John. "Sovereign Individuals and Organic Networks: Political Cultures in Conflict During the Progressive Era." *American Quarterly* 40 (June 1988): 187–204.

Burke, Robert. "Bertha Ethel Knight Landes." In *Notable American Women, 1607–1950,* ed. Edward James and Janet James. 3 vols. Cambridge: Harvard University Press, 1971.

Burnham, John. "New Perspectives on the Prohibition Experiment of the 1920s." *Journal of Social History* 2 (1968): 457–65.

———. *Paths into American Culture: Psychology, Medicine, and Morals.* Philadelphia: Temple University Press, 1988.

Carroll, Susan. *Women as Candidates in American Politics.* Bloomington: Indiana University Press, 1985.

Chapman, Robert L., ed. *New Dictionary of American Slang.* New York: Harper and Row, 1986.

———. *Thesaurus of American Slang.* New York: Harper and Row, 1989.

Clark, Norman. *The Dry Years: Prohibition and Social Change in Washington.* Seattle: University of Washington Press, 1965.

Clark, Thomas. *Indiana University: Midwestern Pioneer.* 4 vols. Bloomington: Indiana University Press, 1970–77.

Conway, Jill. "Women Reformers and American Culture." *Journal of Social History* 5, no. 2 (Winter 1971–72): 164–77.

Cook, Blanche W. "Female Support Networks and Political Activism." In *A Heritage of Her Own: Toward a New Social History of American Women,* ed. Nancy Cott and Elizabeth Pleck. New York: Simon and Schuster, 1979.

Cott, Nancy. *The Bonds of Womanhood: "Woman's Sphere" in New England, 1780–1835.* New Haven: Yale University Press, 1978.

———. "Feminist Politics in the 1920s: The National Women's Party." *Journal of American History* 71, no. 1 (June 1984): 43–68.

———. *The Grounding of Modern Feminism.* New Haven: Yale University Press, 1987.
———. "What's in a Name? The Limits of 'Social Feminism'; or, Expanding the Vocabulary of Women's History." *Journal of American History* 76, no. 3 (December 1989): 809–29.
Cousins, Mark, and Athar Hussain. *Michel Foucault.* Theoretical Traditions in the Social Sciences. London: Macmillan, 1984.
Cowan, Ruth S. *More Work for Mother: The Ironies of Household Technology, from the Open Hearth to the Microwave.* New York: Basic Books, 1983.
Curtis, Bruce. "The Wimp Factor." *American Heritage,* November 1989, 40–50.
Dannenbaum, Jed. "The Origins of Temperance Activism and Militancy Among American Women." *Journal of Social History* 15 (Winter 1981): 235–52.
Dembo, Jonathan. *Unions and Politics in Washington State, 1885–1935.* New York: Garland, 1983.
Dennison, Meg. "Washington, Idaho Among Top Women's Legislatures." Associated Press. *Moscow-Pullman Daily News,* November 12, 1992.
Dorpat, Paul. *Seattle: Now and Then.* Seattle: Tartu Publications, 1984.
Dreyfus, Hubert L., and Paul Rabinow. *Michel Foucault: Beyond Structuralism and Hermeneutics.* Chicago: University of Chicago Press, 1982.
Dryden, Cecil. *History of Washington.* Portland: Binfords and Mort, 1968.
Epstein, Barbara Leslie. *The Politics of Domesticity: Women, Evangelism, and Temperance in Nineteenth-Century America.* Middletown, Conn.: Wesleyan University Press, 1981.
Evans, Sara. *Born for Liberty: A History of Women in America.* New York: Free Press, 1989.
———. "Toward a Usable Past: Feminism as History and Politics." *Minnesota History* 48 (Summer 1983): 231–35.
"Fact File." *Chronicle of Higher Education,* Feburary 7, 1990, A15–16.
Ferree, Myra M., and Beth Hess. *Controvery and Coalition: The New Feminist Movement.* Boston: Twayne, 1985.
Ficken, Robert, and Charles LeWarne. *Washington: A Centennial History.* Seattle: University of Washington Press, 1988.
Foucault, Michel. *Archaeology of Knowledge.* Translated by A. M. Sheridan Smith. New York: Random House/Pantheon, 1972.
———. *Discipline and Punish: The Birth of the Prison.* Translated by Alan Sheridan. New York: Pantheon, 1977.
———. *Discourse on Language.* Translated by Rupert Swyer. Appendix to *Archaeology of Knowledge.* New York: Random House/Pantheon, 1972.
———. *History of Sexuality.* Translated by Robert Hurley. New York: Random House, 1978.
———. *Language, Counter-memory, and Practice: Selected Essays and Interviews.* Edited by Donald Bouchard. Ithaca, N.Y.: Cornell University Press, 1977.
Freedman, Estelle. "Separatism as Strategy: Female Institution Building and American Feminism, 1870–1930." *Feminist Studies* 5, no. 3 (Fall 1979): 512–29.
Friedheim, Robert L. "The Seattle General Strike of 1919." *Pacific Northwest Quarterly* 52, no. 3 (July 1961): 81–98.
Gaustad, Edwin S. *A Religious History of America.* San Francisco: HarperCollins, 1990.
Gearhart, Susanne. "History as Criticism: The Dialogue of History and Literature." *Diacritics* 17 (1987): 56–65.
Glazer-Malbin, Nona. "Housework." *Signs* 1, no. 4 (1976): 905–22.
Gordon, Ann. "Writing the Lives of Women." *NWSA Journal* 1 (Winter 1988–89): 221–37.
Gordon, Linda. "What's New in Women's History." In *Feminist Studies/Critical Studies,* ed. Teresa de Lauretis. Bloomington: Indiana University Press, 1988.

Gordon, Lynn. *Gender and Higher Education in the Progressive Era.* New Haven: Yale University Press, 1990.

Greenwald, Maurine Weiner. "Working-Class Feminism and the Family Wage Ideal: The Seattle Debate on Married Women's Right to Work, 1914–1920." *Journal of American History* 76, no. 1 (June 1989): 118–49.

Gunns, Albert. *Civil Liberties in Crisis: The Pacific Northwest, 1917–1940.* New York: Garland, 1983.

Hartmann, Heidi. "The Family as the Locus of Gender, Class, and Political Struggle: The Example of Housework." In *Feminism and Methodology: Social Science Issues,* ed. Sandra Harding. Bloomington: Indiana University Press, 1987.

Heilbrun, Carolyn. *Writing a Woman's Life.* New York: W. W. Norton, 1988.

Hofstadter, Richard. *Social Darwinism in American Thought.* Philadelphia: University of Pennsylvania Press/Beacon, 1955.

Holli, Melvin, and Peter Jones. *Biographical Dictionary of American Mayors, 1820–1980.* Westport, Conn.: Greenwood Press, 1981.

Hoy, David Couzens, ed. *Foucault: A Critical Reader.* Oxford: Basil Blackwell, 1986.

Jensen, Joan M. "All Pink Sisters: The War Department and the Feminist Movement in the 1920s." In *Decades of Discontent: The Women's Movement, 1920–40,* ed. Lois Scharf and Joan M. Jensen. Westport, Conn.: Greenwood Press, 1983.

Johnson, Warren B. "Muckraking in the Northwest: Joe Smith and Seattle Reform." *Pacific Historical Review* 40 (November 1971): 478–500.

Jones, Nard. *Seattle.* New York: Doubleday, 1972.

Kennedy, David M. *Over Here: The First World War and American Society.* New York: Oxford University Press, 1980.

Kerber, Linda. "Separate Spheres, Female Worlds, Woman's Place: The Rhetoric of Women's History." *Journal of American History* 75 (June 1988): 9–39.

Kerr, K. Austin. *Organized for Prohibition: A New History of the Anti-Saloon League.* New Haven: Yale University Press, 1985.

Kerr, William, Jr. "The Progressives of Washington, 1910–1912." *Pacific Northwest Quarterly* 55 (January 1964): 16–27.

Kessler-Harris, Alice. *Out to Work: A History of Wage-Earning Women in the United States.* New York: Oxford University Press, 1982.

———. "Where Are the Organized Women Workers?" *Feminist Studies,* Fall 1975: 92–110.

———. *Women Have Always Worked: A Historical Overview.* Old Westbury, N.Y.: Feminist Press, 1981.

Koven, Seth, and Sonya Michel. "Gender and the Origins of the Welfare State." *Radical History Review* 43 (1989): 112–19.

Kraditor, Aileen. *The Ideas of the Woman Suffrage Movement, 1890–1920.* New York: Columbia University Press, 1965.

Kyvig, David. *Repealing National Prohibition.* Chicago: University of Chicago Press, 1979.

Larson, T. A. "The Woman Suffrage Movement in Washington." *Pacific Northwest Quarterly* 67 (April 1976): 49–62.

Lazier-Smith, Linda. "A New 'Genderation' of Images to Women." In *Women in Mass Communications: Challenging Gender Values,* ed. Pamela Creedon. Newbury Park, Calif.: Sage, 1989.

Lemons, J. Stanley. *The Woman Citizen: Social Feminism in the 1920s.* Urbana: University of Illinois Press, 1973.

Lerner, Gerda. "The Lady and the Mill Girl." In *A Heritage of Her Own: Toward a New Social History of American Women,* ed. Nancy Cott and Elizabeth Pleck. New York: Simon and Schuster, 1979.

———. "Women's Rights and American Feminism." *American Scholar* 40, no. 2 (Spring 1971): 235–45.

Lippmann, Walter. *Public Opinion.* New York: Free Press, 1922.

"Little Improvement Noted in Women's Page One Status." *Media Report to Women,* May–June 1990, 3–4.

MacDonald, Norbert. "The Business Leaders of Seattle, 1880–1910." *Pacific Northwest Quarterly* 50 (January 1959): 1–13.

Meagher, Paul, Thomas O'Brien, and Consuelo Maria Aherne, eds. *Encyclopedic Dictionary of Religion.* Washington, D.C.: Corpus Publications, 1979. S.v. "Unity School of Christianity" and "New Thought," by R. K. MacMaster.

More, Ellen S. " 'A Certain Restless Ambition': Women Physicians and World War I." *American Quarterly* 41 (December 1989): 636–60.

Morgan, Murray. *Skid Road: An Informal Portrait of Seattle.* New York: Viking Press, 1951.

Moss, Rosalind Urbach. "The 'Girls' from Syracuse: Sex Role Negotiation of Kansas Women in Politics, 1887–1890." In *The Women's West,* ed. Susan Armitage and Elizabeth Jameson. Norman: University of Oklahoma Press, 1987.

Muncy, Robyn. *Creating a Female Dominion in American Reform,* 1890–1935. New York: Oxford University Press, 1991.

Murray, Keith. "Issues and Personalities of Pacific Northwest Politics, 1889–1950." *Pacific Northwest Quarterly* 41 (July 1950): 213–33.

Myres, Sandra L. *Westering Women and the Frontier Experience, 1899–1915.* Albuquerque: University of New Mexico Press, 1982.

Newell, Gordon. *Rogues, Buffoons, and Statesmen.* Seattle: Superior Publishing, 1975.

"NFPW Study: Women Grossly Underrepresented in Newspaper Content, Editorial Decisions." *Media Report to Women,* July–August 1990, 2–4.

Paulson, Ross Evans. *Women's Suffrage and Prohibition: A Comparative Study of Equality and Social Control.* Glenview, Ill.: Scott, Foresman, 1973.

Peiss, Kathy. *Cheap Amusements: Working Women and Leisure in Turn-of-the-Century New York.* Philadelphia: Temple University Press, 1986.

Pieroth, Doris. "Bertha Knight Landes: The Woman Who Was Mayor." In *Women in Pacific Northwest History,* ed. Karen Blair, 83–106. Seattle: University of Washington Press, 1988.

Potts, Ralph Bushnell. *Seattle Heritage.* Seattle: Superior Publishing, 1955.

Powell, Rosalind. *Women and Power.* London: MacDonald, 1985.

Rapp, Rayna, and Ellen Ross. "The 1920s: Feminism, Consumerism, and Political Backlash in the United States." In *Women in Culture and Politics: A Century of Change,* ed. Judith Friedlander, Blanche W. Cook, Alice Kessler-Harris, and Carroll Smith-Rosenberg. Bloomington: Indiana University Press, 1986.

Riley, Denise. *Am I That Name? Feminism and the Category of "Women" in History.* Minneapolis: University of Minnesota Press, 1988.

Rosenberg, Rosalind. *Beyond Separate Spheres: Intellectual Roots of Modern Feminism.* New Haven: Yale University Press, 1982.

Rowbotham, Sheila. *Hidden from History: Three Hundred Years of Women's Oppression and the Fight Against It.* London: Pluto Press, 1973.

Sale, Roger. *Seattle, Past to Present.* Seattle: University of Washington Press, 1976.

Scharf, Lois. " 'The Forgotten Woman': Working Women, the New Deal, and Women's Organizations." In *Decades of Discontent: The Women's Movement, 1920–40,* ed. Lois Scharf and Joan M. Jensen. Westport, Conn.: Greenwood Press, 1983.

Schear, Rillmond. "Our One and Only Madame Mayor." *Seattle Magazine,* February 1965, 18–22.

Schiesl, Martin J. *The Politics of Efficiency: Municipal Administration and Reform in America, 1800–1920.* Berkeley: University of California Press, 1977.

Schwantes, Carlos. "Leftward Tilt on the Pacific Slope." *Pacific Northwest Quarterly* 70 (January 1979): 24–35.

Scott, Joan. "Gender: A Useful Category of Historical Analysis." In *Coming to Terms: Feminism, Theory, Politics,* ed. Elizabeth Weed. New York: Routledge, 1989.

Silber, Nina. "Intemperate Men, Spiteful Women, and Jefferson Davis: Northern Views of the Defeated South." *American Quarterly* 41, no. 4 (December 1989): 614–35.

Simpson, J. A., and E. S. C. Weiner. *Oxford English Dictionary.* Vol. 11. Oxford: Clarendon Press, 1989.

Sklar, Kathryn Kish. "Hull House in the 1890s: A Community of Women Reformers." *Signs* 10 (Summer 1985): 658–77.

Smith, Daniel Scott. "Family Limitation, Sexual Control, and Domestic Feminism in Victorian America." *Feminist Studies* 1 (1973): 41–57.

Smith-Rosenberg, Carroll. "The Hysterical Woman: Sex Roles and Role Conflict in Nineteenth-Century America." In *Disorderly Conduct: Visions of Gender in Victorian America,* 197–216. New York: Alfred A. Knopf, 1985.

Stead, Peter. *Film and the Working Class: The Feature Film in British and American Society.* New York: Routledge, 1989.

Strasser, Susan. *Never Done: A History of American Housework.* New York: Pantheon, 1982.

"Teacher Education Update." *Chronicle of Higher Education,* June 6, 1990, A14.

Teaford, Jon C. *The Twentieth-Century American City.* Baltimore: Johns Hopkins University Press, 1986.

Toews, John. "Intellectual History after the Linguistic Turn: The Autonomy of Meaning and the Irreducibility of Experience." *American Historical Review* 92 (October 1987): 879–907.

Turner, Victor. *Dramas, Fields, and Metaphors: Symbolic Action in Human Society.* Ithaca, N.Y.: Cornell University Press, 1974.

———. "Frame, Flow, and Reflection." In *Performance in Postmodern Culture,* ed. Michel Benamou and Charles Caramello. Madison: Center for Twentieth Century Studies, University of Wisconsin, 1977.

———. *From Ritual to Theatre: The Human Seriousness of Play.* New York City: Performing Arts Journal Publications, 1982.

———. *Process, Performance, and Pilgrimage: A Study in Comparative Symbology.* New Delhi: Concept Publishing, 1979.

———. "Ritual Aspects of Conflict Control in African Micropolitics." In *Political Anthropology,* ed. Victor Turner, Marc Swartz, and Arthur Tuden. Chicago: Aldine Publishing, 1966.

Turner, Victor, Marc Schwartz, and Arthur Tuden. "Introduction." In *Political Anthropology,* ed. Turner, Schwartz, and Tuden. Chicago: Aldine Publishing, 1966.

Van Voris, Jacqueline. *Carrie Chapman Catt: A Public Life.* New York: Feminist Press, 1987.

Ware, Susan. *Beyond Suffrage: Women in the New Deal.* Cambridge: Harvard University Press, 1981.

Warren, James. *King County and Its Queen City: Seattle.* Woodland Hills, Calif.: Windsor Publishing, 1981.

Weimann, Jeanne M. *The Fair Women.* Chicago: Academy Chicago, 1981.

Wiebe, Robert. *The Search for Order, 1877–1920.* New York: Hill and Wang, 1967.

———. *The Segmented Society: An Introduction to the Meaning of America.* New York: Oxford University Press, 1975.

Williams, G. O. "The History of the Seattle Police Department: The Prohibition Era in Seattle." *Sheriff & Police Reporter,* February 1951, 8.

Young-Eisendrath, Polly. "The Female Person and How We Talk About Her." In *Feminist Thought and the Structure of Knowledge,* ed. Mary McCanney Gergen. New York: New York University Press, 1988.

Unpublished Works

Acena, Albert A. "The Washington Commonwealth Federation: Reform Politics and the Popular Front." Ph.D. diss., University of Washington, 1975.

Deacon, Florence. "Why Wasn't Bertha Knight Landes Re-elected?" Master's thesis, University of Washington, 1978.

Gooding, Barbara. "Women in the Washington State Legislature." Senior thesis, Evergreen College, 1983.

Henry, Susan. "Near-Sightedness and Blind Spots in Studying the History of Women in Journalism." Paper presented at the annual meeting of American Journalism Historians Association, Coeur d'Alene, Idaho, October 4–6, 1990.

Kessler, Lauren. "A Siege of the Citadels: Access of Woman Suffrage Ideas to the Oregon Press, 1884–1912." Ph.D. diss., University of Washington, 1980.

Pendergrass, Lee Forrest. "Urban Reform and Voluntary Association: A Case Study of the Seattle Municipal League, 1910–1929." Ph.D. diss., University of Washington, 1972.

Pitzer, Paul. "J. D. Ross and the Old Skagit Tour." Paper presented at Pacific Northwest History Conference, Walla Walla, Washington, February 27, 1990.

Reiff, Janice. "Urbanization and the Social Structure: Seattle, Washington, 1852–1910." Ph.D. diss., University of Washington, 1981.

Saltvig, Robert D. "The Progressive Movement in Washington." Ph.D. diss., University of Washington, 1966.

Sparks, William O'Dell. "J. D. Ross and Seattle City Light, 1917–1932." Master's thesis, University of Washington, 1964.

Tripp, Joseph. F. "Progressive Labor Laws in Washington State (1900–1925)." Ph.D. diss., University of Washington, 1973.

INDEX